During the 1950s and 1960s, research on the prewar British economy was influenced strongly by ideas from Keynesian macroeconomics. After two decades of onslaught on Keynesian macroeconomics, it is important to reexamine this period of history, asking to what extent the Keynesian vision still offers useful insights into the behaviour of the economy at this time. The essays in this volume make use of advances in time series analysis as well as developments in macroeconomics to answer this question. They show that a modified Keynesian approach continues to offer useful insights into this period of history. In particular, in the face of wage and price rigidities, shocks to aggregate demand are seen as an important source of fluctuations in real output and unemployment. Furthermore, a rigid attachment to simple rules rather than the exercise of discretion in policy making is seen to have had serious costs in the disturbed environment of the interwar period.

T0328426

Britain in the international economy

Studies in Monetary and Financial History

Editors: Michael Bordo and Forrest Capie

Britain in the international economy

edited by

S. N. BROADBERRY and N. F. R. CRAFTS

University of Warwick

CAMBRIDGE UNIVERSITY PRESS
Cambridge, New York, Melbourne, Madrid, Cape Town, Singapore,
São Paulo, Delhi, Dubai, Tokyo

Cambridge University Press
The Edinburgh Building, Cambridge CB2 8RU, UK

Published in the United States of America by Cambridge University Press, New York

www.cambridge.org
Information on this title: www.cambridge.org/9780521122603

First published 1992
This digitally printed version 2009

A catalogue record for this publication is available from the British Library

Library of Congress Cataloguing in Publication data

Britain in the international economy / edited by S.N. Broadberry and
N.F.R. Crafts.
    p. cm.
Papers presented at a festschrift held in July 1989 in honour of Alec Ford,
chairman of the Dept. of Economics at the University of Warwick.
Includes bibliographical references and index.
ISBN 0 521 41859 3
1. Prices – Great Britain – History – Congresses. 2. Money – Great Britain –
History – Congresses. 3. Great Britain – Economic conditions – Congresses.
4. International finance – History – Congresses. 5. Ford, A.G. (Alec George)
I. Broadberry, S.N. II. Crafts, N.F.R. III. Ford, A.G. (Alec George)
HB235.G7B75 1992
332′.042′0941–dc20 91–46713 CIP

ISBN 978-0-521-41859-1 Hardback
ISBN 978-0-521-12260-3 Paperback

For Alec Ford

Contents

Foreword

When it became known that Alec Ford was to retire from his Chair in the Department of Economics at the University of Warwick after twenty-five years, his colleagues and friends decided to hold a Festschrift in his honour. The papers in this volume were presented on that occasion in July 1989 and are a tribute to his academic work. That the occasion was funded by the University of Warwick was a tribute to his contribution to the growth and success of that University both in the heady days of its inception and, perhaps more importantly, during the financial cuts of the eighties. The papers here can be categorised as both 'quantitative' and 'non-quantitative', their topics as 'economics' and as 'economic history'. And that is as it should be, for Alec Ford was both an economist and an economic historian who used the developing techniques of his profession as tools and not as shibboleths.

Alec is an old friend and I count it an honour to join in this celebration. We first met in 1966 when, interviewing me for a post in economic history at Warwick, he first railroaded me with Fogel and then gave me a hard time over flexible exchange rates. Rather to my surprise we became colleagues and it was then that I discovered the cheerful, gentle, ever-helpful, private man that is Alec Ford. His presence in a new, rapidly growing, Department of Economics was a boon; unflappable and totally reliable he became a bulwark around which washed the troubled tides of dissent and experiment, of disappointment and excitement. In those early years at Warwick he was as much concerned with the establishment of the University as with the Department and his subject. The Student's Union – and the Athletics Union in particular – benefited from his help and he was rewarded, almost uniquely, with an Honorary Life Membership. The reputation he gained at that time was to stand him in good stead during the troubles that beset Warwick in the late sixties and early seventies.

When Alec joined Leicester's Wyggeston Grammar School in 1934 at the age of eight, few would have thought him a potential Professor of Economics at Warwick. His parents, both teachers, set him on a Classical path but there were, perhaps, two auguries of the future. The first was his insistence on taking mathematics with classics for his Higher Schools Certificate, a blasphemy accomplished only with the connivance of his father who overcame the school's opposition by threatening an even greater sin, a transfer to science. The second was his paternal grandfather, a Suffolk blacksmith, whose unique skill in repairing reapers overcame the wrath of his farmer customers and allowed him to join Warwick's Joseph Arch in promoting the Agricultural Workers Union. At Wyggeston, Alec shone as both scholar and sportsman, he acquired a life-long love for rugby, set a school mile record that stood for ten years and won a Major Classical Scholarship to Wadham College, Oxford. The war intervened. Called to the colours in 1944, Alec served in the Middle East as a sergeant with the Royal Artillery (the fate of many economic historians, John Saville and Tom Kemp to name but two) until his demobilisation in 1947.

January 1948 saw him at Wadham, taking up his Classical Scholarship but after Classical Moderations in March 1949 he changed to philosophy, politics and economics. Part cause of this was some disillusion with ancient history and philosophy but a greater factor was his growing interest in economics, stimulated both by his reading of the *Economist* and by his service in the Royal Artillery. The khaki-clad Alec, to the intense delight of his classical senses, had served in Palestine, Egypt and Greece, but his joy at seeing the cradle of civilisation was severely tempered by the shock of the poverty and underdevelopment in which that world was now clad. And he had wanted to know why. None the less, a change of course at that stage brought problems, but Alec was encouraged by the knowledge that a previous Wyggeston pupil, Michael Parkin, had studied economics to become the school's first First and their first Professor. In the event, a still athletic Alec nimbly covered the field and, in the summer of 1951, scored a First in PPE, was awarded the Webb Medley Senior Scholarship for Research in Economics, and gained a Studentship of Nuffield College.

At Nuffield his choice of research topic was guided by Donald MacDougall with 'Why don't you look at gold?' and furthered by John Hicks' suggestion 'try South America, some funny things happened there'. The result was a thesis 'The gold standard and Argentina 1880–1914' rewarded with a DPhil in 1956 and with the publication of his *The Gold Standard 1880–1914. Britain and Argentina* by Oxford University Press in 1962. One result of this work was that although he considered himself an economist he developed a deep interest in economic history – and came to enjoy tackling historical problems and issues using economic analysis and quantitative methods, the latter a somewhat *avant-garde* approach at that time. This proved to be his life work, the gold standard led him to British overseas lending and the transfer problem, the trade cycle and economic development followed. His contribution to the Cambridge Economic History of Europe he believes, encapsulates his work – not least in its demonstration of the superiority of Keynes to the classics in explaining the world economy and capital flows in the period before 1914. He has also had a long-term interest in the development of quantitative methods in economic history. Whilst modestly describing himself as a 'competent arithmetician' he has been associated with the Quantitative Economic History workshop since its inception and used his position on the Economic History Section of the Social Science Research Council to push the development of quantitative methods in the hope that we might catch up with the Americans.

In 1953 he was appointed an Assistant Lecturer in Economics at the University College of Leicester, was promoted to Lecturer in 1956 and, in 1963, to Senior Lecturer in what had become the University. Leicester brought contact with Arthur Poole, Peter Donaldson and Harold Dyos, all of whom served to further enhance his interest in economic history. It had also provided experience of 'all hands to the pumps' teaching in a three-man economics department and of the problems of rapid growth in a new institution, all that was to stand him in good stead at Warwick. Appointed Reader in Economics at Warwick in 1965 with dewy-cheeked Professors Dick Sargent and Graham Pyatt, he was one of the five founders of a bright, bushy-tailed economics department devoted to the new quantitative approach to the discipline. Alec also found the opportunity to teach more economic history and to teach it to economists, offering in those first prospectuses – with but a single colleague – no less than eight economic history courses as well as a substantial contribution to core economics teaching. A personal chair followed in 1970, the result, I hasten to add, of the quality of his work rather than the quantity of his teaching! A measure of that quality is that no less than five current UK economic historians – Steve Broadberry, Ian Gazeley, Tim Hatton, Peter Howlett and John Redmond – are products of the Ford/Warwick stable, probably the largest group coming from a single source since the sixties. This achievement, in Nick Craft's words, is 'pretty amazing when you think of what has happened to Universities in general and to Economic History in particular'.

A new university, however, demanded more of its founders than the simple ploughing of an academic furrow. A university must be created and, to be successful, some of its academic staff must be people of imagination and administrative ability as well as devotees of their disciplines. Alec was one of those, and, after some jolly days helping to found the Student's Union, the Rugby Club and the Athletics Union he was drawn into a more serious involvement. Voted a Pro-Vice Chancellor during Warwick's crisis years of 1971–2, he was elected Chairman of the Department of Economics 1972–5. In 1977 he was again pressured into a Pro-Vice Chancellorship and Chairmanship of the Estimates and Grants Committee (the Treasury of the University) and was maintained in that position until 1989. That last was not a trivial matter, the University contrived to hold him in place for twelve years despite Charters and Statutes to the contrary by resort to some imaginative 'early resignations' and 're-elections'. It did so for good reason. Allocating scarce resources during a sustained assault by successive governments on university finances required not only allocative skills but, more importantly for the health of the institution, the creation of an atmosphere of trust, of a belief that the distribution is just. Alec Ford was the just man, the honest broker who, almost single handedly, created that trust. As one very senior source put it: 'He succeeded where others might have failed, simply because he was known to be a thoroughly decent man.' It would be hard to find a better testimonial.

But it must not be thought that Alec Ford is a man of righteous solemnity. He is not. He is a very cheerful chap, much given to swapping jokes, to Wadham gaudys, to supping ale of the right quality, a steam railway enthusiast, a railway photographer of great skill and even greater modesty, a family man, a kind man and a good colleague.

BRYAN H. SADLER

1 British macroeconomic history 1870–1939: overview and key issues

S.N. BROADBERRY and N.F.R. CRAFTS

During the 1950s and 1960s, research on the prewar British economy was influenced strongly by ideas from Keynesian macroeconomics. A central figure here was Alec Ford, who produced a widely used introductory macroeconomics textbook (1971) and also wrote extensively on British economic fluctuations and the gold standard. After more than two decades of onslaught on Keynesian macroeconomics, it is important to reexamine this period of history, asking to what extent the Keynesian vision still offers useful insights into the behaviour of the economy at this time.

As well as changes in macroeconomic thought, there have been major changes in quantitative techniques during the last twenty years or so. Since many of the chapters in this volume make use of modern time series methods, a separate chapter is provided by Terry Mills as an introduction to time series analysis for economic historians.

In the rest of this chapter we provide an overview of British macroeconomic history 1870–1939, paying particular attention to the issues on which modern macroeconomic analysis has shed new light. We see that a modified Keynesian approach continues to yield useful insights into this period of history. In particular, in the face of wage and price rigidities, shocks to aggregate demand were an important source of fluctuations in real output and unemployment. Furthermore, rigid attachment to simple rules rather than the exercise of discretion in policy making is seen to have had serious costs in the disturbed environment of the interwar period. Hence, Ford's emphasis on the special circumstances that permitted the smooth functioning of the pre-1914 gold standard continues to have relevance.

Great Britain and fluctuations under the gold standard 1870–1914

Alec Ford's major contribution to the analysis of fluctuations in Britain during the period 1870–1914 is very firmly in the Keynesian tradition.

Growing out of his classic work on the gold standard (1962), Ford's (1969) analysis of fluctuations was based on an examination of the major categories of expenditure, drawing in particular on earlier papers concerning exports (1963) and overseas lending (1965). Although monetary factors were considered, they were clearly seen as passive and what modern macroeconomists now call supply factors did not play a role in Ford's analysis. Fluctuations in output and employment were seen as determined by fluctuations in aggregate demand, resulting in involuntary unemployment.

As economists have come to see monetary and supply side factors as increasingly important during the 1970s and 1980s, these aspects have received attention in the historical literature. The three chapters in the first part of this volume clearly reflect these developments. They also reflect developments in quantitative techniques.

It will be helpful to briefly restate Ford's conclusions and the methods that he used. In Ford's view, the key determinant of fluctuations in Britain during the 1870–1914 period was exports, although he allowed a supporting role for investment as a 'junior partner' (1969: 143). A typical boom, then, can be seen as export-led, with home investment also rising through an accelerator mechanism. The current account of the balance of payments thus improved. Despite this, Ford noted, Bank Rate typically rose during booms. This can be understood in terms of the Bank of England's desire to maintain the external value of the pound on the gold standard. Bank Rate was raised when the Bank was experiencing strain on its reserves or felt the reserves to be inadequate (1969: 138). Although during the boom exports rose and the current account improved, thus lessening the external drain on reserves, there were two offsetting factors. First, the rise in home incomes led to an internal drain, since there was an increase in the transactions demand for sovereigns and notes. But secondly, and more importantly, there was an external drain through the capital account as overseas investment also tended to rise in booms.

Ford was at pains to argue that if Bank Rate was raised in a boom, it did not cause the subsequent slump. Thus monetary factors could be regarded as purely passive. In support of this view, he argued that home investment was not very sensitive to interest rates (1969: 141–2), although he acknowledged a closer link between overseas investment and Bank Rate (p. 142). Importantly, Ford viewed the money supply as endogenous, adjusting passively to demands for accommodation (pp. 143–4). Although this was not particularly emphasised by Ford, writing in the hey-day of the Radcliffe Report era when the quantity theory of money was out of fashion, it was later to be taken up enthusiastically by proponents of the monetary approach to the balance of payments (McCloskey and Zecher, 1976).

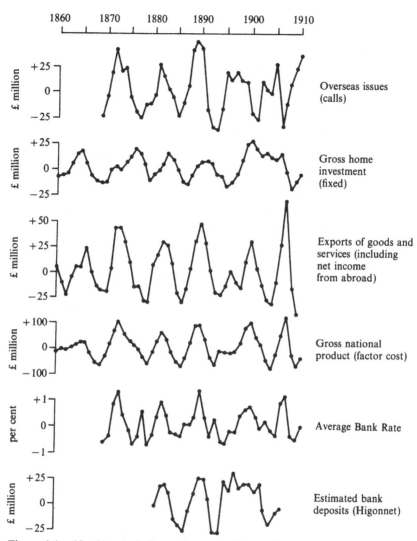

Figure 1.1 Absolute deviations of overseas issues, home investments, exports, GNP, Bank Rate and bank deposits from 9-year moving averages (current values) UK 1860–1910. Source: Ford (1981).

Ford's view of the cycle can be summarised graphically as in figure 1.1, taken from Ford (1981). The key determinants of cycles in GNP were exports and to a lesser extent home investment, exports were significantly affected by overseas issues and Bank Rate moved procyclically as the Bank of England moved to defend the gold parity.

Breaking down the export cycle by geographical areas, Ford noted that Europe was the most important region in terms of both the amplitude of fluctuations and the timing of turning points, thus casting doubt upon the importance attached to the 'North Atlantic economy' in much of the literature on fluctuations (Thomas, 1973). He also noted that British exports were influenced to some extent by fluctuations in overseas investment, although he was careful to point out that in the short 7–10 year cycles, home and overseas investment tended to move together rather than at the expense of each other as in the long 18–20 year cycles.

Ford thus agreed with Keynes in his emphasis on 'animal spirits' affecting home and overseas investment. He also sympathised with Robertson's view that British fluctuations were 'linked with affairs on far-off Prairies and Pampas' (Ford, 1969: 158–9), although he also felt that the European contribution had been undervalued relative to the North American.

Turning to methods, Ford's identification of cycles depended on a filtering of the raw data using 9-year moving averages. Although there appeared to be 18–20 year swings in home and overseas investment in the smoothed data, Ford was sceptical of these cycles since they disappeared when home and overseas investment were added together (1969: 133). Rather, Ford concentrated on the shorter 7–10-year cycles which were apparent in the detrended series, or absolute deviations from 9-year moving averages.

It is clear that Ford was concerned about the possibility of spurious cycles being introduced by the filtering procedure (hence his scepticism about long swings). Modern time series analysis provides a solution to this problem. In Part I of this volume, all three chapters use modern time series methods to filter the data in a way that is statistically admissible. The cyclical properties of the time series are thus extracted from rather than imposed upon the data (Mills, this volume).

Another feature of Ford's analysis was that it was conducted mainly with series in current prices. Since the key variables were exports and investment, cycles could be seen as due to fluctuations in nominal aggregate demand. In a classical model, fluctuations in nominal demand could be consistent with continuous full employment if wages and prices adjusted to ensure continuous market clearing. Ford must be implicitly assuming, then, that there were nominal rigidities so that nominal demand fluctuations were translated into real fluctuations.

Ford's view of fluctuations as arising from exogenous shocks to a weak multiplier-accelerator mechanism is consistent with the standard Keynesian view of the 1950s and 1960s, after it had been realised that the conditions for endogenous cycles in a deterministic framework were extremely restrictive (Matthews, 1959; Evans, 1969). More recently, whilst retaining the stochastic environment, 'real business cycle' theorists have stressed the importance of shocks to aggregate supply rather than aggregate demand. Shocks to aggregate supply generate fluctuations in real output and employment, with continuous market clearing (Plosser, 1988). It should be noted, however, that in an open economy a supply shock abroad translates into a demand shock from the viewpoint of the domestic economy, through the change in exports.

An important book by Edelstein (1982) extends Ford's analysis. Ford emphasised the role of overseas rather than home investment. A rise in overseas investment was seen as stimulating exports, which in turn stimulated home investment through an accelerator relationship. Edelstein provides a detailed evaluation of the interaction between home savings (S), home investment (I^h) and overseas investment (I^o). All three variables are seen as functions of the rate of interest (i), but with each function also subject to shifts reflecting pressures at home and pressures abroad. Income (Y) and wealth (W) are the shift factors for the home savings function, home investment shifts with the marginal efficiency of domestic capital (MEC^h) and the overseas demand for investment funds shifts with the marginal efficiency of overseas capital (MEC^o) and overseas savings behaviour (Z). The model is illustrated in figure 1.2. In this simple equilibrium model, overseas investment can increase if the home savings function moves outwards, if the home investment function moves inwards or if the overseas investment function moves outwards. By seeking to identify such shifts over time, Edelstein attempts to locate periods when pull or push factors were dominant.

Edelstein examines the issue of whether fluctuations in home investment can be treated as exogenous rather than as occurring in response to movements in overseas investment. This is analysed using Granger causality tests, which essentially check whether the turning points in one series precede the turning points in the other series. If home investment typically peaked just before overseas investment, we can treat home investment as the exogenous variable determining overseas investment, while we would not be justified in treating overseas investment as the exogenous variable determining home investment. Edelstein's finding that home investment Granger-caused overseas investment suggests that push factors were of some importance in determining overseas investment. In addition, he suggests that pull factors were important, but varied by region over the period 1850–1914. He finds that the American pull on British savings was strongest during the period 1854–71 and had all but disappeared by 1900. The Australian pull was strongest during the 1860s and 1880s but again had all but disappeared by the turn of the century. The

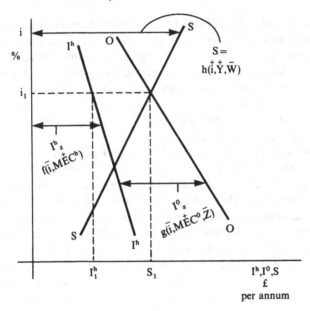

Figure 1.2 The process of savings and investment: a partial model. Source: Edelstein (1982).

Canadian pull was especially strong in the early twentieth century as the prairies were settled. Edelstein's book, then, can be seen as extending Ford's analysis in several ways. As well as clarifying the interactions between home and overseas investment with a simple equilibrium model, Edelstein confirms the importance of overseas factors in British fluctuations and provides clear evidence of an exogenous role for home investment. Edelstein's work also provides an early example of the use of modern time series techniques in economic history, with the Granger causality tests.

Turning now to the papers in Part I, Barry Eichengreen provides a survey of work on the operation of the classical gold standard published since Ford's (1962) major work, before drawing upon this literature to present his own 'Ford-like' model of how the gold standard worked. Eichengreen places more emphasis than Ford on monetary management by the Bank of England and rather less emphasis than Ford on the linkages between British overseas investment and exports.

As Eichengreen notes, Ford's (1962) study predated the open economy IS/LM/BP model and the monetary approach to the balance of payments. This work clarified the issues surrounding the endogeneity of the money supply under a fixed exchange rate regime. If the central bank tried to expand the money supply, this would lower the domestic interest rate and hence lead to a capital outflow. The resultant excess supply of domestic currency would force the central bank to intervene in foreign exchange markets to maintain the value of the currency. This would require the central bank to run down its reserves of gold and foreign currency, which it would sell in exchange for domestic currency. Hence, the amount of domestic currency in circulation would fall, offsetting the initial expansion of the money supply. Although it was possible for the central bank to offset these forces by buying bonds and hence offsetting the contraction of the money supply, such 'sterilisation' could only occur over the short run, as eventually the central bank would run out of reserves. This analysis would provide a rationale for Ford's treatment of the money supply as endogenous and his playing down of the role of the Bank of England's monetary policy.

However, such a vision of the gold standard as an anonymous, self-equilibrating balance of payments adjustment mechanism with no possibility of monetary autonomy fits uneasily with Keynes' graphic description of the Bank of England as 'the conductor of the international orchestra' (1930: II, 307). Indeed, McCloskey and Zecher (1976), applying the monetary approach to the balance of payments in their study of how the gold standard worked, concluded that 'the Bank was no more than the second violinist, not to say the triangle player, in the world's orchestra' (1976: 359).

Eichengreen, however, retains a leading role for the Bank of England by considering the strategic interactions between central banks. In an earlier important paper, Eichengreen (1987) showed that the reserve currency status of sterling provides a rationale for leadership by the Bank of England under the gold standard. There is a simple intuition behind this result. Each central bank is assumed to care about its share of the world's gold reserves and domestic economic conditions. In a symmetric two-country world, a change in the discount rate by the domestic central bank would be matched by a change in the foreign central bank's discount rate, since both banks care about their gold reserves. Changes in prices and output in the two countries would also be symmetric, determined by interest rate changes. Hence, there would be no advantage in adopting a leadership role. Suppose, however, that the foreign country holds part of its international reserves in the form of interest-bearing assets denominated in the domestic country's currency. Now if the discount rate changes in both countries there are different effects in the two economies. If the discount rate rises in both countries, there is an incentive for the foreign central bank to augment its stock of interest bearing foreign exchange reserves. The supply of money available to domestic residents is correspondingly reduced, requiring a reduction in domestic money demand through a fall in domestic prices and income. Similarly, a discount rate fall leads to a greater rise in nominal income in the domestic economy. Hence, there is an incentive for the domestic central bank to act as leader. It is also clear that the domestic central bank exercises a more powerful pull over gold flows, since if both central banks raise their discount rates, the foreign central bank increases its holding of foreign exchange reserves rather than gold. Hence, the international reserve status of sterling is sufficient to explain both the leadership role of the Bank of England and the powerful effects of Bank Rate on gold flows. This also fits in with Ford's (1962) emphasis on the different experiences of the gold standard at the centre and at the periphery.

Eichengreen examines the interaction between time series on a number of key variables, very much in the spirit of Ford's (1969) trade cycle analysis, but using modern time series techniques. Eichengreen estimates a vector autoregression (VAR) for exports, imports, the terms of trade, Bank Rate, gold reserves and overseas lending. Each variable is regressed on three own lags and three lags of each of the other variables. Causality can be investigated by examining F-statistics for the joint significance of lagged values of an explanatory variable. Eichengreen here builds on his earlier work which established a key causal role for the money supply (1983). He finds that despite a high contemporaneous correlation between overseas lending and exports, overseas lending did not statistically cause exports.

To focus on the general equilibrium repercussions, the VAR system is subjected to random shocks. One of the equations is perturbed and the impact on the other variables is traced through. The results suggest a greater role for monetary management by the Bank of England and a smaller role for the linkage between overseas lending and exports than in the work of Ford. However, many of the Keynesian features of the Ford approach are supported. In particular, Eichengreen sees adjustment of real variables as an important part of the balance of payments adjustment mechanism.

The monetary statistics available to Ford during the 1960s were very rudimentary and subsequent scholarship has provided improved estimates, particularly for the money supply. Forrest Capie utilises the data set constructed by Capie and Webber (1985) to examine the role of money in British economic fluctuations. Capie analyses the cyclical behaviour of money, real income and prices using a number of techniques. In the simplest approach, the series are detrended using polynomial trends. A second technique, based on the work of Barro (1984), calculates the shortfall of a variable in a trough by extrapolation forward of the trend during the five years before the previous peak. In addition to these *ad hoc* approaches to the identification of cycles, Capie also reports results obtained with the Kalman filter (see Mills, this volume). In all cases, Capie fails to detect a significant relationship between fluctuations in money and real income. Indeed, using the Kalman filter, the money data show no evidence of cyclicality at all.

This absence of cyclicality in the money data and hence the absence of a causal relationship between money and real income for Britain before the First World War is in marked contrast to the situation for the same period in the US (Friedman and Schwartz, 1963). Capie speculates that the key difference between the two countries was the absence of banking panics or financial crises in Britain. He argues that in turn, this financial stability in Britain resulted from the lender of last-resort behaviour of the Bank of England and the structure of the British banking system, with its widespread branch network. The argument is strengthened by Collins' (1988) finding of a significant relationship between money and real income in the mid nineteenth century when British banks did fail. Dimsdale's (1990) analysis of fluctuations since 1830 also attributes a key role to financial crises before 1870 and emphasises real factors thereafter.

The paper by Nick Crafts and Terry Mills turns to the supply side of the economy, drawing upon the recent real business cycle literature (Plosser, 1988; Lucas, 1987). Fluctuations are seen as arising due to shocks to aggregate supply. Markets are assumed to clear instantaneously, so there is no involuntary unemployment. Fluctuations in real output and employment are explained by the intertemporal substitution of leisure. When there is a positive technology shock which raises the marginal product of labour above its long-run trend, the real wage rises and people choose to take less leisure, since this is a propitious time to work hard. Conversely, when the marginal product of labour is below trend, people choose to take more leisure. Hence, the model is consistent with the fact that unemployment is low in booms and high in slumps.

One advantage of the real business cycle approach is that it makes explicit the links between growth and cycles. Essentially cycles are caused by shocks to a neoclassical growth model. Short-run and long-run analysis are thus inextricably tied together. An interesting issue here is whether the time series on output is trend stationary or difference stationary, since in the trend stationary case shocks do not have a persistent effect on the level of output (see Mills, this volume). Recently, macroeconomists have come to view the world as predominantly difference stationary, with shocks having a persistent effect on the level of output. However, for the UK Mills (1991) finds that although GDP is difference stationary after the First World War, for the 1870–1913 period it is trend stationary. This would appear to cast some doubt on approaches such as that of Solomou (1987) which see the cycle as generated by shocks to growth trajectories.

Crafts and Mills devote some time to explaining this ability to reject the unit root hypothesis, drawing on the work of West (1988). It turns out that the key factors are the slope of the short-run aggregate supply curve and the degree of monetary accommodation. If a shock is to have a persistent effect on output, so that the output series has a unit root, we require a relatively flat short-run aggregate supply curve or the main effect of shocks will be on the price level. Hence the finding of trend stationarity for pre-1914 Britain suggests a relatively steep short-run aggregate supply curve, which is consistent with Hatton's findings for the pre-1914 Phillips curve (this volume). In addition, if the central bank follows a money supply rule but does not offset previous errors, we would expect shocks to have persistent effects and hence produce the unit root result. For the case of pre-1914 Britain, however, the Bank of England could not follow such an accommodating policy, since it was required to maintain the gold standard parity of the pound. Hence, the relatively low degree of monetary accommodation by the Bank of England also plays a role in explaining the finding of trend stationarity for pre-1914 Britain.

Crafts and Mills find that the basic neoclassical growth model with serial correlation in technology shocks and trend stationary growth is a useful starting point for the analysis of pre-1914 fluctuations, but has a number of limitations.

One major problem is that the real business cycle approach requires procyclical real wages. Slumps are caused by negative technology shocks which lower the marginal product of labour and hence lower the real wage, thus inducing people to substitute more leisure for work. Thus real wages fall in slumps and rise in booms. This contrasts strongly with the Keynesian approach, which predicts countercyclical real wages. Slumps are caused by negative shocks to demand, which cause prices to be lower than expected. Given money wage rigidity, the real wage rises, causing a reduction in the demand for labour and hence a rise in involuntary unemployment. In fact, Crafts and Mills find virtually no correlation between output and real wages, which suggests that both demand and supply shocks were present, with neither dominant.

In addition, Crafts and Mills note that although the model is fairly successful in explaining the behaviour of output and consumption, it is rather less successful in explaining investment behaviour. Investment in pre-1914 Britain was substantially more volatile than predicted by the simple real business cycle model. They argue that this excess volatility in investment can be explained by excess volatility in share prices, affecting Tobin's q, the ratio of the stock market valuation of capital to the replacement cost of capital. They demonstrate the excess volatility of share prices by calculating an *ex post* rational price or 'perfect foresight' series, which is much more stable than the actual share price series. The excess volatility of investment can then be attributed to waves of undue pessimism or optimism among investors. This would appear to be consistent with Ford's emphasis on the importance of changes in confidence and expectations (1969: 158).

Price behaviour 1870–1914

Ford's underlying Keynesian view of the world can be seen as relying on wage and price rigidity, so that shocks to nominal aggregate demand resulted in fluctuations of real output and employment. The chapters in Part II look in more detail at the behaviour of prices.

In a world of perfectly flexible prices, we should expect to see purchasing power parity (PPP). This doctrine holds that with a fixed exchange rate of £1 = $4.86, a basket of goods that costs £1 in Britain should cost $4.86 in America. If it were possible to buy the same basket of goods for less than $4.86 in America, it would pay for an arbitrageur to buy up the goods in America and resell them in Britain. However, the increased demand in America would raise the dollar price and the increased supply in Britain would lower the sterling price, bringing the relative prices back into line at the equilibrium ratio of 1 : 4.86.

In practice, of course, some deviations from purchasing power parity would be expected, since there are transport costs involved and information is unlikely to be perfect. Furthermore, many goods and services are simply not traded. Nevertheless, the doctrine of PPP suggests that for an open economy such as Britain in the late nineteenth century, the trend in the price level should be essentially determined by the trend in overseas prices rather than by domestic factors.

Tim Hatton looks again at the evidence for PPP in Britain over the period 1880–1913. Like McCloskey and Zecher (1976), he finds that correlations between the rate of change of British and other countries' price levels are fairly strong, although he notes that the correlation is stronger for wholesale prices than for GDP deflators or wage rates. This would be expected since wholesale price indices are based only on traded goods.

Hatton also examines PPP using modern time series techniques, reporting the results of cointegration tests, since PPP implies that domestic and foreign price levels should move together in the long run (see Mills, this volume, for an introduction to cointegration techniques). The results suggest that there is only very weak evidence for cointegration. However, since there are doubts about the power of the tests, particularly in a small sample, Hatton also calculates the average lag in a specification that imposes long run PPP. He finds an average lag for GDP deflators of 3.4 years and for whole sale prices an average lag of 1.8 years.

If PPP holds strictly, domestic price change should be determined by changes in foreign prices, with no role for changes in domestic costs or variations in domestic economic activity. Estimating a simple structural econometric model, Hatton demonstrates that domestic costs played an important role in determining domestic price change. In addition, he notes that domestic costs, reflected in wage rates, were influenced by the level of economic activity, as in the original Phillips curve model.

Hatton's results suggest an important role for domestic factors in price determination, particularly in the short run, when there were significant departures from PPP. In the long run, however, Hatton's evidence is consistent with a return to PPP and an important role for foreign prices. Neil Blake's paper attempts to show that the major swings in the British price level during 1870–1913 can be explained by swings in import prices, caused by the changing balance of supply and demand for major commodities.

Blake estimates a large macroeconometric model of the UK over the 1870–1913 period, which he then uses for counterfactual simulations. The model is essentially a Keynesian income-expenditure model and can thus be seen as consistent with the work of Alec Ford, who views cyclical fluctuations as the result of erratic shocks to a weak multiplier-accelerator mechanism (1969: 159). In addition, however, much of Blake's model is concerned with the determination of prices, through a cost-plus pricing mechanism. Like Ford, Blake views monetary factors as passive and there is no explicit role for money in the model.

The model is used for a number of counterfactual simulations, to evaluate the extent to which the large swings in the GDP deflator can be explained by swings in import prices. Blake shows that if import prices are held at their 1871 level, the trend fall in the GDP deflator down to the mid-1890s is eliminated. He further shows that if import prices are held at their 1895 level, the trend rise in the GDP deflator through to 1913 is eliminated. Thus Blake argues that the swings in British prices over the 1870–1913 period can be largely accounted for by the swings in import prices. He also shows that the swings in domestic investment are not sufficient to account for the observed swings in the GDP deflator. Hence the Schumpeterian explanation of price trends in terms of investment behaviour is not supported.

Blake explains the trend of foreign prices in terms of supply shocks abroad, which would be consistent with Ford's analysis, although the possibility that the world price level was determined by world monetary trends cannot be ruled out. Blake also notes that if supply shocks were responsible for price trends, this would provide an explanation for the Gibson paradox, or positive correlation between the rate of interest and the price level, illustrated in figure 1.3 which is taken from Harley (1977). Since

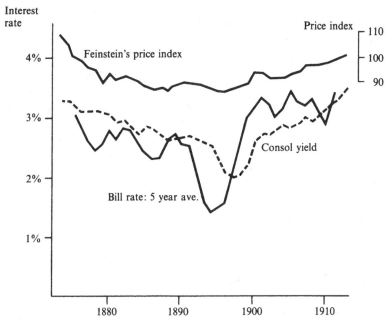

Figure 1.3   Prices and interest rates, 1873–1913. Source: Harley (1977).

the real rate of interest is defined as the nominal interest rate minus the expected rate of inflation, we should expect to see a positive correlation between the nominal rate of interest and the rate of inflation rather than between the nominal rate of interest and the price level.

As Blake notes, however, if there is a positive supply shock which lowers the price level, this raises the real money supply and lowers the rate of interest. Hence, both the price level and the rate of interest fall. Conversely, a real shock that raises the price level also raises the rate of interest. Hence supply shocks are capable of explaining the Gibson paradox.

The chapter by Terry Mills and Geoffrey Wood offers an alternative explanation of the Gibson paradox, which allows a more important role for monetary factors in the determination of prices. Starting from a stable price level, the quantity theory of money tells us that a fall in the money supply leads to a fall in the price level. If the money supply contracts by the same amount in future years, there will be a period of continually falling prices. If expectations adjust to this negative inflation, there is a one-off fall in the nominal rate of interest, to keep the real rate of interest constant. If, however, expectations are slow to adjust, there may be a series of downward movements in the nominal rate of interest. Thus, with lags in the adjustment of expectations, we may expect to observe the Gibson Paradox of a positive correlation between the price level and the rate of interest. This argument was originally proposed by Irving Fisher and is supported by Mills and Wood in their assessment of the modern empirical evidence.

Mills and Wood base their judgement on an analysis of the impact of money on output, prices and interest rates, allowing for possible feedbacks between the series using vector autoregression (VAR) techniques. An equation modelling one variable can be subjected to shocks to trace through the impact on the other variables (as in Eichengreen, this volume). Mills and Wood conclude that the results are consistent with Fisher's explanation of the Gibson paradox, since a positive shock to M0 initially raises both the interest rate and the price level. However, the simulations also appear to be consistent with the supply shock explanation since a positive shock to the price level raises the interest rate.

The open economy context of price and output movements 1870–1914

We have already established that during 1870–1914 participation in the world economy had a major influence on domestic prices and investment in Britain while the exchange rate regime was fundamental to monetary conditions and business cycle fluctuations. In order to provide a better understanding of the background to the events analysed in earlier chapters, the contributions in Part III explore policy choices between the rival monetary arrangements of the gold standard and bimetallism and developments in the supply of food imports as transport costs fell and world population rose. Both of these aspects of international economic relations had important effects on the British economy in this period yet they have been relatively neglected by researchers until very recently.

Membership of a fixed exchange rate regime implies convergence of price trends over the long run; although the mechanisms by which this link is maintained may vary in different circumstances or be the subject of disputed analyses by economists, this basic proposition is not at issue. Indeed, as we have noted earlier, Hatton's chapter confirms that this was the case among the gold standard countries between 1880 and 1913. Given that changes in the world velocity of circulation are minor, we can predict that the common rate of inflation in a gold standard world depends on the difference between the rate of expansion of the world output and of the world money supply which will, in turn, be related to the rate of growth of world monetary gold.

In the mid nineteenth century, Britain's adherence to a gold standard was unusual; most major countries such as France and the United States were on a bimetallic standard based on gold and silver, i.e., their governments had entered a legal commitment to buy either gold or silver at fixed prices.

In practice, divergences in the free market price ratio between gold and silver from the legal ratio would often mean that monometallism would result from such rules, as in the United States from 1837 to the Civil War when the legal ratio was 16:1 but the market ratio was less than this with the result that there was a *de facto* gold standard as the cheaper metal drove the dearer out of circulation.

Under either system the supply and demand balance of precious metals had a major role in price movements. In the gold standard case sizeable discoveries of gold would be inflationary while a failure to add to world monetary gold would tend to reduce the price level in the face of growth in productive potential. With bimetallism, if in the free market either metal became significantly cheaper than the legal ratio it would displace the other, and a *de facto* silver or gold standard would result with the potential for switches from one to the other as relative metal prices changed. In turn, the relative prices of the metals depended (through the demand implications) partly on the number of countries adopting particular metal standards. Switches in and out of gold by bimetallic countries would tend to mitigate the effects on world prices of erratic expansion of gold supplies, although they might involve a high cost to individual agents or central banks.

The history of wholesale price movements in this period is well known – falls between 1872 and 1896 of 50% in the US, 39% in the UK, 36% in Germany and 43% in France while world monetary gold grew at 1.4% per year followed by rises between 1896 and 1913 of 49%, 32%, 41% and 41% respectively while gold increased at the rate of 3.7% per year (Triffin, 1985: 131, 135). In the last quarter of the nineteenth century the major countries of the world moved rapidly to the adoption of the gold standard while the price of silver fell markedly relative to gold. *De facto* silver-standard countries would have experienced a devaluation relative to gold standard countries and consequently to maintain PPP would have experienced lower price falls from the mid-1870s to the mid-1890s.

It follows that choices made concerning the monetary regime in the 1870s had an important impact on prices for the world economy as a whole as well as for particular countries. Friedman (1990) has investigated the consequences for the United States of the stabilisation of the currency after the Civil War on the basis of a gold standard rather than a return to bimetallism. He concluded that bimetallism would have led to a considerably more stable price level in the United States, in particular by obviating at least half the decline in prices prior to the mid-1890s. Moreover, by precluding the large rise in US demand for monetary gold, there would also have been a reduction of downward pressure on prices elsewhere – in the UK by 0.3% per year from 1875 to 1895 (Friedman, 1990: 1176).

Phil Cottrell's chapter revisits the debate over the merits of different monetary standards in the second half of the nineteenth century and explores the international negotiating process involved in the transition from bimetallism to gold. He highlights the important impact of perturbations arising from the impact of the erratic gold discovery process on central banks and pressure groups. In the 1850s and 1860s a falling relative price of gold and consequent withdrawal of silver from circulation is seen as promoting a general move to the gold standard. Nevertheless, for the next two decades he shows that a return to bimetallism was a continuing issue on the international agenda. In particular, he notes not only the lobbying of the silver interest in the United States but also more general continuing worries about the unduly deflationary nature of the gold standard in the 1880s and 1890s.

From a British perspective, Cottrell's chapter is especially useful in establishing the strength of the controversy and the advocacy of bimetallism on into the 1890s in the face of price falls, worries about increasing international competition and low levels of domestic economic activity. This palliative for British economic ills has been unduly neglected by comparison with the considerable attention which has been given to proposals for Tariff Reform. No one has so far attempted counterfactual calculations for a British adoption of bimetallism in the 1870s but, given the importance of the import price transmission mechanism linking world supply and monetary shocks to British prices and, in the short run, activity levels highlighted in Blakes's chapter, it is clear that these alternative monetary policy proposals are worthy of some serious econometric study.

Blake's chapter explores the effects of the large fall in British import prices during the late nineteenth century followed by a subsequent increase. To complement this analysis, Harley's paper examines the factors leading to changes in the real supply price of imported food. His chapter also throws further light on some of the pull factors attracting foreign investment to which Edelstein (1982) drew attention and on the terms of trade which have featured prominently in discussions of living standards and division of the gains from trade in the period, notably in the work of Lewis (1978).

In general, both falling transport costs and rising populations in importing regions can, by raising prices for exporters, lead to rising exports by food-producing regions. Falling transport costs also create the possibility that the net barter terms of trade can improve simultaneously for both exporters and importers of primary products.

Harley draws a sharp distinction between the sources of the expansion of wheat imports from the mid-western United States and meat imports from the Southern Hemisphere and indeed generally between the factors encouraging the greater integration of world product markets before and after 1890. Between 1860 and 1890 the key factor was a huge decline in transport costs based on the use of steam and iron in rail and sea transport, whereas after 1890 rising population continued to encourage greater international trade in food while refrigeration and vertical integration transformed the meat trade but transport costs stabilised. In discussing this later period, Harley makes use of the Argentine experience to clarify the processes involved much as Ford (1962) used it as an example to understand the workings of the pre-1914 gold standard.

While population growth and falls in transport costs both imply rising prices for food exporters they have very different implications for food consumers in importing countries like Britain, as Harley's table 10.1 makes clear. His results are based on a calibrated model of supply and demand drawing on existing econometric estimates of relevant parameters. Because demand for wheat was inelastic and supply elastic the gains from transportation improvement were mainly obtained by consumers who experienced improved terms of trade and decidedly lower food import prices. From the 1890s, as the transport improvements slowed down, the improvement in the British terms of trade was reversed as population increases tended to push food prices up. Together with the changes in world gold supplies, this largely explains the change in nominal import price trends.

It is certainly worth examining the terms of trade in considering the growth of real incomes in late Victorian and Edwardian Britain. Using the Hamada–Iwata weighting procedure, Irwin (1991) found that for 1870–99 growth of real GDP at 2.35% per year was augmented by improved terms of trade worth a further 0.15% to give real income growth at 2.50% per year whereas in 1900–13 the deterioration in the terms of trade reduced real GDP growth of 1.50% by 0.06% per year to 1.44%. As far as real wages are concerned, the terms of trade play only a small part in the end-century slowdown in their growth; Feinstein (1990: 344–9) calculates that between 1882–99 and 1899–1913 labour productivity growth fell by 1.1% per year while the terms of trade had an adverse impact of about 0.2% per year. It seems safe therefore to reject Lewis' claim that 'the basic answer to the question why real wages decelerated after 1899 is the turnaround in the terms of trade' (1978: 111).

Nevertheless, in interpreting the British terms of trade it is important not to forget the role of falling transport costs of which Harley's table 10.1 serves to remind us so strongly. Over the second half of the nineteenth century as a whole they did make a sizeable contribution to gains in British real wages. The improvement in transport also is seen to allow higher prices in Chicago as well as lower prices in Britain and suggests that using the British terms of trade in the 1870s through the 1890s to infer adverse moves in the terms of trade for primary producers as did Prebisch (1950) may be quite seriously misleading.

The macroeconomy in the interwar years

Earlier sections of this introduction have suggested that, although the research findings of Ford's generation of Keynesian economic historians need considerable modification in the light of refinements to theory and econometric procedure, nevertheless a substantial part of their basic view of the world remains plausible. We now turn to the interwar economy with similar questions in mind. How well does the traditional Keynesian analysis of macroeconomic disequilibrium stand up in the light of the intense scrutiny of the past decade which has come about with the resurgence of economists' interest in the period? Does the interpretation of the pre-1914 economy suggested above help us to understand the apparent failure of the interwar years? Do the traditional criticisms of British economic policy need to be revised?

To Keynesians the most striking, and disturbing, feature of the interwar economy was the level of unemployment, which was persistently high, averaging around 9%, and rose to over 15% of the labour force in 1932 (Feinstein, 1972). Both the aftermath of World War I and the world depression after 1929 produced major adverse shocks for the economy, but policy errors bore an important responsibility for this situation, notably the decision to return to gold at an overvalued parity of $4.86 in 1925, a perverse refusal to use deficit finance to stimulate demand especially in the early 1930s, the prevalence of beggar-my-neighbour policies and absence of coordinated monetary policy among the major countries (Ford, 1983; Stewart, 1967: Winch, 1969). Moreover, a failure to understand the true underpinnings of the prewar gold standard, especially in terms of the special position which Britain enjoyed as its leader – or 'hegemonic power' – led not only to the mistaken decision of 1925 but also to the collapse of the interwar gold exchange standard and the triumph of protectionism (Kindleberger, 1973).

Keynesian analysis tended to ignore explicit modelling of the supply-side and expectations, to assume that money wages were very sticky, at least from the mid-1920s onwards, to presume that there was generally a chronic tendency to insufficient aggregate demand and to structural/regional problems such that unemployment was involuntary, and to be highly critical of the Bank of England and the Treasury for sticking to rules like a commitment to the Gold Standard and a balanced budget, thus failing to use suitable discretion in macro policy or to accept new ideas.

The general tendency among economists away from Keynesian views

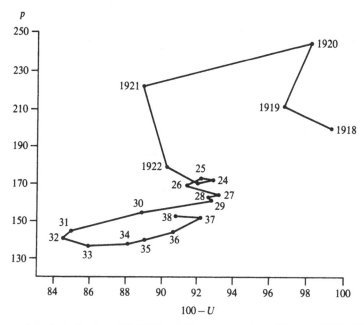

Figure 1.4 Retail prices (*P*) (1913 = 100) and capacity utilisation (100 − *U*) (%). Source: Broadberry (1986).

since the early 1970s has, of course, been reflected in the economic history of interwar Britain along with a subtler or reconstructed Keynesianism. In particular, it has been strongly argued by some, notably Benjamin and Kochin (1979) and Matthews (1986), that the economy was characterised by a high natural rate of unemployment – indeed, Matthews goes on to suggest that taking this into account the exchange rate was, if anything, undervalued at $4.86 in 1925. There has been a general acceptance that real wages did significantly affect the demand for labour (Dimsdale, 1984; Beenstock and Warburton, 1986). A considerable reassessment of Treasury policymaking has led to a clearer appreciation of the constraints under which it operated, of the justifications for a preference for rules rather than discretion and of the existence of a workable strategy to mitigate the adverse shock of the early 1930s (Booth, 1987; Middleton, 1985).

Macromodelling of the interwar economy now very much embraces both aggregate supply and aggregate demand and the flavour of mainstream contributions is reflected in the recent analyses of the depression reproduced in figures 1.4 and 1.5.

Figure 1.4 should be seen as a sequence of equilibrium points where short run aggregate supply and aggregate demand curves intersect and the horizontal axis is to be interpreted as the level of real output. Broadberry

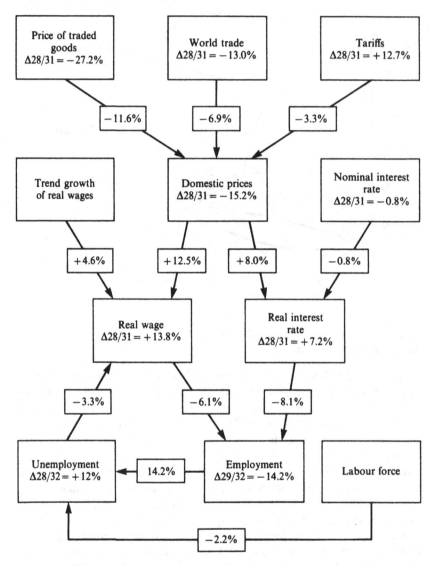

Figure 1.5   Linkages in the Great Depression. Source: Newell and Symons (1988).

(1986) used this device in particular to examine the onset of the depression in Britain. He suggested that the combination of declines in prices with falling output in the early 1930s reversed in the later 1930s indicated that the major shifts were in the aggregate demand schedule and that this largely justified the traditional Keynesian interpretation. By contrast, he pointed to an apparent adverse shock to aggregate supply associated with rising wage costs shortly after World War I which may have led to a persistently higher natural rate of unemployment throughout the 1920s and 1930s.

The post-1929 decline in demand came principally from declining exports and was transmitted in the context of a fixed exchange rate system which tended to amplify the initial effect by imposing pressure for tight monetary policy. Newell and Symons (1988) have performed an econometric analysis of a short-run macro model with money wages which are inflexible downwards to capture the average experience of a European gold standard country in 1928–31. Their analysis, which complements and extends that of Broadberry, is summarised in figure 1.5 which brings out the transmission mechanisms involved in the international recession. In particular, their work stresses the huge impact of the demand decline on real wages and real interest rates for countries on a fixed exchange rate as output prices fell. There was a real wage problem but its origin was in the demand shock and the appropriate action to counter this was to devalue. Countries which did so tended to recover relatively quickly (Eichengreen and Sachs, 1985) and not surprisingly therefore the world recession destroyed the interwar gold standard.

Despite considerable progress from the application of more sophisticated theory and quantification, the interwar macroeconomic experience remains controversial in many ways, partly as a result of data deficiencies and the small number of annual observations available for econometric modelling. The chapters in Part IV of the book dealing with labour market issues attempt to throw further light on some of these still unresolved issues.

The chapter by Mark Thomas focuses on the institutional arrangements of the interwar labour market especially in terms of their implications for wage setting behaviour. Thomas emphasises the need for clear conceptualisation of propositions about wage flexibility/rigidity and the danger of too readily accepting commonplace assertions about the 'institutional peculiarities' of post-1918 Britain. He argues that the data collected by the Ministry of Labour probably overstate the degree of flexibility in wages and that Britain is more similar to other countries of the time than is widely believed.

Nevertheless, a regression analysis of wage behaviour confirms that there were important rigidities, notably that while real wages responded readily to excess demand in the labour market they did not fall in times of excess supply. Thomas suggests that a number of clues indicate that insider-outsider models (in which the unemployed have little or no influence on bargains struck between those still employed and firms) are an appropriate way to understand this phenomenon and at the same time to reappraise the problems of the staple industries so often consigned to an ill-defined notion of structural unemployment. Thomas' chapter does go some way to justifying pre-Keynesian beliefs about the labour market but it also illuminates the transmission mechanism which made the world slump so threatening along the lines proposed by Newell and Symons (1988) and given additional econometric support in a Layard and Nickell type analysis in Dimsdale *et al.* (1989).

Ian Gazeley and Pat Rice in their contribution concentrate on a microlevel investigation of the importance of real wages for labour demand in the staple industries. Their work should be seen as complementing, and in the sophistication of its econometric technique improving upon, the macroeconomic studies of labour demand undertaken by Dimsdale (1984) and Beenstock and Warburton (1986). By considering the staple industries they also shed further light on the issue of structural unemployment between the wars.

Gazeley and Rice make two important advances from the earlier research of Casson (1983), namely they construct new quarterly data series for employment, prices and wages and they employ a flexible functional form for the estimated employment function. Their econometric approach is in the general to specific tradition and involves careful consideration of lag structures. In each of the four staple industries they study, own-product real wages are an important determinant of labour demand; in three cases, the long-run real wage elasticity of labour demand is in the range -0.15 to -0.32 but shipbuilding is an outlier with an estimated elasticity of -5.27. These results imply that any insider dominated bargaining of the kind stressed by Thomas could have adversely affected employment by raising wages. As they remark, however, these results may be biased upward by virtue of their reliance on a perfect competition assumption and there is a clear opening for further exploration of this point.

The other chapters in Part IV deal with the international monetary system which had a crucial influence on domestic policy and which was central to the transmission of shocks between economies. John Redmond provides an overview of the resurrection and ultimate collapse of the gold standard between the wars which also gives further insight into the workings of the pre-1914 gold standard.

Redmond's literature survey leads him to the following conclusions. First, he sees the problems of the system coming above all from a lack of cooperation and policy coordination. Second, he argues that the smooth working of the pre-World War I gold standard depended on special circumstances no longer to be found between the wars and he notes especially the changed position of Britain, the leader of the pre-1914 system. Third, he reasserts his well-known view that the pound was overvalued by the return to gold in 1925, while admitting that this is difficult to quantify, and that this was a fundamentally misconceived policy. Redmond remains, therefore, basically sympathetic to many elements of the Keynesian position.

Redmond's first two conclusions are, however, derived from reasoning which is somewhat more sophisticated than was common twenty years ago. Modern analysis, following Barro and Gordon (1983) has tended to accept the virtue of pre-commitment to policy rules rather than full discretion as an important safeguard against inflationary policies but also to recognise that the choice of an optimal rule depends crucially on the nature of the shocks to which the economy is exposed (Artis and Currie, 1981). Moreover, relationships between central banks are now explicitly modelled in strategic terms much as oligopoly might be analysed (Eichengreen, 1984; 1987).

Seen in these terms both the general desire to return to gold and the demise of the gold standard make sense. A commitment to a fixed exchange rate is a good rule with which to combat irresponsible monetary policy and was attractive in the face of the worries promoted by the spectacle of hyperinflation in the early 1920s but, as conventional Mundell-Fleming analysis suggests, will tend to amplify the deflationary consequences of shocks to exports which turned out to be *the* problem after 1929. Indeed, faced with such a shock the requirement would be for coordinated fiscal and monetary expansion in all major countries to obviate exhaustion of reserves and loss of credibility of the exchange rate, if the rules were to remain helpful. Eichengreen's papers (1984; 1987; 1990) point to the result that the system was more prone to high interest rates and a deflationary bias not only because it failed to achieve a cooperative equilibrium due to incompatibility of beliefs and objectives and deep mutual suspicion among major players but also through the absence of a Stackelberg leader, the role played by pre-war Britain.

Figure 1.6 conveys the essence of Eichengreen's approach. Here r and r^* are the home and foreign interest rates while B and B^* are the reaction functions of the home and foreign central banks who care about gold reserves and domestic economic activity. They are upward sloping because in response to a foreign interest rate increase protecting the reserves outweighs losses from deflation. N represents the noncooperative (Cournot-Nash) equilibrium, S a case where the home country is Stackelberg leader and C the cooperative outcome. N has the highest interest rates and is the

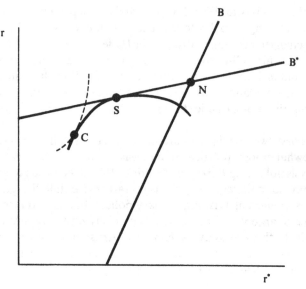

Figure 1.6   Central bank rivalry and interest rates (adapted from Eichengreen, 1984).

most deflationary outcome, C is the least deflationary case. With reaction functions like these, however, each country can do better by following rather than leading – the arguments in Eichengreen (1987) suggest a downward sloping reaction function for pre- but not post-1914 Britain (see Part I). Cooperation requires multilateral expansionary action but suffers from Prisoner's Dilemma type problems; Broadberry (1989) provides calculations which suggest an equilibrium like N prevailed in Anglo-American relations in which unilateral expansion would lead to welfare losses while persuading the other country to expand but failing to go along with it gives welfare gains.

Redmond's third conclusion is also based on a richer analysis than used to be undertaken. He reports the calculations in his (1984) paper which show that the 1925 decision meant a higher real exchange rate relative to 1913 if multilateral rather than bilateral UK–US figures are taken but he also recognises that the equilibrium real exchange rate consistent with internal and external balance might have changed since 1913. Although adverse external circumstances argued for a lower real exchange rate, if internally there was now a higher NAIRU this would imply lower imports in equilibrium and thus, ceteris paribus, a higher real exchange rate, as Matthews (1986) argued. Thus the net effect of the changes is *a priori* ambiguous. At present, however, we do not have estimates of the NAIRU for the interwar economy which command general acceptance and thus uncertainty must remain about the initial degree of overvaluation, which is harder to estimate than a reader of, say, Moggridge (1969) would have been led to believe.

The final chapter by Steve Broadberry and Mark Taylor looks again at purchasing power parity in the 1930s, using much more powerful econometric techniques than were available to earlier investigators. This was a protectionist era and also one of switches in exchange rate regimes which might be expected to be unpromising territory for PPP. The chapter is based on tests using cointegration and Granger-causality techniques (see Mills, this volume). Broadberry and Taylor find results which are broadly supportive of long-run PPP for the pound, dollar and french franc, if allowance is made for tariffs and asymmetric price responses. The Granger causality tests indicate that generally prices adjusted to the exchange rate rather than vice versa, a finding which is consistent with adjustment through commodity rather than asset market arbitrage. By contrast, bilateral exchange rates involving the mark do not exhibit PPP which the authors attribute to the extreme interference with market transactions in Nazi Germany and they conclude that only very drastic controls prevented tendencies to long-run PPP through arbitrage.

The implications of these results are that leaving gold in 1931 had a major payoff for Britain in reducing downward pressures on prices and (with sticky wages) upward pressures on real wages but that devaluation would not be expected to give permanent gains in international competitiveness, as is confirmed by the calculations in Dimsdale (1981). Similarly, opting for an exchange rate too high by PPP standards in 1925 would set in motion changes in relative prices which would gradually restore PPP, a tendency which again is found in recent estimates (Dimsdale, 1981; Redmond, 1984).

A modified Keynesian approach still offers key insights into the British economy in the interwar period. In particular, the primacy of demand rather than supply shocks in instigating the high unemployment of the early 1930s and the importance of adjustment problems resulting from the stickiness of wages are confirmed. In this context the failure of the interwar gold standard becomes readily comprehensible – in the absence of international cooperation it was to be expected that the shocks after 1929 which had no precedent prior to 1914 would destroy the system. Ford's emphasis on the role of special circumstances in permitting the apparently smooth functioning of the pre-1914 gold standard is still appropriate. In neither period were the adjustment mechanisms envisaged in the simple quantity theory world strong or immediate enough to obviate Keynesian problems.

The main thrust of recent research, strongly reflected in these chapters, has been to consider price and wage setting behaviour more seriously, especially in terms of its implications for the response of the economy to shocks. It must be said that so far this has produced more in the way of econometric results (notably those in Dimsdale et al., 1989) than in understanding of the underlying reasons for them.

Nevertheless, enough has been accomplished to suggest the need for some rethinking of the very critical treatment of the Treasury commonplace twenty years ago. Archival work has suggested that Treasury thinking in the early 1930s was essentially aware of the transmission mechanisms operating in a world of sticky wages and designed a policy response which was geared to restraining the threatened increase in real wages by actions to limit price decreases (devaluation, tariffs, support for cartels) while retaining rules like the balanced budget to avoid undesirable signals to agents about future inflation (Booth, 1987). If not an optimal policy, this was quite sensible given the scope for shocks to have persistent effects on unemployment through insider-outsider effects and given what we know about the international pattern of recovery in the 1930s.

Concluding comments

Much progress has been made in our understanding of the British economy 1870–1939. However, a number of important questions remain, providing a promising agenda for future research. Two in particular deserve to be highlighted here. On the issue of aggregate supply, although it has been clearly established that rigidities existed in wage and price setting behaviour, the reasons behind the rigidities are less clearly understood. The casting of these issues within a bargaining framework holds out the promise of further insights here. The chapter by Thomas in this volume shows a little of this promise with its use of the Nash bargaining model for interwar wage determination.

The second area where new thinking seems likely to lead to significant progress is growth. Much of the work in this volume focuses on fluctuations, while much of the debate surrounding British economic performance during this period is concerned with growth. Clearly, as McCloskey (1970) effectively demonstrates, it is naive to simply assume, as does Mayer (1955), that growth would have been faster if demand had been higher without considering supply constraints. Nevertheless, it is equally true that much recent work in macroeconomics has stressed the link between cycles and growth. If output follows a unit root process, shocks have persistent effects and the trend is not independent of the cycle. Thus large shocks, such as those that occurred between the wars have significant effects on growth. The chapter by Crafts and Mills in this volume shows the promise of this approach, which is still in its infancy. A further promising strand in the new thinking on growth is the work on endogenous theories of growth by Romer (1986; 1990). The challenge here is to integrate these theories into a historical framework.

Our understanding of the British economy 1870–1939 has been advanced greatly by the application of modern macroeconomic ideas and modern time series techniques over the last two decades, as reflected by the chapters in this volume. We now look forward to further progress over future decades.

2 An economic historians' introduction to modern time series techniques in econometrics

TERENCE C. MILLS

Trends and cycles in macroeconomic time series

Researchers studying the growth and cyclical behaviour of industrialised economies are immediately faced with the problem of separating out cyclical fluctuations from the longer-term trend, or secular, movements. The difficulties in doing this are certainly well appreciated by economic historians such as Aldcroft and Fearon (1972) and Ford (1981), but the methods of trend and cycle decomposition used by them are essentially *ad hoc*, designed primarily for ease of computation without real regard for the statistical properties of the time series (or set of series) under analysis; for statements supporting this position, see Aldcroft and Fearon (1972: 7) and Matthews, Feinstein and Odling-Smee (1982: 556).[1]

The underlying model in such analyses is that of an additive decomposition of a time series y_t, observed over the time period $t = 1, 2, \ldots, T$, into a trend, μ_t, and a cyclical component, ε_t, assumed to be statistically independent of each other, i.e.

$$y_t = \mu_t + \varepsilon_t, \ t = 1, 2, \ldots, T, \ \mathrm{E}(\mu_t \varepsilon_s) = 0, \ \text{for all } t \text{ and } s. \tag{1}$$

The observed series $\{y_t\}$ is often the logarithm of the series under consideration, while the data are usually observed annually.

The trend and cycle components are, of course, unobservable, and hence need to be estimated.[2] The methods of estimation traditionally employed by economic historians are termed *ad hoc* above because they do not arise from any formal statistical analysis of y_t or its components. Perhaps the simplest model for μ_t that we might consider is the linear time trend

$$\mu_t = \alpha + \beta t, \ t = 1, 2, \ldots, T, \tag{2}$$

which, if y_t is measured in logarithms, assumes constant exponential growth. Estimation of the regression model

$$y_t = \alpha + \beta t + u_t, \ t = 1,2, \ldots, T, \tag{3}$$

by ordinary least squares (OLS) thus produces asymptotically efficient estimates of α and β, although the variances of these estimates will be biased unless the errors u_t are serially uncorrelated and homoskedastic (Fuller, 1976: ch. 9). Given such estimates $\hat{\alpha}$ and $\hat{\beta}$, the trend component is thus

$$\hat{\mu}_t = \hat{\alpha} + \hat{\beta} t, \ t = 1,2, \ldots, T,$$

and the cyclical component is obtained by residual as

$$\hat{\varepsilon}_t = y_t - \hat{\mu}_t, \ t = 1,2, \ldots, T.$$

Note that the trend component will only be efficiently estimated in small samples, an important proviso given the limited number of observations usually available on historical time series, if the cyclical component is, *inter alia*, serially uncorrelated. This is unlikely to be the case if cycles, often defined as 'recurring alternations of expansion and contraction' (Aldcroft and Fearon, 1972: 4), are in fact present in the data, in which case generalised least squares (GLS) or an equivalent technique is required for efficient trend estimation.

Although the linear trend model has been used on occasions, most notably by Frickey (1947) and Hoffmann (1955), economic historians have typically rejected the view that trend growth is constant through time, preferring models that allow for variable trend growth rates. The linear trend model can be readily adapted to allow trend growth to vary across cycles, or *growth phases* as they are sometimes referred to, the terminal years of which are chosen through *a priori* considerations. Thus, if T_1 and $T_2 = T_1 + k$ are the terminal years of two successive cycles, the trend growth rate across the cycle spanning the years T_1 and T_2 is given by the least squares estimate of β_k in the regression[3]

$$y_t = \alpha_k + \beta_k t + u_{kt}, \ t = T_1, T_1 + 1, \ldots, T_2. \tag{4}$$

More efficient estimates of trend growth across cycles can be obtained by extending the model (4) in at least three ways. The first is to incorporate the models for individual cycles into a single composite model, where it is assumed that the end points of the cycles are at times $T_1, T_2, \ldots, T_m = T$:

$$Y_t = \alpha + \beta t + \sum_{i=1}^{m} \gamma_i d_{it} + \sum_{i=1}^{m} \delta_i t d_{it} + u_t, \tag{5}$$

where the d_{it} are $0-1$ dummies, $i = 1,2, \ldots, m$, taking the value 1 in the ith cycle and the value 0 elsewhere. The second extension is to estimate (5) by a variant of GLS to take account of possible serial correlation in the cyclical error component u_t. This will allow hypothesis tests of, for example, a constant growth rate across the sample period ($H_o : \delta_1 = \ldots \delta_m = 0$) to be carried out efficiently (see Crafts, Leybourne and Mills, 1989a).

Thirdly, note that equation (5) does not allow the trend function to be continuous: even if H_o is not rejected, the presence of nonzero γ_is will result in horizontal shifts in the trend. Since commonsense suggests that the trend function should be smooth, continuity can be imposed by considering the class of *segmented trend* models, to use the terminology of Rappoport and Reichlin (1989), these being a special case of *grafted polynomials*; see Fuller (1976: ch. 9.2) and also Hausman and Watts (1980). A segmented linear trend can be written as

$$ y_t = \alpha + \beta t + \sum_{i=1}^{m} \delta_i \phi_{it} + u_t, \tag{6} $$

where the functions ϕ_{it} are given by

$$ \phi_{it} = \begin{cases} t - T_i, & t > T_i \\ 0, & \text{otherwise}, \end{cases} $$

and extensions to higher order trend polynomials are straightforward.

The common feature of the linear trend model and its extensions is that trend growth across cycles is regarded as being *deterministic*, so that *all* fluctuations in y_t must be attributable to the cyclical component. Furthermore, any fluctuation from trend is only temporary: since the cyclical component u_t is estimated by the residual from a regression, it must have zero mean and be *stationary* (for a formal definition of this term, see note 5), so that any shocks to y_t that force it away from its trend path must dissipate through time. The importance of this implication is discussed in more detail later in the chapter. The other potential drawback of these models is that the 'break points' $T_1, \ldots, T_{m-1}$ have to be determined *a priori*, so that such choices could be subjectively biased.

Because of these shortcomings, many historians favour an alternative method of trend estimation. This is the technique of *moving averages*: the usual moving average, or *filter* as it is often known in time series analysis, used to isolate trend in annual macroeconomic time series is the nine-year one (as used, for example, both by Aldcroft and Fearon, 1972, and by Ford, 1969; 1981). Formally, a trend component estimated by a $(2h+1)$-moving average of y_t can be defined using the lag operator B as

$$ \dot{\mu}_t = M(B)y_t = \frac{1}{2h+1} \left(\sum_{j=-h}^{h} B^j \right) y_t, \quad t = h+1, \ldots, T-h-1, \tag{7} $$

where $B^j y_t \equiv y_{t-j}$. Hence, setting $h = 4$ gives the nine-year moving average referred to above. An advantage of using a moving average to estimate the trend component, apart from the obvious one of computational simplicity, is that the trend now becomes stochastic and, although 'smooth', is influenced by the local behaviour of y_t: fluctuations in y are therefore not entirely allocated to the cyclical component.

A property of moving averages is that a $(2h+1)$-moving average will smooth out a $2h+1$ year cycle from the data. Since most economic historians believe that British business cycles are between seven and eleven years in duration, the setting of $h = 4$ is thus seen to have a rational basis, at least in terms of prior beliefs.

One obvious disadvantage of moving averages is that $2h$ trend observations, equally allocated at the beginning and end of the sample period, are necessarily lost. As Aldcroft and Fearon (1972) note, this can cause major difficulties when the available number of observations is limited. An important illustration of this is the estimation of trends during the interwar years, when less than twenty annual observations are available: Aldcroft and Fearon have to resort to linear trends in their analysis of this period.

A less well known disadvantage of using moving averages of the form (7) is that, although they eliminate a linear trend, which is certainly what is required, they also tend to smooth the detrended series too much: this is particularly so for series that are only weakly autocorrelated after differencing, a feature of many historical macroeconomic series. The result is the injection, rather than elimination, of trend into the cyclical component, manifesting itself in the form of low-order autocorrelation. As a consequence, the cycles obtained by residual from this procedure may be spuriously smooth, thus leading to erroneous conclusions concerning their regularity and stability.[4]

From this discussion it is clear that both the linear trend and the moving average filter can have important defects when used to decompose an observed series into trend and cyclical components. While we are certainly not arguing that these techniques are *necessarily* defective, it would obviously be desirable if alternatives existed and methods were available to discriminate between different decompositions. This is particularly so given that the allocation of fluctuations to components, and the determination of whether such fluctuations have permanent or transitory effects, are both heavily dependent upon the decomposition chosen. Recent developments in time series analysis have, fortunately, made available a set of techniques and models designed to do just this and they have already begun to be employed with some success in a number of areas of macroeconomics and economic history.

Discriminating between trend stationary and difference stationary processes

By way of introduction, consider again the simple linear trend model of equation (3):

$$y_t = \alpha + \beta t + u_t, \tag{8}$$

where the series of residuals $\{u_t\}$ is now explicitly assumed to be *stationary*, but not necessarily serially uncorrelated.[5] Secular (trend) movement need not be modelled by a deterministic function of time, however, and one alternative, popularised by Box and Jenkins (1976), allows y_t to be the accumulation of changes that are themselves stationary, so that

$$y_t = y_{t-1} + \beta + e_t, \tag{9}$$

where $\{e_t\}$ is a stationary, but again not necessarily serially uncorrelated, series with mean zero and variance σ_e^2, and where β is the (fixed) mean of the changes. Accumulating these changes from an initial value, y_0 say, yields

$$y_t = y_0 + \beta t + \sum_{i=1}^{t} e_i, \tag{10}$$

which looks superficially like (8), but has two fundamental differences. The intercept is no longer a fixed parameter but now depends upon the initial value y_0, and the error is not stationary, for its variance and covariances all depend on time. For example, if the $\{e_t\}$ do happen to be serially uncorrelated, so that y_t is a *random walk with drift* (of β), then the error variance is $t\sigma_e^2$, which obviously increases as t increases. Nelson and Plosser (1982) refer to models of the class (9) as *trend stationary* (TS) processes and those of class (10) as *difference stationary* (DS) processes.

The distinction between these two processes has important implications for the analysis of both economic growth and business cycles. If y_t is of the TS class then, as was pointed out in Section I, all variation in the series is attributable to fluctuations in the cyclical component. If the series is a DS process, however, its trend component must be a nonstationary stochastic process rather than a deterministic function of time, so that a shock (or *innovation*) to it has an enduring effect on the future path of the series. Hence treating y_t as a TS rather than as a DS process[6] is likely to lead to an overstatement of the magnitude and duration of the cyclical component and to an understatement of the importance and persistence of the trend component.[7]

Given that the properties of the two classes of models are so different, it is essential to correctly distinguish between them. Moreover, the importance of such discrimination is exacerbated by the consequences of incorrectly assuming that a series is TS when, in fact, it is a member of the DS class. Nelson and Kang (1981; 1984) have considered the effects of such misspecification in some detail and their conclusions may be summarised as follows:

1 Regressing the levels of a driftless random walk ($\beta = 0$ in equation (9)) on time by OLS will produce R^2 values of around 0.44, regardless of sample size. For random walks with drift, R^2 will increase with sample size, reaching unity in the limit regardless of the actual rate of drift of the random walk or its variability.

2 The residuals obtained from such a regression will have a variance that is much smaller than the true variance of the series. It is thus very easy to mistake a DS process for a TS process if one simply fits a linear trend without considering alternative specifications.

3 The sample autocorrelations of a so 'detrended' random walk oscillate with a period of about $(2/3)T$, so the detrended series exhibits a completely spurious long cycle.

4 The conventional t-statistic for the OLS estimate of β in a regression of (8) is a very poor test for the presence of trend, and attempts to correct for residual serial correlation, estimating by GLS for example, will only partially alleviate the problem.[8]

Given that modelling a DS process as TS is fraught with potential pitfalls, what dangers are attached to the converse misspecification? Very few it would seem, for the OLS estimator of β will still be unbiased and will have approximately a normal (or Student-t) distribution, and although the efficiency of the estimator is reduced, this will not be serious if the induced serial correlation in u_t is simultaneously modelled.

These conclusions are neatly illustrated by the following simulated example. Figure 2.1 plots TS and DS processes generated for $T = 100$ by assuming $\beta = 2$, $\alpha = y_0 = 10$, and the sequences $\{u_t\}$ and $\{e_t\}$ to be both normal and serially uncorrelated with zero mean and variance 25. It is readily apparent from this figure that the observed TS series is generated from such a process and, indeed, OLS regression of the series on a constant and a time trend yields intercept and slope estimates of 9.46 and 2.001, respectively, and a residual variance estimate of 25.7.

Visual inspection of the DS series might also suggest that it too was generated by a TS process, albeit with a flatter slope. In fact, a similar OLS regression obtains a slope estimate of 1.71, which is accompanied by a t-ratio in excess of 50, and an R^2 statistic of 0.963! Moreover, the residual variance of the regression is 95.1, whereas the true innovation variance of the random walk should be $T\sigma_e^2 = 2500$.

The appropriate estimation method for the DS process is to regress the first differences of the series on a constant: OLS estimation yields an

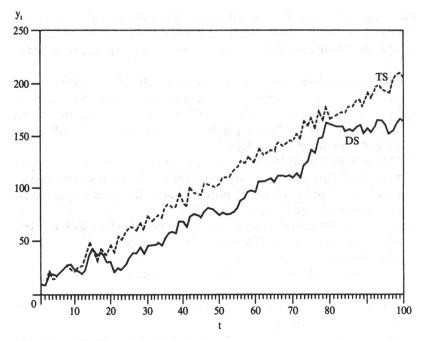

Figure 2.1   Simulated TS and DS series.

intercept estimate of 1.55 with a standard error of 0.51, and an estimate for σ_e^2 of 25.7. However, regressing the first difference of the TS generated series on a constant yields an estimate of 1.97, thus illustrating how misspecifying a TS process as a DS process nevertheless still enables an accurate estimate of the slope coefficient β to be obtained.

How can a researcher distinguish whether an observed time series is a member of the TS or DS class of processes? An easily implemented method has been proposed by Nelson and Plosser (1982), building on the earlier work of Dickey and Fuller (1979; 1981) on testing for *unit roots* in univariate time series. In its simplest form, this takes the DS model as the null hypothesis, embodied in the regression

$$y_t = \alpha + \rho y_{t-1} + \beta t + v_t, \tag{11}$$

where v_t is a residual, as $H_o: \rho = 1$, $\beta = 0$. Under this null, standard t-ratio testing procedures are strongly biased towards finding stationarity around a trend, that is, they are biased towards rejecting a DS process in favour of a TS process, tending to reject the unit root hypothesis of $\rho = 1$ when it is true in favour of the stationary alternative $\rho < 1$, and tending to reject the hypothesis $\beta = 0$ when it is true in favour of the typical alternative $\beta > 0$.

Assuming that $\{e_t\}$ in equation (9) is serially uncorrelated then, following Perron (1988) for example, the appropriate testing strategy is to use the standard t-ratio $\hat{t}_\rho = (\hat{\rho} - 1)/s(\hat{\rho})$, where $s(\hat{\rho})$ is the standard error of the least squares estimator $\hat{\rho}$, to test the null hypothesis $\rho = 1$ against the alternative $\rho < 1$, but to use the critical values given originally in Fuller (1976: 373), and recently extended by Guilkey and Schmidt (1989), rather than the conventional critical values taken from Student-t tables.[9]

The importance of using the correct critical values is seen by comparing, for example, the .01 critical values for an infinite sample size: the correct value is $\hat{t}_\rho.01 = -3.96$, while the incorrect value from the t-distribution is -2.58. A joint test of $H_o : \rho = 1$, $\beta = 0$ may be carried out by computing the standard F-ratio, denoted Φ_3, but now comparing the resultant test statistic to the critical values of the statistic given in Dickey and Fuller (1981: 1062).[10] The hypothesis that y_t is a DS process is rejected in favour of the alternative that it is a TS process if the test statistics *exceed* (in absolute value) their critical values.

How powerful are such tests? The limited number of observations available on many historical economic time series, usually only recorded annually, may be thought to be an obvious problem. As discussed in Perron (1988) and Shiller and Perron (1985), however, the power of unit root tests depends much more on the *span* of the data than on the number of observations *per se*. This has the implication that increasing the number of observations does not necessarily lead to tests having higher power if there is also a change in the sampling interval, e.g. if quarterly rather than annual observations are used but the sample period remains unaltered. With historical economic time series, the relevant alternative to a DS process is often a TS process exhibiting *mean reversion* over a period of an order similar to business cycles. Hence, a long span of annual data is to be preferred to a shorter span with, say, quarterly observations even if the latter affords a greater number of values.

Nevertheless, any test of a unit root will have low power against stationary alternatives with roots close to unity. Such roots would imply that mean reversion occurs over very long periods of time and theoretical models embodying just this property have been developed by West (1987) and would, for example, be implied by the behaviour of the price level during the gold standard (see Mills, 1990b). Again, this highlights the importance of the span of available data rather than merely the number of observations and is a point that has also been made, albeit with a somewhat different emphasis, by Cochrane (1988).

Bearing in mind the earlier discussion concerning structural changes and segmented trend models, an alternative argument as to why unit root tests may have low power is that a TS process, embodying as it does the hypothesis of constant trend growth, is not sufficiently well parameterised to capture the infrequent changes in trend growth which Rappoport and Reichlin (1989) and Perron (1989) argue may well be a better characterisation of the behaviour of macroeconomic time series than are the frequent changes implied by the DS model. The testing procedure outlined above can be extended to consider segmented trend models of the form (6) as an alternative to the DS model of equation (9). Consider the following extension to equation (11):

$$Y_t = \alpha + \beta t + \sum_{i=1}^{m} \delta_i \phi_{it} + \rho y_{t-1} + v_t. \tag{12}$$

The null hypothesis of a DS process is now $H_o: \rho = 1$, $\beta = \delta_1 = \ldots = \delta_m = 0$ and can again be tested by computing the $\hat{t}_\rho$ statistic. However, the critical values of this statistic will differ from those obtained for the simpler model and Rappoport and Reichlin (1989) present critical values, obtained by Monte Carlo simulation, for a sample size of $T = 100$. These values tend to be appreciably larger than those for the TS alternative: with $m = 1$, $\hat{t}_{\rho,.05} = -4.23$ for $T_1 = 50$ and -4.08 for $T_1 = 25$, while for $m = 2$ and break points at $T_1 = 25$ and $T_2 = 75$, $\hat{t}_{\rho,.05} = -4.76$, the usual critical value being -3.45. They also find that the critical values are not biased towards rejecting the DS model if, as would naturally be the case in practice, the break points are selected after viewing the data. Further analysis of segmented trend models is provided by Perron (1989; 1990), where detailed critical values are tabulated for various types of structural change, although only one shift is allowed for.

The methods developed above are predicated on the assumption that the innovation sequence $\{e_t\}$ is uncorrelated but, from equation (9), there is no reason why this should be so. However, if the innovation sequence is correlated, then either the estimation method must be changed (i.e. another regression model must be adopted) or the statistics described above must be modified. Adopting the first approach, Said and Dickey (1984) show that if $\{e_t\}$ is a general ARMA(p,q) process with p and q unknown, then the regression model (11) can be amended to

$$y_t = \alpha + \rho y_{t-1} + \beta t + \sum_{j=1}^{l} \gamma_j \nabla y_{t-j} + v_t, \tag{13}$$

where the number of lags, l, of $\nabla y_t = y_t - y_{t-1}$ introduced as regressors increases with the sample size at the controlled rate ($T^{\frac{1}{3}}$). In this case the $\hat{t}_\rho$ statistic computed from the estimate of $\hat{\rho}$ has the same limiting distribution, and hence critical values, as the statistic calculated from the regression (11).

A potential difficulty with this approach is that if the moving average component of $\{e_t\}$ is important, then the number of extra lags of ∇y_t needed as regressors in the autoregressive correction may be quite large. Since one effective observation is lost for each extra ∇y_t introduced, this approach may have substantially lower power than when the innovations are serially uncorrelated if the series under consideration is relatively short, a relevant consideration in many historical applications. Furthermore, as shown by Schwert (1987; 1989), the correction does not work well, in the sense that the distribution of the test statistic is far different from the distribution of $\hat{\tau}_\rho$ reported by Dickey and Fuller (1979), if the moving average parameter is large. Since it is generally believed, and much empirical work supports this view, that moving average terms are present in many macroeconomic time series after first-differencing, the above approach may face serious practical difficulties.

Phillips and Perron (1988) adopt the second approach, that of modifying the test statistics, to account for serial correlation and, indeed, some forms of heteroskedasticity. The exact forms of their modified test statistics are conveniently set out in Perron (1988: table 1) and will not be repeated here. Their disadvantage is that the modifications necessitate corrections to the standard error of $\hat{\rho}$ and hence the modified statistics cannot be taken directly from the output of a standard regression package. Moreover, their performance in the presence of important moving average components can be worse than that of the autoregressive corrections outlined above, and this leads Schwert (1989) to recommend that the Said and Dickey test should be the one to use when errors are serially correlated, perhaps setting the number of lags of ∇y_t at $l = T^{\frac{1}{4}}$, rounded to the nearest integer, so that when $T = 25, l = 2$; when $T = 50, l = 3$; when $T = 200, l = 4$, etc. Nevertheless, it is strongly recommended that extreme care is taken to establish the presence and form of serial correlation *before* tests of unit roots are carried out, since the importance of making correct inferences is essential to the appropriate analysis of trend and cycle.

One question that needs to be considered is the form of the trend component of a DS process. To develop this, we may assume that the innovation series $\{e_t\}$ in (9) can be written as a linear combination of the present and past values of a series $\{a_t\}$, whose values are independent and identically distributed with common variance σ_a^2: the sequence $\{a_t\}$ is known as *white noise*:[11]

$$y_t = y_{t-1} + \beta + a_t + \sum_{j=1}^{\infty} \psi_j a_{t-j}. \tag{14}$$

Given the trend-cycle decomposition (1), in which μ_t and ε_t are independent, Watson (1986) shows that often an admissible unobserved components (UC) model is

$$\mu_t = \mu_{t-1} + \beta + a_t^\mu, \quad \text{var}(a_t^\mu) = \sigma_{a\mu}^2, \tag{15}$$

and

$$\varepsilon_t = a_t^\varepsilon + \sum_{j=1}^{\infty} \psi_{\varepsilon j} a_{t-j}^\varepsilon, \ \mathrm{var}(a_t^\varepsilon) = \sigma_{a\varepsilon}^2, \ E(a_t^\varepsilon a_{t-j}^\mu) = 0, \ \text{for all } j. \tag{16}$$

Here the trend component follows a random walk with drift, while the cycle is a zero mean stationary stochastic process evolving independently of the trend. The linear trend model is a special case of this UC model and corresponds to the restriction $\sigma_{a\mu}^2 = 0$.

It is not always possible to decompose a process into a random walk trend and an independent stationary cycle, as both Watson (1986) and Nelson and Plosser (1982) point out. For example, the popular ARIMA(1,1,0) process

$$y_t = y_{t-1} + \beta + \theta(y_{t-1} - y_{t-2}) + a_t,$$

for which $\psi_j = \theta^j$, is ruled out. Moreover, the independent component assumption can be replaced by one of *perfect correlation* between components. In this case the trend and cycle are driven by the *same* innovations, and this provides the basis for the Beveridge and Nelson (1981) decomposition, although many economists may feel uncomfortable with such an assumption.

Given that an admissable decomposition exists, an optimal estimate of the trend component is then given by a *weighted* moving average of the observed values of y_t,

$$\mu_t = \Lambda(B)y_t = \left(\sum_{j=-\infty}^{\infty} \lambda_j B^j \right) y_t, \tag{17}$$

where the λ_j weights, which sum to unity, are functions of the variances σ_a^2 and $\sigma_{a\mu}^2$ as well as the ψ_j weights. The moving average introduced earlier as equation (7) is thus seen to be a special case of (17), obtained by setting λ_j equal to $(2h+1)^{-1}$ for $-h \leq j \leq h$ and zero elsewhere, and does not correspond to any model of the form (14).[12]

A more general formulation of the UC model (15) is to let the drift parameter β vary through time by also allowing it to be a random walk, i.e.

$$\mu_t = \mu_{t-1} + \beta_t + a_t^\mu, \ \mathrm{var}(a_t^\mu) = \sigma_{a\mu}^2, \tag{18}$$

where

$$\beta_t = \beta_{t-1} + a_t^\beta, \ \mathrm{var}(a_t^\beta) = \sigma_{a\beta}^2. \tag{19}$$

where a_t^μ and a_t^β are independent white noise processes. With such a setup it is usual to specify the form of the cyclical component explicitly. Clark (1987) and Crafts, Leybourne and Mills (1989b; 1990; 1991), for example, use the AR(2) process

$$\varepsilon_t = \phi_1 \varepsilon_{t-1} + \phi_2 \varepsilon_{t-2} + a_t^\varepsilon, \tag{20}$$

while Harvey (1985; 1990) prefers a sinusoidal process that explicitly exhibits cyclical behaviour.

Granger causality and vector autoregressions

The discussion so far has concentrated on analysing single time series. When two or more series are to be modelled jointly, it is often important to analyse the causal links existing between them. Suppose we consider the relationship between two time series, y_t and x_t. It is well known that the presence of a high correlation between them does not constitute evidence of any relationship between the underlying variables, y and x. Moreover, an assumption such as 'x causes y' cannot be established on the basis of data alone: indeed, such an assumption is often taken for granted on the basis of economic theory.

Given the limitations imposed by non-experimental data, some researchers have thus taken the view that fitting a regression model is primarily an exercise in measurement. That a relationship exists is not actually questioned: what is important is the measured effect of one variable on another. While this approach has underlain a good deal of econometric modelling in the past, it does seem to place an inordinate amount of faith in prior knowledge from economic theory and certainly implies that untestable assumptions are brought into the model.

The wish to examine the assumptions underlying an econometric model estimated from non-experimental time series data has led to a particular concept of causality being developed. It must be stressed, however, that this notion of causality is purely statistical and does not correspond to any acceptable definition of cause and effect in the philosophical sense. Instead, this idea of causality, formalised by Granger (1969), refers to the more limited concept of *predictability*. Two basic rules are taken to apply. The first is that the future cannot predict the past. The second is that it is assumed that it is only meaningful to discuss causality for a group of *stochastic* variables. The variable x is then said to *Granger-cause y* if taking account of past values of x enables better predictions to be made for y, all other things being equal: formal definitions of Granger-causality may be found in, for example, Granger (1969) and Pierce and Haugh (1977).

There are various ways in which tests of Granger-causality may be carried out. Perhaps the most straightforward is the *direct test*. Consider the regression of y_t on lagged values of itself and lagged values of another series x_t:

$$y_t = \sum_{i=1}^{m} \gamma_i y_{t-1} + \sum_{i=1}^{n} \delta_i x_{t-i} + v_t. \tag{21}$$

The hypothesis that x Granger-causes y can then be examined by testing the joint significance of the lagged values of x in (20): if $H_o: \delta_1 = \delta_2 = \ldots = \delta_n = 0$ can be rejected, then x Granger-causes y. The hypothesis can be tested by conventional procedures such as an F-test or a likelihood ratio test, the only problem being to choose the lag lengths m and n so to ensure that the residual v_t is white noise and that all relevant lags of x_t are included in the regression.

An alternative procedure is the *Sims-test* (Sims, 1972), in which x_t is regressed on past and future values of y_t:

$$x_t = \sum_{i=n}^{-m} \pi_i y_{t-i} + w_t. \tag{22}$$

The hypothesis that x Granger-causes y is then equivalent to no future values of y_t appearing in the regression (22), i.e. if $H_o: \pi_{-1} = \pi_{-2} = \ldots \pi_{-m} = 0$ can be rejected, then x Granger-causes y. In implementing this procedure, it is important to take account of any serial correlation in the residual w_t, since otherwise F-tests, etc. of H_o will be misleading. A simple way of modelling such serial correlation is to include an appropriate number of lags of x_t as additional regressors in (22).

Tests of the hypothesis that y Granger-causes x can be carried out simply by transposing x_t and y_t in the regressions (21) and (22), but there is no reason to preclude the possibility that y Granger-causes x and x Granger-causes y, i.e. that there is *feedback* between x and y. This is most easily analysed using a *vector autoregression* (VAR) of the two variables. A VAR of order p in x and y can be written as

$$x_t = \sum_{i=1}^{p} \theta_{11i} x_{t-i} + \sum_{i=1}^{p} \theta_{12i} y_{t-i} + v_{1t}$$

$$y_t = \sum_{i=1}^{p} \theta_{21i} x_{t-i} + \sum_{i=1}^{p} \theta_{22i} y_{t-i} + v_{2t} \tag{23}$$

The hypothesis that y does not Granger-cause x is thus $H_o: \theta_{121} = \theta_{122} = \ldots \theta_{12p} = 0$, while x does not Granger-cause y is encapsulated in $H_o: \theta_{211} = \theta_{212} = \ldots \theta_{21p} = 0$. If both hypotheses are rejected then there is feedback between the variables.

The VAR framework also allows *spurious causality* resulting from the omission of, say, a third variable z to be investigated: lags of z are simply introduced into the VAR equations (23), while patterns of causality within the trivariate system (x,y,z) can be investigated using a VAR of dimension 3: for a development of causality testing in VARs, see Mills (1990a: ch. 14.4).

It should be noted, however, that these multivariate procedures typically assume that the series are stationary in a multivariate sense. This is a highly technical concept that is outside our remit here, but suffice it to say that the presence of nonstationarities results in some difficult, and yet to be completely resolved, inferential problems: see, for example, Sims, Stock and Watson (1990). An analysis of certain key issues in this area is the topic of the next section.

Nonstationarity, differencing and cointegration

As intimated above, when building multivariate models involving non-stationary variables, care must be taken to ensure that any inferences drawn from the models are valid. To see this, consider the well known problem in econometrics of 'nonsense' or 'spurious' regressions. Granger and Newbold (1974) have examined the likely empirical consequences of such regressions, focusing attention on the standard textbook warning about the presence of serially correlated errors invalidating conventional procedures of inference. In particular, they were concerned with the specification of regression equations in terms of the *levels* of economic time series, which, as has been shown above, are typically nonstationary, often appearing to be near random walks. Such regression equations, argue Granger and Newbold, frequently have high R^2 statistics yet also typically display highly autocorrelated residuals, indicated by very low Durbin-Watson (DW) statistics. They contend that, in such situations, the usual significance tests performed on the regression coefficients can be very misleading, and they provide Monte Carlo simulation evidence to show that conventional significance tests are seriously biased towards rejection of the null hypothesis of no relationship, and hence towards acceptance of a spurious relationship, even when the series are generated as statistically independent random walks.

These findings led Granger and Newbold (1974) to suggest that, in the joint circumstances of a high R^2 and a low DW statistic (a useful rule of thumb being $R^2 > DW$), regressions should be run on the first differences of the variables, and these essentially empirical conclusions have since been placed on a firm analytical foundation by Phillips (1986) and Phillips and Durlauf (1986).

Nevertheless, even given the strong implication from these studies that regression analysis using the levels of economic time series can only be undertaken with great care, many economists feel unhappy about analysing regressions fitted to first differences, which is the obvious 'time series analyst' solution to the nonstationarity problem. Phrases like 'throwing the baby out with the bath water' and, less prosaically, 'valuable long-run information being lost' are often heard. These worries centre around the existence of long-run, steady state equilibria, a concept that (primarily static) economic theory devotes considerable attention to.

To develop this argument, consider a simple dynamic model of the form

$$y_t = \alpha + \beta x_t + \gamma x_{t-1} + \delta y_{t-1} + u_t, \qquad (24)$$

where, as usual, all variables are measured in logarithms. In steady state equilibrium, where $y_t = y_{t-1} = y_e$, $x_t = x_{t-1} = x_e$ and $u_e = 0$, we have the solution

$$y_e = \alpha' + \beta' x_e,$$

where $\alpha' = \alpha/(1-\delta)$ and $\beta' = (\beta+\gamma)/(1-\delta)$. If, on the other hand, the differenced model

$$\nabla y_t = \beta \nabla x_t + \gamma \nabla x_{t-1} + \delta \nabla y_{t-1} + v_t \qquad (25)$$

is considered, all differences are zero in the steady state and so no solution is obtainable: we can say nothing about the long-run relationship between y_t and x_t. Moreover, in a constant growth equilibrium, where $\nabla y = \nabla x = g$, the levels model (23) has the solution

$$y_e = \alpha'' + \beta'' x_e,$$

where $\alpha'' = (\alpha - g(\gamma + \delta))/(1-\delta)$; this, of course, reducing to the steady state equilibrium solution when $g = 0$. The differenced equation (24) again has no such solution in terms of y_e and x_e.

Of course, models relating series generated by DS, or *integrated*, processes may indeed not provide any information about long-run relationships; such relationships may simply not exist. But it is obviously important to allow for their possibility when building models between economic time series, which just using differenced variables will fail to do.

There is, in fact, a linkage between these two, seemingly diametrically opposed, views of the model building process. This is the concept of *cointegration*, which offers a connection between relationships between integrated processes and the concept of (steady state) equilibrium. This was originally introduced by Granger (1981) and a formal development is contained in Engle and Granger (1987); useful elementary discussion of the concept may be found in Granger (1986) and the implications it has for econometric modelling are discussed in Hendry (1986) and reviewed in Dolado, Jenkinson and Sosvilla-Rivero (1990).

Some useful notation is needed to develop the concept of cointegration. A time series that requires differencing d times for it to be stationary is said to be an *integrated-process of order d*, denoted $I(d)$. Thus a series that is already stationary is $I(0)$, while if a series is $I(1)$ its first difference is stationary. These two processes are sufficient for our purposes, although a completely general analysis in terms of vector $I(d)$ processes is available in Engle and Granger (1987).

An $I(1)$ series will be rather smooth, with dominant long swings, when compared to an $I(0)$ series. Because the variance of an $I(1)$ series goes to infinity, while an $I(0)$ series has finite variance, the sum of an $I(0)$ and an $I(1)$ series will be $I(1)$. Moreover, if x_t and y_t are both $I(1)$, then it is *generally* true that the linear combination

$$z_t = y_t - \alpha x_t \tag{26}$$

will also be $I(1)$. However, it is possible that z_t is $I(0)$ and, when this occurs, a special constraint operates on the long-run components of x_t and y_t. Since x_t and y_t are both $I(1)$, they will be dominated by 'long wave' components, but z_t, being $I(0)$, will not be: y_t and αx_t must therefore have long run components that virtually cancel out to produce z_t. In such circumstances, x_t and y_t are said to be cointegrated, with α being called the cointegrating parameter; equivalently, they can be said to contain a *common trend* (Stock and Watson, 1988).

To relate this idea to the concept of long-run equilibrium, suppose that such an equilibrium is defined by the relationship

$$y_t = \alpha x_t$$

or

$$y_t - \alpha x_t = 0.$$

Thus, z_t given by (25) measures the extent to which the system (x_t, y_t) is out of equilibrium, and can therefore be termed the 'equilibrium error'. Hence if x_t and y_t are both $I(1)$, then the equilibrium error will be $I(0)$ and z_t will rarely drift far from zero, if it has zero mean, and will often cross the zero line. In other words, equilibrium will occasionally occur, whereas if x_t and y_t are not cointegrated, so that z_t is $I(1)$, the equilibrium error can wander widely and zero-crossings would be rare, suggesting that under such circumstances the concept of equilibrium has no practical implications.

It is this feature of cointegration that links it with the spurious regression analysis discussed earlier. A regression on the differences of time series provides no information about the long-run equilibrium relationship, which can only be provided by a regression estimated on the levels of the data. But, if the series are integrated, standard statistical inference on levels regression breaks down completely, except in one special case: when the series are cointegrated![13] Thus, only if integrated series are cointegrated can inference be carried out on models estimated in levels, and only if they are cointegrated is there a meaningful equilibrium relationship between them. If the series are not cointegrated, then there is no equilibrium relationship existing between them and analysis *should* therefore be undertaken on their differences.

The importance of being able to test whether a pair, or in general a vector, of integrated time series are cointegrated is thus clear. Furthermore, given that such series are cointegrated, estimation of the cointegrating parameter (in general, the cointegrating vector) is then an essential second step. In fact, such testing and estimation are intimately related.

As a prerequisite it must first be determined whether x_t and y_t are $I(1)$ processes: this can be done using the unit root tests introduced earlier. Given that both series are indeed $I(1)$ processes, a convenient method of testing whether they are cointegrated is to estimate the 'cointegrating regression'

$$y_t = \beta_0 + \beta_1 x_t + u_t \tag{27}$$

and then test if the residual $\hat{u}_t$ appears to be $I(0)$ or not. Although a number of tests have been proposed, the one that seems to work best is to perform a unit root test on the residuals, i.e. to estimate the regression

$$\hat{u}_t = \rho \hat{u}_{t-1} + \sum_{j=1}^{l} \gamma_j \nabla \hat{u}_{t-j} + e_t$$

and compute the usual $\hat{\tau}_\rho$ statistic to test the hypothesis that $\rho = 1$. The use of residuals in this test invalidates the Fuller (1976) critical values, but Engle and Yoo (1987) provide the appropriate tables, extended to situations when there are more than two variables being considered.

When x_t and y_t are cointegrated, the OLS estimate of the slope coefficient β_1 in (26) should provide, in large samples, an excellent estimate of the true cointegration parameter α, even though the error u_t will typically be highly serially correlated. The reasoning for this is as follows. If x_t and y_t are cointegrated for $\beta_1 = \alpha$, then u_t will be $I(0)$ and will have a finite variance. All omitted dynamics in (26) can be reparameterised purely in terms of ∇y_{t-i}, ∇x_{t-j} and $(y_{t-k} - \hat{\alpha} x_{t-k})$, all of which are $I(0)$ under cointegration and therefore can be subsumed within u_t. Thus α can be *consistently* estimated despite the complete omission of all dynamics. Furthermore, it is also the case that OLS estimates of α are highly efficient, with $\hat{\alpha}(=\hat{\beta}_1)$ converging rapidly to α at a rate that is much faster than that of standard econometric estimators. Of course, the conventional least squares formula for estimating the variance of $\hat{\alpha}$ remains invalid due to the serial correlation in u_t.

How, though, does the existence of cointegration between y_t and x_t enable equilibrium relationships to be modelled while at the same time avoiding difficult problems of statistical inference? It does so through the Granger Representation Theorem (Engle and Granger, 1987). This shows that if y_t and x_t are both $I(1)$ and cointegrated, then there exists an *error correction representation*, a simple form of which is

$$\nabla y_t = \omega_0 + \omega_1 \nabla x_t - \gamma(y_{t-1} - \alpha x_{t-1}) + \varepsilon_t. \tag{28}$$

All terms in (27) are $I(0)$, so that no inferential difficulties arise. When $\nabla y_t = \nabla x_t = 0$ the 'no change' steady state equilibrium of

$$y_t = \alpha x_t + \omega_0/\gamma$$

is reproduced, while the steady state growth path, obtained when $\nabla y_t = \nabla x_t = g$, takes the form

$$y_t = \alpha x_t + (\omega_0 - g(1 - \omega_1))/\gamma.$$

Models of this simple form have been shown to be capable of being generated by a variety of economic mechanisms based upon minimising adjustment costs in a partial manner: for a survey, see Alogoskoufis and Smith (1991).

Notes

1 In what follows, we explicitly assume that trend and cycle can be separated out. This may not necessarily be the case, as was emphasised by Schumpeter in his classic study of economic development and fluctuations (1939), and was later more formally analysed by Goodwin (1953) and Higgins (1955). Hicks (1965: 4) gives an excellent summary of these arguments. None the less, the assumption that trend and cycle are distinct has been maintained by the vast majority of business cycle researchers and justification for their position can be found in Aldcroft and Fearon (1972: 5–7).

2 This framework leads to the general class of *unobserved component* models, which have been widely employed in the analysis of economic time series; for an extended development of such models, see Harvey (1990).

3 Feinstein, Matthews and Odling-Smee (1982) prefer to estimate β_k by connecting the actual values of the series in the chosen terminal years. This estimate is approximately given by $\beta_k^* \simeq k^{-1}(y_{T_2} - y_{T_1})$, but Crafts, Leybourne and Mills (1989a) show that β_k^* is never a more efficient estimator than the OLS estimator β_k.

4 This result is proved in Pierce (1978), albeit in the context of seasonal adjustment. It is also natural to ask for what model of the observed series y will a moving average provide an optimal trend estimate. This question has been considered by Tiao and Hillmer (1978), unfortunately only in the limited case when the cyclical component is assumed to be serially uncorrelated. However, in this case the models for y would appear to be autoregressive processes of order $h-1$ in the first differences, thus again pointing towards the procedure being

suboptimal for the typical series having only weakly autocorrelated first differences.

5 A series is said to be stationary (or, to be more precise, *weakly* stationary) if its mean and variance are constant through time and its autocovariances (the covariance between u_t and u_{t-k} for values of k) depend only on the time lag k and not on time itself (for further discussion see, for example, Mills (1990a: ch. 5.1)).

6 A related distinction between the two processes is in their forecasting properties. The forecast errors from a TS process are bounded no matter how far into the future forecasts are made because u_t has finite variance. Moreover, while autocorrelation in u_t can be exploited in making short-term (cyclical) forecasts, over long horizons the only relevant information about a future y is its mean, $\alpha + \beta t$, so that neither current nor past events will alter long-term expectations. Contrast this with forecasts made from a DS process. Here, the forecast error variance will increase without bound, since it is an increasing function of time, while long-term forecasts will always be influenced by historical events through the accumulation of the shocks e_t. The actual form of the trend component of a DS process will be discussed later in the chapter.

7 Furthermore, as West (1987) points out, if y is DS then, since all innovations are permanent, the concept of a stationary natural rate of growth will have little meaning, for 'a shock will, on average, never be offset by a return to some constant trend growth rate.'

8 This result, which was originally obtained through Monte Carlo simulation, has now been obtained analytically by Durlauf and Phillips (1988).

9 Note that the test can also be carried out by using the conventional t-statistic for testing whether the coefficient of y_{t-1} is zero in the regression of $(y_t - y_{t-1})$ on a constant, t and y_{t-1}.

10 Both $\hat{t}_\rho$ and Φ_3 are invariant with respect to y_0 and α, but they are not invariant with respect to β, the trend parameter, even asymptotically. In practice this is not a problem in the type of situations typically of interest to economic historians, since one usually wishes to test for a series with a unit root and a drift *against* the hypothesis that the series is stationary around a linear trend. The hypothesis of a unit root with a trend is usually excluded *a priori* since, if y is in logarithms, it implies an ever increasing (or decreasing) rate of change. More general testing procedures are discussed in Dolado, Jenkinson and Sosvilla-Rivero (1990).

11 This representation, known as the Wold decomposition, is a perfectly general one and is the foundation of time series analysis (see, for example, Mills, 1990a: ch. 5.2).

12 The formula for generating the λ_j weights may be found in, for example, Watson (1986). Note that, in general, $\Lambda(B)$ is an *infinite* two-sided moving average. In practice, with only a finite sample of observations $Y^T = \{y_0, y_1, \ldots, y_T\}$ available, unknown values $y_{-1}, y_{-2}, \ldots$ and $y_{T+1}, y_{T+2}, \ldots$ may be replaced by their forecasts constructed from Y^T and the model for y_t.

13 The formal development of these arguments may be found in Stock (1987), Phillips and Durlauf (1986) and Sims, Stock and Watson (1990). Mills (1990a: ch. 13.4) provides a textbook discussion of these matters.

Part I

Great Britain and fluctuations under the gold standard 1870–1914

3 The gold standard since Alec Ford

BARRY EICHENGREEN

Alec Ford's *The Gold Standard 1880–1914: Britain and Argentina* is one of a handful of classics on the gold standard written in the twentieth century. The book made three contributions. First, it elaborated a new model of the balance-of-payments adjustment mechanism. Analysing the experience of Britain, Ford argued that adjustment worked through different channels than the price-specie flow mechanism emphasised by Hume or the interest-rate-induced capital flows emphasised by Whale.[1] Ford's Keynesian model highlighted the tendency of gold outflows to raise interest rates, lower domestic demand, and restore external balance through the reduction of output, employment and import demand.[2] Relative price movements, or changes in interest rates induced by central banks playing by the rules of the game, might aid adjustment but their role was subsidiary.

The second contribution of the book was to contrast the very different nature of gold standard experience in general, and of the adjustment mechanism in particular, in less-developed primary-producing countries. Analysing the experience of Argentina, Ford argued that the record of stability under the gold standard was less satisfactory at the periphery than the centre. As at the centre, at the periphery adjustment worked through changes in income and demand. An inflow of long-term capital, for example, tended to stimulate demand, increasing imports and thereby tending to restore balance to the external accounts. But at the periphery exceptionally large fluctuations in income were required. Given the underdeveloped state of domestic financial markets and even the absence of a central bank, there was little scope for interest rate changes to induce accommodating short-term capital flows. The commodity prices facing primary-producing countries were dictated by world commodity markets. Hence, the burden of adjustment fell squarely on changes in demand, often brought about by fluctuations in employment.

Ford's third contribution was to indicate how countries of both types fit together in an equilibrium system. He showed how the operation of markets throughout the international economy facilitated adjustment to balance-of-payments disturbances. An increase in long-term foreign lending by London, for example, automatically induced an increase in the recipient country's demand for commodity imports from Britain. The fall in British output and employment that otherwise would be caused by the shift from domestic to foreign investment was attenuated by the export boom. But Ford also emphasised the extent to which the operation of these markets depended on 'the social and political environments, as well as economic, of the countries concerned'.[3] Specifically, the maintenance of international equilibrium depended on the fortuitously rapid growth of the world economy, which subdued domestic devaluation lobbies. It depended on the propensity of capital-importing nations to use foreign funds to finance investment rather than consumption. It depended on the fact that the leading capital-exporting nation was also an exporter of capital goods.

Ford's model, with its prominent Keynesian features, was a product of its time. The subsequent quarter of a century has seen a radical change of fashion in macroeconomics, and a recasting of the literature on the gold standard. The rise of monetarism has produced monetarist models of the gold standard. The rise of efficient-markets models of the macroeconomy has led to efficient-markets models of the gold standard. The literature on rules versus discretion and on the credibility and time consistency of macroeconomic policy has led recent authors to view the gold standard in this light.

In this chapter I assess the recent literature on the gold standard. I limit my attention to contributions which postdate Ford's 1962 book, concentrating on publications from the last decade. This review suggests that recent developments have been very much of the character 'two steps forward, one step back'. Most recent work on the gold standard has been driven by a theoretical agenda, not an historical one. Advances in theory have helped to illuminate dark corners of the gold standard adjustment mechanism. But they have led investigators to pay exaggerated attention to certain features of the system at the neglect of others. The literature on the gold standard may have moved forward, but not without suffering significant reversals.

In the second part of the chapter I offer a synthesis of the literature on how the gold standard worked. The model turns out to be very much in the spirit of the work of Alec Ford.

The literature since Alec Ford[4]

The Gold Standard 1880–1914 postdated integration of the IS-LM model into the mainstream of theoretical macroeconomics but preceded the elaboration of its open-economy variant. This awaited the work of Fleming

(1962) and Mundell (1963). These authors showed how, in an open economy with sticky prices, the response of employment and the balance of payments to monetary and fiscal impulses depended on the degree of international capital mobility. The Mundell-Fleming model formalised the elements of income and balance-of-payments determination suggested by Meade (1951) and discussed in a gold standard context by Ford. The adjustment mechanism – the translation of flows into stocks along the traverse from temporary to steady-state equilibrium – was not treated explicitly, but its nature was clear. If demand expansion raised absorption or reduced interest rates relative to combinations consistent with balance-of-payments equilibrium, income would have to fall or interest rates would have to rise, perhaps through contraction of the money supply, for the fixed exchange rate (or gold convertibility) to be maintained.

From there it was a small step to specify a two-country version of the model, as in Mundell (1968), and to analyse internal and external balance under different assumptions about capital mobility. The problem with these models was the assumption that capital flows responded to interest differentials. Flows were not tracked into stocks, which had uncomfortable implications. In two-country models, for instance, residents of both countries would have wished to accumulate assets of the country with the higher yield, which was patently impossible.[5]

It is as a response to these contradictions that the monetary approach to the balance of payments (Frenkel, 1971; Mundell, 1971; Johnson, 1973) must be understood. The monetary approach was the simplest way of analysing balance-of-payments adjustment with stock equilibrium in asset markets. As in the Mundell-Fleming model, each country possessed a money demand function (the stock equilibrium condition). But flows cumulated into changes in stocks. Money supply equalled the sum of domestic credit and foreign reserves.[6] Under fixed rates, the authorities stood ready to purchase domestic currency for reserves when money demand exceeded money supply at the fixed domestic currency price of foreign exchange, and to swap domestic currency for reserves when supply exceeded demand. If domestic credit was held constant, money supplies responded to demand exclusively through reserve flows – that is, through the balance of payments. An excess of money demand over money supply caused reserves to be imported from abroad. An injection of domestic credit which raised money supply relative to demand caused a loss of reserves, leading ultimately to a convertibility crisis. It was straightforward to combine two such countries (Mundell, 1971) and to show how the level of commodity prices had to adjust to ensure that global excess demands for money and reserves equalled zero.

Application to the gold standard was direct (Mundell, 1971; McCloskey and Zecher, 1976). In the simplest formulation, the supply of domestic credit was fixed. Money supplies responded to changes in demand through international specie flows. It was a simple extension to add to this framework the rules of the gold standard game. If central banks adjusted domestic credit in the same direction as changes in their foreign reserves (in other words, played by the rules of the game), the need for actual gold movements would be minimised. Changes in the discount rate might be utilised to bring about the same result through changes in the money multiplier.

Consistent treatment of stock-flow relationships was a step forward. But much of this literature also took on board a whole array of monetarist assumptions and assumptions from efficient markets models with which monetarism is sometimes confused. The money market was assumed to clear instantaneously. Domestic and foreign interest-bearing assets were assumed to be perfect substitutes. Capital was assumed to be perfectly mobile internationally. Real variables were assumed to be determined independently of financial stocks and flows. Purchasing power parity was assumed to hold continuously.

These assumptions combined to yield a particular model of the adjustment mechanism, one very different from its predecessors. With purchasing power parity holding continuously, adjustment entailed no relative price movements like those predicted by Hume. With interest parity holding continuously, it entailed no relative interest rate movements like those predicted by Whale. With full employment maintained continuously, it entailed no relative income movements like those predicted by Ford. When money demand exceeded supply and the incipient excess demand put upward pressure on interest rates, capital simply flowed in, reserves accumulated, and money supply expanded instantaneously to ensure that interest rates remained pegged at world levels.

Changes in spending and other adjustments remained in the background. But if one paused to think about the issue, they were of the utmost importance. If little or no decline in spending occurred in the short run, the capital inflow took the form of increased claims by foreigners on domestic residents. Spending would have to be reduced subsequently to generate the current account surpluses necessary to service the debt. If spending fell in the short run, the accumulation of reserves could be financed with current account surpluses. In this case, no decline in spending would be needed in the future to service foreign debt.

What combination of these extremes operated to restore external balance depended on the consumption-smoothing motives of households and the investment decisions of firms. Early examples of the monetary approach, including those applied to the gold standard, did not address this question. Nor did they ask what change in relative prices was needed to render foreigners willing to absorb the exports consequent on changes in domestic absorption. They assumed away the question by imposing the assumption of absolute purchasing power parity (McCloskey and Zecher, 1984) and by ignoring nontraded goods (and their relative price) entirely. Finally, they failed to pursue the implications of imperfect substitutability between domestic and foreign interest-bearing assets.

Subsequent work, which relaxed many of these restrictive assumptions, demonstrated that the emphasis of the monetary approach on stock equilibrium was entirely compatible with the adjustment mechanisms emphasised by Hume, Whale and Ford.[7] If domestic and foreign goods were imperfect substitutes in consumption, adjustment which entailed a decline in domestic absorption required precisely the change in relative prices predicted by Hume. Domestic prices would have to fall to render foreigners willing to absorb an increasing volume of imports. The stock-flow relationships central to the monetary approach survive this extension.[8] If wages or other costs of production were sticky in nominal terms, the fall in prices might move firms down their supply curves, reducing output and employment as predicted by Ford. If domestic and foreign financial assets were imperfect substitutes in portfolios, adjustment which entailed a capital account deficit required precisely the change in relative interest rates predicted by Whale. The yield on domestic bonds would have to rise to render foreigners willing to devote to them an increasing share of their portfolios.[9] There was nothing incompatible in the alternative formulations. They were all special cases of a more general model. Which mechanisms bore the burden of adjustment depended both on the structure of the economies involved and the nature of the disturbances in response to which adjustment was required.[10]

Unfortunately, the compatibility of these formulations was not widely appreciated. The monetary approach was characterised as a radical departure and a fundamental challenge to existing models.

The monetary approach found widespread application. McCloskey and Zecher (1976) used it to analyse gold flows between the US and Britain. Jonung (1984) analysed Swedish experience under the gold standard using a framework featuring both the monetary model of adjustment and purchasing power parity. McKinnon (1988) used the model to assess the performance of the gold standard in other countries. The relative prices of domestic and foreign traded goods played little role in these authors' description of the adjustment mechanism. According to McKinnon (1988: 9), for example, 'generalized commodity price arbitrage became sufficiently strong [under the gold standard] to prevent the prices (exclusive of tariffs) of any particular tradeable good – say cotton shirts – from differing significantly more across countries than they did interregionally within a country'.

McKinnon did not assume that purchasing power parity is an economic fact of life, however. Rather, he suggested that its presence was a function precisely of the fact that exchange rates had been fixed for substantial periods of time. Absent exchange risk, arbitragers had an incentive to develop the capacity to exploit and eliminate international commodity price differentials. This hypothesis suggests that the price-specie flow mechanism may have been more important during the early years of the gold standard as an international system.[11]

Like Jonung for Sweden, Calomiris and Hubbard (1987) for the United States argued that a monetary model best explains balance-of-payments adjustment under the gold standard. They argued that shocks to money supply and money demand had little persistent impact on prices, output or the balance of payments. Rather, such disturbances appear to have been quickly offset (in the case of money supply shocks) or accommodated (in the case of money demand shocks) by the rapid response of international gold flows. But in contrast to their predecessors, Calomiris and Hubbard acknowledged the compatibility of the essential element of the monetary approach – stock equilibrium in asset markets – with relative price movements inconsistent with strict purchasing power parity. In their analysis, a trade-balance shock might very well require a change in relative prices in order for balance-of-payments equilibrium to be restored. But in their model all of the price adjustment occurred immediately. Gold quickly flowed in or out to equilibrate asset markets. There was no need for the gradual or persistent adjustment characteristic of the price-specie flow model.

A logical problem raised by these conclusions is that it is not clear, in the absence of nominal inertia and in the presence of perfect international capital mobility, how to account for business cycles.[12] Calomiris and Hubbard's answer is credit rationing. In their model, deflationary disturbances erode the value of collateral, threatening the solvency of banks and producing a spread between interest rates in the customer markets frequented by borrowers dependent on bank credit and the internationally-arbitraged spot rates at which governments and other reputable agents can borrow and lend. A widening of these interest differentials signals credit rationing, which is the driving force behind business cycles in the Calomiris-Hubbard model.

The problem with attempting to apply this model to an actual historical episode is that interest differentials can arise also for a variety of other reasons. One, acknowledged by Calomiris and Hubbard themselves, is exchange risk. If, for example, there is a danger that a country will suspend gold convertibility and devalue, investors will demand a higher return. Garber and Grilli (1986) among others explain the high level of interest rates in the United States in the 1890s, when the free silver movement raised the spectre of monetary inflation and devaluation, on these grounds. Fratianni and Spinelli (1984) make a similar argument for Italy, a country threatened repeatedly with inconvertibility due to balance of payments problems.[13]

More generally, investors will demand to be compensated with a premium in order to devote a growing share of their portfolios to the liabilities of a specific country, as in the model of the gold standard developed in Floyd (1984: ch. 4). Balance-of-payments adjustment will be associated with changes in international interest differentials even if asset and commodity markets are perfectly integrated, interest rates rising in the deficit country and falling in the surplus country.[14] Observed interest differentials are likely to reflect some combination of credit rationing and these portfolio effects.

Complementing the literature suggesting that the gold standard was conducive to the equalisation of commodity prices across countries is a second literature emphasising the tendency of the gold standard to stabilise the price level over time. Barro (1979) formalised the argument, due to Mill (1865) and Mundell (1971), that the gold standard stabilised price levels through the reaction of gold supplies. Given gold stocks and money supplies, economic growth tended to put downward pressure on price levels througn the operation of the quantity equation. With national monetary authorities pegging the own-currency price of gold, the decline in commodity prices was equivalent to a rise in the relative price of gold. Insofar as commodity prices and costs of gold mining move together, the decline in prices should have induced a reallocation of resources toward the gold-mining industry and elicited increased production, augmenting the monetary gold stock and reversing the fall in the price level. These conclusions are modified when the characteristics of gold as a depletable resource are acknowledged, of course. Bordo and Ellson (1985) show that there is an inescapable tendency to long-run deflation when account is taken of the resource constraint.

Empirical support for the operation of this mechanism is less than compelling. Rockoff (1984) concluded from his study of mining and prospecting that gold supplies depended more on chance discoveries than on changes in the real price of gold. McKinnon (1988) went further, arguing that gold discoveries largely unrelated to price-level trends were the main source of instability in the operation of the classical gold standard. Other authors such as Bordo (1981) look not at gold mining *per se* but at the price-level stability that it was supposed to produce. Bordo's conclusions are mixed: he finds for Britain that the standard deviation of prices was somewhat lower during the four decades of the classical gold standard than during the post-1913 period; for the United States, it was slightly higher. This sceptical position is buttressed by Cooper (1982) and Callahan (1984), who find little evidence that prices were easier to predict in the gold standard years.

Another approach is to consider short- rather than long-run price-level movements, and to focus not on mining but on shifts of existing gold between monetary and non-monetary uses. Barsky and Summers (1988) and Lee and Petruzzi (1986) observe that asset market equilibrium implies a relationship between rates of return on gold and other non-monetary assets. If a productivity disturbance increases the real return on financial capital, investors will reduce the share of their portfolios devoted to alternative assets such as gold. Investors discouraged from holding gold by the incipient fall in its relative rate of return will sell it to the monetary authorites, who will use it to expand the money supply, raising the price level. Hence the positive correlation between the interest rate and the price level known as Gibson's Paradox.[15]

The implication is that the price level may be unstable under a gold standard not just because of chance gold discoveries, as emphasised by McKinnon, and because of developments affecting the demand for money, but also because of shocks affecting portfolio behaviour that induce shifts in the demand for non-monetary gold, destabilising the money supply. The quantitative importance of the mechanism remains to be adduced, however.

This literature also has implications for the debate over the validity of the Fisher effect in the gold standard years. If productivity disturbances were random and unpredictable, the same would have been true of the price-level changes they produced. Agents' best estimate of the inflation rate would have been zero. Hence, actual (current and lagged) inflation would not have been incorporated into nominal interest rates, even had investors been prepared to respond to anticipated inflation in the manner predicted by Irving Fisher. This is the conclusion reached by Barsky (1987). But if the Mill-Barro gold mining mechanism also comes into play, there may be serial correlation in inflation rates over long intervals. The British data in fact display some evidence of negative serial correlation at longer lags. If so, price-level changes may have been predictable, but their effects still would not be captured by investigators who use only lagged inflation as a proxy for expected inflation.[16]

The alternative to the monetary approach is represented by contributions emphasising not stock equilibrium in money markets but stock-flow interactions in bond markets, itself a central element of Ford's analysis.

Contributions that followed quickly on the heels of Ford's 1962 book include Lindert's (1969) study documenting reliance on foreign exchange reserves in the pre-1913 period; Bloomfield's (1968) study documenting the importance of long-term capital movements in provoking imbalances in the international accounts; and Bloomfield's (1963) study documenting the importance of short-term capital movements in accommodating those imbalances. The unifying theme running through this work was that international capital markets played a more important role in the operation of the gold standard than suggested in traditional accounts.

The introduction of capital movements into models of the gold standard drew attention to the role of central banks in managing the monetary mechanism. The *locus classicus* of this literature is the work by Nurkse (1944) and Bloomfield (1959) on the rules of the gold standard game. Using annual data for a cross section of countries in the 1920s and 1930s, Nurkse demonstrated that the domestic and foreign assets of central banks moved together, as required by the rules of the game, on only a minority of occasions. He concluded that the stability of the classical gold standard relative to its interwar successor was attributable to the greater propensity of central bankers to play by the rules of the game. Upon replicating Nurkse's analysis for the pre-1914 period, Bloomfield found no greater tendency to obey the rules, however. This finding was paradoxical, since it raised the question of how the classical gold standard had operated so successfully if central banks systematically sterilised reserve flows.

The paradox led subsequent investigators to study the behaviour of individual central banks in an effort to better characterise their behaviour. Goodhart (1972) estimated one of the first central bank reaction functions for the gold standard years, finding little evidence that the Bank of England played by the rules of the game. A resolution to the paradox was suggested by Pippinger (1984), who argued that existing studies failed to distinguish adequately between short- and long-run responses. Short-run sterilisation may have been compatible with the stability of the gold standard so long as it was reversed subsequently. In the long run, central banks had to reduce monetary liabilities in response to a decline in gold reserves or risk the suspension of convertibility. Pippinger's specification distinguished the short- and long-run responses of the Bank of England, and led him to conclude that there was considerable sterilisation in the short run but validation of reserve movements in the long run.[17]

Discount policy depended not only on current gold flows, of course, but also on anticipated future gold flows. And anticipated future flows depended in part on changes in policy abroad. Eichengreen (1987) and Giovannini (1989) therefore analysed the strategic interaction of central banks, using discount rates as a measure of policy stance, Eichengreen arguing in favour of more extensive strategic interaction than Giovannini. But both authors found evidence of asymmetries in the behaviour of different central banks. Certain central banks, like the Bank of England, seem to have played a disproportionate role in the determination of discount rates world-wide. When the Bank of England raised her rate, the Bank of France and the Reichsbank were quick to follow. While the Bank of England also responded to changes in monetary policy abroad, it did so to a lesser extent.

The recognition that the gold standard was actively managed by national central banks interacting in an international setting can be developed in two directions. One is additional study of the political economy of economic policymaking, as in de Cecco (1974) and Gallarotti (1988). The other is to search for economic foundations of the asymmetries that characterised international monetary interactions. Lindert (1969), for example, argues that asymmetries stemmed from differences across countries in the depth of domestic financial markets and the value of foreign investments. Deep domestic markets and extensive foreign investments rendered some discount rates, notably that of the Bank of England, more powerful than others. Hence, foreign central banks concerned with their reserve positions were forced to respond quickly to Bank Rate changes in London, while the Bank of England could restore her reserve position to desired levels with only modest changes in interest rates, even after considerable delay.[18]

Another possible source of asymmetry, popularised by Hawtrey, was London's prominence in primary commodity markets. Not only was Britain the leading importer of primary products, but London provided the bulk of the short-term credits that financed inventories of primary commodities. A higher Bank Rate increased inventory-carrying costs, causing stocks of raw materials to be dumped on the market. Thus, a rise in Bank Rate had an exceptional ability to strengthen the British balance of payments: in addition to its other effects, it induced the liquidation of commodity stocks, depressing their price, improving Britain's terms of trade, and reducing the cost of her imports. The time-series evidence does not lend overwhelming support to this interpretation (Moggridge, 1972), although a careful study remains to be done.

These asymmetries may help to shed light on the very different experiences of countries at the centre and the periphery of the gold standard system. All too few authors have followed Ford's lead in focusing on the special difficulties of less developed countries in maintaining gold convertibility. The gap is surprising, since a useful by-product of the asset market approach to modelling the balance of payments has been models of balance of payments crises (Krugman, 1979). These are directly applicable to the problem of a run on the gold reserves of a central bank striving to maintain a gold standard parity. Analyses of stability and crisis under the gold standard remain rare. One of the few examples is Dornbusch and Frenkel (1984), who develop a model of central bank management of the gold standard and suggest that, if the central bank's reserve-deposit ratio falls to low enough levels, actions which normally attract bullion from abroad instead may undermine confidence, with destabilising effects.

Those few studies which have considered the question from the perspective of the periphery analyse the gold standard in conjunction with the periods of inconvertibility with which it alternated. Fishlow (1987) has considered the factors that tended to produce balance-of-payments difficulties for Latin American countries in the gold standard years.[19] His conclusions are consistent with Ford's interpretation of Argentine experience: that the countries of the periphery endured special difficulties due to the synchronisation of capital- and commodity-market shocks. When countries like Britain suffered a decline in exports, the Bank of England could restore external balance by raising interest rates so as to discourage foreign investment. But the countries of Latin America, many of which lacked even a central bank, had no control over the direction of international capital flows. Moreover, disruptions to their export markets rendered them less desirable places to invest. Hence, they simultaneously suffered declines in export revenues and in capital inflows. Fishlow concluded that the relative importance of the shocks varied across countries, however. Fluctuations in capital inflows mattered more for Argentina and Chile than for Brazil. Changes in real export receipts mattered more for Argentina and Brazil than for Chile. Thus, the 'Ford hypothesis' that Latin American countries were buffeted simultaneously by capital- and commodity-market shocks seems to have been primarily a hypothesis applicable to Argentina, logically enough since that was the country studied by Ford.

Even after controlling for external disturbances, Fishlow found that the balance of payments of all three countries was significantly affected by changes in domestic money supply. In other words, the failure of these countries to adhere to the rules of the game, and not merely the severity of the external shocks they suffered, explains their repeated bouts of inconvertibility. The traditional interpretation of this failure is the political power of export and debtor interests: inflation and depreciation benefited politically influential landowners with mortgages and exporters competing in world markets. Fishlow suggests, however, that this interpretation may impute too much foresight and influence to these special interests. Responsibility for the excesses of monetary policy resided, ironically, with the banking and financial communities. There was a growing feeling throughout Latin America in the late nineteenth century that banking and financial development had lagged behind the needs of the economy. Ample liquidity was seen as conducive to the expansion of the banking system and to the invigoration of financial markets. Unfortunately, more than liquidity was needed to promote the financial deepening. Rather than financial development, the result of rapid monetary expansion was inflation, inconvertibility and depreciation.

The view that domestic policy was responsible for external difficulties at the periphery was common among foreign investors. Creditors rightly focused on the incompatibility of domestic monetary policy with gold convertibility. In their view, exchange rate instability resulted not from periodic shortfalls of export receipts but from domestic profligacy. It mattered little whether the exchange rate was marginally overvalued so long as the growth of global export markets was maintained. What mattered was to restrain the tendency toward excess on the part of Latin American governments. Hence the propensity of foreign lenders to require restoration of the gold standard as a prerequisite for renewed foreign lending (Fishlow, 1989). Going off the gold standard could be embarrassing and damaging to a government which had invested considerable import-ance in its restoration. Having associated their reputations with successful maintenance of the gold standard, governments had an incentive to exercise discipline in their conduct of monetary and fiscal policies. This incentive vested their promises to pursue policies consistent with exchange rate and price stability with new credibility.[20] Somewhat ironically, the role of the gold standard as a credibility-creating device was most prominent on the fringes of the gold standard system.

Notes on the working of the gold standard before 1914[21]

This review of the literature provides another opportunity to pose the perennial question of how the gold standard worked. In this section I essay a provisional answer to that question. The methodology employs economic theory and historical data very much in the manner of Alec Ford.

In *The Gold Standard 1880–1914*, Ford analysed time series data for Britain and Argentina, without estimating a formal structural model of their balances of payments. Using time-series plots, he described first differences of exports, imports, foreign lending, net gold movements and the like. He then calculated correlation coefficients for pairs of these variables, and used them to inform his story of how the gold standard worked.

In this section, I proceed in similar fashion. Rather than specifying and estimating a structural model, I begin with significantly less structured data analysis, which considers correlations among the relevant variables in the time domain. The technique is a straightforward extension of Ford's methodology – namely, vector autoregression. I regress each element of a vector of endogenous variables on lagged values of itself and lagged values of the other variables. The estimated coefficients can be used to summarise the correlations between a variable of interest and lagged values of the other variables. Impulse-response functions, in which the error term in one of these equations is perturbed and the dynamic response of the system is traced out, can be used to analyse the consequences of various disturbances.

Vector autoregression reveals little about economic or historical causality. It is unlikely to tell us much about the ultimate causes of balance-of-payments problems under the gold standard.[22] It simply summarises the relevant correlations in a digestible form. Simulations using the estimated coefficients may help us to narrow the range of plausible models consistent with the facts, although there may be more than one model which satisfies this consistency criterion. Ultimately, other economic or historical evidence will be required to arrive at a satisfying interpretation.

Britain's experience is only one part of the larger gold standard story, as Ford's work makes clear. But an analysis of international adjustment by Britain, the centre country of the international gold standard, is a logical starting point for any such study. Here I limit the statistical analysis to data for Britain.

The six variables upon which I concentrate are the volume of British exports, the volume of British imports, Britain's international terms of trade (export prices relative to import prices), the Bank of England's discount rate, gold reserves, and the volume of British foreign lending. This is the minimal list of variables necessary to capture the most important disturbances to the British balance of payments and the most important channels through which balance-of-payments equilibrium was restored. The foreign lending variable is new issues for overseas borrowers (calls) on the London capital market, from Simon (1968), transformed to constant prices using the GNP deflator. Gold reserves (gold in the Issue Department of the Bank of England) are drawn from Mitchell and Deane (1962). The Bank of England's discount rate is drawn from Palgrave (1903), as supplemented by the *Economist Magazine*. The remaining variables are drawn from Feinstein's (1972) national income accounts. All variables are for the period 1871–1913.

Statistical analysis

Figures 3.1 to 3.5 juxtapose the gold flows against the other five variables. Figure 3.1 shows the well-known tendency of the Bank of England to adjust Bank Rate in response to changes in its gold reserve. Generally, as the

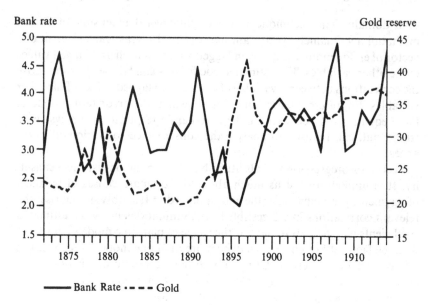

Figure 3.1   Bank Rate and gold reserve, 1872–1914.

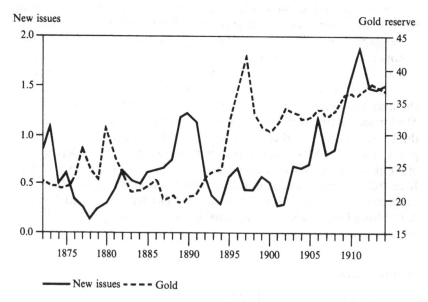

Figure 3.2   New issues and gold reserve, 1872–1914.

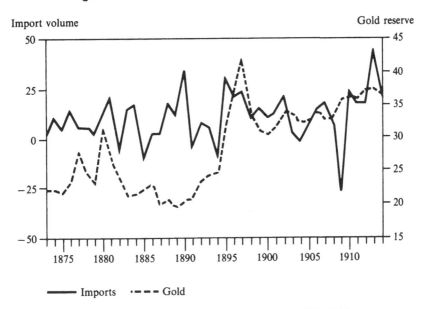

Figure 3.3   Change in import volume and gold reserve, 1872–1914.

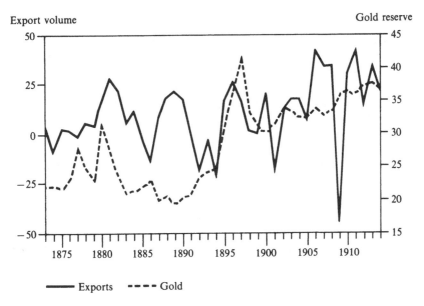

Figure 3.4   Change in export volume and gold reserve, 1872–1914.

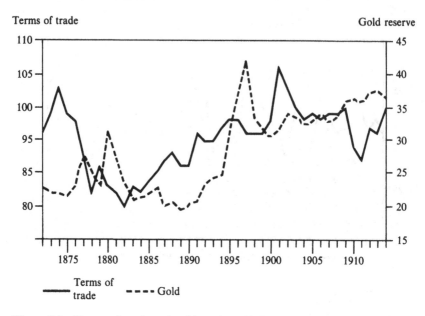

Figure 3.5   Terms of trade and gold reserve, 1872–1914.

reserve rises Bank Rate is reduced, although there are exceptions to the
rule. Figure 3.2 juxtaposes the gold reserve and the real value of new issues
on behalf of overseas borrowers. Here, too, there is some evidence of the
expected inverse correlation. Generally speaking, as the volume of overseas
lending rises, the gold reserve tends to fall.

Interpretation of the remaining three figures is less straightforward.
Figures 3.3 and 3.4 display the change in the volume of British imports and
exports along with the gold reserve. (Since import and export volumes
trend strongly upward over the period, first differences are displayed in
figures 3.3 and 3.4.) Although there is some rather weak evidence in figure
3.3 of positive comovements between imports and gold reserves (as if the
accumulation of reserves allowed an expansion of money supply which
fueled the demand for foreign goods), a notable feature of figure 3.3 is that
the upward shift in the gold reserve in the 1890s was not accompanied by a
comparable shift in the growth of imports. Figure 3.4 makes a similar
impression: export volumes and gold reserves move together (with notable
exceptions like the 1907 panic), but once again there is little noticeable
upward shift in export growth in the 1890s.

Finally, figure 3.5 juxtaposes the terms of trade against the Bank of
England's gold reserves. There is some evidence of sympathetic movements

Table 3.1. *Correlation coefficients*

	New issues	Exports	Imports	Terms of trade	Gold reserve
Bank Rate	0.291	0.295	0.224	0.315	−0.114
New Issues	—	0.701	0.535	0.084	0.293
Exports	—	—	0.961	0.332	0.723
Imports	—	—	—	0.462	0.801
Terms of Trade	—	—	—	—	0.432

Note: Sample period for all variables is 1871–1914.

in the two series, albeit with long and variable lags. In the 1870s and 1880s, movements in gold seem to lag behind the terms of trade, while in the 1890s and 1900s, the opposite, if anything, is true.

Table 3.1 shows correlation coefficients for the six variables, all expressed in level form. The strongest correlation is between exports and imports. The important question is whether fluctuations in one component of the trade balance responded to fluctuations in the other, or whether both responded contemporaneously to movements in other variables. Both exports and imports appear to have been tightly linked to the level of the gold reserve. There is evidence of a strong contemporaneous correlation between foreign lending and exports, as noted previously by Ford, raising anew the question of the direction of causality.

Table 3.2 reports the results of regressing each of these variables on three own lags and three lags of each of the other variables.[23] The sample is 1874–1913 to allow for lags. The figures reported are the confidence intervals implied by F-statistics testing the joint significance of lagged values of an explanatory variable. The null hypothesis is that lagged values of a variable are jointly unrelated to current values of the dependent variable. An entry of 0.05, for example, indicates that the null hypothesis of no association can be rejected at the 95% confidence level.

The first column summarises influences on the Bank of England's discount rate. By far the most important determinant of changes in Bank Rate (other than its own lags) is changes in gold in the Issue Department, plausibly enough given the Directors' concern with changes in gold reserves. There is some evidence that Bank Rate was raised in response to increases in the volume of imports and foreign lending. The obvious

Table 3.2. *Statistical significance of independent variables (confidence levels at which F-statistics indicate null hypothesis can be rejected)*

Independent variable	Bank Rate	New issues	Dependent variable			
			Exports	Imports	Terms of trade	Gold reserve
Bank Rate	0.049	0.810	0.334	0.403	0.281	0.766
New issues	0.051	0.019	0.143	0.242	0.714	0.518
Exports	0.448	0.114	0.006	0.913	0.584	0.482
Imports	0.049	0.043	0.098	0.044	0.272	0.456
Terms of trade	0.078	0.554	0.340	0.241	0.015	0.021
Gold reserve	0.002	0.616	0.712	0.781	0.161	0.008

interpretation is that these variables were viewed as leading indicators of balance of payments trends and hence of future gold flows.

The second column, which summarises influences on the volume of overseas lending, paints a different picture. Changes in Bank Rate, in gold flows, and in the terms of trade display little association with movements in new foreign issues. Only lagged changes in British imports (and, to a lesser extent, exports) have much tendency to 'produce' a change in new foreign lending. It is difficult to determine, on the basis of these correlations, whether it is more appropriate to regard fluctuations in new foreign lending as induced by swings in other components of the balance of payments or as relatively autonomous, as suggested by Ford.[24]

The strongest influence on British exports (other than their own lagged values) is British imports. The two variables covary positively. Apparently, business cycle movements which raised British imports subsequently induced a rise in British exports which served to moderate the deterioration in the balance of trade. One can imagine a two-country model in which the rise in British imports stimulated economic activity abroad through the export multiplier, raising foreign incomes and stimulating demands overseas for British exports. There is also evidence of a less definitive nature that a rise in British foreign lending was followed by a rise in commodity exports. Ford suggested that British funds lent to regions of recent European settlement were disproportionately devoted to investment projects, creating a demand for imported capital goods and stimulating British exports. There is some support in the table for what Ford called the 'sensitivity' of British exports 'directly and indirectly' to British overseas lending, but the evidence is far from overwhelming.[25]

Imports appear to have been little affected by changes in Bank Rate or other variables. If monetary policy was effective in influencing the evolution of the balance of payments, it appears to have operated mainly by influencing other components of the external accounts. Similarly, the terms of trade do not appear to have been *directly* responsive to the Bank of England's discount rate. There is little evidence in table 3.2 of the 'Triffin Effect' – the tendency of a rise in Bank Rate to induce liquidation of commodity stocks and strengthen Britain's terms of trade, although the impact of changes in Bank Rate on the terms of trade is more pronounced than its impact on foreign lending, exports, imports or gold flows.[26] Indeed, the dominant impression that emerges from the first row of the table is that Bank Rate had only a weak impact on the British balance of payments. This is consistent with Sayers' (1936) conclusion that, for much of the period, the Bank of England was still struggling, with mixed success, to render its discount rate effective, and with Ford's conclusion that the power and influence of Bank of England monetary policy has been exaggerated.

The final column of table 3.2 shows that lagged values of most of the variables under consideration had only a weak direct impact on the Bank of England's gold reserve. (Those variables still could have affected the reserve indirectly, a possibility considered below.) However, lagged values of the terms of trade do exhibit an association with the Bank of England's reserve, which may give pause to those inclined to dismiss the relevance of the price-specie flow mechanism.

The above are partial equilibrium inferences. To focus attention on general equilibrium repercussions, Figures 3.6 to 3.11 show the response of the system to perturbations to the disturbance terms in three of these equations. (The equations are first transformed to moving-average form, as is standard in the literature.) The resulting system is then perturbed, in turn, by a one standard deviation shock to the disturbances to the foreign issue, export, and gold equations.[27] I interpret the three disturbances as temporary shocks to the capital account, the current account, and to confidence.

Consider first the response, depicted in figures 3.6 and 3.7, to a temporary increase in new foreign lending. The autonomous weakening of the balance of payments produces an immediate gold outflow. The Bank of England's discount rate is raised, presumably in an effort to damp the loss of reserves. The volume of new foreign issues falls back toward pre-disturbance levels, as if higher British interest rates increase the attractiveness of domestic investment. Indeed, the volume of new foreign issues declines temporarily below its steady state level, due one supposes to higher domestic interest rates.

The response of the current account of the balance of payments is less straightforward. Exports rise relative to imports with the initial weakening of the capital account (figure 3.7). The rise in exports is associated initially with some deterioration in Britain's terms of trade, as if the relative price of British goods had to decline in order to stimulate their increased absorption overseas. But by the second year following the shock, the terms of trade have recovered fully. From years three to seven, they are above their steady state level, as if the surge in foreign lending, once it had time to work its way through the system, shifted rightward the foreign demand curve for British goods.

Figures 3.6 and 3.7 may say something about the geographical source of shocks to British foreign lending. If shifts from domestic to foreign investment had been produced by increases in the marginal efficiency of capital overseas, this should have provoked a rise in import demand overseas at the same time as it attracted financial capital from Britain. The rise in foreign demand should then have strengthened Britain's terms of trade. If, in contrast, shifts from domestic to foreign investment had been produced mainly by inward shifts in the marginal efficiency of capital schedule at home, this should have provoked a decline in domestic demand and a deterioration in Britain's terms of trade sufficient for an increased share of domestic output to be willingly absorbed abroad. There is support for this interpretation in the fact that Britain's terms of trade deteriorate on impact, although their subsequent tendency to strengthen is subversive of that conclusion.

A possible resolution of the paradox may be to argue that foreign shocks in fact drove the fluctuation of foreign lending over the cycle, but that foreign households and firms could not finance their increased notional demand for imports from Britain due to a binding balance-of-payments constraint. They had to wait for the response by British investors and the receipt of long-term capital inflows before increasing their purchases of British goods. Figures 3.6 and 3.7 support this interpretation. Thus, the domestic demand for British goods declined initially, as financial capital was shifted from home to overseas investment in response to the productivity shock abroad. Over time, overseas investors begin to devote their increased sterling balances to purchases of British goods, driving up British export prices. Thus, following their initial deterioration, Britain's terms of trade quickly strengthen. Exports rise steadily. It indeed appears that in the short run an increase in British foreign lending provoked or facilitated little rightward shift in the demand schedule for British exports, but that over time British lending began to translate into a rise in foreign expenditure, including expenditure on imports. Eventually, these effects damp out, as exports, foreign lending and the terms of trade return to their

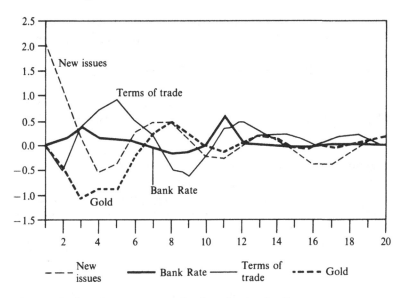

Figure 3.6   Impulse response to shock to foreign lending.

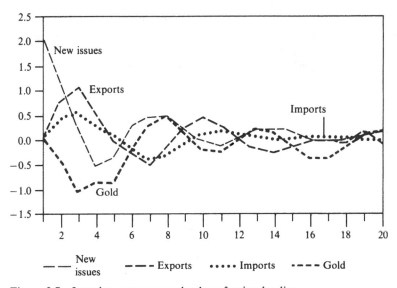

Figure 3.7   Impulse response to shock to foreign lending.

steady state levels. But over the intermediate run, from two to six years following the shock, the terms of trade strengthen relative to their steady state level.

Figures 3.8 and 3.9 show the response to a temporary increase in exports. The autonomous rise in export revenues strengthens the balance of payments and leads initially to an accumulation of gold reserves. But the gold inflow is quickly attenuated. Imports rise in response to the export boom. Long-term foreign lending also rises (figure 3.9). Presumably, the rise in demand overseas for the products of British industry increased British incomes, provoking the rise in import demand.

That foreign lending rises rather than falls following the autonomous increase in exports is helpful for distinguishing between two competing interpretations of the export shocks experienced by the British economy. If exports had tended to fluctuate mainly in response to productivity shocks at home, the logical consequence of a positive shock to export capacity would have been to render domestic investment more attractive relative to foreign investment, and to produce a decline in new foreign issues. If, in contrast, exports tended to fluctuate primarily because of external shocks to incomes overseas, a positive shock to exports would have rendered foreign investment more attractive relative to domestic investment, and one would have expected foreign lending to rise. It is the second case that is observed. The notion that the fluctuation of British export markets was driven mainly by disturbances abroad is supported by the initial improvement in the terms of trade following the positive export shock. If fluctuations in capacity at home rather than in demand abroad had been the primary source of British export cycles, one would expect to see the relative price of British exports decline (the terms of trade deteriorate) following a positive export shock, whereas they improve initially. The explanation for the subsequent deterioration in the terms of trade is less evident.

Figures 3.10 and 3.11 show the response to a temporary, one standard deviation fall in gold reserves. By construction, the initial gold outflow is not associated with a rise in imports, a fall in exports, or an increase in long-term lending abroad. Thus, the disturbance can be interpreted as a purely financial shock – say an autonomous short-term capital outflow. In response to the loss of reserves, the Bank of England raises its discount rate. Reserves recover quickly. It would appear that the principal channel through which adjustment to short-term capital outflows took place was the response of the Bank of England and its capacity to attract capital flows. Interestingly, there is little evidence of an improvement in the trade balance following the loss of gold reserves. To the contrary, the fall in export volume which takes place in response to the loss of reserves and the rise in Bank

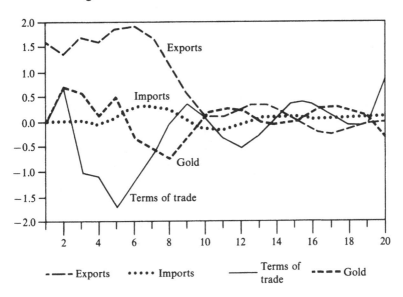

Figure 3.8 Impulse response to shock to exports.

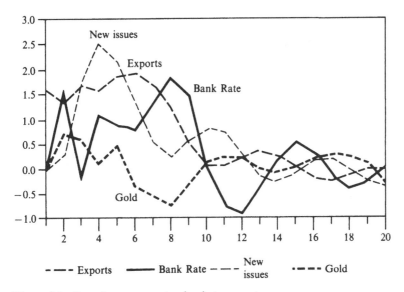

Figure 3.9 Impulse response to shock to exports.

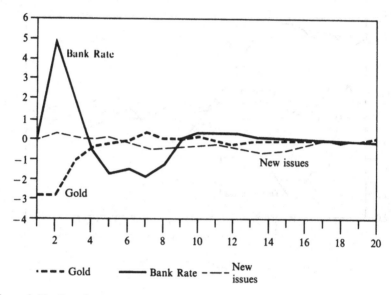

Figure 3.10   Impulse response to shock to gold.

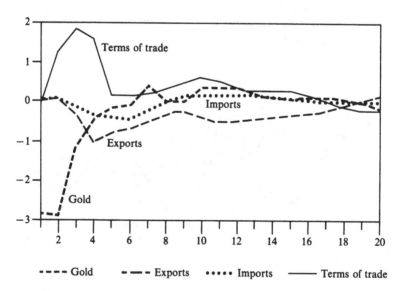

Figure 3.11   Impulse response to shock to gold.

Rate swamps the fall in import volume. The behaviour of exports is attributable, presumably, to the decline in economic activity induced by the financial market disturbance and the higher interest rates it provokes. The decline in export volumes is offset, however, by some improvement in the terms of trade. The two effects roughly cancel, yielding little net change in the current account of the balance of payments.

Interpretation

The metaphor for the balance-of-payments adjustment mechanism that the statistical analysis suggests is a slim man in a winter storm. Like a slim man with little flesh on his bones, the Bank of England had only a slim gold reserve surrounding a vulnerable gold standard frame. To survive in a winter storm, a slim man must dress in layers of clothing to insulate himself from the cold. The Bank of England similarly possessed several layers of insulation to protect itself from the elements. I describe the nature of this insulation by considering export, foreign lending and confidence shocks in turn.

The first layer of insulation from export fluctuations was provided by parallel movements in imports. A foreign expansion which raised the volume of British exports induced parallel movements in imports through two channels: first, the terms-of-trade improvement provoked by the rise in the overseas demand for British exports reduced the relative price of British imports; second, the rise in export demand stimulated domestic production in Britain, increasing the need for intermediate imports and, by raising real incomes, further augmenting the demand for imported consumer goods. Thus, even when trade flows were the source of the external imbalance, they also provided the first layer of insulation.

But induced changes in imports financed only a fraction of autonomous fluctuations in exports. The second layer of insulation was provided by changes in foreign deposits and security holdings. Countries which made up Britain's principal overseas markets tended to hold sterling balances in London. Instead of demanding that the Bank of England convert into gold any sterling balances they acquired from export sales, often they invested in securities in London. In effect, a British trade deficit automatically generated a short-term capital inflow which helped to relieve the pressure on the external accounts.

The third layer of insulation was provided by the banking system through the mechanism emphasised by Whale. Insofar as the autonomous rise in export demand stimulated industrial activity, it increased domestic demands for money and credit. Interest rates were driven up, and short-term capital was attracted from abroad. The increase in circulating media was provided by the banking system, partly in response to its receipt of short-term deposits from abroad.

The fourth and final layer of insulation was provided by the Bank of England. The Bank could raise its discount rate in response to gold losses to attract capital inflows. Characterising the Bank's role in this way serves to remind that, while the balance-of-payments adjustment process was far from automatic, neither did it hinge exclusively on discretionary management by the Bank of England.

The sources of insulation that came into play in response to swings in foreign lending were essentially the same, although their relative importance differed. When new issues for an overseas borrower were floated, the proceeds would be deposited to the borrower's London account. In the first instance, then, new foreign lending led to no change in Britain's balance of payments position. Only over time, as those deposits were drawn down, would the British balance of payments weaken and might the Bank of England begin to lose gold. In the short run, therefore, foreign deposits were Britain's first layer of insulation and the only insulation required.

As the borrower subsequently drew down its deposits to finance purchases of imports, British exports would begin to rise. The importance of this mechanism should not be exaggerated. Typically, a borrower like Canada or Australia would use only a portion of any increae in foreign funds to import commodities and equipment. Only a portion of any such purchases would come from Britain. It is possible, of course, that the demand for British exports was stimulated indirectly. If Canada purchased imports from the United States, the stimulus to US incomes might lead to increased American imports of British goods. But this circular mechanism was subject to leakages which attenuated its operation and built lags into the response of British commodity exports to prior foreign lending.

There was, none the less, at least some response of commodity exports to prior foreign lending. At the same time, since investment had shifted from the domestic to the foreign market, economic activity at home would decelerate, generating a sympathetic fall in British imports. Thus, a strengthening of the trade balance was Britain's second layer of insulation.

The final layer of insulation was again provided by the Bank of England. The Bank could raise its discount rate and induce an inflow of short-term capital to partially offset the outflow of long-term funds.

The response to an autonomous outflow of gold not associated with a fall in exports or a rise in foreign lending – in other words, a shock to confidence – was very different. There was no reason for foreign deposits to rise or for the trade balance to strengthen. Thus, Britain's two outer layers of insulation were stripped away. The burden of adjustment was placed squarely on the Bank of England.

It is not obvious how the Bank of England so successfully shouldered this burden. Part of the explanation is that the British authorities attached clear priority to defence of the gold standard. If the nation simultaneously experienced gold losses and a cyclical downturn, or gold losses and financial panic, there was no question that the authorities attached priority to defence of the monetary standard, even if this implied an intensification of domestic difficulties. They had demonstrated their commitment to the gold standard in 1847, in 1866, and on numerous other occasions. The impact of monetary policy on domestic activity, while vaguely understood, had not been clearly articulated, as it was by Keynes and others in the 1920s. Prior to the extension of the franchise and the rise of the Parliamentary Labour Party, there could be little effective pressure to adapt monetary policy toward employment targets.

To use modern terminology, the Bank of England had acquired a reputation for action that rendered its commitment to the gold standard fully credible. There was no need for domestic or foreign depositors to run on the Bank as a way of testing that commitment. To the contrary, in times of difficulty, short-term capital would tend to flow toward Britain in anticipation of official intervention. If sterling fell toward the gold export point, speculators purchased it in anticipation of official actions designed to strengthen the exchange rate. Intervention would be rendered largely redundant.

The Bank's gold reserve was small in comparison with Britain's external obligations. It is not obvious, therefore, how it succeeded in defending its reserve and maintaining convertibility in instances like 1890 and 1907 when the shock to confidence and consequent gold flows were large relative to the Bank's reserve. Part of the explanation is that by 1890 the official commitment to the gold standard was not merely national but international. The Bank of England could rely on assistance from abroad, notably from the Bank of France. The resources available for sterling's defence were not limited to those of the Bank of England. In 1890, in response to the Baring Crisis, the Bank of England obtained, with the aid of Rothschilds, a loan of £2 million of gold from the Bank of France. It secured £1.5 million in gold from the Russian government.[28] The mere announcement that these funds had been made available proved sufficient to stem the drain from the Bank of England. There was no need for much of the French gold to be ferried across the Channel. Anticipating that concerted international action to defend the sterling parity would be forthcoming, speculators reversed the direction of capital flows so as to render that action unnecessary.

The 1907 crisis provides an even more telling illustration of the point. Bank failures led to a shift out of deposits and into gold in the United States, and to a flow of specie from Britain to America. In response to the loss of gold reserves, the Bank of England first borrowed on the market. Next it raised Bank Rate in an effort to attract gold from third countries, and restricted discounts to short-dated paper only. Finally it obtained support from abroad. But with memory of 1890 still fresh, it was not even necessary for foreign support to be actively solicited. The Bank of France purchased sterling bills, presumably on its own initiative. Apparently aware that the Bank of France was intervening on behalf of its British counterpart, speculators reversed course, repurchasing the sterling assets they had liquidated previously. Again, the response of the market minimised the need for official intervention. The credibility of the commitment to the sterling parity, which extended beyond British shores, did much to relieve the pressure on the Bank of England.

Conclusion

In this chapter I have provided a 'Ford-like' model of how the gold standard worked. The model suggests that the gold standard's smooth operation – smooth from the perspective of the centre – depended on a particular constellation of market forces. Many of those relationships are the very ones first emphasised by Ford more than a quarter of a century ago. My model differs by attaching somewhat less weight than did Ford to the linkage running from British capital exports to capital-good imports by the recipient countries and to exports of capital goods by Britain. It attaches more weight than did Ford to monetary management by the Bank of England. But in emphasising the adjustment of real variables to monetary impulses as well as adjustments in the other direction, and in its retention of certain Keynesian features, the model is very much in the spirit of the one developed by Ford.

The final element of my explanation for the stability of the British gold standard is the credibility of the official commitment to gold. Policy-makers in Britain were unwavering in their commitment to gold convertibility. To the extent to which there existed other goals of policy, these were accorded lower priority. Knowing that policy-makers would intervene in defence of the gold standard, markets responded in the same direction in anticipation of official action. Hence, the need for actual intervention was minimised. Credibility and stability were by-products of a reputation for willingness to take the necessary action. But a central element of my argument is that credibility derived from the fact that the commitment to the gold standard was international. Central banks like the Bank of England could rely on foreign assistance in times of exceptional stress. Again, the need for actual assistance was minimised because the commitment to offer it was fully credible. The markets anticipated the actions of the central bankers, basing their anticipations on the policy-makers' track records. Their anticipations and consequent actions rendered official intervention largely redundant.

In fact, this point was understood well before the recent literature on credibility and reputation. '[D]omestic confidence in convertibility was nourished on its past success', wrote Ford in 1962. '[F]or some countries the maintenance of specie payments was never endangered by domestic speculative runs on gold, while for others a less successful history meant that the additional threat of a domestic speculative drain was ever present . . .'[29]

Notes

1 See Hume (1952) and Whale (1937).
2 Precursors who also emphasised the output and employment effects of international reserve flows include Angell (1926), Ohlin (1929) and White (1933). Hints of the approach can be discerned even earlier, in the debate between Taussig (1917) and Wicksell (1918). None of these authors elaborated a fully-articulated Keynesian model, obviously. But Ford's model owed much to Meade's (1951) seminal work on income determination in the open economy.
3 Ford (1962), p. 189.
4 This is a highly selective survey. I beg the forgiveness of authors whose work I neglect.
5 Floyd (1984: ch. 4, app. II) neatly discusses the inconsistencies implicit in the interest differential formulation of capital flows.
6 For simplicity, I discuss money supply and demand in terms of the monetary base, for the time being ignoring the money multiplier and broader monetary aggregates.
7 The discussion here retraces ground covered in Eichengreen (1985). A catalogue of the relevant models is provided by Dornbusch (1980).
8 See for example Dornbusch and Jaffee (1978) and even McCloskey and Zecher (1984: 122).
9 A general analysis of portfolio balance under the gold standard is provided by Floyd (1985).
10 It is perhaps useful to present some examples that illustrate the compatibility of the monetary and price specie flow models. Consider a country which is small in international capital markets and which cannot affect the world price of its imports. Capital is perfectly mobile and domestic and foreign interest-bearing assets (bonds for short) are perfect substitutes in portfolios. However, domestic- and foreign-produced goods are imperfect substitutes in consumption. To increase the volume of exports, domestic producers must reduce the (relative) price of what they sell.

What is the response of such an economy to an increase in money demand? If this increase in money demand arises out of a shift in portfolio preference – a desire to shift out of a certain quantity of bonds in favour of money – the adjustment mechanism highlighted by the monetary approach bears the entire burden of adjustment. Domestic residents sell bonds in an effort to obtain money, driving down bond prices and driving up bond yields. But the incipient rise in yields renders domestic bonds attractive to foreign investors. They bring gold to the domestic central bank, exchange it for currency, and use that currency to purchase domestic bonds until yields fall (bond prices rise) to world levels. This adjustment can occur quickly (instantaneously under perfect capital mobility) with no accompanying change in relative commodity prices.

But if, in contrast, the increase in money demand is not accompanied by a decline in the demand for bonds, domestic residents can obtain additional domestic currency (and its requisite gold backing) only by exchanging domestic commodities for foreign gold. They reduce their absorption relative to their production, and export the excess in return for gold. Given the desire to smooth consumption over time, the decline in domestic absorption and the consequent balance of trade surplus should, in each period, be small relative to the overall increase in money demand and persist for some time. To enable the increase in exports to be willingly absorbed abroad, their relative price must decline. Thus, adjustment occurs gradually and is accompanied by precisely the kind of relative price movements predicted by the price specie flow model.

11 Just as beauty is in the eye of the beholder, the implications to be drawn from the literature on the efficiency of commodity arbitrage under the gold standard (McCloskey and Zecher, 1976; 1984) depend very much on the tastes of the reader. The one commodity for which detailed studies of the efficiency of international markets have been conducted, namely gold, has led to conflicting conclusions. Clark (1984) argued that there were many violations of market efficiency in the period 1890–1908. Subsequent estimates by Officer (1986; 1989) challenge Clark's conclusions. Interestingly, both authors agree that there were fewer instances of market inefficiency in the second of these decades than in the first.

12 One possible answer is productivity shocks, as in the real business cycle literature. It is hard to imagine a period to which productivity shocks due to changing technology could be more relevant than the century prior to 1913. The problem with this approach is the absence of an obvious propagation mechanism. I discuss some implications of productivity shocks in a gold standard setting later in this section.

13 Fratianni and Spinelli also find little support in Italian experience for the purchasing power parity assumption. Given Italy's record of exchange rate changes, their finding is consistent with McKinnon's view that exchange rate stability fosters commodity market arbitrage.

14 Dick and Floyd (1987) demonstrate how this approach can be applied to Canadian experience under the classical gold standard.

15 An alternative view, that of Benjamin and Kochin (1984), rejects Gibson's

Paradox as a spurious correlation. I am convinced by Barsky and Summers' rejection of their rejection.

16 Barsky and DeLong (1988) present some evidence that lagged changes in gold supplies were useful for predicting price-level changes during the gold standard years.

17 A different conclusion, that central banks systematically violated the rules of the game, is reached by Dutton (1984). Some authors (e.g. Giovannini, 1987) challenge the validity of the entire reaction function literature. The question also has been considered using the case study approach *sans* econometrics; see McGouldrick (1984) and Rich (1984) on Germany and Canada, respectively.

18 De Cecco (1974) elaborated many of the same points when contrasting the operation of the London, Paris, Berlin and New York financial markets.

19 Much of Fishlow's analysis applies to the period when the gold convertibility was in suspension and currency was inconvertible. But many of the same points carry over to the years in which their gold standards prevailed.

20 For a sympathetic perspective, see Bordo and Kydland (1989).

21 The title of this section is lifted directly from Ford (1960).

22 I have utilised vector autoregression in another context, where I present my views of its applicability to questions of causality and justify my preferred interpretation of such results. See Eichengreen (1983).

23 A constant term and time trend also were included but are not reported in the table.

24 Ford (1962), p. 190.

25 Ford (1962), p. 190.

26 Note the emphasis of the word 'directly' in the preceding sentence. Gold flows also appear to have had some impact on the subsequent evolution of the terms of trade. Hence it may be premature to conclude in favour of or against this hypothesis on the basis of the coefficients on Bank Rate alone. It could be that Bank Rate affected the terms of trade indirectly (by attracting gold flows, which altered the terms of trade). This hypothesis is pursued in pp. 67–73 below.

27 Given the order in which the variables are entered, the Choleski Factorisation chooses Bank Rate as the 'most exogenous' variable. That is, the error term in the moving average representation of its equation is uncorrelated with the other error terms. It is followed, in order, by new issues, exports, imports, the terms of trade, and the gold reserve (the 'most endogenous' variable). I experimented with other orthoganalisations and found them to have little impact on the results. For the diagram, I have multiplied the results for Bank rate by ten and divided those for imports and exports by ten. Otherwise, movements in variables other than imports and exports (especially Bank Rate) would not be apparent to the naked eye.

28 Sayers (1936), p. 103.

29 Ford (1962), p. 189.

4 British economic fluctuations in the nineteenth century: is there a role for money?

FORREST CAPIE

Alec Ford made several important contributions to our subject and central amongst them was an explanation of British economic fluctuations, particularly those of the second half of the nineteenth century. At the centre of his explanation for fluctuations were exports. He argued in a series of publications that exports were the key element in fluctuations: 'the proximate cause of cyclical fluctuations in the United Kingdom from 1860 to 1914 lay in the behaviour of exports of goods and services, aided sometimes by home investment' (1981: 35). This is a view in fact that has been offered for almost the whole of modern British history from 1790 to the recent past. Some variants of the explanation allow a supplementary role for both domestic, and overseas investment.

There has almost never been room for a monetary explanation. Indeed, Alec Ford has recently specifically rejected such an explanation: 'monetary influences were not a significant internal cyclical factor in the United Kingdom (1981: 48). It is true that Hawtrey regarded the cycle as 'a purely monetary phenomenon' and he wrote extensively on the subject, drawing on British experience in the late nineteenth century albeit without the benefit of robust data. One interpretation of Hawtrey (Haberler, 1964) is that depression came when demand fell following a shrinkage in the quantity of money. The solution lay in stabilising the flow of money. A shrinkage in the money stock led directly to a fall in consumer spending and recession followed since producers could not dispose of their output at anticipated prices. Stocks rose, production fell, unemployment rose and wages fell. In the upswing the opposite happened. But what lay behind changes in the money supply? And recently Barry Eichengreen in questioning the usefulness of available structural models, turned to time series methods. In using vector autoregression techniques that are in essence tests of antecedence, he was careful to emphasise the limitations of the tests and to stress that they merely provided guidance for specifying

80

reasonable structural relationships. The results were sufficiently strong for him to conclude that 'for the late Victorian period (1869–1901) fluctuations in the monetary base emerge as the single most important determinant of the trade cycle' (Eichengreen, 1983a: 161). But this line is rare.

This chapter therefore sets out to examine the pattern and role of money in late nineteenth century Britain and question its cyclical role. It is guided by the work of Friedman and Schwartz (1963) on the United States whose focus was on the money stock and changes in that in relation to a business cycle chronology defined by the National Bureau. They aimed primarily at establishing some empirical relationships and their principal conclusion was that changes in the money stock conformed to *major* movements in the reference cycle chronology with a long lead. The statistical evidence that they brought to bear was supported by detailed historical study of some *major* recessions in the economy the most notable being the contraction of 1929–33. This chapter seeks to follow the first part of their work, an examination of the course of money and economic activity. It has become quite widely accepted that monetary shocks have been important in causing fluctuations. Lucas puts it strongly: 'Everything points to a monetary shock as the force triggering the real business cycle' (1981: 233).

So the exercise is in the main one of measurement and before this is dismissed as measurement without theory it is worth pondering Friedman's defence of Wesley Mitchell when the same accusation was made:

In the study of any class of phenomena it is necessary first to examine the phenomena themselves, and to find empirical regularities, in order to provide a basis for generalization and abstraction; and at this stage the orderly organization of empirical data is more important than the elaboration and refinement of abstract hypotheses. (Friedman 1950: 469)

This paper in fact finds very little evidence for the kinds of regularities found by Friedman and Schwartz, and very little support for a cyclical relationship between money and economic activity in Britain. It offers instead an explanation for the lack of a strong cyclical pattern in money.

I

The monetary series used are taken from Capie and Webber (1985), and the reference cycle used is that of the NBER. Where output is used it is that of Feinstein (1972). Friedman and Schwartz had occasion to refine some of the NBER's turning points for Britain in their work on Britain and these modifications are also taken into account in this study.

The first objective is to describe the course of these monetary series both in raw form, to give a feel for the data, and then as deviations from trend. The establishment of trend is never straightforward but the first method used is as follows. A polynomial was specified of the form:

$$Y_t = B_o + B_1 T_t + B_2 T_t^2 + B_3 T_t^3 + \ldots e_t$$

where Y_t is the dependent variable, T_t is the time variable and e_t is the error term.

A variety of specifications was estimated, the data determining which one was used. This method of detrending is particularly suited to series in which there is no obvious pattern but in which the data display considerable variation. When the appropriate polynomial for each data set has been specified it is possible to regard the residuals as the cyclical component and plots of these were used to identify turning points in the series.

The raw data for the monetary base show a gentle upward trend from 1889 to 1914, and then a very large increase during the crisis occurring at the onset of World War I. This end-of-period burst requires a little comment. The base increased by 36% between June and December 1914 (Capie and Webber, 1985: Tbl. 1). The source of this increase was the declaration by the Bank of England in August 1914 that it would discount any approved Bill of Exchange, giving up the normal right of repayment when the bill fell due. This scheme was further extended several weeks later when it was decided that if the acceptor was not in a position to pay when the bill matured, the Bank would lend to the acceptor at Bank rate plus 2%, and would not demand repayment until one year following the end of hostilities. The primary aim of this measure was to increase market liquidity. But this remarkable episode is the only jump in the series in the whole period.

The detrended series shows much more variation, and there appears to be some cyclical pattern apparent at least over 1870–91. However, there is no clear correspondence with either of the two business-cycle chronologies. After 1891 some sort of positive relationship exists between the residuals and Friedman and Schwartz (1963) (henceforth F&S) cycle dates, but this is fairly weak.

The broad money series (M3) rises steadily with no major fluctuations visible in the raw data. Trend certainly dominates cyclical fluctuations. Again the de-trended series shows much more variation, corresponding fairly closely (positively) with the F&S chronology, but not as closely with that of Burns and Mitchell (1946) (henceforth B&M). The F&S relationship is especially good between 1877 and 1909. After 1902, the B&M chronology gives almost an inverse correlation.

The money multiplier displays an upward trend but there is a substantial variation about this trend. And that variation around trend when compared with the F&S chronology gives similar timed peaks and troughs, but the multiplier sometimes leads the cycle by one period (NB: annual data). The B&M chronology gives similar results (but without the lead) up to 1886, after which the relationship seems to break down.

The currency–deposit ratio shows a downward trend over the period as a whole, but with a lot of fluctuation. The main reason for this secular decline in the currency–deposit ratio is the growth of banking. More and more people were using banks as a repository for funds and thus were holding a larger proportion of their money holdings in the form of bank deposits.

In the detrended series there is some indication of a positive relationship with the F&S chronology, but this is fairly weak. There is a very weak relationship with B&M: often, what little exists is negative.

The reserve–deposit ratio rises slowly, especially after 1890, in keeping with the widespread pressure for a greater holding of reserves. Initially there was an increase in the ratio, but then it fell (with fluctuations) until 1890, at which point it was 7.7% lower than its 1871 value. It then increased for the rest of the period, still with a great deal of fluctuation, and finally a large jump in 1914. The reasons for the increase in this ratio also concern the changes in the banking system which were occurring at this time. The level of bank deposits over the period was increasing, but this downward influence on the reserve–deposit ratio was outweighed by the upward one of the amalgamation movement. Originally, provincial banks had kept a portion of their reserves with London banks; it was only the London banks themselves that kept reserves at the Bank of England. Once these smaller banks had been swallowed up by larger, frequently London, banks, their reserves became part of the larger banks' reserves at the Bank of England, and thus were included in the calculation of the reserve–deposit ratio.

This exercise has used one means of detrending all the series and regarding the residuals from that trend as the cyclical component. These resulting cycles have then been placed in relation to the reference cycle chronology and their turning points examined in relation to business cycle peaks and troughs. The first thing to be said is that it is encouraging that the measures of income correspond closely with the cycle. It is encouraging since many studies use real income to date the cycle. However, there were one or two differences and given the relatively small number of cycles in the period a difference of one or two years here and there could affect the results.

What is more interesting though is the rather weak and sometimes perverse relationship between the monetary series and the cycle. We saw that it depended in part on which chronology was used but that there was often no obvious association between the monetary base the monetary stock or the money multiplier and the business cycle. The individual elements in the multiplier are more difficult to discuss and we leave that until later.

II

Alternative approaches

Friedman and Schwartz took the logarithm of first differences – a measure of the percentage rate of change from one time period to the next. When this is done for Britain for the period 1870–1914, no obvious relationship between money and output emerges. There is no clear demonstration of unambiguous precedence either way. There is a case for a comparison of money and output or with money and the turning points of the NBER chronology. This latter comparison of money growth with the activity level has been criticised for biasing the case in favour of the monetarist view. And yet even in spite of this bias no result is found for Britain.

Friedman and Schwartz also stressed that it was in *major* movements that money was important. To capture amplitude they compared the moving standard deviation of the annual percentage rate of change in the series. These standard deviations provide a measure of the variability of the respective rates of change of money and income. The objective is to see how the amplitude of cycles in the rate of change in the money stock is related to the severity of business cycles. The latter are now proxied by the measure of real output. Again for Britain there was little correspondence.

Where the early discussion focused on accelerating and decelerating money growth, current discussion would substitute unanticipated money growth; it is alleged that only the unanticipated portion of the change in the money stock affects real variables. Barro (1977–8) pioneered a methodology that separated anticipated from unanticipated change. The methods used have been criticised on various counts and Barro himself resorted to a much simpler approach in his recently revised textbook. The approach is to take a proxy of recent trend in the variable and call that the normal path, then to extend that to the year being considered with the difference between actual and extended being taken to represent the unexpected.

Following Barro (1984) we carry out this exercise here to illustrate the movements and interactions between nominal and real variables. The focus is on shocks or surprises in money and prices in order to find interesting relationships with real variables. Table 4.1 does this for 1870–1914.

The table provides the shortfall of each variable in each recession across the period. The shortfall is calculated in the following way. The trough year of recession is taken. The previous peak year is the base year. The average rate of growth of the variable over the five years prior to the peak (which will usually include some downswing and upswing and hence approximate trend) is taken to represent normal. The 'normal' growth is then projected from the base year to show what a normal or expected figure would be in the

Table 4.1. *Real and nominal variables during recessions 1870–1914*

Final year of recession:	1879	1886	1893	1904	1908	1914
Base year for comparison:	1874	1882	1890	1900	1907	1913

Real income						
Y	1239	1399	1547	2031	2041	2359
Y°	1371	1477	1594	2144	2140	2403
Y° – as % shortfall	10.7	5.6	3.1	5.6	4.9	1.9
Prices						
P	87	82	84	87	90	95
P°	113	91	87	100	91	103
P° – P as % shortfall	30.5	10.4	4.0	14.9	0.9	8.1
Money (1)						
B	15.6	14.0	16.0	19.7	20.8	28.8
B°	16.8	13.5	15.3	20.9	21.1	24.3
B° – B as % shortfall	7.6	– 3.7	– 3.9	6.0	1.4	– 15.6
Money (2)						
M	56.4	61.5	72.2	89.8	96.7	119.8
M°	67.9	61.8	72.0	101.8	97.6	113.9
M° – M as % shortfall	20.4	0.4	– 0.3	13.3	0.9	– 4.9

Note: Y is real GDP, P is the GNP deflator, B the monetary base, and M broad money (M3 equivalent).

year of deepest recession. The difference between the actual and the projected is the shortfall. Thus real GDP in 1908 was £2041m. In the previous peak (1907) it had been £2115m. Had income continued to grow at its normal rate it would have been £2140m in 1908, or 4.9% greater than it actually was. The shortfall is therefore 4.9%. Therefore any negative shortfall is evidence of a higher figure in recession than expected.

The data on real income show recessions of roughly similar size in the nineteenth century except for the first which was twice normal severity and the last which was rather feeble.

Turning to the behaviour of the monetary base (B). For the first recession there is a 7.6% shortfall. In the following two recessions there is an excess of base money – i.e. base money is larger than would have been provided, had previous trend growth continued. The next two are unremarkable and the final one should be treated with caution this being the 1914 financial crisis when war broke out, the gold standard abandoned, and the monetary base hugely expanded by the monetary authorities. So over these six recessions before World War I there is no clear relationship between contractions in output and shortfalls in the monetary base. The broader definition of money yields no clearer picture of any relationship. In three of five recessions there is virtually no shortfall, while in the other two it is rather substantial.

Finally prices. Here we find quite substantial shortfalls – by over 30% in the first recession and by more than 8% in three others. Given that there are no banking panics in the British economy over these years, so there should be no abnormal change in the real demand for base money. In the two largest recessions there is a close correspondence between prices and broad money.

Recent time series techniques

The exercise this far has proceeded within the conventional framework of measurement and reference cycle chronology. But there have been serious challenges to these approaches. While it is obvious that modern industrial economies move unevenly through time, and the up and down movements have been seen as fluctuations about a trend it is possible to regard the movements as the result of a series of shocks that simply leave the impression of a cyclical pattern. The conventional approach to trend-cycle analysis has been to use *ad hoc* filters to detrend series using techniques such as moving averages (many of the results discussed above use just such a technique). But recent research effort has focused on the nature of the movement in the series, in the jargon to discover whether the data are generated by a trend stationary or a difference stationary process and to see whether oscillations are transitory or persistent. Most of the work done has been on US data but some work on the UK (e.g. Mills and Taylor, 1989) reports a difference stationary process for the post World War II period but a trend stationary process for the period 1860–1914 (Crafts, Leybourne & Mills, 1989, on an industrial production series).

In this section I report briefly on some work in progress (Capie and Mills, 1989) that employs structural time series models to establish the path of the trend growth of money and output and hence the extent and timing of fluctuations around the trend.

The Kalman filter is used to decompose our respective series on income and money into their trend and cycle components. The technique allows such decomposition to estimate not on an *ad hoc* moving average but rather by an optimal linear filter derived by signal extraction techniques from the actual stochastic process generating the data. What the technique reveals is that there is indeed a cycle in British income data over this period. However the cycle does not agree closely with the conventional (NBER) dating of the business cycle. There is occasional coincidence in the turning points in the two chronologies, and at other points quite close correspondence. But there are also some large differences, the most extreme being that the revised series shows 1874 as a trough whereas it is a peak in the conventional dating.

The most interesting result, though, is that the monetary data do not show any cyclicality at all. This result may be confirmation of a kind, of our inability to detect cyclical relationship by other means. If we accept this result we would conclude that it was not monetary shocks that produced fluctuations in income in this period.

When the relationship is pursued more rigorously this result is confirmed – a weak or non-existent relationship between money and the cycle in real output.

III

Monetary determinants and the cycle

We turn now to an examination of the behaviour of the proximate determinants of the money supply. Friedman and Schwartz suggested, and used, a method of determining the contribution of each proximate determinant of the money stock for the US. Table 4.2 gives the results of all applications of this method to the UK. The method gives the fraction of monetary change which was produced by each of the determinants between the beginning and the end of the period, and for sub-periods, selected first in order to allow comparisons with other studies. Over the period as a whole it was high-powered money (the base) that explained by far the greater part of the change in M3 – 70%. A slightly rising reserve–deposit ratio was acting to slow monetary expansion after the late 1880s, and a falling currency–deposit ratio was acting to offset this. The effect of the currency–deposit was considerably stronger taken over the whole period. In the sub-periods 1870–9, 1880–96, and for 1880–1913 the respective contribution of each of these factors was more or less the same. For the period 1897–1913 monetary base is the very powerful explanation, reserve–deposit is strong and currency–deposit has lost a little of its importance. In summary, whichever way we look at it the monetary base was the prime determinant of money supply in this period.

However, it is the behaviour of those determinants over the course of the business cycle that is of prime interest. Table 4.2 brings together the relevant figures, these being the percentage change in the proximate determinants of the money supply, over the downswing and the upswing of

Table 4.2. *The overall growth (with the annual average growth rate in brackets)*

	Currency–deposit ratio	Reserve–deposit ratio	H	£M3
Peak→trough				
1873–9	−3.4%	1.8%	1.6%	−1.8%
	(−0.58)	(2.80)	(0.26)	(−0.30)
1883–6	−6.9%	2.97%	−1.6%	0.87%
	(−2.40)	(0.98)	(−0.54)	(0.29)
1890–4	−10.5%	10.2%	5.6%	7.6%
	(−2.80)	(2.40)	(1.40)	(1.80)
1900–04	−0.15%	14.4%	3.2%	−2.6%
	(−0.04)	(3.40)	(0.79)	(−0.66)
1907–08	6.3%	0.9%	6.95%	4.0%
The *arithmetic mean*	−2.93	9.3	3.15	1.61
Trough→Peak				
1870*–3	−0.2%	−4.6%	12.8%	14.5%
	(−0.07)	(−1.60)	(4.00)	(4.50)
1879–83	−17.5%	−14.8%	−8.02%	6.6%
	(−4.80)	(−4.00)	(2.10)	(1.60)
1886–90	−5.1%	−9.9%	6.8%	13.6%
	(−1.30)	(−2.60)	(1.60)	(3.20)
1894–1900	−11.3%	−1.7%	15.8%	23.3%
	(−2.00)	(−0.29)	(2.40)	(3.50)
1904–07	−18.1%	8.7%	1.4%	5.6%
	(−6.60)	(2.80)	(0.47)	(1.80)
1908–13	4.1%	3.4%	19.4%	15.5%
	(0.80)	(0.67)	(0.50)	(2.90)
The *arithmetic mean*	−8.02	−3.15	8.03	13.18

*1870 not a trough – but it is our starting date.

the cycle. Figures 4.1 and 4.2 illustrate the path of variables against the backdrop of recession and expansion. The shaded areas of the figure show the contractionary periods. There are five and a half cycles over the period 1870–1913.

First, the reserve–deposit ratio of the banking system. The total of reserves available to the banks is limited by the total amount of high-powered money. It is also dependent on the desire of the public for base money and so on the willingness of the public to hold deposits rather than currency. *A priori* we would expect the reserve–deposit ratio to increase in the downswing of the cycle and to decrease in the phase of business expansion, the argument being that the slowdown or actual fall in economic activity is accompanied by a slower growth or fall in bank deposits and the banks are left with 'excess' reserves. In the expansionary phase of the cycle opposite tendencies are at work so that the ratio falls.

In Cagan's (1965) study of the US he found this tendency for the ratio to rise when economic activity slowed, and to fall when business improved. When panic developed the reserve–deposit ratio rose steeply and continued for some time after as banks sought safety in ample reserves until all danger had passed. The broad conclusion was that reserves fell to uncomfortably low levels during business expansion and 'when the demand for loams slackens after a business peak, banks take the first opportunity to augment their reserves'. Figure 4.2 shows that something of this expected pattern can be seen in Britain in the late nineteenth century. The reserve–deposit ratio grew in every downswing in the period with the average change for the five downswings being 9.3%.

The opposite should hold in the upswing with deposits increasing and the banks allowing the ratio to fall back to the lower end of its desired band. Again this is what happened. In almost every cycle the ratio fell so that the average fall over the six upswings was 3.2%.

Interpretation of the currency–deposit ratio is more difficult. Cagan (1965), for example, found that the tendency was for the currency/money ratio to decline at a diminishing rate during the course of the expansionary phase of the cycle, and that banking panics, which sharply increase the demand for currency, and so the ratio, did not account for cyclical fluctuations in the ratio. The net result was that cycles in the currency ratio rise through the latter part of an expansion and continue through the first half of the contraction. And there was no clear evidence on whether the ratio was leading or lagging economic activity. Our analysis does not as yet permit this kind of comment; as it stands at the moment our evidence is mixed. In the five downswings the currency deposit ratio fell, but in the upswings it fell by a greater amount.

High-powered money is more difficult to deal with. If under the gold

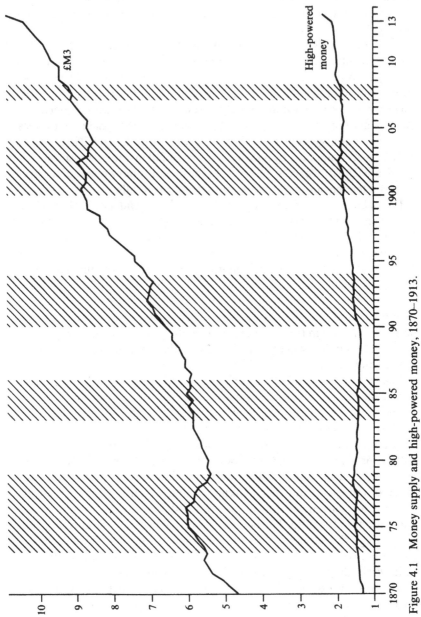

Figure 4.1 Money supply and high-powered money, 1870–1913.

R–d; c–d ratios

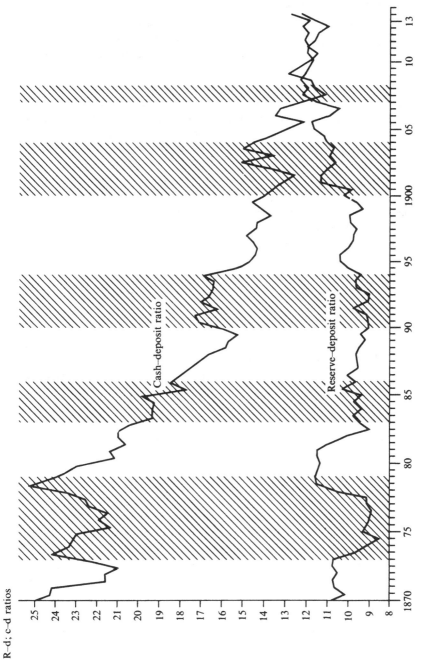

Figure 4.2 Cash-deposit and reserve-deposit ratios, 1870–1913.

standard base money were determined exclusively by the balance of payments, then in the downswing of the cycle with a surplus anticipated (as import growth slows and export growth is steady or expands) high-powered money should grow. This happened in four of the five cycles so that overall the average growth was 3.2%. In the upswing, the reverse should happen: as imports grow and exportables are diverted to the domestic market, a deficit, or at least a worsening in the current-account balance should develop, and so bring a fall in high powered money. But this happened in only one episode and the average over all the upswings is a growth of 8%. However this story is certainly too simple. In the first place, the United Kingdom was somewhat unusual at this time in that the current account tended to improve during the upswing and deteriorate in the downswing (Ford, 1981). Secondly, it ignores the capital/account. Here the difficulties multiply. There are some suggestions that the short-term capital balance may have improved in the upswing, since during a world boom the demand for the key currency, sterling would have increased. Also, when monetary stringency was anticipated and the demand for liquidity increased, the role of Bank rate was strengthened (Bloomfield, 1968). Further evidence on the movement of short-term capital and gold is that when Germany, France and the UK all raised their rates gold eventually flowed into the UK. Of course there was not always or even often a coincidence of rate increases. Clearly then there could have been offsetting long- and short-term capital movements. As we mentioned earlier the Bank of England could influence gold flows and short term capital movements and therefore change the relationship predicted between high powered money and the cycle. A tentative conclusion at this point is that at least from the late 1880s onwards the monetary authorities influenced the movement of funds so that the balance of payments did not determine the base.

IV

The role that banking panics and financial crises play may be important for monetary volatility. Their absence in Britain at this time could provide much of the explanation for comparative stability in Britain.

The approach the monetarists take to the question identifies financial crises with banking panics and regards these as responsible for monetary contractions and therefore for the consequences of that contraction. (By implication if banking panics were removed a major source of monetary movements would be removed.) Where there is a loss of confidence in institutions, that leads the public to convert bank deposits into currency and results in a large contraction of deposits. The currency–deposit ratio rises sharply as does the reserve–deposit ratio. That behaviour in turn damages economic activity.

The principal alternative strain in the literature (Minsky, 1968; Kindleberger, 1989) sees financial crises, 'as an essential part of the upper turning point of the business cycle – as a necessary consequence of the previous boom' (Bordo, 1986a). The mechanism at work in this view is different from the monetarist, but what is important (and similar) for our purposes is that at some point there is a huge shift from real assets into cash and the consequences are the same, a contraction in the broad measure of money supply. There is also a downturn in activity though of course in this explanation the connection between money and output is viewed differently.

Gorton (1988) discusses the relationship between banking panics and business cycles in the US. He sets out to demonstrate that panics are explicable in rational terms. He shows that for the period 1870–1914 they were systematic responses by depositors to changing perceptions of risk: 'every time a variable predicting a recession reached a threshold level, a panic occurred' (1988: 753). The suggested explanation was that since banks tended to fail in recession, depositors would withdraw deposits in advance to avoid losses due to bank failure. He found that at ten business cycle peaks between 1870 and 1913 six banking panics either coincided or closely corresponded with those peaks. In other words sharp monetary contractions had their origins in the anticipated recession in activity, and the monetary contractions were followed by deep recessions (this of course must have important implications for the causality debate). Anticipation of the depression leads to bank panics and so to monetary volatility. So bank panics make for bigger depressions and by this route money remains causal. But the important point is that the monetary contractions had their source in the fragile banking system.

The experience in Britain was quite different. There were no financial crises, no banking panics in Britain in this period and the principal reasons for stability are to be found in the behaviour of the Bank of England as a lender of last resort, and in the structure of the commercial banking system and allied to the latter, the banks' freedom to locate and hence diversify their portfolios. The nature of the financial system meant that even if there were anticipations of recession this did not lead to bank panics and real activity was as a result, less volatile. The assertion that there were no financial crises in this period may seem provocative and requires some substantiation. Schwartz (1985) has provided what seems a very useful definition and distinction. The distinction is between what she calls real and pseudo crises. A real crisis is one that threatens the financial system, one that involves a banking panic and widespread banking failure. Banks like other firms will fail but such a failure, however large, should not be seen as a crisis unless it threatened to lead to a collapse of the system. A panic occurs only when the demand by depositors to convert deposits into currency exceeds the capacity of the *system* to supply. And with that definition in view she stated that there had been no financial crisis in Britain since 1866 and none in the United States since 1933.

There were some episodes in Britain in this period that continue to go under the name of crises and are often cited as evidence of fragility in the system. The most common is the collapse of Barings in 1890 but the collapse of the City of Glasgow bank in 1878 is also said to have presaged a crisis (Collins, 1988). The City of Glasgow Bank, an unlimited liability firm, failed in October 1878. It was not simply badly managed but corruptly managed and there were criminal prosecutions. Clapham was surely right to view this as simply a bank failure that had few ramifications for the rest of the country. Morgan too claimed that 'the failure did not create a crisis in the money market' (1943: 200). More recently, however, Collins has argued that this did constitute a crisis. Collins argues that in the 1870s there were still important elements of instability in banking structure and practice. This is no doubt true as the system was evolving towards its more stable form but Collins himself surely supports my position when he says, 'It is clear that a general panic was but a hair's breadth away . . .' (1988: 4). Being close to a panic and having one are different states and it is part of the argument of this chapter that the evolving structure prevented incipient panics becoming actual panics.

The other principal episode was that of Barings in 1890. This case is more straightforward. Barings, an investment bank, had overcommitted themselves in Latin America and failed. The Bank of England stepped in and organised a lifeboat that allowed Barings to be reconstituted and the name was saved. Other banks were not involved in serious pressure. It could be argued that the Bank should not have performed this bail-out. The Bank's concern is with the stock of money and it should not come to the rescue of an individual bank but rather, as Bagehot argued, simply lend to the market.

The point that we want to stress here though is that in neither case was there a threat to the monetary system. There were no panics. The public did not rush to convert deposits into currency and so there was no great contraction in the money stock. The currency–deposit ratio, which began the period at just over 20% was on a downward trend, with the spread of banking. In 1877 it was 18.5%. In 1878 it rose to 19% and in 1879 slightly further to 19.4%. The following year it fell to 17.6%. So there is clearly a retardation in the fall but it can be considered no more than a blip and does not constitute the kind of change that would distort the money multiplier significantly. There is slightly greater change in the banks' reserve–deposit ratio. They had begun the period at round 10%. However, there was criticism of low reserve positions and several factors were at work to raise this. In 1877 the ratio stood at 10.7%. In 1878 it was 11.3%, and in 1879 it reached 13.2%. Thereafter, as we have seen, there were fluctuations but the point here is that there was no dramatic change in the banks' behaviour that would have led to significant contraction of the money stock.

In the nineteenth century there had been genuine financial crises. In the period immediately prior to the one examined here there is evidence broadly consistent with the results for the US. In a recent article Collins (1988b) took up the Friedman and Schwartz framework and applied it to mid-nineteenth-century Britain. This was a period of regular financial crises, crises appearing at the peak of the cycle, and there is a different behaviour found than in the later century when financial crises disappear.

After placing great emphasis on the extreme fragility of the data, Collins carried out a detailed historical study of the three mid-century cycles. In particular he examined the behaviour of the commercial banking sector through the course of quite sharp oscillations in banking conditions. He points out that there was a pattern of a rise in the cash ratio at the peak of the cycle. He also noted the sharp fall in a measure of banks' 'liquidity' as an economic upswing petered out. In his examination of the individual cycles of the 1850s, 1860s, and 1870s, a fairly close correspondence was found between the monetary series, economic activity and prices. But Collins concludes tentatively; whether the banks 'were initiators of change, and the more general question of the direction of causation may not have been resolved'.

But these experiences coupled with Bagehot's exhortations and changing opinion led eventually to the Bank of England, around 1870, accepting its role of lender of last resort ready to provide liquidity to the market in times of difficulty. The Bank had for a long time acted in the last resort to supply the system with funds but Bagehot's particular contribution was to insist that the Bank should commit itself in advance to that position. His emphasis on precommitment was to assure the market that sound banks would always find sufficient liquidity (at a price) even when unsound banks were failing. From the fact that there were no crises of the kind defined it does not of course automatically follow that the Bank's behaviour was responsible. But in a recent interesting investigation of the issue Ogden (1988) examined the period in detail (much of it on daily data from the Bank's archives) particularly periods of pressure – that is where there seemed to be 'excessive' discounting – and found evidence of the Bank's responding quickly and adequately to ease liquidity needs of the market. This undoubtedly contributed to avoiding any pressure developing into widespread fear of and actual failure.

Table 4.3. *British branch banking 1870–1910*

	London banks		Provincial banks		All UK banks	
	Banks	Branches	Banks	Branches	Banks	Branches
1870	56	84	299	1092	387	2728
1880	54	109	258	1396	358	3454
1890	65	149	200	1795	303	4347
1900	39	135	108	1875	188	5822
1910	27	36	47	1516	122	7565

Source: Capie and Webber (1985)

There was another important institutional aspect that undoubtedly promoted stability in British banking and perhaps in the economy too and it is one that contrasts with the US. It is the structure of the banking system. By 1870 British banking had evolved to its modern form, with a large number of commercial banks the larger of which had many branches throughout the country. This structure continued to develop as the summary in table 4.3 shows.

As early as 1870 there were more than 3,000 bank offices in the country (0.73 offices per 10,000 of the population). Although the total number of banks in all categories fell fairly steadily throughout the period there were still over 100 banks in 1914 and there were around 8,000 bank offices at that point (1.63 per 10,000 of the population). The fall in total number of banks was in part a consequence of the contemporary concern with size associated as it was with security and prestige, and so of the mergers/acquisitions that took place at an accelerating pace in the 1890s. But the main point to make is that there was a great growth from an already substantial base in 1870 of this branching network. This meant that any one bank, usually with headquarters in London, had loans and sources of funds in most if not all parts of the country covering the whole spectrum of industry, agriculture and services. This branch network meant that if a branch (or even several branches) were in trouble in an area adversely affected by a fall in demand for its product, the resources of the bank could readily be diverted to ease the pressure. This could be done without any indication being given to a wider public and so could remove an important potential source of apprehension for the depositor.

This structure, of course, contrasts starkly with the structure in the United States where branch banking or certainly inter-state branching was prohibited. A small bank failure could therefore lead to another and so on to a run, particularly in the absence of a clearly recognised lender of last resort.

There continued to be many banks in Britain without branches and there were fairly frequent bank failures, and there were also regular new entrants to the system every year. But these failures did not result in runs, they were simply accepted as part of the pattern of business enterprise. There were even occasionally quite large bank failures such as that of the City of Glasgow bank in 1878. This was a badly run bank, with corrupt practices, which was clearly insolvent and allowed to fail. It had close connections with a number of other banks all of which were affected. But there was no run on banks, no banking panic, no financial crisis, no significant rise in current–deposit or reserve–deposit ratios.

Conclusion

In summary, this exercise in measurement has shown that the relationship between money and the business cycle in Britain is far from unambiguous. A variety of measures fails to reveal the kind of correspondence that has been found for the US? The question then becomes, how can this contrast with the US be explained. But it is worth stressing that the contrast should not be overdrawn since Friedman and Schwartz's position was a cautious one and one that relied not only on average statistical results but in good part on evidence from *major* downturns. There were no major downturns in this period in the United Kingdom of the kind found in the United States.

There were far fewer turning points in Britain than in the US: that is, much less fluctuation. And the movement there was was much less severe than in the US. Thus, using percentage deviations from trend, of average annual real output growth from peak to trough, Bordo (1986b) shows that the British trough of 1894 was −0.19 whereas the corresponding figure for the US was −9.5. The worst British experience of the whole period was that of 1907–08 when the deviation was −4.7. The corresponding fall in the US was 14.7. And there were no banking panics or financial crises. The suggested explanation for this essential difference may lie in the fact that there was in Britain an accepted lender of last resort by the start of this period; there was also a well established and expanding branch banking system that operated without restrictive regulation. The result of these elements was that there were no threats to the financial system, little volatility in the monetary series. Some of the movement in monetary series in the US undoubtedly arises from the recurrent financial crises that were an essential part of the business cycle.

Notes

I should like to thank Anna Schwarz and Michael Bordo for their comments.

5 British economic fluctuations 1851–1913: a perspective based on growth theory

N.F.R. CRAFTS and TERENCE C. MILLS

Introduction

Alec Ford's analysis of economic fluctuations, synthesised in his contributions to Aldcroft and Fearon (1972) and Floud and McCloskey (1981), remains the focal point of discussions of the trade cycle before 1914. Perhaps the best known element of this work concentrates on the statistical investigation of nominal demand variables, notably in terms of deviations from nine-year moving averages. The most widely cited recent paper on pre-1914 business cycles (Eichengreen, 1983a) also concentrates its quantitative analysis on short-term correlations between changes in money, exports, output, prices etc. by using a vector autoregression approach.

Although Ford's exposition takes changes in effective demand as central to the analysis, he does not favour an endogenous cycle of a multiplier-accelerator kind as capturing the essential nature of the Victorian economy. His view of the underlying sources of fluctuations in this period places its emphasis on long run real factors associated with an international process of capital accumulation and long run economic development such that he would

support the use of a weak multiplier-accelerator model with erratic shocks (autonomous investment abroad could be one strong source) with emphasis on 'real' forces, although the monetary or interest rate factor must not be neglected. The 'trade cycle' in this period for Britain is seen as inextricably linked with the growth and development process not only of Britain but of the primary producers and borrowers. (1972: 159)

Many other authors have argued for the importance of this perspective: for example, Matthews argued that the apparent phenomenon of a 7 to 10 year cycle inherent in the working of the economy was illusory, being a reflection of unsynchronised long waves of capital accumulation at home and abroad (1959: 220–6). This argument has since been significantly developed by Edelstein (1982) and Solomou (1987).

Edelstein established that British savings were sensitive to interest rates and that shocks to foreign investment would impact on home investment and vice versa. Solomou produced some statistical evidence in favour of long swings, which he interpreted as episodic events (based on investment shocks associated with structural changes) leading to transitions between steady-state growth paths. Nevertheless, such approaches have not been embedded in the basic models of economic growth which have been analysed in a hitherto separate new economic history literature concerned with the alleged failure of the late Victorian economy: see, for example, Crafts (1979), Kennedy (1974; 1987) and McCloskey (1970).

In this chapter we analyse a formal model looking, in particular, at links between growth and cycles in order to provide some statistical evidence relevant to Ford's underlying view, given that these recent contributions have emphasised its general plausibility. We would argue that it is important to consider economic fluctuations and growth explicitly together, since it seems probable that there were strong interactions between the two.

The strong likelihood that this is the case has dominated recent developments in macroeconomics which follow up insights from the real business cycle literature and the econometric testing for unit roots in output to develop the notion that unforecasted changes in long run economic prospects, working in the context of a neoclassical growth model, can generate fluctuations much like the conventional conception of the business cycle (Stock and Watson, 1988). A major concern of this approach is whether trend growth should be seen as deterministic or stochastic. This in its turn is reflected (much less formally, of course) in the controversy over late-nineteenth-century British growth, with McCloskey firmly of the deterministic position while Kennedy and earlier writers like Phelps-Brown and Handfield Jones (1952), in their famous account of the climacteric, seem much more inclined to the stochastic view.

Time series analysis of British growth has already thrown up some important results in this context. Mills (1991), whose work is summarised below, has demonstrated by using a variety of tests that World War I appears to mark a boundary between an earlier period in which the growth process was trend stationary and a later period when the appropriate characterisation was of a random walk with drift, a result which seems to be rather general for twentieth century Western economies (see, for example: Campbell and Mankiw, 1989; Kormendi and Meguire, 1990). Such results are essentially statistical, however, and leave unanswered the question of what model may have generated the observed behaviour. Resolution of this issue is central to any serious attempt to view economic fluctuations as arising from shocks to a (neoclassical) growth process. Given Mills' results, we might expect the basic neoclassical growth model, which embodies trend stationarity, to be a good starting point for the analysis of pre-World War I fluctuations, although not for later periods.

Our main concern is then with the question of whether an essentially neoclassical growth model of the refined types presented in the recent literature, notably King, Plosser and Rebelo (1988a, b), is capable of replicating the British experience of fluctuations, particularly before 1914. A further issue needs also to be addressed, however. In some circumstances it should be very difficult (indeed impossible with realistic sample sizes) to reject correctly the hypothesis of a unit root in output. For example, West (1988) shows that there are configurations of aggregate demand and supply relations which, when combined with particular policy rules followed by the authorities, will give near unit root behaviour of output. A full understanding of growth and fluctuations in the pre-1914 world needs to be able to explain the absence of this near unit root outcome.

Models of persistence in output

Before proceeding to an analysis of a formal real business cycle model, it is important to clarify some basic statistical ideas concerning the effects of shocks on output growth and future levels of output.

We begin by assuming that the logarithm of output, denoted y_t, follows a first-difference stationary linear process: in other words, that the growth rate of output is stationary. If this is the case, y_t has a moving average representation of the form

$$\nabla y_t = (1 - B)y_t = \mu + A(B)\varepsilon_t = \mu + \sum_{j=0}^{\infty} a_j \varepsilon_{t-j}, \tag{1}$$

where B is the lag operator, defined such that $B^k y_t = y_{t-k}$, the first equality defines the equivalent notations ∇y_t and $(1 - B)y_t$, for first differences of y_t, and the last equality defines the lag polynomial notation $A(B)$. The ε_t are independent and identically distributed errors with common variance σ_ε^2: i.e. ε_t is white noise. The constant μ is the 'drift', representing the long-run growth of y_t.

From (1), the impact of a shock in period t on the growth rate of output in period $t + k$, ∇y_{t+k}, is a_k. The impact of the shock on the level of output in period $t + k$, y_{t+k}, is therefore $1 + a_1 + \ldots + a_k$. The ultimate impact of the shock on the level of output is the infinite sum of these moving average coefficients, defined as

$$A(1) = 1 + a_1 + a_2 + \ldots = \sum_{j=0}^{\infty} a_j.$$

The value $A(1) = \Sigma a_j$ can then be taken as a measure of how persistent shocks to output are. For example, $A(1) = 0$ for any trend stationary series, since $A(B)$ must contain a factor $(1 - B)$, whereas $A(1) = 1$ for a random walk, since $a_j = 0$ for $j > 0$. Other positive values of $A(1)$ are, of course, possible, depending upon the size and signs of the a_j.

Difficulties arise in estimating $A(1)$ because it is an infinite sum, thus requiring the estimation of an infinite number of coefficients. Various measures have thus been proposed in the literature to circumvent this problem. Mills (1991) compares the results of tests based on the approaches proposed by Campbell and Mankiw (1987), Cochrane (1988) and Clark (1987): these being, respectively, an ARMA model approach, a non-parametric model of persistence, and a structural time series model.

These alternative estimates of the persistence of output innovations for the UK are remarkably consistent, in contrast to the analogous findings for the US summarised, for example, in Stock and Watson (1988). For the post-World War II quarterly data and for annual data post-1921, innovations to output have been largely persistent: a 1% unforecasted increase in output will change the forecast of the long-run level of output by around 1%. For the pre-1919 data, however, innovations were largely temporary: a forecasted increase in output would tend to have no impact on the long-run forecast. This last finding is consistent with the results of unit root tests reported in Crafts, Leybourne and Mills (1989a) and Mills and Taylor (1989), and the evidence in favour of trend stationarity in the pre-World War I period thus appears quite strong.

There are several implications of this discussion of persistence in output which are of interest for this chapter. First, it suggests that it may well be that a different model of growth and cycles is required for the Victorian economy than would be appropriate under modern conditions, as Ford's work itself strongly suggests. Second, also in line with Ford's expectations, there would be a reversion to long run trend following shocks such as changes in home or foreign investment opportunities in the pre-1914 economy but not after World War I. This could be consistent with Ford's emphasis on fluctuations in planned spending around a steady growth in productive potential (1981: 32). It also corresponds with the constant natural rate of growth idea at the heart of McCloskey's discussion of growth (1970), though it is not so easy to square with Solomou's (1987) emphasis on growth traverses. Third, the finding of no persistence prior to 1914 could be compatible with a neoclassical model of growth and cycles such as that put forward by King, Plosser and Rebelo (1988a), which is considered in detail in the next section.

This model is in the Real Business Cycle tradition, however, which, while stressing real shocks as an explanation of fluctuations, as does Ford, has a different emphasis from the Keynesian tradition, in that it seeks to work out predicted implications in a choice theoretic framework in markets that clear. Nevertheless, the Real Business Cycle viewpoint is similar to Ford's in stressing real shocks rather than monetary disturbances as providing a very sizeable fraction of output fluctuations, and it seems to offer an interesting way of formalising the underlying Ford view of pre-1914 fluctuations. We proceed next to investigate how well the basic neoclassical model performs in attempts to replicate British cyclical experience.

A formal modelling approach to growth and cycles

The basic neoclassical model

We begin by setting out briefly the key features of the basic one-sector, neoclassical model of capital accumulation that forms the basis of King, Plosser and Rebelo's (1988a) analysis of real business cycles.

The preferences, technology and endowments of the environment are defined in the following manner.

PREFERENCES

The economy is assumed to be populated by many identical infinitely-lived individuals, of sufficient number that each perceives his influence on aggregate quantities to be insignificant, and whose preferences over goods and leisure are represented by the utility function

$$U = \sum_{t=0}^{\infty} \beta^t u(C_t, L_t), \ \beta < 1, \tag{2}$$

where C_t and L_t are commodity consumption and leisure in period t, respectively. Momentary utility, $u(\cdot)$, is assumed to be strictly increasing, concave, twice continuously differentiable and to satisfy Inada-type conditions that ensure that the optimal solution for C_t and L_t is always (if feasible) interior. Restrictions can also be imposed on β to guarantee that life-time utility U is finite.

PRODUCTION TECHNOLOGY

The economy has only one final good, Y_t, and it is produced according to a constant returns to scale production technology given by

$$Y_t = A_t F_t(K_t, N_t X_t), \tag{3}$$

where K_t is the predetermined capital stock (chosen at $t-1$) and N_t is labour input. By allowing the scale variable A_t to be time varying, temporary changes in total factor productivity are permitted, although, as we discuss below, permanent technology variations are restricted to be in labour productivity, X_t. We assume that $F(\cdot)$ has standard neoclassical properties, i.e. that it is concave, twice continuously differentiable, satisfies the Inada conditions, and implies that both factors of production are essential.

CAPITAL ACCUMULATION
In this simple neoclassical framework the single commodity can either be consumed or invested, i.e. stored for use in production next period. The evolution of the capital stock is thus

$$K_{t+1} = (1 - \delta_K)K_t + I_t, \tag{4}$$

where I_t is gross investment and δ_k is the rate of depreciation of capital.

RESOURCE CONSTRAINTS
In each period, an individual faces two resource constraints: (i) total time allocated to work and leisure cannot exceed the endowment, which is normalised to unity, and (ii) total uses of the commodity must not exceed output. These conditions are

$$L_t + N_t \leq 1, \tag{5}$$

and

$$C_t + I_t \leq Y_t. \tag{6}$$

There are also the non-negativity constraints $L_t \geq 0$, $N_t \geq 0$, $C_t \geq 0$ and $K_t \geq 0$.

STEADY STATE GROWTH
A characteristic of most industrialised economies is that variables such as output per capita and consumption per capita exhibit sustained growth over long periods of time: this long-run growth occurring at rates that are roughly constant over time within economies but which differ across economies. King, Plosser and Rebelo (1988a) interpret this pattern as evidence of steady state growth: that levels of certain key variables grow at constant, but possibly different, rates. For the economic system described by equations (2)–(6) to exhibit steady state growth, additional restrictions on preferences are required.

RESTRICTIONS ON PRODUCTION
For steady state growth to be feasible, permanent technical change must be expressible in a labour augmenting form. While there are various functional forms for $F(\cdot)$ that will ensure this, the most tractable is the Cobb-Douglas:

$$Y_t = A_t K_t^{1-\alpha}(N_t X_t)^\alpha. \tag{7}$$

Since variation in A_t is assumed to be temporary, it can be ignored in terms of steady growth, so that we can work with the assumption that A_t is constant for all time, i.e. $A_t = A$. As the amount of time devoted to work (N) has to be between zero and one, the only feasible per capita constant growth rate for N is zero, i.e. on denoting $\gamma_N = N_{t+1}/N_t$, we must have $\gamma_N = 1$. The production function (7) (indeed, *any* constant returns to scale production function) and the capital accumulation equation (4) then imply that the steady state rates of growth of output, consumption, capital and investment per capita are all equal to the growth rate of labour augmenting technical progress, i.e.

$$\gamma_Y = \gamma_C = \gamma_K = \gamma_I = \gamma_X \tag{8}$$

RESTRICTIONS ON PREFERENCES

The feasible steady state given by the growth rates above will be compatible with an (optimal) competitive equilibrium if two restrictions on preferences are imposed: (i) the intertemporal elasticity of substitution in consumption must be invariant to the scale of consumption, and (ii) the income and substitution effects associated with sustained growth in labour productivity must not alter labour supply per person. These conditions imply the following class of admissible utility functions:

$$u(C,L) = \frac{1}{(1-\sigma)} C^{1-\sigma} v(1-N) \tag{9a}$$

for $0 < \sigma < 1$ and $\sigma > 1$, while for $\sigma = 1$,

$$u(C,L) = \log(C) + v(1-N). \tag{9b}$$

For this class of utility functions, the constant intertemporal elasticity of substitution in consumption is $1/\sigma$.

STATIONARY ECONOMIES AND STEADY STATES

The standard method of analysing models with steady state growth is to transform the economy into a stationary one, which can be done here by dividing all variables by the growth component X, so that $c = C/X$, $k = K/X$ etc. This alters the capital accumulation equation (4) to

$$\gamma_X k_{t+1} = (1-\delta_K)k_t + i_t \tag{10}$$

and transforms the utility function (2) to

$$U = \sum_{t=0}^{\infty} (\beta^*)^t u(C_t, L_t), \tag{11}$$

where $\beta^* = \beta(\gamma_X)^{1-\sigma} < 1$ to guarantee finiteness of lifetime utility. Substituting (5) into (10) and combining (3), (6) and (9) into a general resource constraint, we can form the Lagrangian

$$\mathscr{L} = \sum_{t=0}^{\infty} (\beta^*)^t u(c_t, 1-N_t) + \sum_{t=0}^{\infty} \Lambda_t [A_t F(k_t, N_t) - c_t - \gamma_X k_{t+1} + (1-\delta_K)k_t] \quad (12)$$

The first order (efficiency) conditions for this transformed economy are given below as equations (13)–(16), in which $\mathscr{D}_i$ is the first partial derivative operator with respect to the ith argument and, for convenience, we discount the Lagrange multipliers to current values, i.e. $\lambda_t = \Lambda_t/(\beta^*)^t$.

$$\mathscr{D}_1 u(c_t, 1-N_t) - \lambda_t = 0 \tag{13}$$

$$\mathscr{D}_2 u(c_t, 1-N_t) - \lambda_t A_t \mathscr{D}_2 F(k_t, N_t) = 0 \tag{14}$$

$$\beta^* \lambda_{t+1} [A_{t+1} \mathscr{D}_1 F(k_{t+1}, N_{t+1}) + (1-\delta_K)] - \lambda_t \gamma_X = 0 \tag{15}$$

$$A_t F(k_t, N_t) + (1-\delta_K)k_t - \gamma_X k_{t+1} - c_t = 0 \tag{16}$$

for all $t = 1, 2, \ldots$. There is also a 'transversality condition',

$$\lim_{t \to \infty} (\beta^*)^t \lambda_t k_{t+1} = 0 \tag{17}$$

which ensures that the non-negativity constraint on k_t is imposed as $t \to \infty$ (the economy's initial capital stock, k_0, is assumed to be given).

For a given sequence, $\{A_t\}_{t=0}^{\infty}$, of technology shifts, optimal per capita quantities for this economy are sequences of consumption, $\{c_t\}_{t=0}^{\infty}$, work effort, $\{N_t\}_{t=0}^{\infty}$, capital stock, $\{k_t\}_{t=0}^{\infty}$, and shadow prices, $\{\lambda_t\}_{t=0}^{\infty}$, that satisfy the efficiency conditions (13)–(17), which are both necessary and sufficient for an optimum to be achieved. Thus, as real shocks impact on A_t, the economy will be characterised by intertemporal substitutions which will temporarily change investment, consumption, work effort, etc. and these transitory dynamics lie at the heart of fluctuations. It should further be noted that, although it is common in expositions of this type of model to think of A_t as the outcome of technology shocks, other factors could have similar effects. In general, any shock to the value of Tobin's q (Tobin, 1961) which triggers off a change in the desired capital stock will have similar effects, and in an open economy such as late Victorian Britain the source of such changes might well be developments abroad rather than at home, as Edelstein (1982) and Solomou (1987) have suggested.

Near steady state dynamics

The basic one-sector neoclassical model with stationary technology has the property that the optimal capital stock converges monotonically to a stationary point. Our focus of attention will be on the approximate *linear* dynamics of the model in the neighbourhood of the steady state denoted by $(A, k, N, c$ and $y)$.

The initial step in obtaining a system of linear difference equations is to approximate (13)–(16) near the stationary point. This is done by expressing each condition in terms of the percentage deviation from the stationary value, which we indicate using a circumflex [e.g. $\hat{c}_t = \log(c_t/c)$, $\hat{k}_t = \log(k_t/k)$, etc.], and then linearising each condition in terms of these deviations. Equations (13) and (14) imply that

$$\xi_{cc}\hat{c}_t - \xi_{cl}\frac{N}{1-N}\hat{N}_t - \hat{\lambda}_t = 0, \tag{18}$$

$$\xi_{lc}\hat{c}_t - \frac{N}{1-N}\xi_{ll}\hat{N}_t - \hat{\lambda}_t - \hat{A}_t - (1-\alpha)\hat{k}_t + (1-\alpha)\hat{N}_t = 0, \tag{19}$$

where ξ_{ab} is the elasticity of the marginal utility of a with respect to b and where we have used the Cobb-Douglas production function (7). The ξ's depend on the utility function employed. We shall use the additively separable function (9b), from which it follows that $\xi_{cc} = -1$, $\xi_{cl} = \xi_{lc} = 0$ and $\xi_{ll} = L\mathcal{D}^2 v(L)/v(L)$.

Approximation of the intertemporal efficiency condition (15) implies that

$$\hat{\lambda}_{t+1} + \eta_A\hat{A}_{t+1} + \eta_k\hat{k}_{t+1} + \eta_N\hat{N}_{t+1} = \hat{\lambda}_t, \tag{20}$$

where η_A is the elasticity of the gross marginal product of capital with respect to A evaluated at the steady state, etc. With the Cobb-Douglas assumption, it follows that $\eta_A = [\gamma_X - \beta^*(1-\delta_K)]$, $\eta_k = -\alpha\eta_A$ and $\eta_N = \alpha\eta_A$. Approximation of the resource constraint (16) implies

$$\begin{aligned}\hat{Y}_t &= \hat{A}_t + \alpha\hat{N}_t + (1-\alpha)\hat{K}_t \\ &= s_c\hat{c}_t + s_i\phi\hat{K}_{t+1} - s_i(\phi-1)\hat{k}_t,\end{aligned} \tag{21}$$

where s_c and s_i are consumption and investment shares in output and $\phi = K_{t+1}/I_t = \alpha_X/[\gamma_X - (1-\delta_K)] > 1$.

Equations (18)–(20) can be combined to eliminate $\hat{c}_t$, $\hat{N}_t$ and $\hat{y}_t$, yielding a difference equation system in $\hat{k}$ and $\hat{\lambda}$, which can then be solved, subject to the transversality condition, to produce unique solution sequences for capital accumulation $\{\hat{k}_t\}_{t=0}^{\infty}$ and shadow prices $\{\hat{\lambda}_t\}_{t=0}^{\infty}$, given a specification for the exogenous sequence $\{\hat{A}_t\}_{t=0}^{\infty}$. The time path of capital accumulation can, in fact, be written in the form

$$\hat{K}_{t+1} = \mu_1\hat{K}_t + \psi_1\hat{A}_t + \psi_2 \sum_{j=0}^{\infty} \mu_2^{-j}\hat{A}_{t+j+1}, \tag{22}$$

where μ_1 and μ_2 are the roots of the quadratic

$$\mu^2 - [1/\beta^* - s_c\eta_k/\sigma s_i\phi + 1]\mu + 1/\beta^* = 0,$$

and which satisfy the inequalities $\mu_1 < 1 < \beta^{*-1} < \mu_2$. The parameters ψ_1 and ψ_2 are given by

$$\psi_1 = \frac{1}{\mu_2\phi s_i}$$

and

$$\psi_2 = \psi_1\left[\left(\frac{s_c}{\sigma}\eta_A - 1\right) + \mu_2^{-1}\right]$$

and are thus complicated functions of the underlying parameters of preferences and technology.

Real business cycles

We now incorporate uncertainty, in the form of temporary productivity shocks, into the basic neoclassical model discussed above. The time path of efficient capital production, given by equation (22), contains the future time path of productivity shocks 'discounted' by μ_2. If we posit a particular stochastic process for $\hat{A}$, we may replace the sequence $\{\hat{A}_{t+j}\}_{j=1}^{\infty}$ with its conditional expectation given information available at t. In particular, if $\hat{A}_t$ follows a first-order autoregressive process with parameter ρ, then $\hat{A}_{t+j}$ can be replaced by $\rho^j\hat{A}_t$. This then allows the 'state dynamics' of the model to be given by the linear system

$$s_{t+1} \equiv \begin{bmatrix} \hat{K}_{t+1} \\ \hat{A}_{t+1} \end{bmatrix} = \begin{bmatrix} \mu_1 & \pi_{kA} \\ 0 & \rho \end{bmatrix}\begin{bmatrix} \hat{k}_t \\ \hat{A}_t \end{bmatrix} + \begin{bmatrix} 0 \\ \varepsilon_{A,t+1} \end{bmatrix} = Ms_t + \varepsilon_{t+1} \qquad (23)$$

where $\pi_{kA} = \psi_1 + \psi_2\rho/(1 - \rho\mu_2^{-1})$ and $s_t \equiv (\hat{k}_t, \hat{A}_t)$ is the state vector.

Given (23), the efficiency conditions (18)–(21) and the further equations

$$\hat{w}_t = \hat{y}_t - \hat{N}_t, \qquad (24)$$

and

$$\hat{i}_t = \frac{1}{s_i}\hat{y}_t - \frac{s_c}{s_i}\hat{c}_t, \qquad (25)$$

then the vector $z_t' = (\hat{c}_t, \hat{N}_t, \hat{y}_t, \hat{i}_t, \hat{w}_t)$ is related to the state variables through the system of linear equations

$$
z_t = \begin{bmatrix} \hat{c}_t \\ \hat{N}_t \\ \hat{y}_t \\ \hat{i}_t \\ \hat{w}_t \end{bmatrix} = \begin{bmatrix} \pi_{ck} & \pi_{kA} \\ \pi_{Nk} & \pi_{NA} \\ \pi_{yk} & \pi_{yA} \\ \pi_{ik} & \pi_{iA} \\ \pi_{wk} & \pi_{wA} \end{bmatrix} \begin{bmatrix} \hat{K}_t \\ \hat{A}_t \end{bmatrix} = \Pi s_t \tag{26}
$$

where the π coefficients, which are elasticities with respect to deviations of the capital stock from its stationary values, are complicated functions of the parameters of the model, i.e. α, σ, δ_K, β and γ_X. This formulation allows computation of impulse response functions for the system and population moments of the joint (z_t, s_t) process.

IMPULSE RESPONSES

Impulse response functions provide information on the system's average *conditional* response to a technology shock at date t, given the posited stochastic process for $\hat{A}_t$. The response of the system in period $t+m$ to a technology shock at $t+1$ is

$$
s_{t+m} - E(s_{t+m} \mid s_t) = M^{m-1} \varepsilon_{t+1}
$$

and

$$
z_{t+m} - E(z_{t+m} \mid s_t) = \Pi M^{m-1} \varepsilon_{t+1}.
$$

POPULATION MOMENTS

Population moments provide additional, *unconditional*, properties of the time series generated by this model economy. The linearity of the system implies that it is relatively straightforward to calculate population moments. The following procedure may be employed. The system matrix M is first decomposed as

$$
M = PM \cdot DM \cdot PM^{-1},
$$

where PM is the matrix of eigenvectors of M and DM contains the eigenvalues on its diagonal (and zeros elsewhere). Transformed states and innovations are then defined as

$$
s_t^* = PM^{-1} s_t
$$

and

$$
\varepsilon_t^* = PM^{-1} \varepsilon_t
$$

respectively. The covariance between any two elements of s_t^*, s_{jt}^* and s_{it}^*, say, is given by

$$
E[s_{jt}^* s_{it}^*] = [1 - dm_j dm_i]^{-1} E[\varepsilon_{jt}^* \varepsilon_{it}^*],
$$

where dm_i is the ith diagonal element of DM. Calculation of the variance-covariance matrix of the original (untransformed) state variables is then given by reversing the transformation:

$$\Sigma_{ss} = E[s_t s_t'] = PM \cdot E[s_t^* s_t^{*'}] \cdot PM^{-1}.$$

The autocovariance of the states at any desired lead or lag $m \geq 0$ is then given by

lags: $E[s_t s_{t-m}'] = M^m \cdot \Sigma_{ss}$
leads: $E[s_t s_{t+m}'] = \Sigma_{ss}(M')^m$,

while the autocovariance of z is given similarly by

lags: $E[z_t z_{t-m}'] = \Pi M^m \Sigma_{ss} \Pi'$
leads: $E[z_t z_{t+m}'] = \Pi \Sigma_{ss}(M')^m \Pi'$.

Alternative parameterisations of the model

To complete the M and Π matrices, and hence obtain, for example, the population moments, values are required for the taste and technology parameters σ, α, s_c, γ_X, β^*, ξ_{cc}, ξ_{cl}, ξ_{ll}, ξ_{lc}, N, ρ and δ_K. Labour's share of output was set at $\alpha = 0.52$, the mean share over the period 1855–1913. Consumption's share of output was similarly set at its mean value over the period of $s_c = 0.87$, so that s_i was thus 0.13 (Feinstein, 1972). The growth parameter was set at $\gamma_X = 1.02$, using the common growth rate estimated from the deterministic trend models reported later in the text. As noted above, we assume that the momentary utility function is of the additively separable form (9b): this specification implies zero cross-elasticities ($\xi_{lc} = \xi_{cl} = 0$) and unitary elasticity of consumption ($\sigma = -\xi_{cc} = 1$). The steady state value of work effort was set at $N = 0.35$, reflecting the fact that hours worked per person has been estimated as 65 hours per week until 1870 and 56 hours thereafter (Matthews *et al.*, 1982: 566). Given this value, and an estimate of the elasticity of labour supply of 0.4, taken from Beenstock and Warburton's (1986: 164) research on interwar Britain, the elasticity of the marginal utility of leisure with respect to leisure (ξ_{ll}) is then estimated to be $\xi_{ll} = -4.5$ (cf. King, Plosser and Rebelo, 1988a: 28). It should be recognised, however, that econometric evidence on labour supply elasticities is negligible and quite possibly unreliable.

Since the price level was stationary over this period (see Mills, 1990b), the real interest rate and the nominal interest rate coincide. This averaged approximately 3% per annum during the sample period, thus yielding a value of $\beta^* = 0.99$. The remaining pair of parameters, the rate of depreciation of capital (δ_K) and the persistence of technology shocks (ρ), were

Table 5.1. *Parameter values for the linear system (23) and (26)*

			Persistence			
	None	$(\rho=0)$	Moderate	$(\rho=0.5)$	Strong	$(\rho=0.9)$
δ_K	0.017	0.100	0.017	0.100	0.017	0.100
μ_1	0.931	0.801	0.931	0.801	0.931	0.801
π_{kA}	0.257	0.718	0.248	0.661	0.206	0.500
π_{ck}	0.649	0.625	0.649	0.625	0.649	0.625
π_{cA}	0.246	0.369	0.277	0.429	0.422	0.598
π_{Nk}	-0.059	-0.050	-0.059	-0.050	-0.059	-0.050
π_{NA}	0.262	0.219	0.251	0.198	0.201	0.140
π_{yk}	0.449	0.454	0.449	0.454	0.449	0.454
π_{yA}	1.136	1.114	1.131	1.103	1.104	1.073
π_{ik}	-0.889	-0.689	-0.889	-0.689	-0.889	-0.689
π_{iA}	7.096	6.104	6.846	5.616	5.672	4.247
π_{wk}	0.508	0.504	0.508	0.504	0.508	0.504
π_{wA}	0.874	0.895	0.879	0.905	0.904	0.933

allowed to vary, taking the values 0.017 and 0.10 (the latter as in King, Plosser and Rebelo, 1988a) and 0, 0.5 and 0.9, respectively. There is no way of estimating the value of ρ, but Feinstein (1988: 427) tentatively suggests a lifetime of about 60 years for capital (i.e. $\delta_K=0.017$).

The coefficients of the M and Π matrices obtained under these various combinations are shown in table 5.1, while the implied population moments, i.e. relative standard deviations, correlations and auto- and cross-correlations, are shown in tables 5.2 and 5.3.

The Feinstein depreciation coefficient is much lower than King, Plosser and Rebelo's (1988a) 'realistic depreciation'. As table 5.1 shows, this has a number of implications. The adjustment parameter μ_1 increases as δ_K falls, indicating that the capital stock adjusts more slowly at lower depreciation rates. The elasticity π_{kA}, on the other hand, declines as δ_K falls but, unlike μ_1, is sensitive to the serial correlation properties of $\hat{A}$, declining as ρ increases. These responses can be explained in terms of the basic economics of lowering the depreciation rate. First, when there is a lower depreciation rate, it follows that there is a higher steady state capital stock and a lower output-capital ratio: using the result that $(y/k)=(\gamma_X-\beta^*(1-\delta_K))/\beta^*(1-\alpha)$, then as δ_K goes from 0.10 to 0.017, y/k falls from 0.19 to 0.015. This suggests a substantial decline in the elasticity π_{kA}. Second, the change in μ_1 and the sensitivity of π_{kA} to ρ reflect the implications that δ_K has for the relative

Table 5.2. *Population moments for the linear system (23) and (26): relative variability*

		Standard deviation relative to $\hat{A}$					Standard deviation relative to $\hat{y}$			
δ_K	ρ	$\hat{y}$	$\hat{c}$	$\hat{I}$	$\hat{N}$	$\hat{w}$	$\hat{c}$	$\hat{i}$	$\hat{N}$	$\hat{w}$
0.017	0	1.18	0.52	7.12	0.27	0.95	0.44	6.04	0.22	0.80
0.017	0.5	1.54	0.97	7.75	0.28	1.32	0.63	5.04	0.18	0.86
0.017	0.9	4.03	3.51	11.10	0.37	3.84	0.87	2.76	0.09	0.95
0.100	0	1.24	0.84	6.16	0.23	1.08	0.67	4.97	0.18	0.87
0.100	0.5	1.77	1.46	6.17	0.22	1.65	0.82	3.49	0.12	0.93
0.100	0.9	4.36	4.13	7.49	0.20	4.28	0.95	1.72	0.05	0.98

importance of wealth and intertemporal substitution effects. With lower depreciation, the intertemporal technology that links consumption today with consumption tomorrow becomes more linear near the stationary point. This means that the representative agent faces less sharply diminishing returns in intertemporal production possibilities and will choose a temporally smooth consumption profile that requires more gradual elimination of deviations of the capital stock from its stationary level. The depreciation rate also impinges on the relative importance of substitution and wealth effects associated with future shifts in technology.

Capital accumulation is less responsive to technological conditions when shocks are more persistent (i.e. π_{kA} falls as ρ rises). For the same reason, more persistent technology shocks imply that consumption is more responsive (π_{cA} rises as ρ rises) and investment is less responsive (π_{iA} falls). Altering the character of intertemporal tradeoffs also has implications for labour supply via intertemporal substitution channels, with more persistent shifts in technology producing smaller, but still positive, changes in work effort ($\pi_{NA} > 0$, but falls as ρ rises). Alternative parameterisations of the model imply then that the nature of the intertemporal substitutions will change and thus, as we now discuss, different patterns of variability in the time series properties of the key variables.

Time series implications

A major feature of economic fluctuations is the differential variability in the use of inputs (labour and capital) and in the components of output

Table 5.3. *Population moments for the linear system (23) and (26): auto- and cross-correlations*

Variable	Autocorrelations				Cross-correlations with $\hat{y}_{-j}$								
	1	2	3	4	−4	−3	−2	−1	0	1	2	3	4
$\rho=0;\ \delta_K=0.017$													
$\hat{y}$	0.16	0.09	0.06	0.05	0.05	0.06	0.09	0.16	1.00	0.16	0.09	0.06	0.05
$\hat{c}$	0.88	1.71	0.64	0.59	0.18	0.21	0.29	0.53	0.69	0.26	0.22	0.20	0.18
$\hat{\imath}$	−0.02	0.00	0.00	0.01	−0.02	−0.02	−0.03	−0.05	0.94	0.08	0.00	−0.01	−0.02
$\hat{N}$	−0.03	0.01	0.02	0.02	−0.03	−0.04	−0.05	−0.09	0.91	0.06	−0.01	−0.03	−0.03
$\hat{w}$	0.26	0.16	0.13	1.00	0.08	0.09	0.12	0.23	0.99	0.19	0.11	0.09	0.08
$\rho=0;\ \delta_K=0.10$													
$\hat{y}$	0.39	0.29	0.22	0.17	0.17	0.22	0.29	0.39	1.00	0.39	0.29	0.22	0.17
$\hat{c}$	0.88	0.69	0.54	0.42	0.34	0.45	0.60	0.80	0.79	0.43	0.34	0.26	0.21
$\hat{\imath}$	−0.07	−0.05	−0.03	−0.02	−0.05	−0.07	−0.09	−0.12	0.83	0.21	0.15	0.10	0.07
$\hat{N}$	−0.10	−0.06	−0.04	−0.03	−0.10	−0.13	−0.18	−0.24	0.75	0.16	0.11	0.07	0.05
$\hat{w}$	0.53	0.40	0.30	0.23	0.21	0.28	0.37	0.50	0.99	0.41	0.31	0.24	0.18
$\rho=0.5;\ \delta_K=0.017$													
$\hat{y}$	0.67	0.40	0.27	0.21	0.21	0.27	0.40	0.67	1.00	0.67	0.40	0.27	0.21
$\hat{c}$	0.96	0.79	0.70	0.64	0.30	0.35	0.43	0.60	0.80	0.79	0.54	0.44	0.39
$\hat{\imath}$	0.46	0.24	0.12	0.06	0.07	0.13	0.25	0.52	0.86	0.36	0.16	0.05	0.00
$\hat{N}$	0.45	0.25	0.13	0.07	0.04	0.09	0.20	0.47	0.80	0.28	0.09	−0.01	−0.05
$\hat{w}$	0.74	0.48	0.36	0.29	0.24	0.30	0.42	0.68	0.99	0.72	0.45	0.32	0.26

$\rho=0.5;\ \delta_K=0.10$

$\hat{y}$	0.78	0.51	0.34	0.24	0.24	0.34	0.51	0.78	1.00	0.78	0.51	0.34	0.24
$\hat{c}$	0.94	0.69	0.52	0.40	0.35	0.48	0.66	0.93	0.91	0.72	0.49	0.35	0.26
$\hat{\imath}$	0.41	0.18	0.08	0.03	−0.03	0.00	0.08	0.26	0.77	0.59	0.34	0.20	0.12
$\hat{N}$	0.36	0.16	0.07	0.03	−0.12	−0.12	−0.08	0.04	0.60	0.46	0.25	0.13	0.07
$\hat{w}$	0.84	0.56	0.39	0.28	0.27	0.38	0.56	0.83	0.99	0.78	0.51	0.35	0.25

$\rho=0.9;\ \delta_K=0.017$

$\hat{y}$	0.96	0.84	0.76	0.70	0.70	0.76	0.84	0.96	1.00	0.96	0.84	0.76	0.70
$\hat{c}$	0.99	0.87	0.79	0.73	0.69	0.75	0.83	0.96	0.95	0.91	0.81	0.73	0.67
$\hat{\imath}$	0.86	0.80	0.72	0.64	0.48	0.54	0.60	0.65	0.78	0.75	0.65	0.58	0.53
$\hat{N}$	0.84	0.80	0.72	0.65	0.30	0.35	0.39	0.40	0.55	0.54	0.45	0.40	0.36
$\hat{w}$	0.97	0.85	0.77	0.71	0.70	0.77	0.85	0.97	0.99	0.96	0.84	0.76	0.70

$\rho=0.9;\ \delta_K=0.10$

$\hat{y}$	0.97	0.79	0.66	0.56	0.56	0.66	0.79	0.97	1.00	0.97	0.79	0.66	0.56
$\hat{c}$	0.99	0.77	0.62	0.53	0.51	0.62	0.77	0.99	0.99	0.95	0.77	0.64	0.54
$\hat{\imath}$	0.82	0.80	0.76	0.70	0.63	0.67	0.69	0.68	0.83	0.83	0.68	0.57	0.49
$\hat{N}$	0.72	0.72	0.69	0.65	0.50	0.46	0.37	0.20	0.40	0.44	0.36	0.31	0.27
$\hat{w}$	0.97	0.78	0.65	0.54	0.54	0.65	0.79	0.98	1.00	0.96	0.79	0.66	0.55

(consumption and investment). With purely temporary technology shocks ($\rho = 0$), consumption is much less variable than output (about a half as variable), while investment is far more variable (about five times as variable). Labour input $\hat{N}$ is somewhat less variable than consumption while the real wage rate $\hat{w}$ is rather more variable.

When shifts in technology become more persistent, there are important changes in the relative variabilities. Consumption increases in variability relative to output, although it is still less volatile in absolute terms, and this accords with the permanent income perspective. Real wages become somewhat more variable relative to output while labour input becomes much less variable, this fundamentally reflecting the diminished desirability of intertemporal substitution of effort in the face of more persistent technology shocks. Investment declines in variability relative to output, but still remains considerably more volatile. These relative variabilities appear to be only marginally affected by changes in the rate of depreciation.

A notable feature of the time series implications of the model is that $\hat{y}$, $\hat{i}$ and $\hat{N}$ exhibit almost no serial correlation in the absence of serially correlated technology shocks, irrespective of the rate of depreciation. This is not true of real wages or consumption, however, the latter being considerably smoother and also cross-correlated with output, unlike investment and labour. Serial and cross-correlation patterns become stronger as ρ increases, although again the value of δ_K has little influence.

We have considered deterministic labour augmenting technological change that grows at a constant proportionate rate as the source of sustained growth. The neoclassical model then predicts that all quantity variables (with the exception of N) grow at the same rate γ_X. The non-deterministic components of consumption, output and investment are then

$$\hat{y}_t = \log(Y_t) - \log(X_t) - \log(y)$$
$$\hat{c}_t = \log(C_t) - \log(X_t) - \log(c)$$
$$\hat{i}_t = \log(I_t) - \log(X_t) - \log(i)$$

Assuming that X grows at a constant proportionate rate

$$X_t = X_0 \gamma_X^t$$

i.e.

$$\log(X_t) = \log(X_0) + t \cdot \log(\gamma_X)$$

then

$$\hat{y}_t = \log(Y_t) - \beta_0 - \beta_1 t$$

where

$$\beta_0 = \log(y/X_0) \qquad \beta_1 = \log(\gamma_X)$$

and similarly for $\hat{c}_t$ and $\hat{i}_t$. Hence $\log(Y_t)$, $\log(C_t)$ and $\log(I_t)$ are *trend stationary* and possess a *common* deterministic trend. Therefore we should consider deviations of the log levels of output, consumption and investment from a common linear trend as empirical counterparts to $\hat{y}_t$, $\hat{c}_t$ and $\hat{i}_t$. Work effort, on the other hand, possesses no trend and thus $\hat{N}$ is simply the deviation of the log of hours from its mean. The real wage rate will also be trend stationary, although it will not necessarily have the common growth rate of γ_X.

Data for the period 1851 to 1913 for output, consumption and investment were taken from Mitchell (1988: 837–9). The real wage series is for own-product real wages and was obtained by deflating a money wage series from Mitchell (1988: 149–50) spliced to Feinstein (1990) by the GDP deflator from the national accounts tables in Mitchell. The labour input series N was generated by scaling the percentage employed (Feinstein, 1972: T125) by hours worked per week (65/168 up to 1870 and 56/168 from 1871 onwards). The following trend stationary models were then estimated.

$$\log(Y_t) = 6.12 + 0.0193t, \qquad s = 0.0355,$$
$$\log(C_t) = 6.02 + 0.0193t \qquad s = 0.0364,$$
$$\log(I_t) = 3.67 + 0.0206t, \qquad s = 0.1546,$$
$$\log(W_t) = 4.03 + 0.0081t, \qquad s = 0.0353,$$

where s is the residual standard error of the regression. Note that, as predicted by the model, the slope coefficients (i.e. trend growth rates) are very similar for output, consumption and investment, but not for real wages. Imposition of a common trend yields the following models, which show very little deterioration of fit when compared to the unrestricted trend models:

$$\log(Y_t) = 6.10 + 0.0197t, \qquad s = 0.0363,$$
$$\log(C_t) = 6.00 + 0.0197t, \qquad s = 0.0375,$$
$$\log(I_t) = 3.72 + 0.0197t, \qquad s = 0.1555.$$

Given the above models, the empirical counterparts to $\hat{y}_t, \hat{c}_t, \hat{i}_t$ and $\hat{w}_t$ were generated as

$$\hat{y}_t = \log(Y_t) - 6.10 - 0.02t$$
$$\hat{c}_t = \log(C_t) - 6.00 - 0.02t$$
$$\hat{i}_t = \log(I_t) - 3.72 - 0.02t$$

and

$$\hat{w}_t = \log(W_t) - 4.03 - 0.008t$$

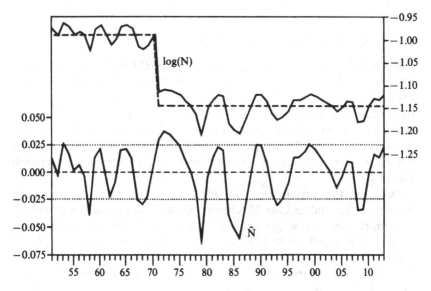

Figure 5.1   Labour input (work effort), 1851–1913.

Figure 5.1 plots $\log(N_t)$ and $\hat{N}_t$, the latter defined as the deviation of $\log(\hat{N}_t)$ from its mean value, which is allowed to shift in 1870 when hours worked per week was reduced. As predicted by the model, work effort shows no trend whatsoever.

Figures 5.2–5.5 show the empirical counterparts to $\hat{c}$, $\hat{i}$, $\hat{w}$ and $\hat{N}$ plotted against the reference variable $\hat{y}$, while table 5.4 presents the sample moments of the series. Consumption is highly cross-correlated with output, investment, work effort and real wages somewhat less so. Consumption, real wages and investment are also more highly serially correlated than output.

Consumption, real wages and output have almost identical variability, while investment is some four times more volatile, but work effort is rather less variable, than output. Comparisons of table 5.4 with tables 5.2 and 5.3 suggests approximate correspondence with a neoclassical growth model having moderate technology shocks and a depreciation rate more in the range of 10% per annum rather than that assumed by Feinstein. Nevertheless, there are some noticeable deviations from the predictions of the model, most particularly in investment, which seems too volatile and serially correlated, and in real wages, which is almost uncorrelated with output. Moreover, the standard deviation of $\hat{N}$ is much larger than in table 5.2. These features are particularly noticeable in the figures, the close

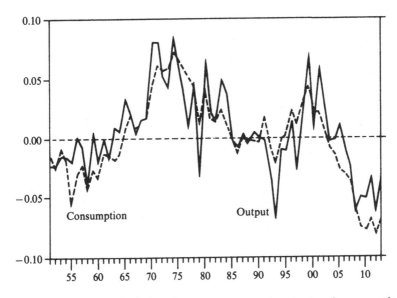

Figure 5.2 Estimated deviations from common trend: output and consumption, 1851–1913.

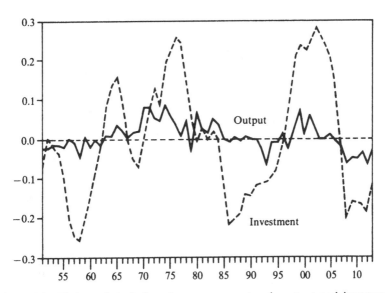

Figure 5.3 Estimated deviations from common trend: output and investment, 1851–1913.

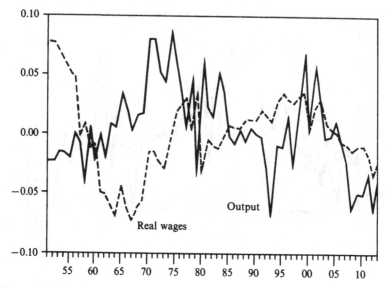

Figure 5.4   Estimated deviations from common trend: output and real wages, 1851–1913.

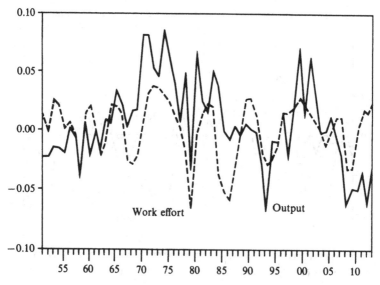

Figure 5.5   Estimated deviations from common trend: output and work effort, 1851–1913.

correspondence in serial correlation and variability between $\hat{c}$ and $\hat{y}$ being clearly seen, as is the markedly more volatile and persistent behaviour of $\hat{i}$.

Further evidence concerning the performance of the model is obtained by examining the processes generating the empirical counterparts to $\hat{y}$, $\hat{c}$ and $\hat{i}$. It is easy to show that these series should be generated by ARMA(2,1) processes with identical autoregressive polynomials, but different moving average parts. Fitting such processes obtains the following models:

$$\hat{y}_t = 0.61\hat{y}_{t-1} + 0.23\hat{y}_{t-2} + \varepsilon_t - 0.27\varepsilon_{t-1}, \qquad \sigma_{\varepsilon_A} = 0.028$$
$$\hat{c}_t = 0.70\hat{c}_{t-1} + 0.24\hat{c}_{t-2} + \varepsilon_t + 0.08\varepsilon_{t-1}, \qquad \sigma_{\varepsilon_A} = 0.016$$
$$\hat{i}_t = 1.52\hat{i}_{t-1} - 0.65\hat{i}_{t-2} + \varepsilon_t - 0.65\varepsilon_{t-1}, \qquad \sigma_{\varepsilon_A} = 0.052$$

The implied ARMA structure is apparent for output and consumption but is not found for investment, the autoregressive parameters of which reflect the cyclical behaviour of $\hat{i}_t$ shown in figure 5.3.

The low and slightly negative correlation between $\hat{w}$ and $\hat{y}$ represents a serious lack of correspondence with the basic neoclassical model. It also represents an interesting difference from the results obtained by King, Plosser and Rebelo (1988a: table 6) in applying the basic neoclassical model to the post-World War II United States. By contrast they found a high correlation between $\hat{w}$ and $\hat{y}$ but a very low correlation between $\hat{N}$ and $\hat{y}$.

Stochastic growth

An alternative growth model has been proposed by King, Plosser and Rebelo (1988b) which might be thought capable of replicating the behaviour of investment more satisfactorily. Rather than assume that labour productivity grows at a constant proportionate rate as in the basic neoclassical growth model, so that consumption, investment and output are trend stationary with a common trend growth rate, here we assume that, in general, labour productivity follows a *stochastic trend*, specifically a random walk:

$$\nabla \log(X_t) = \log(X_t) - \log(X_{t-1}) = \log(\gamma_X) + \varepsilon_t$$

or
$$\tag{27}$$

$$\log(X_t) = \log(X_0) + t \cdot \log(\gamma_X) + \sum_{i=0}^{\infty} \varepsilon_{t-i}.$$

Hence, shocks to the stochastic trend at time t, ε_t, result in a *permanent* shift in the level of X_t. The (transformed) capital stock is then driven by the permanent technology shock ε_t:

$$\hat{k}_t = \mu_1 \hat{k}_{t-1} - \varepsilon_t. \tag{28}$$

Table 5.4. *Sample moments*

Variable	Standard deviation	Standard deviation relative to $\hat{y}$
$\hat{y}$	0.036	1.00
$\hat{c}$	0.037	1.03
$\hat{\imath}$	0.154	4.29
$\hat{N}$	0.024	0.67
$\hat{w}$	0.035	0.97

Variable	Autocorrelations				Cross-correlations with $\hat{y}_{-j}$								
	1	2	3	4	4	3	2	1	0	-1	-2	-3	-4
$\hat{y}$	0.57	0.54	0.44	0.35	0.35	0.44	0.54	0.57	1.00	0.57	0.54	0.44	0.35
$\hat{c}$	0.88	0.79	0.71	0.58	0.43	0.54	0.64	0.71	0.84	0.65	0.59	0.56	0.43
$\hat{\imath}$	0.91	0.73	0.51	0.29	0.33	0.43	0.50	0.57	0.58	0.46	0.35	0.24	0.15
$\hat{N}$	0.58	0.05	-0.32	-0.40	-0.01	0.06	0.13	0.19	0.39	0.19	0.05	-0.12	-0.19
$\hat{w}$	0.82	0.72	0.58	0.46	0.23	0.15	0.03	-0.04	-0.15	-0.15	-0.21	-0.19	-0.18

Since all other stationary variables of the system respond only to the position of the transformed capital stock (there being no transitory components of technology under the random walk assumption), we have

$$\hat{c}_t = \pi_{ck}\hat{k}_t, \qquad \hat{N}_t = \pi_{Nk}\hat{k}_t, \qquad \hat{y}_t = \pi_{yk}\hat{k}_t,$$
$$\hat{i}_t = \pi_{ik}\hat{k}_t, \qquad \hat{w}_t = \pi_{wk}\hat{k}_t \tag{29}$$

Concentrating attention on the behaviour of output, consumption and investment, then substituting the appropriate relationships into

$$\log(Y_t) = \log(X_t) + \log(y) + \hat{y}_t$$
$$\log(C_t) = \log(X_t) + \log(c) + \hat{c}_t$$
$$\log(I_t) = \log(X_t) + \log(i) + \hat{i}_t$$

yields

$$\nabla \log(Y_t) = \log(\gamma_X) + (1 - \pi_{yk})\varepsilon_t + \pi_{yk}(\mu_1 - 1)\hat{k}_{t-1}$$

or

$$\nabla \log(Y_t) = (1 - \mu_1)\log(\gamma_X) + \mu_1 \nabla \log(Y_{t-1}) + (1 - \pi_{yk})\varepsilon_t - (\mu_1 - \pi_{yk})\varepsilon_{t-1}$$

with similar expressions for $\log(C_t)$ and $\log(I_t)$, i.e. the *growth rates* of Y, C and I should follow ARMA(1,1) processes with identical AR parts.

Utilising the parameter values $\mu_1 = 0.8$, $\pi_{yk} = 0.4$, $\pi_{ck} = 0.6$ and $\pi_{ik} = -0.7$, taken as representatives of the values given in table 5.1, the implied processes are

$$(1 - 0.8B)\nabla \log(Y_t) = 0.2 + (1 - 0.7B)\varepsilon^*_{yt}$$
$$(1 - 0.8B)\nabla \log(C_t) = 0.2 + (1 - 0.5B)\varepsilon^*_{ct}$$
$$(1 - 0.8B)\nabla \log(I_t) = 0.2 + (1 - 0.9B)\varepsilon^*_{it}$$

where $\varepsilon^*_{yt} = 0.6\varepsilon_t$, $\varepsilon^*_{ct} = 0.4\varepsilon_t$ and $\varepsilon^*_{it} = 1.7\varepsilon_t$.

Since the autoregressive and moving average parameters are fairly similar, the autocorrelations and cross-correlations of the series will be small, although the contemporaneous correlation between them will be high. Given the above models and taking $\sigma^2_\varepsilon = 1$, the implied standard deviations of the growth rates of the series are $\sigma_y = 0.61$, $\sigma_c = 0.45$ and $\sigma_i = 1.72$, respectively.

The corresponding sample moments are given in table 5.5. The variability of consumption and investment relative to output are both somewhat too low to that implied by the model, while the presence of large autocorrelations and cross-correlations at low lags and leads is also in contrast to that predicted.

Table 5.5. *Sample moments*

Variable	Standard deviation	Standard deviation relative to $\hat{y}$
$\nabla\log(Y_t)$	0.033	1.00
$\nabla\log(C_t)$	0.016	0.48
$\nabla\log(I_t)$	0.064	1.94

Variable	Autocorrelations				Cross-correlations with $\hat{y}_{-j}$								
	1	2	3	4	4	3	2	1	0	-1	-2	-3	-4
$\nabla\log(Y_t)$	-0.48	0.09	-0.02	0.05	0.05	-0.02	0.09	-0.48	1.00	-0.48	0.09	-0.02	0.05
$\nabla\log(C_t)$	-0.22	0.01	0.19	-0.02	-0.05	-0.01	0.14	-0.25	0.75	-0.35	-0.05	0.21	-0.01
$\nabla\log(I_t)$	0.50	0.22	-0.04	-0.09	0.07	0.05	0.01	0.14	0.31	-0.04	0.01	-0.07	0.04

The fitted ARMA(1,1) models confirm these findings:

$$\nabla\log(Y_t) = 0.019 - 0.21\nabla\log(Y_{t-1}) + \varepsilon_{yt}^* - 0.40\varepsilon_{yt-1}^*, \qquad \sigma_\varepsilon = 0.029$$
$$\nabla\log(C_t) = 0.019 - 0.19\nabla\log(C_{t-1}) + \varepsilon_{ct}^* - 0.19\varepsilon_{ct-1}^*, \qquad \sigma_\varepsilon = 0.016$$
$$\nabla\log(I_t) = 0.018 + 0.45\nabla\log(I_{t-1}) + \varepsilon_{it}^* + 0.14\varepsilon_{it-1}^*, \qquad \sigma_\varepsilon = 0.056$$

The models for output and consumption are close to those predicted by the model: the problem is again that of investment, whose parameters are considerably different. This would therefore appear to confirm that assuming stochastic growth is not, in itself, capable of correcting the failure of the basic neoclassical growth model adequately to model the behaviour of investment.

Indeed, we would argue that, of the two variants, the constant growth model is to be favoured, giving overall a better modelling of the growth and fluctuations of the pre-World War I British economy. In particular, the evidence of the various tests discussed earlier seems strong enough to reject the notion of a random walk model of the trend in GDP with some confidence. For the *post*-World War I period, however, we would expect the stochastic growth model to be the better of the two, recollecting that in the Introduction we reported the findings of Mills (1991) to the effect that the behaviour of output was very different before and after World War I: while output was trend stationary in the earlier period, it was difference stationary from 1922 onwards. This suggests that the constant growth model should provide a poor fit to the post-World War I data, being dominated by the stochastic growth variant.

Evidence that this is indeed the case is now provided. Concentrating again on the behaviour just of output, consumption and investment, trend stationary models for the period 1922–86 were estimated to be

$$\log(Y_t) = 5.66 + 0.0206t, \qquad s = 0.0736,$$
$$\log(C_t) = 5.60 + 0.0197t, \qquad s = 0.0753,$$
$$\log(I_t) = 2.14 + 0.0356t, \qquad s = 0.3147,$$

Imposing a common trend considerably worsens the fit of the models, which is not surprising given that the slope coefficient of the investment equation is substantially larger than those of the other two:

$$\log(Y_t) = 5.08 + 0.0253t, \qquad s = 0.1159,$$
$$\log(C_t) = 4.91 + 0.0253t, \qquad s = 0.1303,$$
$$\log(I_t) = 3.42 + 0.0253t, \qquad s = 0.3706.$$

Given the above models, the empirical counterparts to $\hat{y}_t$, $\hat{c}_t$ and $\hat{i}_t$ were generated as

$$\hat{y}_t = \log(Y_t) - 5.08 - 0.025t$$

Table 5.6. *Sample moments*

Variable	Standard deviation	Standard deviation relative to $\hat{y}$
$\hat{y}$	0.111	1.00
$\hat{c}$	0.125	1.13
$\hat{i}$	0.371	3.34

Variable	Autocorrelations				Cross-correlations with $\hat{y}_{-j}$								
	1	2	3	4	4	3	2	1	0	-1	-2	-3	-4
$\hat{y}$	0.93	0.82	0.70	0.56	0.56	0.70	0.82	0.93	1.00	0.93	0.82	0.70	0.56
$\hat{c}$	0.94	0.86	0.77	0.69	0.39	0.42	0.46	0.50	0.57	0.60	0.63	0.66	0.68
$\hat{i}$	0.91	0.77	0.64	0.53	-0.62	-0.66	-0.67	-0.64	-0.56	-0.45	-0.34	-0.21	-0.11

$$\hat{c}_t = \log(C_t) - 4.91 - 0.025t$$
$$\hat{i}_t = \log(I_t) - 3.42 - 0.025t$$

and the sample moments associated with these series are shown in table 5.6. From them we see that it would be difficult to find a constant growth model that would adequately fit the observed data. Indeed, the autocorrelations of the series show that each contains a root that is close to, if not equal to, unity.

The sample moments of the logarithmic first differences for the period 1922–86 are shown in table 5.7. The relatively low autocorrelations and cross-correlations are reasonably consistent with a stochastic growth model in which technology shocks are persistent and thus confirm that such a model presents a better explanation of the post-World War I data than the constant growth model.

Further consideration of the results

The results presented in the previous section are basically consistent with our expectations based on the observed pattern of persistence in output. The basic neoclassical growth model, with serial correlation in technology shocks and trend stationary growth, has some promise as a foundation for the analysis of pre-1914 fluctuations but is not well-suited for the later, post-World War I, period. The first topic to be addressed in this section is the conditions which permitted the absence of the unit root (or random walk) in output in the Victorian economy. We than go on to explore the apparent failings of the real business cycle model revealed in the previous section, namely its inability to replicate the behaviour of investment and the absence of a procyclical pattern of real wage fluctuations.

Near random walk behaviour in output

In a recent paper, West (1988) demonstrated that, in some circumstances, simple aggregate demand and supply models subjected to nominal shocks can generate a highly persistent (near random walk) process for output. Since we can reject the hypothesis of a unit root in pre-1914 output, it is useful to clarify that this outcome would be expected on the basis of West's approach.

In fact, West offers two models: one for a case where the government pursues an interest rate target, and a second for the case of a money supply target. This second model is the one we investigate here, as it is appropriate to the operations of the Bank of England in the pre-1914 gold standard period. It is widely agreed that the overwhelming priority of the Bank of

Table 5.7. *Sample moments*

Variable	Standard deviation	Standard deviation relative to $\hat{y}$
$\nabla\log(Y_t)$	0.034	1.00
$\nabla\log(C_t)$	0.027	0.79
$\nabla\log(I_t)$	0.149	4.38

Variable	Autocorrelations								Cross-correlations with $\hat{y}_{-j}$								
	1	2	3	4	4	3	2	1	0	-1	-2	-3	-4				
$\nabla\log(Y_t)$	0.28	0.14	0.12	-0.14	-0.14	0.12	0.14	0.28	1.00	0.28	0.14	0.12	-0.14				
$\nabla\log(C_t)$	0.44	0.07	-0.08	-0.22	-0.01	-0.13	-0.24	-0.36	-0.19	-0.12	-0.15	0.04	0.29				
$\nabla\log(I_t)$	0.35	-0.03	-0.14	-0.08	-0.22	-0.33	-0.36	-0.39	-0.02	-0.05	-0.12	0.23	0.34				

England's action in the money market was to maintain convertibility and to sustain a target level of reserves (Collins, 1988: 181; Dutton, 1984: 192; Goodhart, 1984: 223). Given the stable behaviour of the money to high-powered money and high-powered money to gold ratios (Bordo and Schwartz, 1981: 114–15), this effectively translates into a money supply rule followed over anything other than the very short term, with the rule chosen so as to be consistent with the fixed exchange rate.

The model is based on overlapping wage contracts as an endogenous source of persistence and where the money supply rule allows a choice as to the degree of accommodation of inflation and of past control errors. The model can be set out as follows.

$$x_t = 0.5x_{t-1} + 0.5\mathrm{E}(x_{t+1|t-1}) + 0.5\gamma\mathrm{E}(\hat{y}_{t|t-1} + \hat{y}_{t+1|t-1}) \tag{30}$$

$$p_t = 0.5(x_t + x_{t-1}) \tag{31}$$

$$\hat{y}_t + p_t = m_t \tag{32}$$

$$m_t = \phi p_t + \lambda(m_{t-1} - \phi p_{t-1}) + u_t \tag{33}$$

In these equations, x_t is the logarithm of the nominal wage rate, $\hat{y}_t$ is the logarithm of output, i_t is the nominal interest rate, p_t is the logarithm of the price level, m_t is the logarithm of the money supply and u_t is a serially uncorrelated shock. All variables are zero mean deviations from trend.

In each period (year), one half of the labour force fixes its nominal wage for the next two periods. Equation (30) then says that the nominal wage depends on actual and expected wages, as well as expected demand pressure, measured by expected deviations of output from trend. Equation (31) is a price markup equation, while (32) is a simple quantity equation. Equation (33) is a money supply target with $0 \leq \lambda \leq 1$.

Values of the unknown parameters γ, ϕ and λ were then obtained by estimating regression counterparts of equations (30) and (33). In the former equation, expectations were replaced by functions of observed values using the results that both x_t and $\hat{y}_t$ can be modelled adequately by AR(2) processes. The estimates thus obtained were $\gamma = 0.2$, $\phi = 0.4$ and $\lambda = 0.9$. West shows that the model has a simple solution when the monetary accommodation parameter λ equals unity, this being

$$\hat{y}_t = a\hat{y}_{t-1} + u_t + 0.5(1-a)u_{t-1},$$

and

$$a = \begin{cases} c - (c^2 - 1)^{1/2}, & \text{if } c > 1 \\ c + (c^2 - 1)^{1/2}, & \text{if } c < -1 \end{cases}$$

with

$$c = (1 + 0.5(1-\phi)\gamma)(1 - 0.5(1-\phi)\gamma)^{-1}$$

Since our estimate of λ is reasonably close to unity, making this approximation and using the estimates of γ and ϕ found above yields

$c = 1.13$ and $a = 0.60$,

so that the implied process for $\hat{y}_t$ is

$$\hat{y}_t = 0.6\hat{y}_{t-1} + u_t + 0.2u_{t-1}$$

or, approximately

$$\hat{y}_t = 0.40\hat{y}_{t-1} + 0.16\hat{y}_{t-2} + u_t.$$

Since the AR(2) model fitted to $\hat{y}_t$ has estimated parameters of 0.38 and 0.36, we see that a reasonably close correspondence is obtained, and that a near unit root result, as would have been implied by a being close to 1, is not found.

Comparison with West's results for the postwar United States (1988: 206) indicates that the absence of the near unit root in output derives both from a rather steeper short-run aggregate supply curve and, especially, from a lower degree of monetary accommodation by the pre-1914 Bank of England than the post-World War II Federal Reserve System. This is not particularly surprising given the evidence for a Phillips Curve in this period (Hatton, 1991) and recent econometric estimates of Bank behaviour (Pippenger, 1984: 208).

The behaviour of home investment

Certain peculiarities of British investment expenditure in the late nineteenth century are well known. In particular, Edelstein has stressed the existence of an inverse pattern of long swings in home and foreign investment and their relative profitability (1982: 30, 153). The tendency to quite long periods where home investment grew consistently well above or below trend is indeed reflected in figure 5.3 above. However, econometric investigation has shown that, in practice, foreign investment conditions had little effect in crowding out home investment, although the volume of foreign investment responded both to surges of opportunity abroad and to the home marginal efficiency of capital (Edelstein, 1982: 224). Within the real business cycle framework, this suggests that our attention can be confined to the domestic determinants of home investment.

The best known recent discussion of home investment in the Victorian economy is that of Eichengreen (1983b). In particular, Eichengreen stressed the positive, though lagged, impact of rising share prices based on optimistic reassessments of home profitability in raising q (the ratio of asset market valuation of capital relative to its replacement cost) in the home investment boom of the 1890s, followed by a subsequent reversal in both q and investment. Share prices exhibited substantial volatility in this period, presumably as investors generally (not merely in the London equity markets) reassessed future prospects. It should be recognised, however, that there is a considerable body of evidence which suggests that even in modern economies there appears to be substantial excess volatility of share prices and thus, presumably, investor confidence about profits, compared with what would have turned out to be *ex post* rational (Bulkley and Tonks, 1989). If this can be shown also to apply to our period, this might account for the divergence of investment from the behaviour predicted by the basic neoclassical model, which embodies *ex post* rational forecasting.

The presence of excess volatility in share prices can be established by utilising the methodology proposed by Shiller (1981) and since used and debated extensively: Bulkley and Tonks (1989) provide a British application. This is based upon a simple efficient markets model, where the detrended real equity price P_t at period t is given by

$$P_t = \sum_{k=0}^{\infty} \delta^{k+1} E(D_{t+k\,|\,t}), \tag{34}$$

where D_t is the detrended real dividend paid at t and δ is the constant detrended real discount factor. This model can also be written in terms of the ex post rational price, or 'perfect foresight', series P_t^*, i.e. P_t^* is the present value of actual subsequent dividends:

$$P_t = E(P_t^*), \tag{35}$$

where

$$P_t^* = \sum_{k=0}^{\infty} \delta^{k+1} D_{t+k}.$$

P_t^* can be approximated by working backwards from a terminal date P_T^* using the recursion

$$P_t^* = \delta(P_{t+1}^* + D_t). \tag{36}$$

From (35) we thus have

$$P_t^* = E(P_t^*) + e_t = P_t + e_t, \tag{37}$$

where $e_t = P_t^* - P_t$ is a 'forecast error' uncorrelated with the 'forecast' P_t of P_t^*: it therefore follows that, since $var(P_t^*) = var(P_t) + var(e_t)$, the inequality

$$var(P_t^*) \geq var(P_t) \tag{38}$$

must hold or else P_t is 'too volatile' to be explained by the simple efficient markets model.

Index

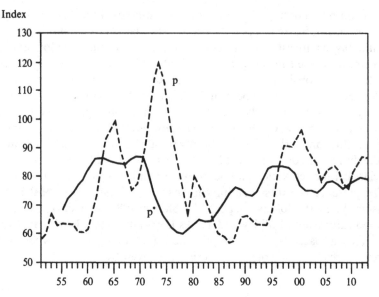

Figure 5.6   Equity prices, 1851–1913.

To investigate the volatility of equity prices in this period, data on detrended real equity prices and dividends are required. The nominal share price index is taken from Mitchell (1988: 687–8) and is deflated by Feinstein's (1972) GDP deflator. The series is then detrended by removing an exponential trend with growth rate of 0.8% per annum, the average rate over the sample period. Real dividends are proxied by Mitchell's (1988: 828–9) profits series, deflated by the GDP deflator and detrended by removing an exponential trend with growth rate 1.8% per annum. The detrended real discount factor δ is given by the ratio of one plus the dividend growth rate to one plus the real interest rate, i.e. $\delta = 0.99$. Using the terminal condition $P^*_{1914} = P_{1914}$, the recursion (36) was then computed, yielding the series shown in figure 5.6. It is quite clear that P^*_t is considerably smoother than P_t: indeed, the standard deviation of P_t, at 15, is almost twice as large as that of P^*_t, calculated to be 7.6. Given P^*_t, a 'perfect foresight' q can be computed: this series, q^*_t, plotted along with q_t itself, is shown in figure 5.7. The perfect foresight series is seen to be much smoother than q, the large increase in the value of this latter series around the turn of the century being entirely absent in q^*_t. (A similar exercise was carried out using a proxy for real dividends given by capital's share of output from the Cobb-Douglas production function of the previous section, i.e. $Y^{1-\alpha}_t$, where $\alpha = 0.52$, detrended and scaled to the equity index. Even greater

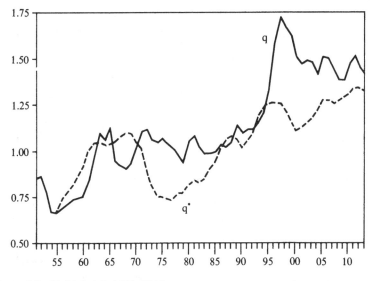

Figure 5.7   Tobin's 'q', 1851–1913.

evidence of excess volatility was found, the ratio of standard deviations in this case being approximately five).

Figures 5.8 and 5.9 show q and q^* plotted against investment. It is clear that the correspondence between investment and q is much closer than that with q^*. We thus conclude that a *prima facie* case exists for the argument that the source of the real business cycle approach's failure to model investment successfully may well lie in a tendency to waves of undue optimism and pessimism among investment decision makers. Arguably, expectations may have been formed in a more Keynesian mode in a world of relatively poor information and a quite imperfect capital market (Kennedy, 1987). Certainly Ford would not be surprised by this, as he pointed to the importance of 'animal spirits', 'exaggerated gloom and revulsion' and 'bloated expectations of gain' during this period (1981: 37).

The absence of procyclical real wages

The real business cycle model proponents in the American literature have wanted to argue that technology shocks are quantitatively more important than monetary disturbances as factors initiating business cycle fluctuations, or even that monetary disturbances are unimportant in that context (McCallum, 1989: 17). In the market clearing tradition, the implication of the recessionary tendency for individuals to increase the amount of leisure

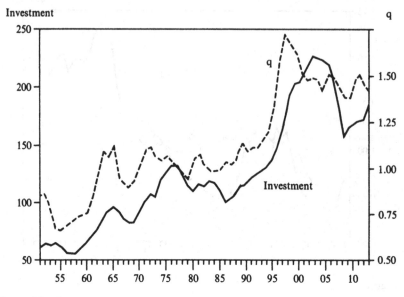

Figure 5.8   Investment and q, 1851–1913.

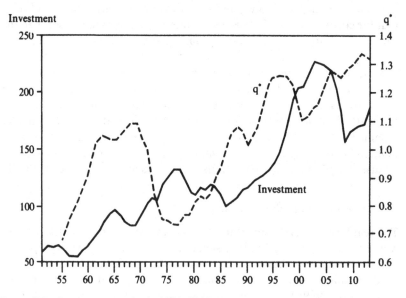

Figure 5.9   Investment and q*, 1851–1913.

they demand simultaneously with reducing their demand for goods must be that the real wage (the price of leisure) has fallen as a result of an adverse technology shock. By contrast, the Phillips Curve or 'Lucas surprise supply function' approaches to short-term macroeconomic fluctuations see output rising as real wages fall through wage-bargainers' failure fully to anticipate changes in monetary policy and inflation. As Mankiw (1989) points out, in a pure real business cycle framework there would be no room for a Phillips Curve.

Hatton (1991) is the latest in a long line of investigators to confirm the existence of a Phillips Curve in pre-war 1914 Britain. Moreover, he finds that wages were relatively insensitive to price changes, as if there were money illusion in the economy. In this context we would expect that any demand shocks or, indeed, monetary disturbances, would tend to generate a tendency for countercyclical movement in real wages. In fact, we observe virtually no correlation between output and real wages, a result also found by some researchers for the recent United States experience (McCallum, 1989: 23). This suggests the possibility that *both* real (technology) shocks *and* demand shocks were present, with neither strongly dominant over the other.

Thus we regard the notion that all short-run movements in output and employment result from real shocks as implausible, but do not believe that this need imply rejection of the view that fluctuations were substantially affected by the long-run growth and development process. In this we arrive at a position which, in important respects, is probably similar to that of Phelps-Brown. He stressed the strong impact on the British economy of a drying-up of technological and investment opportunities at the end of the nineteenth century (Phelps-Brown and Handfield Jones, 1952), while also emphasising the presence of a Phillips Curve in a world where nominal wages were insensitive to prices (Phelps-Brown and Browne, 1968). We would, however, not accept the notion of a climacteric in trend growth which looms large in Phelps-Brown's account of this period, as we have shown elsewhere that the time series evidence appears to reject this hypothesis (Crafts, Leybourne and Mills, 1989a).

Summary and conclusions

1 We have shown that a neoclassical model of growth disturbed by real shocks has some success in accounting for fluctuations in the Victorian and Edwardian economies. Such a model seems to require both serial correlation of shocks and depreciation over realistic time periods to replicate key features of the historical experience.

2 There seems to be strong evidence that shocks to output were not

persistent and that growth tended to revert to a constant trend rate of around 2% per annum. This matches the early vintage (Solow-type) neoclassical growth model, as used in McCloskey (1970), rather than new vintage examples like Romer (1986), which do not have diminishing returns to capital accumulation. It would follow that the very slow growth of 1899–1907 or the very strong growth prior to 1873 should be seen as 'blips'.

3 The major failings of this real business cycle model are its inability to replicate fluctuations in investment and the absence of pro-cyclical real wages in late Victorian Britain. These are serious difficulties and seem likely to result from features of the economy stressed by writers in a more Keynesian tradition, namely, 'animal spirits' and a short-run Phillips Curve.

4 In general, the results of this paper are consistent with Alec Ford's own views of the trade cycle in the late nineteenth century. Real shocks have an important part to play, but so also do 'Keynesian factors' that are assumed away in a perfect-foresight, choice theoretic framework.

Part II

Price behaviour 1870–1914

6 Price determination under the gold standard: Britain 1880–1913

T.J. HATTON

The gold standard and purchasing power parity

The challenge of understanding and explaining how the classical gold standard functioned in its heyday, 1880–1913, and why it worked so 'successfully' has proved an enduring one. Generations of scholars have interpreted and reinterpreted this experience, applying new theoretical frameworks, reviving old ones or introducing variations on established themes. This literature has been ably surveyed by Bordo (1984) and Eichengreen (1985). Many different questions have been raised, including global issues, such as whether the commodity standard contributed to the growth and stability of the world economy and whether other international monetary arrangements might have been preferable. Whether the constraints placed on policy makers by adherence to the gold standard produced 'better' economic outcomes remains an important issue for policy. Much of the discussion has focused on Britain as the major hub of trade and payments and the centre of commodity and financial markets. Questions such as whether and to what extent the Bank of England played the rules of the game, and why gold flows were so small relative to fluctuations elsewhere in the international accounts have occupied centre stage. Above all: how was it possible for Britain to remain on the gold standard with such apparent ease despite such small gold holdings at the Bank of England? This question seems especially pertinent in the light of Britain's experience since the First World War. These issues have been approached through various models of balance of payments adjustment under fixed exchange rates. The purpose of this paper is to further examine one of the more recent reinterpretations – that put forward in two papers by McCloskey and Zecher (1976 and 1984).

In their earlier paper, these authors argued that a number of puzzling features of how the gold standard worked are more easily understood when it is reinterpreted using the insights offered by the monetary approach to the balance of payments (MABP). This paradigm was developed in the

1970s, by Mundell (1971) and Johnson (1976). Elements of this approach were applied to the gold standard by Williamson (1964) and Triffin (1968), and the broader macroeconomic implications for the classical gold standard have been discussed by Eichengreen (this volume). A prominent feature of this approach is that international movements of assets are viewed as adjustments, which take place to maintain portfolio balance. They therefore reflect transitory equilibrating adjustments and not permanent flows arising from disequilibrium nominal or real rates of return. Similarly, international monetary movements, whether in the form of gold or currency, are the expression of domestic excess supply or demand for money. In this view, gold flows do not serve the function of driving macroeconomic adjustments in prices and income, which ultimately rectify the 'disequilibrium' on the balance of payments, which initiated the gold flow. Rather, the gold movement itself reflects the equilibration of supply and demand for money.

In common with many other applications of the monetary approach, McCloskey and Zecher link it with the notion that purchasing power parity (PPP) or the law of one price held.[1] Indeed, establishing this proposition formed a major focus of their 1976 paper and was the central issue in the 1984 one. Invoking the postulate of rationality among economic agents and the process of arbitrage, they argued that competition was sufficiently strong in domestic and international markets to ensure that substantial deviations between the domestic and foreign price level could not occur. Imports and exports of goods and services represent excess demand or supply at the world ruling price, fixed by arbitrage, just as for gold or foreign currency. Furthermore, arbitrage was so strong that through substitution between different markets for goods and through the mobility of factors of production within each economy all prices were tied closely together across countries. General equilibrium adjustments were fast and smooth enough to reallocate resources and reestablish equilibrium prices even in the short run.

Armed with this apparatus, McCloskey and Zecher (1976) argued that it helps explain many of the apparent anomalies that beset the orthodox approach in its many forms. Among these are the overall parallelism rather than divergence in year to year price movements between trading countries, the evidently small magnitude of international gold flows and the fact that many central banks held foreign currency as well as gold. The positive correlation between gold flows and income fluctuations in the UK and US and the alleged failure of the Bank of England and other central banks to play by the rules of the gold standard game are also cited. One point to make about this is that it is far from clear that the preexisting orthodoxy as developed over the century from the 1880s either ignored these stylised facts or failed to incorporate them into coherent accounts of how the gold standard worked. Indeed, much effort has been devoted to explaining the various empirical regularities invoking a variety of mechanisms. Second, as Eichengreen has pointed out (1985, this volume) the various channels of adjustment which form the focus of attention, are not necessarily mutually exclusive and can be considered as part of a general model of balance of payments. Furthermore, in the absence of the PPP assumption, the monetary approach to the balance of payments is largely consistent with accounts that stress the influence of relative prices, interest rates, and levels of activity.[2] To the extent that the monetary approach lays stress of the finding of a stable demand for money function and the fact that the domestic money stock was not rigidly tied to the stock of gold, few would take issue with it.

Thus, the key assumption is the rigid application of PPP. Under this assumption, the relative price changes between domestic and foreign produced goods, which provided the key adjustment mechanism in the Humean model of price-specie flow could not occur. If domestic and foreign prices for tradables are locked together by arbitrage, then changing relative prices in international trade could be neither cause nor effect of gold flows. Similarly, if arbitrage spread through the domestic economy to nontraded goods, then the changing relative prices of traded to nontraded goods envisaged by Taussig (1927) and his students (for instance Viner, 1924) could not be part of the adjustment process either. If capital markets were perfectly arbitraged, then adjustments occurring in response to interest differentials, as envisaged by Barrett Whale (1937), Sayers (1957), and Lindert (1969), would not be relevant. Finally, if, as appears to be the case under the strong version of PPP, prices were perfectly flexible, there could be no Keynesian effects on economic activity arising either from imperfect price adjustment or from sticky wage adjustment. Hence, the income expenditure effects envisaged by Scammell (1965), Triffin (1968), and above all by Alec Ford (1960; 1962) would have no equilibrating role to play in balance of payments adjustment. As McCloskey and Zecher put it, 'if the postulate is accepted, it implies that the wrenching adjustments of prices, interest rates, and incomes that the orthodox theory in its many forms holds necessary for reestablishing equilibrium in the balance of payments were in fact not necessary' (1976: 363).

At this point, the student of the classical gold standard might be tempted to say that the application of the monetary approach to the balance of payments by itself adds little to our understanding of how the gold standard worked and that augmenting it by rigidly applying PPP is unrealistic and, therefore, not worthy of serious consideration. This would be premature. The strong correlation between prices of traded goods produced or sold in different countries and between national aggregate price levels is indeed striking, and this fact has long been known. J.W. Angell, for example, in his 1926 book on international prices noted that 'the prices of commodities exchanged between countries definitely tend to maintain a world equality within assignable limits, or a scale of fairly constant differentials, although the closeness of the equalisation varies for different kinds of commodities' (p. 388). Comparing general price indices of Britain and the United States during the nineteenth century he went on to note that 'at most points a zone not more than 10 percent in width would include all of the deviations of one from the other' (p. 389). Yet, he was unwilling to subscribe wholeheartedly to the view that PPP was closely maintained by arbitrage. Similarly, in a well-known piece, Triffin observed that

as long as stable exchange rates were maintained, national export prices remained strongly bound together among all competing countries by the mere existence of an international market not broken down by any large or frequent changes in trade restrictions. Under these conditions national price and wage levels also remained closely linked together internationally even in the face of divergent rates of monetary and credit expansion as import and export competition constituted a powerful brake on the emergence of any large disparity between internal and external price and cost levels. (1968: 129)

Yet he was willing to admit a range of adjustment mechanisms through relative prices, interest rates, and incomes.

More recently, in their book on *Monetary Trends in the United States and the United Kingdom*, Friedman and Schwartz (1982), also noticed the strong correlation between the GNP deflators for the two countries. Like Angell, they found that between 1870 and 1931 'the purchasing power parity exchange rate fluctuated within a narrow range of plus and minus 10 percent, which seems consistent with a reasonably unified market' (1982: 280). Yet, while they admit to the tendency towards the law of one price through arbitrage, they also stress the adjustment to price levels occurring through something close to the price-specie flow mechanism.[3] A recent paper by Calomiris and Hubbard (1987) can be seen as going some way towards reconciling these views. They stress the efficiency of arbitrage in the rapid adjustment of interest rates, prices, and gold flows. They construct an IS/LM type macro model for the US economy and estimate this on the random shocks obtained as the residuals from vector autoregressions. Thus, the effects of relative prices on trade flows, gold flows on interest rates, interest rates on capital flows, and demand shocks on prices are all short-run responses, which take place against the background of strong equilibrating forces.

In the remaining sections of this chapter I examine some of the issues that arise in applying PPP specifically for Britain during with the period

1880–1913. First is an examination of the correlation between general price levels. Correlation of changes in various countries' prices with those for Britain confirm the findings of McCloskey and Zecher and others. Wholesale prices are more strongly correlated than GDP deflators, wage rates less so. Correlations of changes in output or deviations from trend in output are less strong but still positive. Such findings as these, while broadly consistent with the MABP/PPP approach, are hardly decisive evidence. As an alternative, in the following section I apply the recently developed techniques of cointegration to test for a long-run relationship in levels between British and foreign price levels. These tests prove to be indecisive. The tendency towards a long-run stable relationship appears to be weak. A simple autoregressive model for relative prices suggests that lags in adjustment were quite long, typically one to four years.

In the final section I turn to estimating a simple structural model of domestic price determination. This allows for the effects on domestic price change of changes in foreign prices, changes in domestic costs and variations in economic activity. One problem is that there is strong collinearity between different variables influencing domestic price change but if simple restrictions are placed on the model then the results become much clearer and suggest that domestic costs were the dominant factor. Finally, domestic costs themselves, as reflected in wage rates, respond to activity as reflected in the Phillips curve model of wage adjustment. The chapter concludes by summing up evidence for the classical gold standard period and considering the extent to which the results differ from those obtained for more recent times.

The correlations of prices and economic activity

The major piece of evidence offered by proponents of PPP is the closeness of correlations among different countries' prices. Tests of the homogeneity of prices for certain commodities in different countries can be used to shed light on the efficiency of arbitrage in internationally traded commodities and can be used to form a classification of how far the group of commodities for which unified markets existed can be extended. But if the issue is whether national economies can be described 'as if' they were price takers in a single market, as the MABP/PPP approach demands, then the appropriate comparison is between aggregate price indices. This is the principal evidence offered by McCloskey and Zecher (1976; 1984) as well as by other supporters of PPP.

McCloskey and Zecher found correlation coefficients for annual changes in GNP deflators and wholesale prices between the UK and US of 0.60 and 0.66 respectively. German prices gave lower correlations. The matrix of

Table 6.1. *Correlation coefficients for annual rates of change of prices* (*with the UK, 1880–1913*)

	GNP deflator	Wholesale price	Retail price	Wage rate
Belgium		0.66	0.37	0.56
France		0.77	0.28	
Germany	0.57	0.73	0.66	0.34
Italy	0.26	0.41	0.24	0.06
Norway	0.59			
Sweden	0.57	0.75	0.59	0.57
Denmark	0.69		0.56	
USA	0.57	0.67	0.54	0.30
Canada	0.46	0.72		
Australia	0.24			
Average 1880–1913	0.49	0.67	0.46	0.37
Average 1880–1896	0.51	0.66	0.49	0.31
Average 1897–1913	0.34	0.54	0.20	0.38

Note: GNP deflators obtained from the ratio of nominal to real GNP.
Sources: for tables 6.1 and 6.2 data was taken from Mitchell (1975; 1983) with the following exceptions. Real GNP and GNP deflators for US: Balke and Gordon (1989); Canada: Urquhart (1986). Wage rate for UK and retail price for UK from Feinstein (1972). The series for Italy are adjusted by the exchange rate with sterling given by Fratianni and Spinelli (1984).

correlation coefficients for retail prices among five countries gave four correlation coefficients larger than 0.5 and six below it, (1976: 376–7). Table 6.1 offers further evidence along similar lines. In this case the price indices are correlated in the form of first differences of logs and the correlations presented are for each country with the UK.

There are several observations worth making about these results. First, all the correlation coefficients between British and foreign prices are positive. While positive correlations do not reject the operation of the price specie flow mechanism as sometimes suggested, the array of positive coefficients is none the less impressive. Second, there is some evidence of higher correlations between British and foreign wholesale prices than between British and foreign GDP deflators. To the extent that wholesale prices reflect traded goods more than GDP deflators, this is as would be expected. The evidence for wage rates is more mixed, but there are a few relatively high correlations even among these. Third, almost all countries experienced gradually falling prices until the 1890s and then a reversal of the price trend: It might be suspected that the correlation coefficients reflect the change in trend rather than the closeness of year to year fluctuations. The averages are generally no higher for sub-periods than for the whole period 1880–1913. Finally, these results are similar to those obtained by Kravis and Lipsey (1978: 216) who obtained an average of correlation coefficients with other countries for 1950–73 of 0.44 for GDP deflators and 0.64 for wholesale prices.[4]

Correlations such as these have led recent observers to emphasise the parallelism among different countries. At the same time, recent studies have tended to downplay the parallelism among measures of economic activity. Friedman and Schwartz, for example, found only a weak correlation between the rate of change of real national income in the UK and the US. Similarly, in a detailed study of fluctuations in real output, Easton (1984) found relatively weak and often negative correlations using deviations from trend and similarly weak and sometimes unexpected results from Granger causality tests (p. 519). These findings contrast with the earlier literature, which emphasised the cyclical parallelism among leading countries as a key ingredient of the stability of the gold standard (see Morgenstern, 1959; Ford, 1962; also Lewis, 1978). These studies emphasised, particularly for Britain, that simultaneous increases in activity at home and abroad raised imports and exports at the same time, reducing strain on the balance of payments.

Table 6.2 offers correlations between real GNP and industrial production for a number of countries with Britain. The correlations of rates of change in the first two columns are lower than those for prices. In particular, the correlations for real GNP are lower than for the GNP deflators. But rates of change in other countries' GNP and industrial production are (with one trivial exception) positively correlated with the counterpart British variable. Rates of change are not the same as cycles and, as an alternative, correlations were taken between percentage deviations from trend. As the table shows, these do not seem to be more strongly correlated than the simple rates of change. Interestingly, the correlations are, if anything, stronger for the later years than for earlier.

Measures such as these tell something about the degree of association of prices and quantities but do not provide tests of whether PPP holds. Whether prices are more closely correlated than quantities does not provide an appropriate benchmark. McCloskey and Zecher interpret the evidence from price correlations and regressions as supporting their case, but they argue that there are few appropriate standards of comparison. The

Table 6.2. *Correlation coefficients for activity with UK 1880–1913*

	Annual rates of change		Per cent deviations from trend	
	GNP	Ind. prodn.	GNP	Ind. prodn.
France		0.38		0.34
Germany	0.25	0.20	−0.02	0.32
Italy	0.16	−0.01	−0.08	−0.16
Norway	0.04		0.22	
Sweden	0.28	0.12	0.43	0.41
Denmark	0.40		0.58	
USA	0.36	0.32	0.47	0.37
Canada	0.13		0.07	
Australia	0.43		−0.25	
Average 1880–1913	0.26	0.20	0.18	0.26
Average 1880–1896	0.15	0.19	0.20	0.30
Average 1897–1913	0.25	0.24	0.28	0.31

Note: for sources of data, see note to table 6.1.

one they emphasise (the Genberg-Zecher criterion) compares price correlations between countries with those (for the same commodity or commodity bundle) among different locations in the same country (1976: 372–3; 1984: 140). Yet, this criterion is hardly compelling. National economies may not be well integrated, and there will be regionally nontraded goods as well as internationally nontraded goods. In the following sections, two alternative methods of evaluating the strength of PPP are pursued: tests for cointegration between British and foreign price levels, and a structural model of the price level which tests the direct influence of foreign prices.

Cointegration tests of purchasing power parity

A weak version of PPP demands that prices in different countries move together in the long run. It is possible for the correlation coefficients among price changes to be quite high but for the individual price series to wander apart over time. Hence, correlation coefficients or regression coefficients between price changes are inappropriate as tests for PPP when prices do not move exactly in lockstep. An alternative is to use the tests recently advanced by Granger and Engle (1987) and others for cointegration among economic variables.

An individual time series may not be stationary (or said to be integrated of order zero I (0)). If it is not, then its asymptotic variance is infinite and it cannot have a long run stable relationship with a variable which is I (0). However, two or more variables which follow a random walk and are therefore I (1) can have a long run relationship in levels even through individually they do not revert to some constant means in the long run. In such circumstances cointegration can be used to test for a long-run relationship among variables which are not themselves stationary. This is done by determining whether the disturbance term from the long-run relationship is stationary (or I (0)).

The first step is therefore to take the price series underlying table 6.2 and test for a random walk (or unit root) in each of the individual series. The tests were conducted allowing for a deterministic trend in each series. The results are not reported but two test statistics were derived. The cointegrating regression Durbin-Watson statistic (CRDW) was obtained from the regression of the log of the individual series on a constant and a time trend. The Dickey-Fuller test statistic (DF) was obtained from regressing the residuals from the first regression on the lagged residuals. These tests almost always fail to reject that the series are I (1) at the 5% level against the alternative of I (0). The only exceptions are the wholesale price for Germany and the wage rates for Belgium, Germany and the UK each of which are rejected as I (1) on the CRDW test but not on the DF test.

Given that the overwhelming majority of these series appear to be close to I (1) cointegration tests seem appropriate. Tests were performed between each UK price series and the corresponding foreign series. The cointegrating regression in each case was formed by regressing the relevant UK price series (in logs) on the log of the corresponding foreign price series, a constant and a time trend. This is a relatively weak form of PPP since divergence in relative prices is permitted by the time trend and by the failure to restrict the coefficient on the foreign price to unity. This may be justified on the grounds that there will be differences in the composition of price indices over time. The important point is that this is not a very stringent test which should therefore make it more likely that PPP would be accepted. For further discussion of this form of test for PPP, see Broadberry and Taylor (this volume).

The upper panel of table 6.3 displays the Durbin-Watson statistics from the cointegrating regressions. If the CRDW statistic is greater than 0.39 then we cannot reject that the residuals are I (0) and therefore that the pair of series is not cointegrated. In almost every case the pairs of price series do appear to be cointegrated though in a few cases the test statistic is marginal.

Table 6.3. *Cointegration tests on UK and foreign prices*

	GNP deflator	Wholesale price	Retail price	Wage rate
Cointegrating regression DW statistics				
Belgium		1.22	0.99	0.69
France		1.18	0.36	
Germany	0.89	0.57	0.50	0.66
Italy	0.63	0.78	0.44	0.62
Norway	0.73			
Sweden	1.23	1.03	1.12	0.61
Denmark	1.30		1.13	
USA	0.59	0.68	0.47	0.60
Canada	0.59	0.71		
Australia	0.53			
Dickey-Fuller test statistic				
Belgium		4.01	3.29	2.60
France		3.79	2.10	
Germany	3.10	2.14	2.31	2.54
Italy	2.69	2.96	2.20	2.38
Norway	2.77			
Sweden	3.84	3.32	3.54	2.39
Denmark	4.10		3.62	
USA	2.48	2.82	2.43	2.40
Canada	2.54	3.08		
Australia	2.36			

Note: CRDW is the Durbin-Watson statistic obtained from the regression: $\log P_{UK_t} = a_0 + a_1 t + a_2 \log P_{it} + u_t$, where P_{UK} is the relevant price index for the UK, P_i is for another country, t is the time trend and u_t, the residual. The DF statistic is the computed 't' value for b from the regression: $u_t = b u_{t-1} + e_t$ where u_t is the residual from the previous regression.

The lower panel gives the Dickey-Fuller test statistic for which the critical value is 3.37. Most of the test statistics fall below this, suggesting that the series are not cointegrated. These results indicate that the evidence for cointegration is relatively weak.

It has been argued that tests of cointegration are particularly weak in discriminating between a unit root in the residuals from a cointegrating regression and a case where the residuals have a large autoregressive parameter (e.g. 0.9), especially in small samples. Hence, these results may

Table 6.4. *Autoregressive coefficients for relative price series*

	GNP deflator	Wholesale price	Retail price	Wage rate
Belgium		0.44	0.46	0.64
		(0.15)	(0.15)	(0.15)
France		0.40	0.87	
		(0.16)	(0.08)	
Germany	0.48	0.82	0.74	0.45
	(0.16)	(0.11)	(0.12)	(0.22)
Italy	0.74	0.57	0.74	0.85
	(0.12)	(0.14)	(0.11)	(0.10)
Norway	0.80			
	(0.12)			
Sweden	0.70	0.57	0.02	0.85
	(0.12)	(0.15)	(0.07)	(0.08)
Denmark	0.58		0.65	
	(0.15)		(0.13)	
USA	0.89	0.70	0.78	0.86
	(0.89)	(0.12)	(0.11)	(0.08)
Canada	0.85	0.64		
	(0.11)	(0.13)		
Australia	0.77			
	(0.12)			

Note: The coefficients and standard errors (in brackets) presented are from the regression: $\log(P_{UK}/P_i)t = c_0 + c_1 t + c_2 \log(P_{UK}/P_i)_{t-1} + v_t$ where P_{UK} is the relevant price index for the UK, P_i the corresponding price index for another country, t is the time trend and v the residual.

indicate that a disturbance to the equilibrium price relationship may persist for a long time. To examine this issue further, the ratio of the UK to corresponding foreign price (in logs) was regressed on its lagged value, a constant and a time trend. This imposes the restriction of proportionality between the price series (apart from the time trend).

Table 6.4 displays the coefficient on the lagged dependent variable for each regression with its standard error in parentheses. In most cases the coefficient on the lagged dependent variable is 0.4 or higher with the exceptions of GDP deflators for Italy and Sweden previously noted and the retail price index for Sweden. In this simple model the average lag can be calculated as $\lambda/(1-\lambda)$ where λ is the coefficient on the lagged dependent variable. Thus a coefficient of 0.5 gives an average lag of one year and a coefficient of 0.75, an average lag of three years between a disturbance and the adjustment of the price ratio back to its long run level. Though the importance of contemporaneous year to year adjustments has often been stressed these results suggest that average lags in adjustment were typically in excess of a year and often much longer. With one exception wholesale prices appear to adjust more quickly than GDP deflators. The average of average lags for GDP deflators is 3.4 years and that for wholesale prices is 1.8 years.

These results are not particularly kind to short-run PPP though, for the most part, they are consistent with PPP in the long run. Subject to appropriate qualifications concerning tests on relatively few observations, there is evidence that relative price levels revert to a long-run level or, in some cases, a long-run trend. It is hard to compare the results with those for other periods, most of which use monthly data and concentrate on periods of floating exchange rates. This evidence suggests strong tendencies to PPP in the 1920s (Taylor and McMahon, 1988) weaker tendencies in the 1930s due to trade distortions. (Broadberry and Taylor, this volume), and no tendencies at all in the 1970s and early 1980s (Taylor, 1988). Using annual data and testing over much longer periods of time (but not using cointegration) Officer (1982) found evidence in favour of long-run PPP but also pointed to periods of significant and persistent deviations.

The adjustment of prices and wages

It is clear that prices are positively and, in some cases, closely correlated across countries. For Britain, the price correlations with other countries are quite close and, to a lesser extent, so are those in economic activity. As previously noted, it is precisely this kind of evidence that has been used to support the PPP approach. This contrasts with the long tradition of empirical price and wage equations based on the Phillips curve in which excess supply or demand determines price adjustment. Indeed, it was for Britain in the late nineteenth century that the empirical model of wage adjustment, which spawned such a large literature, was first estimated by Phillips (1958). The PPP approach directly contradicts this in that domestic prices are determined by the world market and there is therefore no role for such 'wrenching adjustments'. In this section I present some simple wage and price adjustment models to see whether foreign prices dominate in determining domestic prices, or whether there is a role both for direct foreign price effects and for variations in economic activity.

Two observations are worth making before turning to the results. First, those who believe in PPP might argue that fluctuations in activity arise from exogenous shocks to the price level. Hence variations in output and employment would be determined by price changes and not the other way round as believers in the Phillips curve would suggest. Tests of Granger causality may help resolve this issue. Initial tests of the causal relationship between the general price level and real GDP deviations and between the wage rate and unemployment yielded uniformly insignificant results. For 1880 to 1913 the only likelihood ratio test which was significant at the 10% level was for causality running from unemployment to the wage rate. This suggests that the important relationships are contemporaneous – at least on annual data[5]. Second, from the point of view of cointegration, regressing rates of change of prices or wages on measures of activity is legitimate since these series all appear to be close to I (0). However, relating domestic price changes to foreign price changes does not ensure that price levels will be related in the long run. The price or wage adjustment is regarded as one structural equation in an economic system. It therefore would be necessary to provide the full system to determine whether long-run PPP would hold.

Table 6.5 presents some simple price change equations, using instrumental variables. In the upper panel the dependent variable is the rate of change of the GDP deflator. This is first regressed on a 'world' GNP deflator constructed from series represented in table 6.1. The result is a significant coefficient of about 0.6 and 28% of the variation explained. In the second equation the deviation from trend of GDP shows a positive correlation with the rate of price change but explains very little of the total variation. The third equation shows the positive relationship between the wage rate and the GDP deflator. In the fourth, both the foreign price index and the wage rate are included and both are reduced to insignificance, although the R^2 now climbs to a half. While it seems likely that both foreign prices and domestic costs contributed to the domestic price level, it proved impossible to precisely estimate the contribution of each.

In the lower panel the same exercise is repeated with the export price index. One might have expected a stronger correlation between this and other countries' export prices (a weighted average of export prices of France, Germany and the US). The result in equation 1 indicates that half the variation is explained, and the coefficient is almost identical to that in the previous table. Equation 2 shows that though there is a positive correlation between export price change and deviations from trend of industrial production, the correlation is weak and explains very little of the price variation. The third equation shows the relationship between the export price index and the wage rate. This gives a surprisingly large coefficient – a finding which is confirmed even in the presence of the index of foreign export prices.

For both the GDP deflator and the export price index, collinearity is a

Table 6.5. *Price adjustment equations 1880–1913*

	(1)	(2)	(3)	(4)
Dependent variable: rate of change of GDP deflator ($\ln P_y$)				
Const ($\times 100$)	0.04	0.28	−0.24	−0.16
	(0.30)	(0.31)	(0.37)	(0.29)
$\Delta \ln P_y$ (World)	0.59			0.36
	(0.19)			(0.24)
ln GDP (Deviation)		0.38		
		(0.15)		
$\Delta \ln W$			0.98	0.45
			(0.46)	(0.43)
R^2	0.28	0.11	0.33	0.51
DW	1.63	1.89	1.82	1.60
LM(1)	0.06	0.00	0.07	0.00
RESET	1.74	0.24	0.06	0.01
HETERO	1.32	0.19	0.58	1.24
Dependent variable: rate of change of export price ($\ln P_x$)				
Const ($\times 100$)	0.08	−0.03	−1.27	−1.24
	(0.05)	(0.66)	(0.78)	(0.72)
$\Delta \ln P_x$ (World)	0.62			0.24
	(0.28)			(0.31)
ln IP (Deviation)		0.27		
		(0.16)		
$\Delta \ln W$			2.34	2.35
			(0.98)	(0.90)
R^2	0.50	0.15	0.36	0.51
DW	1.89	1.88	1.94	1.91
LM(1)	0.03	0.06	0.00	0.01
RESET	1.47	0.01	0.23	0.36
HETERO	0.23	0.05	4.36	4.71

Note: Standard errors are in parentheses. LM(1) is the Lagrange multiplier test statistic for first order serial correlation. RESET is the test statistic based on the square of the fitted values. HETERO is the test statistic for heteroscedasticity based on the regression squared residuals on squared fitted values. These are all distributed as $X^2(1)$.

Table 6.6. *Price ratio adjustment equations 1880–1913*

| | Dependent variable | | | |
| | $\Delta\ln P_y$ $-\Delta\ln P_y$ (World) | | $\Delta\ln P_x$ $-\Delta\ln P_x$ (World) | |
	(1)	(2)	(3)	(4)
Const ($\times 100$)	-0.26	-0.27	-0.34	-0.69
	(0.23)	(0.25)	(0.51)	(0.49)
$\Delta\ln W - \Delta\ln P_y$ (World)	0.67	0.59		
	(0.23)	(0.22)		
$\Delta\ln W - \Delta\ln P_x$ (World)			0.71	0.86
			(0.29)	(0.25)
$\Delta\ln P_m - \Delta\ln P_y$ (World)		-0.02		
		(0.16)		
$\Delta\ln P_m - \Delta\ln P_x$ (World)				0.58
				(0.27)
R^2	0.63	0.59	0.20	0.36
DW	1.57	1.48	1.94	2.10
LM(1)	0.01	0.09	0.002	0.19
RESET	1.22	1.93	0.07	3.35
HETERO	0.42	0.26	0.20	6.29

Note: price of imports of raw materials taken from Schlote, 1952: 176–7. For definition of statistics see table 6.5.

serious problem, making it difficult to separate domestic and foreign influences. An alternative is to specify the equation in ratio form so that the coefficients on foreign prices and domestic costs are constrained to add up to one. The coefficient can then be interpreted as 'weights' on foreign prices and domestic costs in short run price adjustments. The results of using this specification are given in table 6.6. The first equation gives a well-determined coefficient on the wage, giving it a weight of two thirds in price adjustment. Adding the rate of change of imported raw material prices does not improve the explanatory power as equation 2 shows. Equation 3 places slightly higher weight on the wage in the export price equation. It was thought that raw material prices would be more important for exports than for GDP as a whole, a finding borne out in equation 4. But now the coefficients on domestic costs add up to more than one, giving a negative weight to foreign prices.

Apart from this last anomaly, the results obtained appear to be similar to those from a recent study of export price adjustments of the G7 countries. Manufactured export prices were specified as a weighted average of competitors' export prices and a domestic price index. For the UK the weight on domestic prices in the long run was 0.68 (Barrel, 1989: 91). If we use the GDP deflator as the domestic price variable, the resulting equation for 1880–1913 is the following:

$$\Delta \ln P_x - \Delta \ln P_x \text{ (World)} = -0.0015 + 0.70(\Delta \ln P_y - \Delta \ln P_x \text{ (World)})$$
$$(0.0044) \ (0.30)$$
$$R^2 = 0.36 \quad DW = 1.92 \quad LM(1) = 0.006 \quad RESET = 0.42 \quad HETERO = 0.21.$$

Hence the results obtained here seem broadly consistent with recent evidence. However, it may be suspected that the equations, which include wage rates, particularly those for the export price index are biased up and are picking up effects running from export prices to wage adjustment.

Did foreign prices affect wage rates directly? Advocates of a strong version of PPP might argue that a fall in prices in world trade placed direct downward pressure on wage rates through the 'threat' of unemployment. The view that export price variations fed through to wage rates has received some illustrious support. Both Cairncross (1953) and Triffin (1968) noted that wage rates followed export prices more closely than import prices. Similarly, Phelps-Brown and Browne argued that 'an international trend of unit wage costs was set up that at any time acted as an externally imposed constraint upon the wage negotiation, such that so long as profit margins remained unchanged, money wage earnings could rise above the internationl trend of unit wage costs only to the extent that productivity rose' (1968: 131). The emphasis here is on the trend but, in terms of fluctuations, one obvious institutional mechanism linking output prices to wages is the sliding scales. Though these were in decline by the 1880s, empirical evidence suggests that for coal mining at least there was a direct effect of changes in prices on wage rates throughout the period up to 1913.

Table 6.7 presents some simple Phillips curve equations, using the log of the unemployment rate as an explanatory variable. Equation 1 illustrates that a relatively strong negative effect can be discerned over the period 1880–1913, explaining about 40% of the variation. When the rate of change of the GDP deflator is introduced, it raises the explanatory power but does not itself give a significant coefficient. As equation 3 shows, the cost of living index does even less well and adds very little to the explanation of wage change. Most surprising of all is that when the rate of change of the export price index is included, its coefficient is very small and insignificant.

Taken together, these results suggest a rather more traditional view of domestic wage and price setting. Clearly there is evidence that foreign

Table 6.7. *Wage adjustment equations 1880–1913*

Dependent variable: rate of wage change ($\Delta \ln W$)				
Constant	0.03	0.03	0.03	0.03
	(0.01)	(0.01)	(0.01)	(0.01)
log Unempt. rate	−1.96	−1.52	−1.47	−1.77
($\times 100$)	(0.61)	(0.77)	(0.79)	(0.82)
$\Delta \ln P_y$		0.26		
		(0.31)		
$\Delta \ln P_{col}$			0.16	
			(0.21)	
$\Delta \ln P_x$				0.06
				(0.18)
R^2	0.40	0.50	0.43	0.46
DW	1.96	1.91	1.73	1.95
LM(1)	0.01	0.02	0.54	0.01
RESET	4.27	2.61	10.41	2.46
HETERO	3.01	2.07	1.63	3.26

Note: For definition of statistics, see table 6.5.

prices mattered, but their influence is smaller than that of domestic costs. If domestic costs could be measured more exactly rather than relying on wage rates, perhaps the effect of this component would increase further. Variations in activity have relatively weak effects on price change, which disappear altogether when domestic costs or foreign prices are included. It appears that the main effect of domestic activity is working through unemployment to wage adjustment. The wage rate itself, however, does not seem to be influenced much by price changes and hence is characterised by nominal inertia.

PPP and the international economy: then and now

The MABP/PPP model has gone in and out of fashion. It has been tried and tested on data for a wide range of countries on postwar data, for periods of fixed and floating exchange rates and to many people's minds has been found wanting. In a comprehensive study of the international transmission of inflation based on quarterly data for 1955–76, Darby *et al.* (1983) found little evidence that the linkages stressed in the MABP/PPP model were very strong, a conclusion reinforced in successive chapters of the study. Employing Granger causality tests, they found that there was little evidence of price inflation leading changes in the money stock and more often the reverse.[6] Similarly, tests of causality running from world prices to domestic prices yielded little evidence of strong links. The authors summarise their results as 'consistent with the seven foreign economies being independent of the US or alternatively with a chain of transmission running from US money to foreign money and thence to foreign prices' (p. 79). Structural modelling produced, if anything, weaker linkages; relative price effects on trade were found to be weak and slow acting; the effect of variations in the balance of payments on domestic money supplies was often sterilised. Monetary expansion worked through only gradually to prices. Summing up the evidence, they concluded that

Neither goods nor assets appear to be perfect substitutes, but both the trade balance and capital flows are responsive to movements in foreign prices and interest rates relative to their domestic counterparts, with the response increasing over time. Only weak evidence was found in support of either asset substitution effects or money demand or absorption effects on real income. (Darby et al., 1983: 504–5)

In a recent survey, Dornbusch (1988) concluded that the macroeconomic experience of the 1970s and 1980s has not been kind to PPP as a theory of exchange rates. He points to dramatic fluctuations in real exchange rates, deviating from the mean by as much as 25% in either direction and often persisting over a period of years. Correlations of inflation rates among major industrialised countries (converted to US dollars) are, if anything, lower than for the years of the classical gold standard period. In a study more sympathetic to the usefulness and validity of PPP, Officer (1982) found evidence that it held reasonably well in the long run over periods of decades, but that there were substantial short-run deviations.

Should one believe that in the light of evidence for the postwar period the MABP/PPP model would be even less useful to explain adjustments under the classical gold standard? Such a view might be based on the notion that the world economy has become more integrated due to increases in the speed and reductions in the cost of transport and communications and due to the spread of industrialisation leading to more 'intense' competition. But at the same time, according to some observers, restrictions on the free flow of goods, capital and labour have increased. Thus, Friedman and Schwartz state that 'the technological improvements, which might have been expected to unify the world, have been *more* than offset by governmental intervention, which has fragmented the world into separate isolated markets' (1982: 292, emphasis added). With regard to financial openness, it has been argued on the basis of correlations among interest rates and other capital market data that, while the world economy has become more integrated during the post-war period, it is still somewhat less so than during the gold standard era (Zevin, 1989). With regard to labour market, it seems likely that these are less integrated (at least on the evidence of migration) than they were a century ago. What about product markets? There is little evidence that the economies of Europe and North America have become more open (in the sense of trade shares in GNP) than a century ago (Grassman, 1980), but this measure will be affected by the growth of real incomes and shifting pattern of comparative advantage as well as the integration or disintegration of global markets.

The evidence presented here on the causes and effects of price variations suggests that, with regard to international price behaviour, there are strong similarities between then and now, though there are also some differences. First, the overall correlation between rates of price change between Britain and other industrial countries was about the same during the gold standard era as under the Bretton-Woods system, though the correlations appear to have declined during the period of floating exchange rates. Second, tests for long-run purchasing power parity seem consistent with findings for other periods. They suggest that such long-run tendencies existed but the lags are relatively long and could give rise to substantial and persistent deviations in the short and medium term. Third, there is an important domestic cost component to price changes, which takes a weight of about two thirds. This also broadly corresponds to recent findings. Fourth, variations in activity appear to influence price change by affecting wage adjustment. In comparison with the postwar period the degree of real wage rigidity appears to have been similar, but nominal inertia was much greater before the First World War (Hatton, 1988).

Such evidence does not provide us with the answer to the question: why did the gold standard work so well? What it does suggest is that the operation of the law of one price was no stronger then than now. Hence, it was not this factor that conduced to the operation of the gold standard but failed to provide the conditions for the maintenance of fixed exchange rates in later periods. Other features particular to the pre-World War I period probably did make a difference. The free flow of capital and labour internationally, the interaction of manufacturing and primary producing economies, the dominance of a few countries in financial and commodity markets, the actions of central banks, and the relative absence of government intervention are all likely to have contributed to the stability of the gold standard. These issues have been the central focus of much of the writing on the gold standard, and there is no reason to believe that this effort has been misdirected.

Notes

I would like to express my thanks to Beth Kulas for research assistance. I would also like to thank Jeff Williamson and the participants at the conference in honour of Alec Ford for useful comments.

1 There is a distinction between the law of one price, which is usually taken to mean that, for a given commodity, the same price rules everywhere, down to the wedge of transport costs, and purchasing power parity. The latter is normally applied to aggregate price relatives to calculate the 'equilibrium' exchange rate or under fixed exchange rates, to calculate the deviation from equilibrium of relative national (or subnational) price levels. In its strongest form PPP is held to apply to absolute levels of prices, but it is more frequently used in the weaker form of period to period changes or deviations from a base year. These distinctions are discussed by Dornbusch (1988: 265–9).

2 See Frenkel and Johnson (1976: 24). McCloskey and Zecher recognise this explicitly in their later article (1984: 122).

3 Their emphasis on the short-run independence of national money stocks and their effects on national price and output levels led to a sharp exchange with McCloskey and Zecher (see Friedman's comment on McCloskey and Zecher, 1984, and the ensuing discussion).

4 These were for 8 and 11 countries, respectively, and where prices were adjusted for changes in exchange rates.

5 For Britain, during the gold standard period Eichengreen (1983: p. 158) has found some evidence of causality running from domestic activity to the price level before 1870 and from export volumes to the price level for 1870–1913.

6 It should be noted that for the UK opposite directions of causality were found, depending on which statistical series were used (p. 74).

7 Import prices, economic activity and the general price level in the UK 1870–1913

NEIL BLAKE

Introduction

The long swing in prices, both in the UK and elsewhere, over the forty or so years leading up to the First World War is a well-known and key feature of the economic history of the period. Partly as a result of this, there has been considerable controversy over what were the causal features behind this pattern. Two broad schools of thought exist. One, the monetarist explanation, looks to changes in the stock of money relative to real output as the explanatory factor. The other, which may be termed the 'real' or 'supply shock' school focuses instead on the changing balance between the supply and demand of major commodities and the implication for cost-push price changes. In this view, money plays a largely accommodating role.

This chapter argues that the supply shock view is a plausible explanation of the price swing in world prices. The greater part of the chapter, however, is concerned with the effect on UK prices. With major swings in world prices and a fixed exchange rate regime, the transmission mechanism from world to UK prices was through import prices. Just how this worked is explored with the help of a structural macroeconomic model of the UK economy estimated over the 1870–1913 period. Various simulation exercises are carried out to illustrate the impact of 'supply shock' induced import price changes on the UK price level. The use of a structural model has the advantage of being able to trace these changes through the economic system and to show how they impacted on UK output and employment as well as on price changes and how these variables had knock-on implications for prices.

The first section looks at the price swing debate in greater detail. The second then goes on to describe the macroeconomic model used. The counterfactual simulations are then discussed in the third section and the chapter concludes with a summary of the implications and limitations of the exercise.

Background

The price swing: a possible explanation

Kondratieff (1935) identified the downswing in prices from 1873 as the second half of the second long cycle and the subsequent upswing as the beginning of the third and argued that the cyclical phenomena that he claimed to have discovered existed in the real economy as well as in prices. No explanation of the link between prices and real fluctuations was made, but there was an attempt to bring gold production, and hence monetary forces, into the long-cycle framework. It was asserted that gold discoveries and production were not random events, but a function of the profitability of gold mining. Since under the gold standard the price of gold was fixed, the profitability of gold mining would vary in line with costs. As costs would vary with the general price level, the lower the general price level, the more profitable gold production would be. The problems of discovering new gold mines and difficulties in exploiting them inevitably led to a lag in output changes and, consequently, the big increases in output tend to come in the upswing after the initial discoveries have been made towards the end of the downswing.

Kondratieff's paper is largely descriptive. Gold is brought into the long-cycle framework but it is not explicitly ascribed with causing the price cycle. Schumpeter (1939) produced a long-swing theory where long swings were due to the bunching of major technological innovations (the innovations for the upswing beginning in the mid-nineties being electricity, industrial chemical and motor vehicles). The increase in investment opportunities would produce credit expansion, put pressure on resources and force up prices. A problem with Schumpeterian style theories is that evidence linking major bursts in investment with the price swing is lacking. Investment tended to follow a shorter cyclical pattern rather than the long swing observed in prices.

A number of explanations focus on the relative supply and demand of industrial goods and basic commodities (Phelps-Brown and Ozga, 1955; Lewis, 1978; Rostow, 1975; 1978; Rostow and Kennedy, 1979). Lewis and Rostow look to changes in the supply conditions of basic commodities. Referring to other work, Rostow (1975: 727) states,

These studies inevitably raised an issue posed by Kondratieff, explored by the early Kuznets (in his work on secondary movements in prices and production), but pretty well washed out by Schumpeter, the latter day Kuznets, and their followers: that is: the relative abundance or scarcity of supplies of foodstuffs and raw materials.

Wheat prices are quoted as an example of a primary commodity which fits this pattern in the late nineteenth and early twentieth centuries. High prices in the 1860s encouraged the expansion of wheat acreages in the USA and elsewhere following the end of the civil war. This continued after the price decline set in as the earlier investment in infrastructure still made increased acreages profitable. Only after a lag did world wheat prices respond to lower prices, producing the upturn in prices in the mid-1890s. This, in turn, prompted with a lag an increase in investment in further capacity. International capital movements are seen as an accessory, not the prime mover of this pattern. There were examples of increased capital exports to wheat producers during the downswing such as the investment booms in Australia 1883–6, Argentina 1886–90 and Russia in the 1890s, but in each case the investment flows have a specific cause. The Australian case is put down to an increase in domestic rather than export demand and the surge in capital exports to Argentina to the opportunities afforded by the opening up of the pampas following the establishing of political stability.[1]

To this we might add some change to the conditions of industrial supply which, in part, were an integral part of the expansion of agricultural and raw material supply and also contributed a general expansion in the supply of industrial goods. De Cecco (1974: 40–1) writes:

the years of the Great Depression were the years of the Second Industrial Revolution, whose basic feature was the mass production of industrial commodities. They were, in addition, the years of the transport revolution – of the contribution of steam and steel which revolutionised merchant shipping, and the penetration of railways into continents. All of which meant lower prices for raw materials and finished goods, at least at the wholesale level.

To sum up the supply shock argument, the primary force behind the price swing were changes in the rate of growth of the world's output of basic materials. Shifts in the rate of technical change are also seen to have contributed to the swing, but not to have been the major cause. These 'shocks' were sustained rather than sudden because of:

a A relatively long lag between the emergence of a profit possibility and the investment decisions designed to exploit it (in the primary goods sector), as compared to manufactures;
b A relatively longer period of gestation (in the primary goods sector), caused in part by large prior infrastructure outlays before production could begin;
c A longer time between the completion of the investment and its maximum efficient exploitation, often involving large domestic or international migration.[2]

Given that these major changes in supply conditions could have produced sustained movements in world prices we can turn to the effect of the UK. That is done in the third section where we attempt to trace the transmission mechanism from different world prices to UK prices, output and employment. Before that, however, we must consider the alternative arguments to the Rostow/Lewis supply shock school.

Monetary matters

One problem with an approach that sees supply shocks as being the major determinants of the UK price level is that it has little to say about money. The well known equation of exchange $M.V = P.T$ states that the stock of money multiplied by its velocity of circulation is equal to the price level multiplied by the number of transactions. In other words, there must be enough money available to exactly meet the needs of economic transactions. This is a simple identity. However, given assumptions of the exogeneity of the money supply under the gold standard, the stability of the demand for money (i.e. the stability of velocity) and the exogeneity of real output, the equation becomes a theory which states that changes in the aggregate price level can only be due to monetary factors. This approach to explaining price movements over the 1870–1913 period has been taken by, amongst others, Bordo and Schwartz (1980), Bordo and Schwartz (1981) and Friedman and Schwartz (1982).

The theme of the arguments presented above, and of this chapter in general, is that real, not monetary, factors lay behind the observed changes in the aggregate UK price level over the period. Any explanation of price changes which is independent of monetary changes must have something to say about how either the money stock, velocity or real output could have changed to preserve the identity.

That the above mentioned assumptions, which underlie the quantity theory, are valid is by no means obvious. However, there is some evidence that the demand for money was stable, at least in the long run. A more controversial point concerns the exogeneity of the money stock and it is on this point that we will concentrate our attention. Even under the gold standard there were a number of ways in which money could be flexible. Gold could only affect the monetary base not broad money. The links between the monetary base and broad money would be determined by the behaviour of the banking and non-bank private sectors both in the UK and overseas. Further, the world stock of monetary gold was by no means fixed. Not only were there continuous additions from new production, but the ratio of monetary to non-monetary gold could also vary. For 1899–1909, Kitchen (1930) found that just 51% of the world's total gold stock was monetary gold and this had risen from 46% between 1869 and 1879. On a world scale a large degree of monetary flexibility was also made possible by the practice of many countries of keeping foreign currency rather than gold reserves.

A considerable amount of work has been carried out using Sims-Granger type statistical causality tests on the links between nominal incomes and money. Sims (1972) concluded that there was evidence of a causal link between money and incomes in the United States for the 1947–69 period. A similar study, with similar conclusions, was carried out for the 1870–1913 period, also for the United States, by Bessler (1984). An examination of the money-income link for the UK by Williams *et al.* (1976) failed to find any conclusive evidence either way, while Mills and Wood (1978) found evidence of a causal link running from incomes to money. Blake (1988) repeated this exercise using the money stock data compiled by Capie and Weber (1985) and found no evidence of causality in their direction.

Mills and Wood (1978) and Mills (1980) argue that the pursuit of a fixed, or fixed but changeable, exchange rate as under the Bretton Woods system renders the money stock endogenous for all but 'reserve centre' countries. Only a freely floating exchange rate is said to leave money fully autonomous. Thus it is argued that as most of the post-war data used in UK causality tests relates to the Bretton Woods period the ambiguity of the test results should be expected. For a 'reserve centre' such as the United States, however, the expected causality results have been more forthcoming. In the 1870–1913 period the gold standard reached its height and it might be argued that sterling was the dominant reserve currency (even more so than the US dollar under Bretton Woods). This would appear to run counter to Mills & Wood's argument that money was endogenous via the balance of payments. Dwyer (1985) backs up the Mills and Wood position and suggests that under the gold standard the UK approximated to the case of a small open economy (see also McCloskey and Zecher (1975)). Friedman and Schwartz (1982), on the other hand, argue that the exchange rate regime does not affect the causal link between money and incomes and that it only affects the forces determining the quantity of money. Capie and Rodrik-Bali (1983) also argue against the endogeneity of the monetary base via the balance of payments, suggesting that the ability of the monetary authorities to manipulate the movement of funds outweighed movements in the balance of payments.

Where does all of this leave the money-income causality debate? The findings that with the Capie and Wood data for the UK little evidence can be found of any causality either way (Blake, 1988) could be taken to support the Mills and Wood position. That is that the inconclusiveness of the evidence implies that we are observing a mixture of periods when money

was exerting an exogenous influence and times when money was endogenous via the balance of payments. Indeed, this could also fit in with the
Friedman and Schwartz view (1982: 325):

Monetary policy cannot affect the quantity of money except temporarily; nonethe-
less, changes in the quantity of money, however produced, will affect income.
Indeed it is precisely because they do that a gold standard or other fixed exchange
rate regime is self-adjusting. Similarly, while 'income fluctuations [whether in the
country in question or other countries to which it is linked] produce accommodating monetary flows', it is also true that monetary flows produce accommodating
income fluctuations.

In short, the exchange rate regime does not affect the existence of a 'causal'
influence from money to income; it affects the forces determining the quantity of
money and thereby whether the situation is one of largely unidirectional influence
from money to income or of simultaneous determination and interaction.

We should, however, be wary of accepting the results of causality tests when
either positive, negative and inconclusive results are claimed to support a
certain argument.

What is worth noting is that under the gold standard, the money-income
link cannot be considered in the context of a single country, at least outside
the short-run. Bordo and Schwartz (1981) attempt to get around this by
looking at the relationship between money and incomes in the US and UK
added together, though this is not done in a Sims-Granger causality testing
framework. If we take their methodology of summing the UK and US
variables and apply causality tests we get some interesting results. There is
strong evidence that income Granger-causes M0 (high powered money or
the monetary base), but no evidence of any linkage between M3 and
nominal incomes.[3] This introduces yet more confusion. Admittedly the UK
and the USA were not the entire world economy, though they were a
substantial part of it. Evidence of a causal link between incomes and money
appears to refute the monetarist hypothesis. The lack of a link between M3
and nominal incomes is, however, puzzling.

In the absence of clear statistical evidence of the link between nominal
incomes and money one other area is worth considering. There is a
well-known link between interest rates and the level of prices in this period
known as the Gibson Paradox. Although some commentators argue that
the paradox is due to the slow adjustment of inflationary expectations to
changes in the trend change in the price level (Fisher, 1896; 1907; 1930;
Friedman and Schwartz, 1982; Harley, 1977) the length of lags implied
appear to be implausibly long. The basis is of their argument is that
inflationary expectations adjusted with the sustained change in prices and
that this produced the interest rate pattern. The problem with this is that
shifts in the sustained direction of change of prices (as happened in the
mid-1890s) should cause a once and for all change in interest rates and not a

change in their trend. That is, unless expectations took a considerable length of time to adjust.

A non-monetary explanation, on the other hand, fits the historical evidence rather well. If we take nominal incomes to be independent of money, then a decrease in prices, for whatever reason, will reduce interest rates given a stable demand for money function. Conversely, an increase will tend to force up interest rates. Over the period of interest there was a long period of the decline of prices followed by a number of years of sustained increase. If we adopt the view that these price changes were due to supply shocks the parallel movement of interest rates follows. There is no paradox. If we look for a causal link from money to interest rates the Gibson paradox is not observed unless we are willing to believe there were very long lags in adapting inflationary expectations. An extension of the non-monetary explanation would see money accommodating nominal income changes (i.e. there being a causal link from incomes to money). In this case we might expect money to only partially react and with a lag. This would also produce the Gibson Paradox.

Not unrelated to the money-income debate is the question of how the UK (and other countries) managed to maintain a fixed exchange rate over the period.[4] Could the price changes that we are considering (both actual and counterfactual) have occurred independently of monetary changes with fixed exchange rates? Well, there were major supply shocks over the period that we are considering and the exchange rate regime did survive. This was despite the fact that the Bank of England kept very low gold reserves to guard against external drain. The size of the Bank of England's gold reserves may be misleading. As de Cecco (1974) points out, by 1913 although the Banks' reserves were only about £30 million there was in addition about £150 million deposited in London from Empire and Commonwealth states (of which £136.3 million was from India), plus £101.7 million from the Japanese government and the Bank of Japan and some £100 million from other European countries.

Another feature of the gold standard which may have contributed to its stability was its influence on expectations. As long as exchange rates were expected to be fixed there were few reasons to expect speculative flows against a currency (especially sterling). This was in sharp contrast to the Bretton Woods system where the possibility of exchange rate adjustments actually encouraged speculative flows.

To sum up, the point of this section has been to argue that price changes over the period were not necessarily a purely monetary phenomenon and that the world monetary system could and did adapt to autonomous price changes. This view rejects the classical dichotomy between nominal and relative prices and looks to supply shocks as being the root cause of changes to the aggregate price level. We can now go on to look at the construction of a UK macroeconomic model and to consider in detail what it has to say about how international supply shocks affected prices and how this was transmitted to the UK economy.

Model characteristics and performance

Appendix I gives details of a ninety-one equation model which aims to be a simplified representation of the working of the UK economy over the 1870–1913 period. The model is a modified version of that developed in Blake (1988). This section gives an overview of the model and highlights some of its features and characteristics.

In recent years, the fashion has swung away from large-scale structural models in favour of much smaller models. Large models still hold sway for present-day macroeconomic forecasting, however, and they have the advantage of being able to trace shocks through the economic system. The large structural model approach is favoured here as being best able to reproduce the links between various prices, between prices and incomes and between incomes and spending.

Given the data problems involved in modelling the nineteenth century economy, the model is of a considerable size and contains a reasonably comprehensive picture of the economy. One feature to note is that monetary variables do not enter into the model. The price equations are based on a cost plus framework with some role for the cyclical state of demand, but no direct role for money. Likewise, monetary variables do not appear in the expenditure equations. The inclusion of both money balances and interest rates were experimented with in the consumer spending equations but were not found to be significant. Similarly interest rates were not found to be statistically significant in the investment equations where the main explanatory variables are incomes.

One main omission is in the government sector. Government expenditure (as an exogenous variable) and indirect taxes are modelled. There is, however, no attempt made at modelling the government budget constraint and the effects on the rest of the economy of financing government debt. With further extensive research it should be possible to add such a sector. Such a substantial extra effort is however not considered to be worthwhile for the purpose of examining price linkages, particularly in a period where the government sector was relatively unimportant. Similarly, there is no consideration of the effects of the accumulation of domestic financial assets by the personal sector and the possible consequences for future spending patterns. The acquisition of overseas assets, and the subsequent income flows, are, however, endogenous to the model.

Other areas lacking are the linkages between the UK and the international economy and within the international economy. Again, this is beyond the scope of this research. As in most present-day models, international variables are taken to be exogenous. Given the relative size of the UK economy in the world economy in this period this is obviously a major simplification. Further reference will be made to this in qualifying the model simulation results.

Aside from the question of the linkages between overseas demand for UK exports and the level of UK import demand, there is the whole question of the effects of capital exports on overseas demand. Ford (1960) notes that capital exports could have had a direct effect on overseas demand for UK exports. Unfortunately, as with other linkages within the world economy, this cannot be easily incorporated into the model and is omitted.

A related feature to be aware of is the way the relationship between domestic demand and foreign investment is modelled. Domestic investment is a function of UK incomes while net investment overseas (i.e. net capital exports) is determined as the residual of UK incomes less the demand for domestic output, the implicit assumption being that there was a completely elastic foreign demand for UK capital. Given the large international capital movements of the nineteenth century, generated by migration to new areas of recent settlement this is not too unreasonable an assumption. Other interpretations are, however, plausible. In the absence of foreign and domestic investment opportunities British rentiers could have altered their consumption patterns with a consequent impact on domestic demand. For short periods this may well have occurred if overseas investment became for some reason unfashionable for a short time (following the Argentinian default of 1887 for example). Alternatively, rentiers could have chosen to run up their money balances temporarily.

It is also possible that overseas investment had implications for domestic investment through a crowding out process. The lack of contemporary complaints about finance shortage quoted by Cairncross (1953), Kindleberger (1964) and Landes (1969) are, however, evidence against this. Kennedy (1974) asserts that the scale of overseas investment was due to overseas investment opportunities being better suited to the conservative nature of British lenders and that overseas investment did not, directly, reduce the availability of finance for domestic investment. The lack of any reaction of the propensity to consume out of non-employment incomes and the dependence of domestic investment solely on UK incomes in the model can also be judged by the model's tracking performance which is discussed below.

A skeletal framework of the model is shown on the following page. Although the model is built up around a national income accounting

identity   (Income = Consumption + Government   Expenditure + Investment + Exports − Imports) its workings are a little more complex. Imports
(for both food and other goods) depend on the ratio of demand in the
economy to productive capacity as well as on relative prices. In the case of
food, productive capacity is proxied by the index of agricultural output,
itself a function of relative prices. For other goods, capacity is defined as
output at full employment for a given capital stock. As the capital stock is
fully endogenous (depending on accumulated investment and depreciation), this gives the model an inbuilt supply side. The ability of the
economy to grow depends not only on the expansion of demand, but also
on the accumulation of capital, which enables demand to be channelled
into domestic activity rather than imports.

Employment, and hence labour productivity, is also a function of the
capital stock via a technical relationship with output. Increases in the
capital stock lead to a lower labour requirement per unit of output and
hence lower unit labour costs and prices.[5]

Prices are determined in the cost mark-up framework.[6] Wages are a
function of consumer prices, the share of profits in GDP and changes in
unemployment. Profits fall out of the GDP(Y) identity, being the residual
from nominal GDP less income from employment and other income
(chiefly rent). This means that profits depend on the ability of producers to
mark up the price of goods to produce a surplus of total receipts (nominal
GDP) over net costs (mainly wages and imports). Investment is then largely
driven by profits and the demand for replacement investment.

A further category of income which played a major part in the
macroeconomics of the late nineteenth and early twentieth century UK
economy was net property income from abroad. By 1913, net property
income was equal to the equivalent of 9.4% of nominal GDP (income
estimate) and the average for the whole period, 1870–1913, was 6.6%. This
compares with a net property income–GDP(Y) ratio of only 1.4% in 1988.[7]
Net property income also made a substantial contribution to the current
account. The current account averaged a surplus of £78.2 million a year
over the period (1870–1913). Of this however, an average of £94.7 million
came from net property income, leaving a deficit, on average, of £16.5
million on transfers and trade in goods and services. The relative size of this
variable makes it much more important to the characteristics of the model
than would be the case with a model of the modern day economy.

Note that in the model UK export prices are, in part a function of the
world export price of manufactures. The world export price of manufactures, in turn, is assumed to vary with the price deflator for non-food
imports. Hence, when non-food import prices change in the model so do
world manufactures prices and consequently so do UK export prices. This

has implications for UK export prices in the import price simulations discussed below.

GDP(E) $GDP = CE + GVCE + IF + II + TE - TM$

GDP(A) $GDPA = GDP + SDA$

GDP(Y) nominal $GDPYN = PDGDP.GDP/100 - TXCBN + SDYN$

Employment $CVEMP = f(GDPA, KIF)$

Earnings $WRCAN = f(PDCE, \ NRUT/(moving \ average(NRUT))$
   $PROF/PDGDP)$

Profits $PROF = GDPYN - YEMP - OYN$

Incomes

i) $TEMP = WRCAN.CVEMP.SDW$

ii) $YXEMP = PROF + OYN$

Prices $PD_i = f(WRCAN, GDP/CVEMP, PDTM, PC)$

Domestic expenditure

i) $CE_i, TM_i = f(YEMP, YXEMP)$

ii) $IF_i = f((TBPKA - NPROP)/PDIF, PROF/PDGDP)$

Exports $TE_i = f(IP_a, PDTE_i/(WRCAN/PROD), PDTE_i/PHC)$

Capital stock

i) (Gross) $GKIF_{it} = GKIF_{it-1} + IF_{it} - SIF_{it}$

ii) (Net) $KIF_{it} = KIF_{it-1} + IF_{it} - DIF_{it}$

Potential output $YP = f(WPOP - ARMF, KIF)$

Imports

i) (food) $TMFDT = f(CEFDT, CEMF, XGGAGR, PDTMFDT/PDCEFDT)$

ii) (other) $TMO = f(GDP + TM - YP, PDTMO/PDGDP)$

Agricultural output $XGGAGR = f(CEFDT, CEMF, TMFDT)$

Predictive performance

This exercise in macroeconomic modelling has not been carried out, as is usual, with the aim of forecasting the future of the economy. The aim is to see what the simulation properties are (i.e. the changes consequent on asking what if?-type questions about one or more variables). Nevertheless, if we are to have any faith in the simulation results some method of model verification is required. This is done by solving the model over the estimation period (lagged variables and data availability actually constrain the solution period to 1874–1913) using the actual values of the exogenous variables, and then compare the model's predictions for the endogenous variables with the actuals.

The model comprises a total of thirty-three stochastic equations and fifty-eight identities. There are a total of thirty-one exogenous variables. A substantial number of these however, are dummy variables, statistical

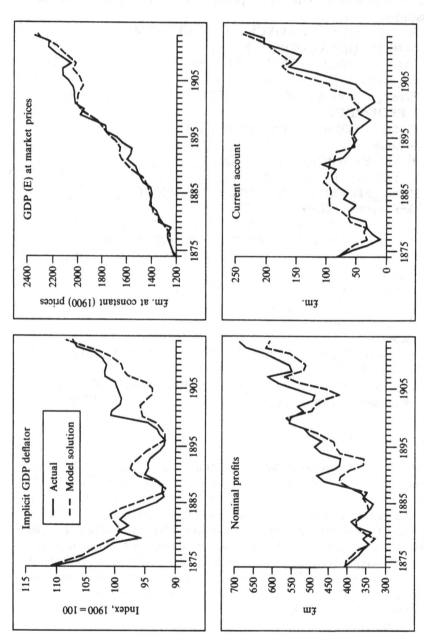

Figure 7.1 Tracking performance for real GDP, GDP deflator, current account and level of profits.

discrepancies, ratios of coal to other prices or trend terms. Excluding these variables, we are left with just ten exogenous variables. This is a relatively small number of 'key' exogenous variables when compared with a total of ninety-one endogenous variables:

Major exogenous variables

WPOP	Working population.
ARMF	Number of armed forces personnel.
GVCE	Government consumption.
PDTXCB	Adjustment to factor cost deflator.
PDTMFDT	Import prices: food, drink & tobacco.
PDTMO	Import prices: other goods.
RATE	Rate of return on overseas assets.
RTXCB	Average rate of indirect taxation.
TRANS	Net transfers abroad.
IPA	US industrial production.
IPE	European industrial production.
V1	Ratio of working population to population.
V2	Natural rate of population increase.

The solution to the model (i.e. the implied values of the endogenous variables for given values of the exogenous variables) is obtained by the Gauss-Seidel algorithm for solving non-linear models. The solution is dynamic in that the predicted, and not the actual, values of lagged endogenous variables are used in generating the current endogenous variables. The solution values differ in two respects from the fitted values from the individual equations. That is they are determined by the entire model system rather than just the right hand side variables, and they are also dependent on predicted rather than the actual values of any lagged endogenous variables. The solution values are therefore, conditional on the values of the exogenous variables and the starting values of the lagged endogenous variables.

Figure 7.1 illustrates the tracking performance of the model for four of the major endogenous variables, real GDP, the GDP deflator, the current account and the level of profits. The results for the first two of these are also summarised quantitatively in table 7.1.

The errors in this table look to be well within the bounds of acceptability. An error of just 1.2% for GDP and 0.9% for the GDP deflator after a forty year simulation may be judged as a creditable performance for any macroeconomic model. By way of comparison, the introduction to a set of counterfactual studies for the period 1970–83 by Saville and Gardiner (1986) using the National Institute's quarterly model found an error of 1.5% in output and 11% in prices (with exchange rates exogenous). The

Table 7.1. *Tracking performance 1874–1913*

	GDP (at market prices)	GDP deflator
Error in 1913 (%)	−1.2	0.9
Maximum error (%)	6.2 (1893)	5.8 (1905)
Mean absolute error (%)	2.1	2.3
Mean error (%)	−0.2	−0.3

simulation period of fourteen years is rather less than that used here, though because the model is quarterly the number of periods is slightly more. Given the effect of the greater volatility of prices since 1970 on the tracking performance for prices found by Saville and Gardiner, the performance of the models looks to be fairly similar.

The time period where the model goes the most off track is in the early years of the century. The investment boom is not reproduced with the consequence that GDP and prices are underpredicted.[9] Despite this, the long-swing pattern in prices is clearly reproduced.

Model based counterfactual results

The previous section has outlined the make up and properties of a macroeconomic model of the UK for the period 1870 to 1913. We now take the model to see what information it can offer regarding changes in the UK price level for that period. The technique by which this is done can be described as 'counterfactual model simulations'. A hypothesised explanation for any particular price change is examined, within the framework provided by the model, by removing the hypothesised cause and solving the model. The 'counterfactual' simulation results should then be able to shed some light on what might have happened to the UK economy had the actual path of the hypothesised causal variable not occurred. Put more simply, if 'A' causes 'B', then if we remove 'A', 'B' should no longer occur. This study uses a model of the UK economy to apply this simple logic to historical events.

Attempts to quantify arguments in economics and economic history have been numerous since the pioneering work of Robert Fogel (1964). Examples of studies similar to this one, which use macroeconomic models to examine various hypotheses about the causes of certain events can also be found in the work of Artis and Green (1982) using the Treasury Model, Artis *et al.* (1984) using the Treasury Model and National Institute Model, and of Saville and Gardiner (1986) using the National Institute model. The approach taken here is undertaken in a similar spirit.

The use of macroeconomic models for counterfactual simulations is open to two main criticisms. One is the general criticism of the use of macroeconomic models for prediction and policy analysis known as the Lucas critique (Lucas, 1978). This argues that the equations in the model are not truly structural, in that the coefficients are likely to alter with the state, or expected state, of the exogenous variables. This is a serious critique of all uses of macroeconomic models, but Sims (1982) has thrown some doubt on the practical importance of the problem. Sims argued that even with quite sharp policy shifts economic agents would be in some doubt as to the likely continuity of the policy and, consequently, would be unwilling to make major changes to their pattern of behaviour. For the 1870–1913 period there is a further factor which mitigates against the Lucas critique. That is that the Lucas critique was aimed largely at the effects of policy shifts and that the entire period, 1870–1913, was characterised by a very stable policy regime. Further, the exogenous shifts which do concern us, such as changing import prices, were very much the subject of uncertainty as far as economic agents were concerned. In this case, Sims' argument, regarding the uncertainty surrounding policy shifts, can be applied even more strongly.

Secondly, and not unconnected with the first criticism, is the problem of using the model with values some distance away from actual values. Econometric estimates of structural coefficients become less reliable the further we go from the values of the data used for estimation. This study, by necessity, is concerned with posing questions involving quite large deviations of the exogenous variables from their historical path. Consequently the results must be interpreted with caution and taken as orders of magnitude rather than exact estimates.

The two main model simulations, or counterfactuals, carried out concern, first of all, the fall in import prices down to the mid-nineties and second, the subsequent rise to the end of the period. Other simulations look at the differential effect of changes in different import prices and the effects of investment fluctuations.[10]

Falling import prices 1872–96

Down to 1881, import prices move, more-or-less, in line with the GDP deflator, first rising in the aftermath of the Franco–Prussian War and then falling away gradually. After 1881 their paths diverge. The GDP deflator fell only modestly, down 5.9% by 1985. Import prices, on the other hand, dropped dramatically, down 30.5% by 1985. The fall is evident in both food and non-food import prices. The 'supply-shock' argument is that these declines were due to two factors. The main argument is that the increase in the supply of agricultural and other basic commodities produced a sustained price fall. The other is that there was also a shift in the supply conditions of industrial commodities associated with the growth of industry outside the UK. There were also knock on effects from the fall in commodity prices onto industrial costs and prices. We are concerned here with the way that these prices were transmitted to the UK price level and the side effects that they had on the real economy in the UK. The simulation sets import prices equal to their 1871 nominal level from 1875. The aim of this is to discover:

i Did the fall in import prices produce the fall in the GDP deflator down to 1881? and:

ii How much of the subsequent fall in the GDP deflator (down to the mid-1890s) was caused by the further decline in import prices? and why did the GDP deflator and import prices cease to move in line from 1881?

Figure 7.2 shows the counterfactual assumption for import prices (note that in the simulation the aggregate import price deflator does not actually remain constant because of changes in the relative weights of food and non-food imports). The difference between assuming nominal import prices at their 1871 level and what actually happened is clearly major. In the simulation this leaves food import prices at a maximum of 64.9% above actual and non-food prices at a maximum of 57.1% above actual (in 1896 and 1898 respectively).

Simulation results for the GDP deflator (together with the actual values) are also shown in figure 7.2. The effects of this counterfactual assumption on prices in the model are dramatic. Not only does the price level fail to fall but from 1886 there is a sustained increase until 1900, from when there is a levelling off. In the counterfactual case prices are roughly stable to 1885, which answers the first of the two questions posed above. Within the context of the model, the fall in import prices did account for the fall in the GDP deflator to 1881. There is also a partial answer to the second question. Import price falls appear to have accounted for more than 100% of the subsequent decline to the mid-nineties. In other words, had import prices not fallen, the implication of the model is that there would have been a period of sustained inflation between 1885 and 1900. Compared to twentieth century experience the rise in prices is not high in the simulation, averaging 1.5% per annum between 1885 and 1899. In the late nineteenth century context, as figure 7.2 shows, it is severe.

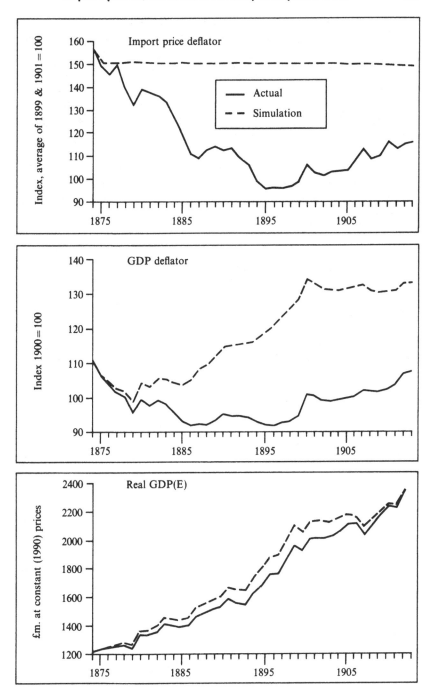

Figure 7.2   Model simulation: 1871 import prices.

This unambiguously establishes the link between import prices and the general price level in the model. The aggregate import price deflator reaches a maximum of 57.1% above actual in 1895. This produces a GDP deflator which is 35.7% higher than actual in 1899. Looking at the individual price deflators the extent of the changes are different, but the pattern of a substantial increase over actual is repeated in each case. Export prices show the largest increase, compared with the actual series, being 49.4% higher in 1898, not surprisingly given the direct effect of world prices on non-coal export prices in the models. Amongst the other deflators, the fixed investment price deflator shows the next highest increase, being 45.4% above actual in 1899, while the maximum effect on the consumer price and the government consumption deflators is slightly less at 30.1% and 31.0% respectively (both in 1899).

Nominal wages are 33.6% above actual by 1899. Increased consumer prices, however, mean that real wages are little changed. Increased employment does produce some increase in real employment incomes, but this peaks in 1895. Real profits, on the other hand, show a very marked increase, reaching 26.3% higher than actual in 1898 (total real non-employment incomes increase considerably less, up 11.6% in 1898). The size of the increase in profits reflects the price mark-up mechanism built into the model. The ability to pass on cost increases tends to lead to a rise in the profits share when import prices increase.

The simulation results also show a marked effect on the quantity, as well as the price variables, in the model. Increases in import prices represent both a gain in competitiveness and a loss of real income, so the results represent the net effect of these two opposing forces. Overall the effects are positive. GDP (expenditure measured at market prices) reaches a maximum of 7.6% above actual in 1898. Agricultural output, benefiting from the rise in food prices, peaks at 9.6% above actual in 1903. The main gains on the expenditure side of GDP come from increased exports and fixed investment. These two series reach 7.0% above actual and 21.6% above actual in 1898 and 1895 respectively. These increases are due in turn to the increase in export prices relative to domestic costs and to the income distributional effects of import price changes. Consumer spending only reaches a more modest 3.4% above actual (in 1898) largely because of the failure of real wages to increase substantially. Total imports are down on the actual for all of the sample period except for a few years at the beginning of the simulation.

Higher output also produces an effect on the labour force. Lower unemployment reduces net emigration (in fact it brings it to a complete halt in the mid-1890s). This in turn has implications for the population and labour force size. The labour force reaches a maximum of 1.9% above actual in 1901, the equivalent in number of an extra 369,000.

After c. 1900, price increases in the simulation level off, while historically, this was the period of rising prices. This phenomenon is largely a result of large increases in investment earlier in the period in the simulation. Extra capital accumulation produces a value (1900 prices) of the net capital stock in the simulation which is 10.4% higher than actual in 1905. Accompanying this increase is a substantial improvement in labour productivity (up by 2.7% by 1908). By then the impetus to aggregate demand produced by higher exports and lower imports is declining (because the ratio of import prices in the simulation to their actual level is declining after the mid-nineties as the actual levels begin to increase). This combination of a higher capital stock and lower aggregate demand reduces employment, increases unemployment and produces a weaker labour market. The consequent easing of nominal wages accounts for the levelling off of the price level in the simulation (note, however, that both nominal wages and prices in general level off at a level which is still considerably above the actual level).

This description of the simulation results is given in order to show how the model reacts to simulated price changes and through that to shed some light on how the late-nineteenth- and early-twentieth-century economy reacted to changes in the international price level. Static nominal import prices between 1875 and 1913 are not, of course, put forward as a serious alternative outcome, just as an extreme case to facilitate analysis. Continuing that analysis we can go on to discuss why falling import prices appear to have been the cause of more than 100% of the actual fall in the GDP deflator. Why, on the basis of the model, was there an inbuilt inflationary bias in the UK economy?

The explanation for this can be found by a brief examination of the model simulation results for consumer prices:

By far the largest impact is on prices of manufactures and food, not surprisingly as import prices enter directly into these equations. Services by contrast, are only affected indirectly through increases in wages. Further, the increase in the price of services represents a movement in the rate of increase of services' prices while for the other two deflators it is a switch from a rate of decrease to a rate of increase. The implications of all of this are that services' prices appear to have a natural tendency to increase as long as there is positive growth in nominal wages. Over the period to the mid-1890s the rising price of services was more than countered by falling prices of other consumer goods. When this is taken away, as in the simulation, we are left with no counter to rising services' prices. Even if we assume that services' prices would have remained unchanged in the face of the changes in import prices even indirectly through wage increases (i.e. services' prices are 'excluded', or 'exogenised' from the model) we still observe a similar though slightly muted effect (the average rate of change of

Table 7.2.*Simulation results (import prices stay at their 1871 level over 1875–1913)*

	Consumer price deflator		
	Average rate of change 1874–99		Per cent above actual in 1899
	Actual	Simulation	
Manufactures	−1.50	0.00	46.0
Food	−0.59	0.66	36.6
Services	0.58	1.49	25.2
Total	−0.54	0.67	35.1

Source: see data appendix for actual; for simulation, see above, p. 000.

the GDP deflator is 1.1% per annum between 1885 and 1899, compared with 1.5% in the full simulation and 0.1% in the actual series). Hence, even the rate of increase of the services' prices deflator in the actual series alone would have been enough to cause a substantial increase in the GDP deflator had actual import prices failed to fall.

Services accounted for 33% of consumer spending and 28% of GDP over the simulation period, so the impact of changes in the price deflator for services was considerable. The reason for the reaction of services' prices is apparent from the equation. The consumer price deflator for services is expressed solely as a function of nominal wages. Neither productivity, or import prices enter into the equation. In interpreting this we must be cautious of the data. The index for services' prices is based to a large extent on wages so the estimated link between wages and prices is only to be expected. Such an assumption is not altogether unreasonable however. There are many examples of how productivity increases could occur in the service sector – in transport for example. Equally, there are examples of areas where there was little potential for productivity changes – domestic service for example (though even here new technology could increase productivity – the introduction of vacuum cleaners and new materials for example). The absence of any productivity effect from the estimated equation (and by implication from the data) may be extreme, but we would expect a far greater role for productivity change in consumer goods industries than in services in this period.

The outcome of this is that productivity increases tend to push up nominal wages outside the service sector. Competition in the labour market then tends to bid up wages in the services sector to a near equal extent. Outside of the services sector productivity changes counter the increases in nominal wages, helping to stabilise prices. In the services sector there is little potential for productivity increases (no potential at all in the model). Consequently, prices increase. For there to be zero inflation in the absence of falling import prices, wages over the economy as a whole would have to increase at only a proportion of the rate of labour productivity growth in the non-services sectors, the proportion being equal to the share of the non-services sectors in the economy. This also requires the price of goods (i.e. output excluding services) to be continually declining. Although it is probable that average earnings over the whole economy did increase at a slower rate than for productivity outside the services sector (difficulties in measuring service and non-service sector output and employment make it difficult to make exact statements), the ratio of wage increases to productivity increases must have been too large to permit price stability in the absence of import price falls.

Had import prices failed to fall in the manner that they did, it can be argued that increases in nominal wages would have been proportionately smaller on the grounds that employers would have been less able to pay. This does not look to have been the case. Increasing import prices increase rather than reduce profit shares in the model, and a positive correlation between the profits share and real import prices can also be found in the data. Further, higher import prices leading to higher consumer prices can be expected to have put upward pressure on nominal wages.

The condition that the price of goods (output excluding services) be in a state of perpetual decline does appear to be difficult to meet. What actually happened in the period to the mid-1890s is that some goods, namely internationally traded goods, did decline in price sufficiently to permit a general price fall in the UK.

The link between the consumer price for services and the GDP deflator also helps explain why the GDP deflator and the import deflator moved so closely down to 1881 but not after, and so provides an answer to question (ii) posed above. The estimate of services' prices remained relatively steady until the mid-1880s as nominal wages returned to their pre-boom levels (i.e. pre-1871). Only after the turn-around in nominal wages does the estimate of the consumer price deflator for services begin to show a great enough rate of increase to force the divergence between the import price deflator and the GDP deflator (between 1875 and 1886 the average annual rate of change of the consumer price deflator for services is 0.26%. Between 1886 and 1910 it is 1%).

Rising import prices 1897–1913

The previous section has argued that falling import prices were the driving force behind the decline in the general UK price level down to the mid-1890s. It remains to demonstrate what the model has to say about what would have happened had import prices not turned around in the mid-nineties. The argument regarding world prices here is that, just as an increase in the relative supply of basic commodities drove down prices before the mid-1890s, a slowdown in the rate of supply growth of commodities after the mid-1890s produced an increase. This had knock on effects for industrial prices as costs increased. Between 1896 and 1912 the price of food imports actually increased by less than the price of other imports (18.2% compared with 20.6%, for 1895/7 to 1911/13). Note, though, that non-food imports contained a substantial amount of basic commodities as well as manufactures.

Figure 7.3 shows what happens in the model when import prices are kept at their 1895 levels. This leaves import prices for food, drink and tobacco at a maximum of 16.5% below actual (in 1909), and other import prices at a maximum of 22.9% below actual (in 1910). In total this produces an aggregate import price deflator which reaches a maximum of 17.7% below base in 1910.

As can be seen from figure 7.3, this still leaves the 1900 peak in the GDP deflator, but after that prices fall back towards their 1896 trough. By 1911 the value of the GDP deflator in the simulation is only 1.6% above the 1896 level. It appears, therefore, that the increase in import prices after 1895 was responsible for the bulk of the increase in the level of the GDP deflator after the mid-1890s. What now needs to be explained is why the tendency of services' prices to rise faster than other prices did not force up the general price level in the absence of any changes to nominal import prices, as hypothesised above.

The answer to this lies in the reaction of the real variables in the model to price changes. Changes in the import price deflators do not have identical effects. Both tend to affect consumer prices and hence real incomes. The effect of non-food import prices on output, through competitiveness effects (a greater willingness to export or the effects of the relative price terms in the import equations), however, are greater than those for food import prices. In the previous simulation the changes to the two deflators was not dissimilar. The counterfactual assumption for food import prices reached a maximum of 64.9% above actual in 1896, and non-food import prices a maximum of 57.1% above actual in 1898. In the case of this simulation the relative changes are the other way around. What is more, the differences are considerably greater. As noted above, the counterfactual assumption for

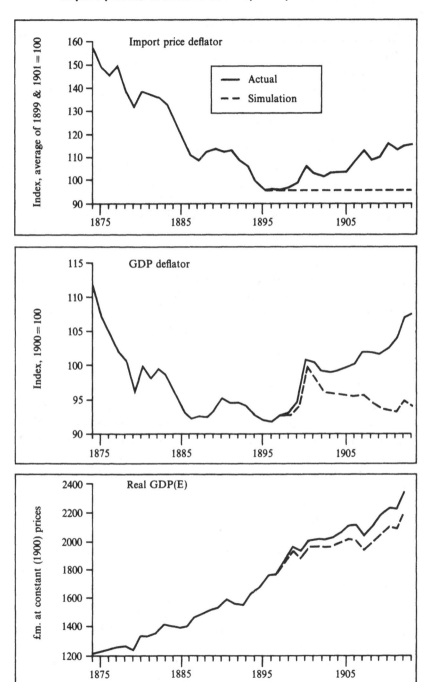

Figure 7.3   Model simulation: 1895 import prices.

non-food import prices reaches a minimum value, relative to actual of 22.9%, while the minimum value of food prices relative to actual is only 16.5%.

One consequence of this is a fall in the volume of non-coal merchandise exports to 5.6% below actual by 1908. Falling profits also have hefty repercussions on fixed investment (down 17.9% relative to actual by 1912). This combines to force up the unemployment rate (to 11.4% or 3.8% above actual in 1908) and weaken the labour market. As a result nominal wages gradually return back towards their 1896 levels. Real wages actually show some decline relative to actual. The levelling off of nominal wages means that services' prices grow at a slower rate than actual to 1903/4 and then level off. Hence, the impetus to a higher price level is removed. The slowdown in demand growth also has a limiting effect on increases in the fixed investment deflators and on the consumer spending on manufactures deflator.

The implications of this for the interpretation of actual events is that without the upturn in import prices (particularly of non-food import prices) the levelling off of real wages would have been even more severe than it actually was. This would no doubt have had further implications for the increasing level of industrial (and social) conflict after the turn of the century.

Divergent movements in import prices

The discussion above of the counterfactual results with import deflators held at their 1895 level raises a need for a further consideration of the differential effects of changes in import prices for food, drink and tobacco and non-food import prices on the economy as a whole. Between 1895 and 1906 the price deflator for non-food imports increased by 17.6%, while food import prices only increased by 4%. This section attempts to investigate the effects of different rates of change in the two import price deflators by carrying out two further simulations. One forces import prices for food, drink and tobacco to follow non-food import prices from 1895, the other lets non-food import prices follow the import price for food, drink and tobacco. The effects on a number of other key variables by 1906 (the date of the maximum divergence of the counterfactual values of the two import price deflators from actual) are illustrated in table 7.3.

The simulations aims to illustrate the asymmetrical effects of the two changes. Increases in food import prices, relative to actual, raise prices and depress GDP and employment (and vice versa). Reductions in non-food imports, on the other hand, reduce the general price level, but still lead to a fall in real GDP and employment. This is because non-food prices contain

Table 7.3. *Simulation results (differing counterfactual assumptions on import prices 1896–1913)*

	Percentage difference from actual in 1906	
	Food import prices follow non-food import prices	Non-food import prices follow food import prices
Import prices:		
Food, drink and tobacco	+23.7	
Other		−19.2
Total	+8.7	−12.2
GDP deflator	+3.1	−4.9
Nominal wages	+3.3	−5.4
Real wages	−1.7	−1.2
Employment	−1.9	−4.2
Real GDP (E)	−1.5	−4.2
Exports	−0.7	−2.8

an element of competing goods and any change has consequences for UK competitiveness. To a certain extent, this is also true of food imports, but their effect on the UK agricultural sector is considerably less in magnitude than the effect of other imports on industry. It is impossible, therefore, to draw conclusions regarding changes in import prices unless the composition of those changes is known.

This illustrates the difficulties in dealing with the concept of a country's terms of trade (as defined by a price index for all exports divided by a price index for all imports). A deterioration in the terms of trade caused by an increase in the price of imported goods which compete with domestic products is likely to increase output. If it is caused by a rise in the price of goods which are essentially inputs into the domestic economy, then real incomes and output will fall. In both cases domestic prices will rise, though this rise will be tempered if output falls.

Neither of the two import price categories considered here fits exactly into these definitions. Food import prices, however tend to be inputs, either directly into consumer goods or into food manufacturing industries. Non-food import prices tended to be more likely to be for competing goods. This could either be directly by acting on import price competitiveness, or indirectly as import prices also represent the international price level which export prices tended to follow. Changes in international prices for food, for example, would be unlikely to have had any direct influence on the level of UK exports of manufactures. There could have been an indirect influence via the effect on the real incomes of importing countries, but that is beyond the present scope of the discussion. Changes in UK import volumes could also impact on producers' incomes. Here again, the full implications are beyond the scope of this paper. Olson (1974), however, points out that even large changes in UK import volumes would have had a relatively minor effect on world markets.

The main flaw in the model is that imports are disaggregated into only two categories. Non-food imports include both inputs and competing goods. Less than half of this category was in fact composed of manufactures, the rest being made up of raw materials and services. Just because goods were categorised as raw materials, it does not mean that they did not compete with UK products but that a large proportion (imports of raw cotton for example) are more properly categorised as inputs and not competing goods. This is a limitation of the model which, as mentioned above, does add some bias to the results. As a future development, the model would benefit from the further disaggregation of visible trade into at least three categories (food, raw materials and manufactures). This does not, however, affect the basis of the argument. Changes in prices of different categories of imports could have been (and still could be) expected to have different macroeconomic implications for the UK.

Applying this argument to the upturn in import prices after the mid-1890s we can see divergent effects on output (though increases in both deflators would tend to push up the GDP deflator). The increase in food import prices was a depressive influence on real wages, while the increase in other import prices would have tended to improve international competitiveness and hence increase output. A similar argument can be applied to an earlier period. Between 1883 and 1887 food import prices fell by a total of 25.2% while other import prices only fell by 12.7%. The fall in food import prices would have helped to sustain real incomes, while the fall in other import prices would have eroded competitiveness and tended to depress output.

Fluctuations in fixed investment

The simulations presented above have clearly identified fluctuations in import prices as the cause of the UK price swing. Before concluding the chapter, it is worth considering one more counterfactual. This concerns changes in the level of fixed investment. One view, associated with Schumpeter (1939), attributes the turn around in price in the mid-1890s to a boom in investment in new technology. This would increase prices through demand-pull increases and increase the money stock by financial intermediaries supplying additional loans to meet the needs of new investment. The price effects can be investigated using the model.

Fixed investment is the most volatile of the expenditure series. Specifically, the data shows falling fixed investment from the mid-1870s to the mid-1880s, followed by a moderate upturn and then a major boom between 1895 and 1904 and then an almost equally spectacular collapse. It is quite plausible that fluctuations of this size could have produced major swings in prices, depressing them in the middle of the period and raising them around the turn of the century.

In the model these changes are presented as an attempt to adjust the stock of fixed capital to a desired level which is determined by real incomes. In the simulation the question of investment determination is left aside and the question 'What if fixed investment had followed a smooth (i.e. constant rate) growth path?' is posed. This is done by calculating a growth rate for each of the three categories of fixed investment in the model which would have left the total volume of investment over the period 1874 to 1913 constant. The aggregate growth rate assumption for fixed investment turns out to be 2.26%.[11] Having excluded the three fixed investment categories from the model, the model is then solved to give the implied values of the remaining endogenous variables. The changes to fixed investment are considerable. The changes to output and prices are, however, much less severe. The GDP deflator still falls steeply to the mid-eighties. From then the fall is moderated by the higher investment levels in the simulation. In 1896 the GDP deflator is 2.2% above actual, but this still represents a fall of 18% on the 1873 level. Prices still increase sharply in 1900 and then grow at a higher rate than actual. The pattern of fixed investment obviously has some effect on the price level in the model, but it is not enough to cause major price swings as with changes to import prices. Additionally, the slump in investment indicated by the Feinstein data at the end of the period moderated the upswing in prices.

The assumed path of fixed investment smooths out some of the fluctuations in real GDP and leaves it slightly higher than the actual value at the end of the period (though little changed over the entire solution period). Some of the fluctuations in the current account are also ironed out to some extent as is shown by a fall in the standard deviation (of the current account) from 55.2 to 46.9.

These results indicate that there are some links between fluctuations in the level of fixed investment and the price level. This is further illustrated in figure 7.4 which plots the deviation of the solution values from the actual values for fixed investment and the GDP deflator against the left axis and

Fixed investment (%)   GDP deflator (%)

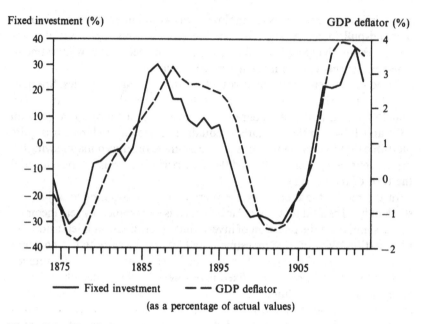

— Fixed investment   – – GDP deflator

(as a percentage of actual values)

Figure 7.4 Model simulation: smoothed fixed investment.

right axis respectively. Shown in this way, the link between prices and investment shows up clearly. The implied responsiveness of prices to fixed investment is quite low. The elasticity implied by a simple regression of the proportional differences from the actual GDP deflator on the lagged value of the proportional difference from base of fixed investment is only 0.08 (a 1% change in fixed investment leads to a 0.08% change in prices). Looking at the overall relationship between quantities and prices, we get a much more sensitive response. The elasticity of price changes with respect to changes in real GDP, calculated in a similar fashion is 0.55. This implies that demand pressures did have a significant effect on prices, but that, in the case of fixed investment at least, these effects were dominated by a price swing of considerably greater magnitude. What the simulation essentially does is to remove the cycle in investment of approximately 20-year duration from the expenditure data in the model (sometimes known as a Kuznets or building cycle). This has some effect on the price level by removing a 20-year cycle from prices but, as figure 7.4 shows, the amplitude is not very large. The long swing pattern still dominates.

Note that the elasticities of prices with respect to quantities quoted above are essentially short-term. In the longer term an increase in investment leads not to a rise in the price level but to a fall as labour productivity rises with the capital stock and hence unit labour costs fall.

Conclusions

This chapter has attempted to assess the degree to which import prices were responsible for the observed swing in prices between 1870 and 1913 by running a series of simulations on a structural macroeconomic model. The results are clear. Changes in import prices were sufficient to have produced the UK price swing.[12] Further, without the steep fall in import prices down to the mid-1890s, the model indicates the UK price level would have had an upward trend. This was because of the tendency of services' prices to increase in line with nominal wages and the absence of any productivity offset. The pattern of investment booms and slumps also had some effect on prices, but these were of secondary importance.

An interesting secondary result concerns the effect of the price changes on the real economy. The simulations indicate that the substantial fall in world prices to the mid-nineties limited UK GDP growth while the subsequent increase provided a boost. The implication that such price changes could have long-term implications for GDP is obviously at odds with theories which see the long-run growth path as fixed in some way (as with many of the monetarist explanations). Two things are worth mentioning here. One is that with the capital stock being endogenous to the model, price changes could lead to changes in the productive potential of the economy. Secondly, implicit in the model is that changes in import prices (under fixed exchange rates) affect the real exchange rate and, hence, competitiveness.

Of course there are problems in using a macroeconomic model in this way, such as the reliability of the estimated coefficients when considering values for variables which are considerably different from those used in estimation. The results are also very much specific to the model. That is that they depend on both the specification of the estimated equation and the structural make up of the model. The process of model development and testing, together with the tracking performance of the model, as detailed in the second section, does show that a structural macroeconomic model of the UK with non-monetarist price determination can be constructed which is able to reasonably reproduce the macroeconomic history of the period. There is, therefore, reason to have faith in the model's performance and some credence must be given to the simulation results.

One outstanding question must concern the cause of the international price movements. The second section above argues that these were due to real, not monetary factors. This argument has not, however, been settled. What if the changes in world prices were determined by world-wide monetary forces? In many ways the interpretation of the simulation results would not be altered. The fact that neither interest rates or money balances could be found to have a significant effect in the expenditure equation still stands. The model would still indicate that the transmission mechanism from world to UK prices was through a cost plus mechanism and not through an increase in the UK money stock leading to an increase in UK prices. As it is, rather than look for a monetary explanation of world prices and a cost plus interpretation for the UK, we believe that the results are more consistent with a supply shock explanation of international price changes which are transmitted to the UK through import price changes.

Notes

1 Another possible cause not mentioned by Rostow, was a lack of domestic investment opportunities in the UK in the 1880s.
2 Rostow and Kennedy, 1979: 727.
3 The F-statistics for the joint US–UK causality tests ($F3,34(5\%)=2.89$) are:
   Nominal GNP 'causes' MO – 8.31
   MO 'causes' nominal GNP – 2.53
   Nominal GNP 'causes' M3 – 0.58
   M3 'causes' nominal GNP – 2.42
4 Note that although compared with recent experiences, exchange rates over the period were extremely stable, they were by no means fixed as not all countries were on the gold standard. The US dollar appreciated against sterling in the years leading up to 1879 when the USA went on to gold. This could help explain why the big falls in UK import prices came after 1880. Most of the less developed countries were on a silver standard and saw their currencies depreciate substantially against gold standard currencies until the mid-1890s. This could have contributed to the sustained decline in the sterling/gold price of basic commodities.
5 The employment function contains a technological change variable. This takes the value 0 in 1869 and then increases by 0.1 in each year down to 1897. Thereafter, it increases by only 0.003 per annum. This change, which was arrived at by experimenting with different changes at different dates, attempts to take into account a major slowdown in labour productivity which occurred sometime around the turn of the century and which cannot be explained by changes in the capital/labour ratio. This can be viewed as a 'climacteric' variable.
6 One exception to this is export prices. Following Barrell (1989), the specification makes the export prices of goods (excluding coal) a function of both domestic costs and the world price of manufactures. Given a fixed-exchange rate regime it might be argued that export prices should have followed world prices exactly in the long run. However, there is ample evidence of divergences in prices between

UK export prices and other countries' export prices over the period and that British domination of colonial export markets helped this to persist (Lewis, 1978: 121–2; De Cecco, 1974). Further, the econometric evidence supports this conclusion.

7 All data is taken from Feinstein (1972) except where stated.

8 Taken from the 'United Kingdom National Accounts' (The CSO Blue Book), 1989 edition.

9 With reference to the debate on the link between foreign and domestic investment made earlier, the mistiming of the investment boom in the model could be due to failure to capture the influence of the foreign demand for capital. Also worth noting, is that the investment data is possibly the least reliable of the expenditure data series.

10 Other simulations concerning changes in nominal wages and coal prices are presented in Blake (1988) but were not found to offer much towards the explanation of the price swing.

11 The disaggregated rates used are: residential investment – 1.78%, other buildings and works – 2.29%, non-construction – 2.45%.

12 The relationship between UK prices should not be interpreted so as to support purchasing power parity as described by McCloskey and Zecher (1976). On the contrary, rather than there being an automatic link between world and UK prices, adjustment is not always rapid and is only partial. Changes to the real exchange rate were possible.

Appendix 1 Variable listing

ARMF	Armed Forces Employment
C1	Ratio of coal prices to the GDP deflator
C2	Ratio of price of exported coal to all coal
C3	Ratio of price of home consumed coal to all coal
CE	Consumer spending: total
CEC	Consumer spending: coal
CECN	Consumer spending: coal, nominal
CEFDT	Consumer spending: food, drink & tobacco
CEFDTN	Consumer spending: food, drink & tobacco, nominal
CEMF	Consumer spending: manufactures
CEMFN	Consumer spending: manufactures, nominal
CESER	Consumer spending: services
CESERN	Consumer spending: services, nominal
CVEMP	Civilian employment
D12	Dummy variable, 1912 = 1

D1900	Dummy variable, 1900–13 = 1
D93	Dummy variable for 1893
DEM2	Cumulative demand variable
DIFOBW	Depreciation: other buildings & works
DIFPMSV	Depreciation: non-construction
DIFRS	Depreciation: residential
GDP	GDP: expenditure estimate at market prices
GDPN	GDP: expenditure estimate at market prices, nominal
GDPA	GDP: average estimate
GDPY	GDP: income estimate, current prices
GIFOBW	Gross capital stock: other buildings & works
GIFPMSV	Gross capital stock: non-construction
GIFRS	Gross capital stock: residential
GVCE	Government consumption
GVCEN	Government consumption, nominal
IF	Fixed investment: total
IFN	Fixed investment: total, nominal
IFCO	Fixed investment: construction total
IFCON	Fixed investment: construction total, nominal
IFOBW	Fixed investment: other buildings & works
IFPM	Fixed investment: non-construction
IFPMN	Fixed investment: non-construction, nominal
IFRS	Fixed investment: residential
IP	Industrial production
IPA	Industrial production: USA
IPE	Industrial production: Europe
KIF	Net capital stock: total
KIFOBW	Net capital stock: other buildings & works
KIFPMSV	Net capital stock: non-construction
KIFRS	Net capital stock: residential
NETP	Net property income from abroad
NINC	Population Increase
NMIG	Net Emigration
NPT	Population
NRUT	Unemployment (%)
OY	Other income (rent), nominal
PDCE	Price deflator: total consumer spending
PDCEC	Price deflator: consumption of coal
PDCEFDT	Price deflator: consumption of food etc.
PDCEMF	Price deflator: consumption of manufactures
PDCESER	Price deflator: consumption of services
PDGDP	Price deflator: GDP(E) at market prices
PDIF	Price deflator: fixed investment, total
PDIFCON	Price deflator: fixed investment, construction
PDIFPM	Price deflator: fixed investment, non-const.
PDII	Price deflator: stockbuilding
PDTE	Price deflator: exports, total

PDTEC	Price deflator: exports, coal
PDTEMXC	Price deflator: exports, merchandise exc. coal
PDTM	Price deflator: imports, total
PDTMFDT	Price deflator: imports, food, drink & tobacco
PDTMFDT	Price deflator: imports, other
PROF	Profits & income from self-employment, nominal
RPROF	Real adjusted profits
RPROP	Rate of return on overseas assets
RYEMP	Real adjusted income from employment
RYXEMP	Real adjusted non-employment incomes
RYXEMP	Real adjusted non-employment incomes, exc. net property income from abroad
SD1	Statistical discrepancy (GDPN(E)GDPN(Y)) trend
SDGDPA	Ratio of GDP(E) to GDP(A)
SDGDPY	Ratio of nominal GDP(E) to nominal GDP(Y)
SF	Discrepancy between average earnings times employment and the income from employment series
SIFOBW	Scrapping: other buildings & works
SIFPMSV	Scrapping: non-construction
SIFRS	Scrapping: residential
T	Time trend, $1870 = 1$
TBPCAN	Current account
TBPCANC	Current account, cumulative
TE	Exports: total goods and services
TEC	Exports: coal
TECH	Technology variable, increases 0.1 p.a. to 1897, then by 0.003 p.a. to 1913
TECN	Exports: coal, nominal
TEMXC	Exports: merchandise excluding coal
TEMXCN	Exports: merchandise excluding coal, nominal
TES	Exports: services
TESN	Exports: services, nominal
TEN	Exports: total goods and services, nominal
TFEFC	Total final expenditure less factor cost adjustment
TM	Imports: total
TMFDT	Imports: food, drink & tobacco
TMFDTN	Imports: food, drink & tobacco, nominal
TMM	Imports: total, nominal
TMO	Imports: other
TMON	Imports: other, nominal
TRANS	Net transfers from abroad, nominal
TXCB	Real Indirect taxes
TXCBN	Indirect taxes, nominal
TXRBN	Average rate of indirect taxation
UNEMP	Unemployment, 000's
V1	Ratio of working population to total population
V2	Ratio of natural population increase to population

WPOP	Working Population
WRCAN	Average nominal earnings from employment
XGGAGR	Index of agricultural output
YP	Potential (full employment) output
YEMP	Earnings from employment, nominal
YXEMP	Earnings not from employment, nominal

Note: all expenditure variables are in real terms except where stated.

Appendix 2 UK model: equation listing

CE_t

$= CEMF_t + CEFD_t + CESER_t + CEC_t$

CEC_t

$= .0205.RYEMP_{t-1} - 5.8320.D12 + 31.2409 + r_{1t}$

$\quad (2.38) \qquad\qquad (-3.18) \qquad\quad (3.54)$

OLS (1900–13)

sum of squares $\quad = 26.9331$ mean of dep. var. $= 51.9429$

standard error $\quad = 1.5648 \qquad\qquad Z(5) = 1.87$

DW $= 1.741$

$CECN_t \qquad = CEC_t.PDCEC_t/100$

$CEFDT_t \qquad = .7002.CEFDT_{t-1} + .1270.RYEMP_t + 59.2092 + r_{2t}$

$\qquad\qquad\quad (10.7) \qquad\qquad (4.51) \qquad\qquad\quad (4.63)$

IV (1871–1911)

sum of squares $\quad = 2188.20$ mean of dep. var. $= 520.409$

standard error $\quad = 7.5884 \qquad\qquad Z(5) = 11.9$

LM(2) $= 3.14$

$CEFDTN_t \qquad = CEFDT_t.PDCEFDT_t/100$

$CEMF_t \qquad = .5085.CEMF_{t-1} + .15425.(RYEMP_t + RYXEMP_t) -$

$\qquad\qquad\quad (2.99) \qquad\qquad (4.57)$

$\qquad\qquad 61.3879 + r_{3t}$

$\qquad\qquad (-3.32)$

IV (1871–1913)

sum of squares $\quad = 6165.67$ mean of dep. var. $= 378.019$

standard error $\quad = 12.4145 \qquad\qquad Z(5) = 7.78$

LM(2) $= 0.22$

$CEMFN_t \qquad = CEMF_t.PDCEMF_t/100$

$CEN_t \qquad = CEMFN_t + CEFD_{tt} + CESER_t + CEC_t$

$CESER_t \qquad = .1495.RYEMP_t + .06766.RYXEMP_{t-1} + 363.374 + r_{4t}$

$\qquad\qquad\quad (1.43) \qquad\qquad (1.27) \qquad\qquad\quad (2.70)$

$\qquad\qquad rho = .8797$

$\qquad\qquad\quad (5.62)$

ALS (1900–13)
sum of squares   = 497.031 mean of dep. var. = 565.027
standard error   = 7.050 $Z(5) = 2.660$
$DW = 1.961$

$CESERN_t$ $= CESER_t.PDCESER_t/100$

$dln(CVEMP_t)$ $= .9128.dln(GDPA_t) - .3687.dln(KIF_{t-1}) + .01565.diff(D93)$
                  $=$ (9.76)   (−1.63)   (1.75)
                  $=$ $-.5697.res_{t-1} + 1.7793$
                  $=$ (−4.59)   (4.57)

OLS (1871–1913)
Sum of Squares   = .0054 Mean of Dep. Var. = 9.673
Standard Error   = .0119 $Z(5) = 3.34$
where 'res' is the residual from:

$ln(CVEMP_t)$ $= 1.2545.ln(GDPA_t) - .28629.ln(KIF_{t-1}) - 1.2765.$
                     $TECH + .0520.D93 + c$
                     $(CRDW = 1.62, DF = 5.16)$

$DIFOBW_t$ $= .0089.GKIFOBW_{t-1} + .4603 + r_{6t}$
                     $= (5.03)$ (−0.18)
                     $= rho = -.4448$
                       (-3.23)

ALS (1871–1913)
$R^2 = 0.69$ $DW(1) = 2.29$

$DIFPM_t$ $= .0298.GKIFPM_{t-1} + .2072 + r_{7t}$
               (26.3)   (1.08)
               $rho = -.4218$
                  (-2.99)

ALS (1871–1913)
$R^2 = 0.90$ $DW(1) = 2.14$

$DIFRS_t$ $= .0084.GKIFRS_{t-1} + .4603 + r_{8t}$
              (13.1)   (0.22)
              $rho = -.4419$
                  (-3.22)

ALS (1871–1913)
$R^2 = 0.36$ $DW(1) = 2.47$

$DEM2_t$ $= DEM2_{t-1} + dln(GDPA_t) - .02$

GDP_t $= CE_t + GVCE_t + IF_t + II_t + TE_t - TM_t$

$GDPA_t$ $= (GDP_t - TXCB_t).SDGDPA_t$

$GDPN_t$ $= CEN_t + GVCEN_t + IFN_t + IIN_t + TEN_t - TMN_t$

$GDPY_t$ $= (GDPN_t - TXCBN_t).SDGDPY_t$

$GKIFPBW_t$ $= GKIFOBW_{t-1} + IFOBW_t - SIFOBW_t$

$GKIFPM_t$ $= GKIFPM_{t-1} + IFPM_t - SIFPM_t$

$GKIFRS_t$ $= GKIFRS_{t-1} + IFRS_t - SIFRS_t$

$GVCEN_t$ $= GVCE_t.PDGVCE_t/100$

IF_t $= IFPM_t + IFCON_t$

$IFCON_t$ $= IFOBW_t + IFRS_t$

$IFCONN_t$ $= IFCON_t.PDIFCON_t/100$

IFN_t $= IFCONN_t + IFPMN_t$

$IFOBW_t$ $= .8448.IFOBW_{t-1} + .0332.RYXEMPX_{t-1} + .0412.$

(20.3)   (2.98)   (7.93)

$RYXEMPX_{t-2} + .0384.RYXEMPX_{t-3} + .0246.$

(4.90)   (3.68)

$RYXEMPX_{t-4} - .0521.KIFOBW_{t-1} + 20.0420 + r_{9t}$

(−8.16)   (5.34)

OLS (1874–1913, second degree polynomial distributed lags with far point restriction)

Sum of squares $= 382.364$ mean of dep. var. $= 53.2250$

standard error $= 3.305$ $Z(5) = 8.73$

$LM(2) = 0.44$

$IFPM_t$ $= .8158.IFPM_{t-1} + .0114.RYXEMPX_{t-1} + .0227.$

(8.40)   (3.16)   (3.16)

$RYXEMPX_{t-2} + .0341.RYXEMPX_{t-3} - .0432.$

(3.16)   (−2.84)

$KIFPM_{t-1} - 8.6870 + r_{10t}$

(−1.29)

OLS (1873–1912, second degree polynomial distributed lags with near point restriction)

Sum of squares $= 1092.91$ mean of dep. var. $= 56.3250$

standard error $= 5.510$ $Z(5) = 10.43$

$LM(2) = 2.29$

$IFRS_t$ $= .8900.IFRS_{t-1} + .0356 RYEMP_{t-3} - .0419.KIFRS_{t-1}$

(9.80)   (3.78)   (−4.29)

$+ 12.1373 + r_{11t}$

(3.78)

rho $= .4063$

(2.25)

ALS (1873–1913)

Sum of squares $= 125.158$ mean of dep. var. $= 24.845$

standard error $= 1.8646$ $Z(5) = 6.91$

$LM(2) = 6.62$

II_t $= .20.(GDP_t - TXCB_t) + .13.(GDP_{t-1} - TXCB_{t-1})$

$+ .07.(GDP_{t-2} - TXCB_{t-2}) + r_{12t}$

OLS (1873–1913, first degree polynomial distributed lags with far point restriction)

Sum of Squares $= 2600.97$ Mean of Dep. Var. $= 14.6341$

Standard Error $= 6.8474$ $Z(5) = 2.93$

R^2 $= 0.6541$ $DW = 1.6087$

IIN_t $= II_t.PDII_t/100$

$\ln(IP_t)$ $= .73.\ln(IP_{t-1}) + 1.47.\ln(GDPA_t) - 1.16.\ln(GDPA_{t-1})$

$- 1.12 + r_{13t}$

KIF_t $= KIFRS_t + KIFOBW_t + KIFPM_t$

$KIFOBW_t$ $= KIFOBW_{t-1} + IFOBW_t - DIFOBW_t$

$KIFPM_t$ $= KIFPM_{t-1} + IFPM_t - DIFPM_t$

$KIFPM_t$ $= KIFPM_{t-1} + IFPM_t - DIFPM_t$

$NETP_t$ $= RPROP_t.TBPCAN_{t-1}$

$NINC_t$ $= V2_t.NPT_{t-1}$

$NMIG_t$ $= .1160.MA(UNEMP)_{t-1} + 49.054 + r_{14t}$
                    (2.63)   (1.03)
                    rho $= .7617$
                    (6.50)

where $MA(UNEMP) = (UNEMP_t + UNEMP_{t-1} + UNEMP_{t-2} + UNEMP_{t-3})/4$

OLS (1876–1913)

Sum of Squares $= 5854.0$ Mean of Dep. var. $= 135.105$

Standard Error $= 40.87$ $Z(5) = 7.41$

DW $= 1.72$ $R^2 = 0.683$

NPT_t $= NPT_{t-1} + NINC_t - NMIG_t$

UR_t $= 100.(WPOP_t - CVEMP_t - ARMF_t)/WPOP_t$

$OY_t.SD1_t$ $= .9647.OY_{t-1} + .0058.(GDPN_t - TXCBN_t) + 1.029 + r_{15t}$
                    (33.2)   (1.71)   (.78)

IV (1871–1913)

Sum of Squares $= 129.448$ Mean of Dep. Var. $= 192.512$

Standard Error $= 1.7989$ $Z(5) = 8.87$

$LM(2) = 1.57$

PC_t $= C1_t.PDGDP_t$

$PDCE_t$ $= 100.CEN_t/CE_t$

$\ln(PDCEC_t)$ $= .4613 \ln(PHC_t) - .0048\ TIME + 5.0700 + r_{16t}$
                    (11.3)   (−6.21)   (82.9)

IV (1871–1913)

standard error $= .0143\ R^2 = .77$ $DW = 1.56$

$Z(5) = 7.462$

$\ln(PDCEFDT_t)$ $= .4886 \ln(PDCEFDT_{t-1}) + .2443 \ln(PDTMFDT_t)$
                    (5.53)   (5.77)
                    $+ .0005\ TRM_t.\ln(PDTMFDT_t) + .1460 \ln(WRCAN_t)$
                    (1.62)   (3.21)
                    $+ .5057 + r_{17t}$
                    (1.71)

IV (1871–1913)

sum of squares $= .0078$ mean of dep. var. $= 4.636$

standard error $= .0143$ $Z(5) = 2.038$

$LM(2) = .69$

$\ln(PDCEMF_t)$ $= .4262 \ln(PDCEMF_{t-1}) + .3257 \ln(PDTM_t)$
                    (4.39)   (4.37)
                    $+ .2069 \ln(WRCAN_t/PROD_t) + .3691\ DEM2_t$
                    (2.54)   (2.82)
                    $+ .0857\ D72 - .3001 + r_{18t}$
                    (3.52)   (−0.64)

IV (1871–1913)

sum of squares $= .0183$ mean of dep. var. $= 4.663$

standard error $= .0223$ $Z(5) = 2.839$

$LM(2) = .79$

$\ln(PDCESER_t)$ $= .9281 \ln(PDCESER_{t-1}) + (.2380 - .1471\ L)\ \ln(WRCAN_t)$
                    $(40.7)\qquad\qquad\qquad (7.58)\ (-4.61)$
                    $-.0696 + r_{19t}$
                    (-1.95)

IV (1871–1913)
sum of squares $= .0011$ mean of dep. var. $= 4.538$
standard error $= .0052\ Z(5) = 5.562$
LM(2) $= .02$

$PDGDP_t$ $= 100.GDPN_t/GDPt$

$\ln(PDGVCE_t)$ $= .4538 \ln(PDGVCE_{t-1}) + .1541 \ln(WRCAN_t)$
                    $(5.26)\qquad\qquad\qquad (7.19)$
                    $+ .1570\ (\ln(PDCE_t) + \ln(PDIF_t)) + .1825\ (1 - L)\ \ln(IP_t)$
                    $(6.52)\qquad\qquad\qquad\qquad\qquad (2.41)$
                    $+ .3843 + r_{20t}$
                    (2.01)

IV (1871–1913)
sum of squares $= .0042$ mean of dep. var. $= 4.584$
standard error $= .0105\ Z(5) = 2.145$
LM(2) $= .26$

$PDIF_t$ $= 100.IFN_t/IF_t$

$\ln(PDIFCON_t)$ $= .8567 \ln(PDIFCON_{t-1}) + .18347 \ln(WRCAN_t/PROD_t)$
                    $(11.4)\qquad\qquad\qquad\qquad (2.19)$
                    $+ .1793\ (1 - L)(PHC_t) + .3246\ (1 - L)\ln(IP_t)$
                    $(6.98)\qquad\qquad\qquad\qquad (3.21)$
                    $- .6149 + r_{21t}$
                    (-1.66)

IV (1871–1913)
Sum of squares $= .0151$ mean of dep. var. $= 4.496$
standard error $= .0200\ Z(5) = 8.164$
LM(2) $= 0.99$

$\ln PDIFO_t)$ $= .7112 \ln(PDIFO_{t-1}) + .3626\ (\ln(WRCAN_t) - \ln(PROD_t))$
                    $(6.62)\qquad\qquad\qquad (3.56)$
                    $+ .1284 \ln(PDTMO_t) + .1470\ (1 - L)\ln(PHC_t)$
                    $(1.55)\qquad\qquad\qquad (3.62)$
                    $+ .6684\ (1 - L)\ln(IP_t) - .0653\ D89 - 2.034 + r_{22t}$
                    $(2.95)\qquad\qquad\qquad (-2.38)\quad (-1.77)$

IV (1871–1913)
sum of squares $= .0218$ mean of dep. var. $= 4.571$
standard error $= .0265\qquad Z(5) = 4.20$
LM(2) $= 1.34$

$\ln(PDII_t)$ $= .8449 \ln(PDTEM_t) + .4718 + r_{23t}$
                    $(3.75)\qquad\qquad\qquad (.416)$

IV (1871–1913)
sum of squares $= 1.998$ mean of dep. var. $= 4.728$
standard error $= .2207\qquad Z(5) = 1.75$
LM(2) $= 4.72$

$PDTE_t$ = $100.TEN_t/TE_t$

$PDTEC_t$ = $C2_t.PC_t$

$PDTEM_t$ = $100.(TEMXCN_t + TECN_t)/(TEMXC_t + TEC_t)$

$dln(PDTEMXC_t)$ = $.6222.dln(WWPDTEMF_t) + .45976.dln(WRCAN_t/$

$\qquad$ (6.15) $\qquad\qquad\qquad\qquad$ (4.00)

$\qquad PROD_t) - .3925.res_{t-1} - .6403$

$\qquad$ (−2.46) $\qquad\qquad$ (−2.47)

OLS (1871–1913)

sum of squares = .0151 mean of dep. var. = −.0051

standard error = .0197 $\quad$ Z(5) = 9.712

LM(2) = 1.64 $\qquad R^2$ = .792

where 'res' is the residual from:

$ln(PDTEMXC_t)$ = $.9458.ln(WWPDTEMXC_t) + .2951.ln(WRCAN_t/$

$\qquad PROD_t) + c$

$\qquad$ (CRDW = 1.232, DF = 4.180)

$PDTES_t$ = $PDTM_t$

$PDTM_t$ = $100.TMN_t/TM_t$

PHC_t = $C3_t.PC_t$

$PROD_t$ = $GDPA_t/CVEMP_t$

$PROF_t$ = $GDPY_t - YEMP_t - OY_t$

$RYEMP_t$ = $100.SD1_t.YEMP_t/PDCE_t$

$RXYEMP_t$ = $100.SD1_t.YXEMP_t/PDCE_t$

$RYXEXPX_t$ = $100.SD1_t.(PROF_t + OY_t)/PDGDP_t$

$SIFPM_t$ = $.94.(IFPM_{t-31} + IFPM_{t-32} + IFPM_{t-33} + IFPM_{t-34} +$

$\qquad IFPM_{t-35})$

$\qquad + r_{25t}$

$TBPCAN_t$ = $TEN_t - TMN_t + NPROP_t + TRANS_t$

$TBPCANC_t$ = $TBPCANC_{t-1} + TBPCAN_t$

TE_t = $TEMXC_t + TEC_t + TES_t$

$ln(TEC_t)$ = $.5264.ln(TEC_{t-1}) + .5272.ln(IPE_t) - .6252 + r_{27t}$

$\qquad$ (4.79) $\qquad\qquad$ (4.26) $\qquad\qquad$ (−3.74)

OLS (1870–1913)

Sum of Squares = .0964, Mean of Dep. Var. = 2.8029

Standard Error = .0964 $\qquad\qquad$ Z(5) = 3.94

DW = 1.776 $\qquad\qquad\qquad R^2$ = .993

$TECN_t$ = $TEC_t.PDTEC_t/100$

$dln(TEMXC_t)$ = $.2721.dln(IPA_t) + 1.008.dln(IPE_t)$

$\qquad$ (4.10) $\qquad\qquad\qquad$ (5.26)

$\qquad - .1383.dln(PHC_{t-1} - 1/PDTEMC_{t-1})$

$\qquad$ (−2.87)

$\qquad - .5996.res_{t-1} + -.0967 + r_{28t}$

$\qquad$ (−4.03) $\qquad\qquad$ (−4.58)

OLS (1871–1913)

Sum of Squares = .0388 Mean of Dep. Var. = .0258

Standard Error = .0320 $\qquad\qquad$ Z(5) = 10.44

LM(2) = 3.310 $\qquad\qquad\qquad R^2$ = .66

where 'res' is the residual from:

$\ln(TEMXC_t)$ $= .3228.\ln(IPA_t) + 1.3186.\ln(IPE_t) - .2291.\ln(PHC_t/PDTEMXC_t)$
$- .3948.\ln((WRCAN_t/PROD_t)/PDTEMXC_t)$
$- .03867.t + c$
$(CRDW = 1.127, DF = 4.068)$

$TEMXCN_t$ $= TEMXCW_t.Q.PDTEMXC_t/100$
TEN_t $= TEMXCN_t + TECN_t + TESN_t$
TES_t $= .5914.TES_{t-1} + .5205.IPEUR_t + 14.2267 + r_{30}$
$\quad\quad (6.09) \quad\quad\quad (4.58) \quad\quad\quad (4.07)$

OLS (1871–1913)
Sum of Squares $= 281.489$ Mean of Dep. var. $= 92.8484$
Standard Error $= 2.6528$ $\quad\quad\quad Z(5) = 1.60$
DW $= 1.692$ $\quad\quad\quad\quad\quad\quad R^2 = .991$

$TFEFC_t$ $= CE_t + GVCE_t + IF_t + II_t + TE_t - TXCB_t$
TM_t $= TMFDT_t + TMO_t$
$\ln(TMFDT_t)$ $= .6702 \ln(TMFDT_{t-1})$
$\quad\quad (9.67)$
$\quad\quad + .2151 \ln(CEFDT_t + .3.CEMF_t - 3.XGAGR_t)$
$\quad\quad (4.01)$
$\quad\quad - .1561 \ln(PDTMFDT_t/PDCEFDT_t) + 0.4651 + r_{31t}$
$\quad\quad (-2.19) \quad\quad\quad\quad\quad\quad\quad\quad (2.93)$
$\quad\quad rho = -.4697$
$\quad\quad\quad (-3.01)$

ALS (1873–1913)
sum of squares $= 0.0369$ mean of dep. var. $= 5.0603$
standard error $= 0.032$ $\quad\quad\quad Z(5) = 2.306$
DW $= 1.998$

$TMFDTN_t$ $= TMFDT_t.PDTMFDT_t/100$
TMN_t $= TMFDTN_t + TMO_t$
$\ln(TMO_t)$ $= .2087 \ln(TFEFC_t - YP_t/SDGDPA_t) + .0883 \ln(TEMXC_t)$
$\quad\quad (7.60) \quad\quad\quad\quad\quad\quad\quad\quad\quad (1.84)$
$\quad\quad + .0027 t.\ln(TEMXC_t) - .3767 \ln(PDTMO_t/PDGDP_t)$
$\quad\quad (11.9) \quad\quad\quad\quad\quad\quad (-7.81)$
$\quad\quad + 3.463 + r_{32t}$
$\quad\quad (12.3)$

IV (1871–1913)
sum of squares $= 0.0111$ mean of dep. var. $= 5.4619$
standard error $= 0.0171$ $\quad\quad Z(5) = 6.76$
DW $= 2.340$

$TMON_t$ $= TMO_t.PDTMO_t/100$
$TXCB_t$ $= 100.TXCBN_t/PDTXCB_t$
$UNEMP_t$ $= WPOP_t - CVEMP_t - ARMF_t$
$WPOP_t$ $= V1_t.NPT_t$

$\text{dln(WRCAN}_t)$ $= .8044 \ (1-L) \ \ln(\text{PDCE}_t)$
$\qquad$ (4.75)
$\qquad$ $+ .1330 \ (1-L) \ \ln(\text{PROF}_t/(\text{GDPN}_t.\text{SD1}_t)$
$\qquad$ (1.90)
$\qquad$ $- .0638 \ \ln(\text{UR}_t) - \ln(\text{UR}_t + \text{UR}_{t-1} + \text{UR}_{t-2})$
$\qquad$ (-4.68)
$\qquad$ $+ r_{33t}$

IV (1871–1913)
sum of squares $= .0101$ mean of dep. var. $= .0097$
standard error $= .0161$ $Z(5) = 5.81$
DW $= 2.02$

$\ln(\text{WWPDTEMF}_t)$ $= .6141 \ \ln(\text{WWPDTEMF}_{t-1}) + .6226 \ \ln(\text{PDTMO}_t)$
$\qquad$ (5.12) $\qquad\qquad\qquad$ (6.52)
$\qquad$ $- .2963 \ \ln(\text{PDTMO}_{t-1}) + .2232 + r_{34t}$
$\qquad$ (-2.40) $\qquad\qquad$ (1.50)

OLS (1872–1913)
sum of squares $= .0294$ mean of dep. var. $= 4.5919$
standard error $= .0278$ $Z(5) = 4.75$
LM(2) $= 4.82$ $\qquad$ $R^2 = .958$

$\ln(\text{XGAGR}_t)$ $= .1820 \ \ln(\text{CEFDT}_t + .3.\text{CEMF}_t - 3.\text{TMFDT}_t)$
$\qquad$ (2.05)
$\qquad$ $+ .0021t + 3.8095 + r_{35t}$
$\qquad$ (1.40) $\qquad$ (10.9)

IV (1871–1913)
sum of squares $= 0.092$ mean of dep. var. $= 4.6153$
standard error $= 0.0475$ $\qquad$ $Z(5) = 4.88$
DW $= 1.862$

YEMP_t $= \text{SF}_t.\text{WRCAN}_t.\text{CVEMP}_t$

$\ln(\text{YP}_t)$ $= (\ln(.98.(\text{WPOP}_t - \text{ARMF}_t)) + .28.\ln(\text{KIF}_{t-1}) - .05.\text{D93}_t +$
$\qquad$ $1.27.\text{TECH}_t - 3.13)/1.25$

YXEMP_t $= \text{PROF}_t + \text{OY}_t + \text{NPROP}_t$

where $\qquad$ ln $\qquad$ natural logarithm.
$\qquad\qquad$ dln $\qquad$ first logarithmic difference.
$\qquad\qquad$ diff $\qquad$ first difference.
$\qquad\qquad$ OLS $\qquad$ Ordinary least squares.
$\qquad\qquad$ IV $\qquad$ Instrumental variables.
$\qquad\qquad$ ALS $\qquad$ Autoregressive least squares (Cochrane-Orcutt).
$\qquad\qquad$ Z(n) $\qquad$ Post sample stability test static for (n years)
$\qquad\qquad$ LM(n) $\qquad$ Lagrange multiplier statistic for up to nth degree
$\qquad\qquad\qquad\qquad$ serial correlation.
$\qquad\qquad$ DW $\qquad$ Durbin-Watson statistic.
$\qquad\qquad$ DF $\qquad$ Dickey-Fuller test statistic.
$\qquad\qquad$ CRDW $\qquad$ Cointegrating Durbin-Watson statistic.
Estimation period is given in parentheses.

Appendix 3 Data sources

All data is taken from Feinstein (1972) except:

a   Dissaggregated Expenditure and Price Data:
   Based on Prest and Adams (1954) and Jeffries and Walters (1955), together with
   unpublished data prepared for Feinstein (1972) and data from the Statistical
   Abstract for the United Kingdom. For details of compilation see Blake (1988).

b   World Price of Manufactures
   Taken from Lewis (1978).

c   Migration Data
   Green and Urquhart (1976).

8 Money and interest rates in Britain from 1870 to 1913

TERENCE C. MILLS and

GEOFFREY E. WOOD

Introduction

Although the phenomenon known today as the Gibson Paradox had been identified and discussed well before the years examined in this chapter (see Cagan, 1984), it was on the basis of data gathered during these years that the phenomenon received its name (from Keynes, 1930), and was explained (by Fisher, 1896). Since then, several further explanations have been advanced. The aim of this chapter is two-fold. We examine the impact of money on output, prices and interest rates in this period, and we use the results of that examination to reconsider Fisher's explanation of the famous paradox.

The plan of the chapter is as follows. First, there is a brief exposition of the theory which organises the paper. There is then a survey of previous work on the Gibson Paradox. After summarising the questions prompted by that research, the data are described. That prepares the way for the statistical work. The chapter then concludes with a discussion of the results.

Money and interest rates

Here we set out the effects of a once and for all shift from one steady rate of money growth to another. (There is, of course, no implication that this is how money behaved in these years: this is purely a device to simplify exposition.) Because of data limitations, we are almost exclusively concerned with the effects of such a shift on the nominal yield of a nominal asset, but we do at points also note the behaviour of certain other yields. The monetary change is unanticipated, but when it occurs, is fully perceived. Also for expository simplicity, it is assumed that the price level is initially constant and is initially expected to remain so.

On the assumption that the general level of prices is slower to change than both nominal interest rates and output, the effects of such a monetary change can be divided into four stages. First, there may be a loanable funds effect, which is succeeded by a liquidity effect. Output then starts to move, and that affects interest rates. There is then an effect on the general level of prices and on price level expectations; this latter in turn produces the ultimate impact of the monetary change on the nominal yield on nominal assets. These various stages are described in order.

LOANABLE FUNDS EFFECT

This comes about because revenue accrues to the issuers of new money. This revenue may be spent on consumption goods but, if the revenue is used to augment wealth, there will be an increase in the supply of loanable funds. As it is being assumed that inflation expectations do not change, this increased supply affects both real and nominal yields on both real and nominal assets. Furthermore, because the shift in money growth was unanticipated, *ex post* yields on all types of assets now differ from *ex ante* ones.

LIQUIDITY PREFERENCE EFFECT

This effect is also an initial reaction to the changed rate of money growth but, unlike the loanable funds effect, it does not depend on choices concerning the disposition of the revenue from money creation, and it produces a sustained decline rather than an immediate drop in rates. (Again, because of the above assumptions, rates on all types of assets). Rates behave in this way because we have moved to a higher growth rate of money. So long as no other variable except interest rates can change, there is a continually rising ratio of real (and nominal) money to output. To induce this to be held, the nominal rate of interest has to fall, and it keeps on falling until the third effect, the income effect, comes into play.

THE INCOME EFFECT

We now have lower real and nominal interest rates on all types of asset. The prices of the services of assets have therefore risen relative to the prices of the assets which supply these services. Nominal expenditure therefore rises, and as prices (including money wages) have not yet changed, so do nominal and real income. This increases the quantity of real cash balances demanded at every opportunity cost, and hence as income rises, the nominal yield on nominal assets also rises, gradually reversing the liquidity effect. (As price expectations have by assumption still not changed, real yields on real assets and real yields on nominal assets also rise.) All these rates rise until they are back at their pre-monetary expansion level, for only then is the stimulus to expenditure dissipated.

PRICE EXPECTATIONS

A higher rate of money growth has been superimposed on an unchanged real economy. The only way, since no real variable changes, that the increased nominal money stock will be held is if prices rise. They rise eventually at the same rate as the rate of growth of money. When prices are rising at this rate, and if price expectations remain unchanged, real rates of interest on all assets must fall again. Price expectations must therefore change until ultimately the inflation is fully anticipated. At that point, nominal yields on nominal assets (both *ex ante* and *ex post*) will have risen by an amount equal to the rate of inflation, while real yields (again both *ex ante* and *ex post*) on real and on nominal assets remain unchanged.

It may seem surprising that scholars wrote of an inflation expectations effect, and that we entertain it as an empirical possibility, in a period of commodity based money. One should, of course, remark that when some authors (such as Henry Thornton (1802), and in his two 1811 speeches on the Bullion Report) wrote, Britain was engaged in the Napoleonic wars. The gold standard had been suspended, and resumption was far from certain. But later authors – notably Irving Fisher, but also Alfred Marshall – paid great attention to the inflation expectations effect.[1] As we shall argue below, there was good reason for this, even when the gold standard was not suspended. We return to this after the empirical work.

The Gibson Paradox

Over the period 1870 to 1913 there appears to be a positive association between the nominal interest rate and the level of prices, an association which Keynes (1930) called the *Gibson Paradox*, after A.H. Gibson, who first drew attention to the relationship.[2]

This association between the price *level* and some measure of the nominal interest rate is not readily deducible from any standard classical model. Double the money supply (and thus the price level), and all real variables, including the rate of interest – which is a variable having the dimension $ per $ per time – are homogeneous of degree zero with respect to such a comparative static change in the nominal variables. What, then, can explain the association between the price level and the interest rate? The answer most in accordance with the theory outlined above was first advanced by Irving Fisher (1896; 1907; 1930) and later given qualified support by Friedman and Schwartz (1982). They argued that because a move from one fully anticipated inflation rate to another would, even with the real return on physical capital unchanged, alter the nominal yield on nominal assets, the *appearance* of a relationship between nominal yields and the *level* (as opposed to the rate of change) of prices could be produced. This relationship would appear if inflation expectations adjusted to inflation with a lag, so that the longer inflation persisted (and thus the higher the price level rose), the higher would the nominal yield rise.

This is not, however, the only explanation that has been offered. Wicksell, and later Keynes, proposed an explanation which was also within the traditional framework but posited a movement in the real rate of return on physical assets. According to both Wicksell (1907) and Keynes (1930), nominal rates on nominal assets were pulled down by a downward drift in the natural rate of interest, reflecting a decline in the marginal physical productivity of capital. This occurred in the first half of the period, and was replaced in the second half by a rise as the American mid- and far-west were opened up. Price level movements were in turn induced because the market rate lagged behind the natural rate.

Some explanations entirely reject this traditional framework by denying the influence of money on prices. Mathias (1983: 367) wrote as follows:

Many vital factors do not fit this thesis. Bullion dealers reported no shortage of gold: the reserves of the Bank of England stayed high . . . Furthermore – a key fact – interest rates on Lombard Street stayed low – consols were under 3 per cent per annum yield and the discount rate between 2 and 3.5 per cent per annum. These depressed interest rates . . . suggest an exactly contrary thesis to the monetary one – that excess savings were seeking investment outlets; that money was overplentiful in relation to investment opportunities of every sort.

Throughout that quotation there is a confusion, made explicit in the last sentence, between money and credit. But what seems to be implied is that there was a persistent abundance of money (an excess supply?), but that *nominal* interest rates stayed low because of *real* factors, with money not affecting prices. What then did determine prices? Phelps-Brown and Ozga (1955) advanced an explanation, which was later taken up by Coppock (1961). Phelps-Brown and Ozga argued that when industrial production grew more slowly than the production of primary goods, primary goods prices fell, and exerted a downward cost-push on prices, with the converse happening when the growth rate of industrial production exceeded that of primary production. Coppock adopted this view, and explained the co-movement of prices and interest rates as a result of the slowing of Britain's growth in the 1870s not being offset in its impact on world industrial production until the German and American growth of the 1890s.

Three comparatively recent studies return to the position that money growth determined the trend of prices, and that the behaviour of interest rates has to be reconciled with that. These are Sargent (1973), Harley (1977), and Friedman and Schwartz (1982). All start from Irving Fisher and

his argument that the phenomenon was produced by inflationary expectations, which depended on past inflation, changing only very slowly. But as
Sargent put it, this explanation of the Gibson Paradox may be 'really only a
redefinition of it' (Sargent, 1973: 387), for Cagan had earlier (1972) pointed
out that the mean adjustment lags estimated by Fisher do seem remarkably
long – ten to thirty *years*. After extensive analysis and empirical work,
Sargent (1973: 447) reached the following main conclusions,

within the context of bivariate models, interest and inflation appear mutually to
influence one another. One implication of this finding is that Irving Fisher's
explanation of the Gibson paradox, which posits a unidirectional influence flowing
from inflation to interest, is inadequate.

Harley (1977) robustly supports a 'Fisherian' explanation. He argues
(p. 73) that 'the money market adjusted to price expectations, and there was
little effect on real interest rates', and that 'the decline in the market rate of
interest in the 1870s can be fully accounted for by price expectations and is
fully consistent with a monetary explanation of price trends'.

Next we come to Friedman and Schwartz (1982). At the beginning of
their chapter (chapter 10) on money and interest rates, they remark of the
Gibson Paradox (p. 479) that 'we are left with no single satisfactory
interpretation of that supposedly well documented phenomenon'. Fair, but
there is more than that to what they find. First, they deduce *analytically* the
length of lag for Fisher's explanation to be correct: 'A close correlation
between rising prices and rising interest rates requires that the time it takes
for people to adjust their anticipations must be roughly comparable to the
duration of long swings in prices' (p. 547). They also observe, following a
suggestion by Klein (1975), that in some money supply regimes it may be
perfectly sensible to forecast inflation on the basis of past price level
behaviour.

They support Fisher's explanation for the Gibson Paradox, partly by
noting that the studies which rejected the explanation actually included in
their data set periods when the paradox did not occur, partly by rejecting
(on Cagan's grounds[3] and also by use of their own series for the real rate of
interest) the Wicksell explanation, and partly by finding shorter lags than
Fisher on price expectations. Their explanation of the end of the Gibson
Paradox is derived from the same analytical framework: there was a change
in the monetary standard, which produced greater incentives to forecast
future price movements.

Finally in this section, we come to two explanations of the paradox
which, unlike those outlined above, we do not examine in some detail
subsequently. The reasons for this subsequent neglect are set out after we
have summarised these explanations. The first is that of Benjamin and

Kochin (1984). This is in the Keynes-Wicksell tradition, in that it gives movements in the real rate of interest a central part in the explanation. Benjamin and Kochin claim that Gibson's paradox was the product of two factors, both of them associated with wars. Wartime fiscal policy lies behind both. These policies raised real rates of interest, as the temporary squeeze on private consumption increased the real rate of time preference. Secondly, as there was inflationary monetary expansion to facilitate the financing of wartime deficits, both nominal interest rates and the general level of prices rose.

The other of these two explanations for the paradox is the most recent. It was advanced by Barsky and Summers (1988) and is both very simple and very elegant. Gold, they say, has two classes of use, monetary and non-monetary. Suppose there is a rise in the real rate of interest – there is no need to specify the reason. As gold is a long-lived asset, this lowers the value of non-monetary gold in terms of other goods. The value of monetary gold, however, is held fixed by the monetary authorities. Accordingly, there is substitution from non-monetary to monetary gold, and therefore an increase in the quantity of money. That in turn produces a rise in the price level and in the nominal rate of interest.

We do not deny that either, and indeed both, of these explanations contributed something to producing the phenomenon called the Gibson Paradox. What we do deny is that either of them is capable fully of explaining the paradox, and thus making other explanations redundant. First Benjamin and Kochin. They claim as evidence for – indeed, it is an essential part of their explanation that the paradox held only in wartime. We, and numerous other authors, find it exists in years of peace.[4]

Turning now to Barsky and Summers, their exposition is based on the premise of a fixed stock of gold. As they acknowledge, gold production, i.e. addition to that stock, was substantial in the years 1870 to 1913. For this period, therefore, other factors must be considered.[5] These are the reasons that attention is paid to the 'traditional' explanations for the paradox in the empirical work that follows.[6]

Before turning to that empirical work, it is desirable to consider the implications of economic openness. Could Britain's being an open economy have produced, or contributed to, the paradox? So far as we can discover, no previous author has considered this explicitly.

In fact, this neglect, albeit perhaps brought about by default rather than intention, is justified. Our reasons for this are as follows. First, Britain remained an open economy after the phenomenon faded away. Second, the phenomenon persisted through periods both of the gold standard and of suspensions of that standard; it was thus unaffected by exchange rate regime. (This is important, as an explanation can be constructed which depends on a floating exchange rate – a monetary expansion depreciates the currency, thereby quickly having a positive impact on the price level, while also raising inflation expectations and thereby bond yields.)

In view of this, we now proceed to empirical matters with no further regard to openness or exchange rate regimes.

The data

Previous studies have used a variety of money supply definitions, each of which has a number of important defects. With the publication of Capie and Webber (1985), many of these defects were removed; that volume (tables I.(1) and I.(3)) was the source of our money stock data. Because the relationships between money and the other variables could perhaps be influenced by the definition of money used, two series are considered here; the narrow, money base, definition, denoted M0, and the broader series, M3. For exact definitions of these, see Capie and Webber (1985).

The interest rate employed is the yield on Consols, which has been used almost exclusively as the measure of the long-term rate of interest in this period. Series for short rates also exist, of course, but these are not as well suited to the examination of hypotheses about, or depending upon, the Fisher effect. The usual Consol yield series, given in Capie and Webber (1985: table III.10) for example, has, as both Harley (1976) and Capie and Webber (1985: 316–20) point out, traditionally been miscalculated for the years 1880 to 1903. This miscalculation leads to an overestimation of the true yield for two reasons. The price of Consols in this period rose above par, thus increasing the possibility of redemption at par and decreasing the true yield, and the details of Goschen's conversion of the National Debt in 1889 affected the way in which Consol yields were calculated. We therefore employ a revised Consol yield series, that given in the appendix to Harley (1977), although related work reported in Capie, Mills and Wood (1991) has used both this and the traditional series in similar exercises and found little difference in the results so obtained.

The output series used is Feinstein's (1972) compromise estimate of GDP, and hence his implicit GDP deflator is used as the price series. While there has been some discussion recently over the reliability of this output series – see the interchange between Greasley (1986, 1989) and Feinstein (1989) and the discussion in Crafts, Leybourne and Mills (1989a) – it would still seem to be the best that is currently available.

Annual observations for all series are available from 1870 to 1913, except for M3, whose initial (1870) observation is missing. Detailed descriptive discussion of the data and univariate analysis of the individual series is to be found in Capie, Mills and Wood (1991). In particular, it is found, using a variety of methods, that the logarithms of both money series, output, and prices are all integrated processes of order one, i.e. $I(1)$, while the interest rate itself is $I(1)$, findings that are confirmed by Taylor (1989).

The empirical work

In order to examine the impact of money on output, prices and interest rates, and to allow for possible feedbacks between these series, multivariate modelling is obviously required. Denoting the logarithms of money, output and prices as m, y, and p, respectively, and the untransformed interest rate as R, we then wish to model the vector $x = (m,y,p,R)'$.

Although each of the individual series in x has been shown to be $I(1)$, it is not necessarily the case that they will need first differencing when being modelled jointly. This result was shown in the time series literature by Lutkepohl (1982) and Tjostheim and Paulsen (1982), but is now more familiar to econometricians as the condition of *cointegration* (Granger, 1981; Engle and Granger, 1987). Put briefly, and in the context of the current application, a vector x is said to be cointegrated if each of its components are $I(1)$ but some linear combination of them, $z = \alpha'x$ say, is $I(0)$, i.e. z is stationary although the components of x are individually nonstationary.[7] Thus, although each of the components of x tend to drift over time, there is a sense in which they are related together through a stable long-run relationship. The extent to which the components are away from this 'equilibrium' is given by the vector z, which may then be interpreted as the 'equilibrium error'.

The vector α is known as the *cointegrating vector*, and may not be unique. Indeed, for a q-dimensional vector x ($q = 4$ in the application here), there can be up to $q - 1$ cointegrating vectors. While this non-uniqueness has been a problem with empirical applications of cointegration, Johansen (1988) has recently developed a maximum likelihood technique of estimating *all* of the cointegrating vectors for a q-dimensional vector x. This has the added advantages of being able to test which of these vectors are significant and to allow restrictions on the cointegrating parameter vectors to be tested.

For the x-vector containing M0 as the money supply, standard tests of cointegration reject the hypothesis that the variables $m0$, q, p and R are cointegrated: analysis should, given the univariate properties of the individual series, use the first differences of each of the variables. When M3 is used as the money supply, however, similar tests cannot reject that $m3$, q, p, and R are, in fact, cointegrated. Moreover, Taylor (1989), using the Johansen (1988) procedure, finds that there is a unique, statistically significant, cointegrating vector. After normalising on $m3$, and imposing unrejected parameter restrictions, he finds that the cointegrating vector is estimated to be $\alpha' = (1, -1, -1, 0.05)$, i.e.

$$z3_t = m3_t - q_t - p_t + 0.05R_t,$$

thus embodying the long-run equilibrium relationships of unit output and price elasticities of money demand and a small, but negative, interest elasticity.

Given that the vectors containing M0 and M3 have different cointegration properties, they need to be analysed in somewhat different ways. We thus consider first modelling the vector $x0_t = (mO_t, q_t, p_t, R_t)$, before analysing the vector $x3_t$, defined in an analogous fashion.

Model containing M0

Since the components making up the $x0_t$ vector have been shown not to be cointegrated, it is appropriate to model the first differences of the series, e.g. $\nabla mO_t = mO_t - mO_{t-1}$. A popular method is to employ a *vector autoregression* (VAR).[8] As is well known, interpreting a VAR as a structural model is hazardous when there are contemporaneous correlations between the innovations of each equation, since an *a priori* recursive causal ordering has to be imposed on the innovations, and this may not correspond to a meaningful model that can be derived from economic theory; see, *inter alia*, Cooley and LeRoy (1985), Leamer (1985) and Bernanke (1986).

This is potentially important since, with annual data, we would expect there to be at least some large contemporaneous correlations between residuals (innovations). The approach taken here is thus similar to those of Blanchard and Watson (1986) and Bernanke (1986). Standard VAR techniques are first employed to determine the lag length k in the model

$$\nabla x_t = \sum_{i=1}^{k} A_i \nabla x_{t-i} + u_t, \tag{1}$$

where the innovations u_t are serially uncorrelated and only cross-correlated contemporaneously, i.e.

$$E(u_t u_t') = \Omega,$$

a positive definite variance-covariance matrix. The estimate of Ω and considerations of economic theory then enable us to specify a structural model accounting for the observed contemporaneous correlations between the elements of u_t, in effect allowing (1) to be written as

$$\nabla x_t = \sum_{i=0}^{k} A_i \nabla x_{t-i} + e_t, \tag{2}$$

where $E(e_t e_t')$ is a diagonal matrix. For consistent estimation of (2), of course, enough identifying restrictions on A_0 need to be imposed.

The lag length was determined as $k=1$, and the following structural model was then developed, embodying the large contemporaneous correlations observed between the output and price innovations and price and interest rate innovations: the former, being negative, is assumed to capture a contemporaneous output-price trade-off in the aggregate supply function, the latter, being positive, the Gibson Paradox itself. Restricting the other elements of A_0 to be zero achieves identification and, indeed, the model is almost recursive, with mO_t and q_t being predetermined and a contemporaneous causal ordering running $q \rightarrow p \rightarrow R$.

Aggregate Demand

$$\nabla q_t = .0222 - .327\nabla mO_{t-1} - .0789\nabla R_{t-1}, \; R^2 = .229, \; s.e. = .0247$$
$$(.0039) \; (.127) \qquad (.0338)$$

Aggregate Supply

$$\nabla p_t = -.355\nabla q_t + .415\nabla q_{t-1} + .375\nabla p_{t-1}, \; R^2 = .318, \; s.e. = .0218$$
$$(.105) \qquad (.106) \qquad (.131)$$

Demand for Money

$$\nabla mO_t = .304\nabla q_{t-1} + .255\nabla mO_{t-1}, \; R^2 = .063, \; s.e. = .0276$$
$$(.128) \qquad (.133)$$

Gibson Paradox

$$\nabla R_t = 1.598\nabla p_t + .425\nabla R_{t-1}, \; R^2 = .420, \; s.e. = .0862$$
$$(0.496) \qquad (.117)$$

While each of these individual equations would seem to have sensible specifications and plausible parameter estimates, the full dynamic response of each variable to innovations in the others can only be ascertained by computing the relevant *impulse response (IR) functions*, obtained from the implied moving average representation of (2), i.e.

$$\nabla x_t = e_t + \sum_{i=1}^{\infty} B_i e_{t-i}, \qquad (3)$$

where the B_i are functions of the A_i's: see, for example, Mills (1990a: ch. 14).
The *cumulative* IR functions, calculated from

$$x_t = e_t + \sum_{i=1}^{\infty} \left(\sum_{j=1}^{i} B_j \right) e_{t-i}, \qquad (4)$$

are shown in figures 8.1 to 8.4 and depict the cumulative response of each normalised variable to a unit innovation in each of the other equations.

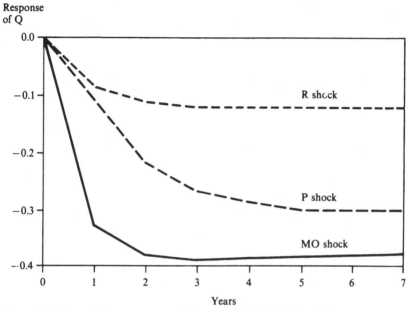

Figure 8.1   Cumulative response of Q to shocks in MO, P and R.

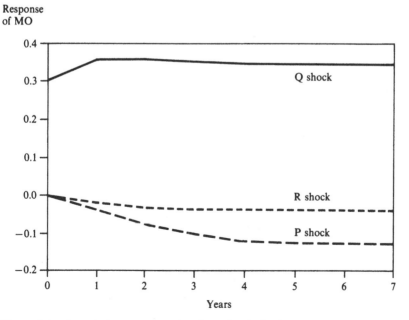

Figure 8.2   Cumulative response of MO to shocks in Q, P and R.

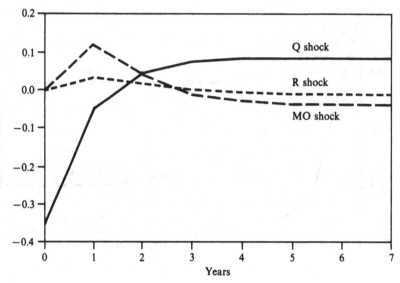

Figure 8.3   Cumulative response of P to shocks in Q, MO and R.

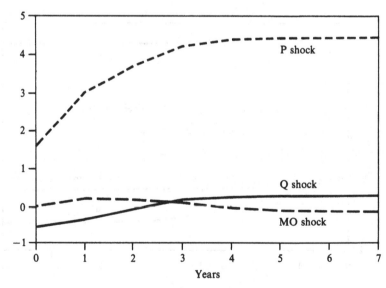

Figure 8.4   Cumulative response of R to shocks in Q, MO and P.

M0 shocks, whether produced by temporary demand or supply fluctuations, have a negative impact on output, an initially small positive, but an overall negative, effect on the price level, and almost no effect whatsoever on interest rates. What little effect there is (a positive response for the first two years) is an indirect one, running from money through both output and prices. There are a number of important feedbacks from, and interactions between, the other variables, however. Output (or aggregate demand) shocks have a positive impact on M0, both immediate and cumulative, and while they have initially negative impacts on both the price level and interest rates, the cumulative response is positive in both cases. Price shocks have negative effects on output and M0, but a large positive impact on interest rates. Interest rate shocks have negative effects on the other three variables in the system. All responses are essentially completed within a maximum of five years, with the most powerful effects being observed in the first three years.[9]

Model containing M3

As discussed above, the vector $x3_t$ is cointegrated with a unique cointegrating vector. From Engle and Granger (1987) and Hylleberg and Mizon (1989), a VAR representation,

$$\mathbf{x}_t = \sum_{i=1}^{p} A_i \mathbf{x}_{t-i} + \mathbf{u}_t, \tag{5}$$

will exist such that the matrix of long-run multipliers, $A(1) = 1 - \Sigma_{i=1}^{p} A_i = \gamma \alpha'$, is of rank 1, where γ is a 4×1 matrix of rank 1 such that $B(1)\gamma = 0$, $B(1)$ being the sum of the coefficients in the vector moving average (Wold representation) of $\nabla \mathbf{x}_t$ given by (3). There then exists an equivalent *error correction mechanism (ECM)*,

$$\nabla \mathbf{x}_t = \sum_{i=1}^{p-1} A_i^{\dagger} \nabla \mathbf{x}_{t-i} - \gamma \mathbf{z}_{t-1} + \mathbf{u}_t \tag{6}$$

where $A_i^{\dagger} = -\Sigma_{j=i+1}^{p} A_j$, $i = 1, 2, \ldots, p-1$ and $\mathbf{z}_t = \alpha' \mathbf{x}_t$.

As in the system containing M0, the lag length p was first determined (here $p = 2$) and then the observed contemporaneous cross-correlations were used to develop a structural model. As in the previous system, a contemporaneous inflation-output trade-off and a Gibson Paradox relationship were observed. Additionally, relationships were found between M3 and both output and interest rates. Given previous research findings (Mills and Wood, 1978, 1982), these were taken to be indicative of a structural demand for money equation, thus leading to the following model:

Aggregate Demand

$$\nabla q_t = -.0937\nabla R_{t-1} - .00948z3_{t-1},\ R^2 = .133,\ s.e. = .0262$$
$$\quad\quad\ (.0360)\quad\quad\ (.00201)$$

Aggregate Supply

$$\nabla p_t = -.339\nabla q_t + .365\nabla q_{t-1} + .357\nabla p_{t-1},\ R^2 = .269,\ s.e. = .0213$$
$$\quad\quad\ (.106)\quad\ (.107)\quad\quad\ (.132)$$

Demand for Money

$$\nabla m3_t = -.616 + .246\nabla q_t + .162\nabla q_{t-1} - .0448\nabla R_t + .235\nabla m3_{t-1}$$
$$\quad\quad\ (.098)\ (.069)\quad\ (.074)\quad\quad\ (.0169)\quad\quad\ (.079)$$

$$-.314z3_{t-1},\ R^2 = .703,\ s.e. = .0125$$
$$(.050)$$

Gibson Paradox

$$\nabla R_t = 1.951\nabla p_t + .436\nabla R_{t-1},\ R^2 = .449,\ s.e. = .0850$$
$$\quad\quad (0.544)\quad\quad (.119)$$

The Gibson Paradox and aggregate supply equations are of the same specification as those in the M0 model. Major differences are found in the aggregate demand and demand for money equations however. A fundamental difference is that both equations contain the error correction term $z3_{t-1}$ while, in addition, both ∇q_t and ∇R_t appear in the demand for money function. A constant term also appears in the demand for money function. Although this may seem a minor extension, it has an important implication when taken in conjunction with the cointegration properties of $x3_t$. As Stock and Watson (1988) and Hylleberg and Mizon (1989) show, the presence of a unique cointegrating vector *and* a non-zero mean in u_t implies that there exists a *common trends representation*,

$$x3_t = \mu t + F\tau_t + v_t,$$

of the variables, where F is a 4×3 matrix of rank 3, τ_t is a 3×1 vector which is a linear transformation of $u_1 + u_2 + \ldots + u_t$ and v_t is a linear combination of the u_t's. The individual series thus contain both deterministic and stochastic trend components, there being three common stochastic trends (cf. the univariate models of output developed for a similar sample period in Crafts, Leybourne and Mills (1989a) and Mills (1991b)).

Again the cumulative impulse response functions may be calculated, these being shown in figures 8.5 to 8.8. M3 demand shocks have a very similar effect to M0 shocks, eliciting only small responses from the other variables. The other three shocks, aggregate demand (output), aggregate

Response
of Q

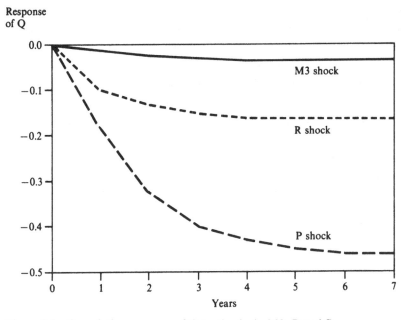

Figure 8.5   Cumulative response of Q to shocks in M3, P and R.

Response
of M3

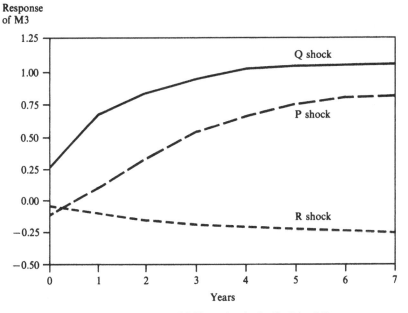

Figure 8.6   Cumulative response of M3 to shocks in Q, P and R.

Response
of P

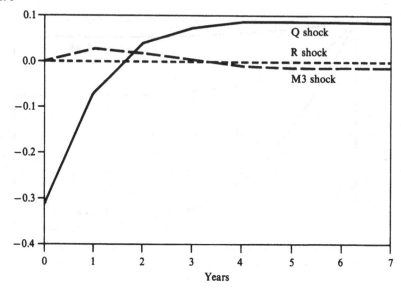

Figure 8.7 Cumulative response of P to shocks in Q, M3 and R.

Response
of R

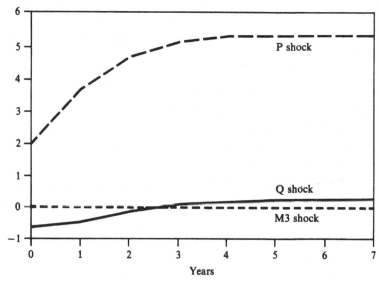

Figure 8.8 Cumulative response of R to shocks in Q, M3 and P.

supply (price), and interest rate shocks, also elicit responses that are similar to those found in the M0 system. The one exception is that the response of M3 is, in each case, somewhat larger in absolute magnitude and, for a price shock, is now positive.

These results for the system containing M3 may be compared with those obtained in the related study of Capie, Mills and Wood (1991). There the cointegration of the $x3_t$ vector was not imposed on the vector autoregression, with the result that M3 was found to be purely passive. As pointed out in both Engle and Granger (1987) and Engle and Yoo (1987), omission of the error correction term from the VAR can constitute a serious model misspecification, and evidence of this is thus provided here, although the major properties of the system are essentially unaltered (see also Mac-Donald and Kearney (1987) for a similar finding using money and income data from the modern era).

Conclusions

This chapter started by briefly setting out the traditional theory of the impact of monetary fluctuations, and then linked this analysis with a series of questions prompted by the substantial body of work on the Gibson Paradox. It is convenient to follow that order in summarising the results.

First, and worthy of emphasis, there is no initial negative effect of either definition of money on the observed nominal yield on nominal assets. This does not mean there is no such effect, but it does mean that, if there is, it is over within our unit of observation, one year (data limitations preclude using a shorter period of observation). This result implies that deviations from the aggregate supply curve which were produced by monetary shocks were over within one year. Whether this is quick or slow depends on prior expectations; it is, however, consistent with Goodhart's (1982) conjecture that only large monetary shocks affect output, for there was very little in the way of monetary disturbance in this period. So far, though, this remains a plausible conjecture looking for an explanation and more general empirical support.

Second, there is a positive reaction of interest rates to money shocks after one year, so that the income effect is indeed observed. Nevertheless, the long-run response of interest rates to a money shock is essentially zero.

Although admittedly containing some oddities, these results clearly do conflict with some explanations of the Gibson Paradox. The existence of the paradox is confirmed, thus further undermining Benjamin and Kochin's (1984) explanation. The persistence of the effect after 1896, when the world stock of monetary gold started to grow substantially, similarly qualifies the Barsky and Summers (1988) explanation. What of the remainder? We disagree with Sargent's (1973) result that prices were affected by interest rate shocks; that was his main objection to Fisher. M0's being exogenous to the system, along with Capie and Webber's (1985) results on the determinants of money growth, weakens the Keynes-Wicksell explanation in exactly the same way as Cagan's (1965) findings on the money multiplier did for the United States. The causal effect of money eliminates the non-monetary explanations.

These findings all constitute 'negative support' for Fisher, by disagreeing with the rival explanations. Can we add any positive support? There are two items. Interest rates rise with money. This, of course, may be the combination of income and inflation expectation effects, perhaps predominantly the first. More telling, the lag lengths between money, prices and interest rates have been shortened substantially over those found in other studies, and thought to be a puzzle by many authors. We doubt that anything more can be said on the basis of detailed analysis of the dynamics of nineteenth century data, and must therefore conclude with a somewhat tentative summary. The results of this paper are inconsistent with all explanations of the Gibson Paradox except Fisher's; and they are consistent with his.

Notes

1 The full process described here, *including the inflation expectations effect*, was also described in Cairns (1874) and Mill (1848). Francis Horner (1802) provides a most succinct statement of the process.
2 An admirable, and brief, survey of explanations of the paradox can be found in Cagan (1984).
3 Wicksell had attributed the decline in the real rate of interest in the first part of the period to an expansion in bank-created money increasing the supply of savings. But Cagan (1965) found that, at any rate for the US, changes in the monetary base dominated money growth.
4 In particular, Mills (1990b) provides a detailed criticism of the econometric methodology followed by Benjamin and Kochin. In that paper it is shown explicitly using data from 1729 onwards that the Gibson Paradox appears even when a variable measuring real defence expenditure is included in the model.
5 It should be observed that there are numerous other puzzles in the Barsky and Summers study. We do not examine them in this paper, as doing so would be a deviation substantial in both direction and extent from our main purpose, but they do require listing. Benjamin and Kochin claim in evidence that they show the paradox holds *only* during wars; Barsky and Summers claim in evidence that it *never* holds during wars. As noted above, Mills (1990b) presents evidence that the paradox holds during *both* war and peacetime. Barsky and Summers require

frequent variation in the real rate of interest; Friedman and Schwartz (1982) found very little variation. Barsky and Summers deny the existence of a Fisher effect; as we will argue below, even under a commodity standard a Fisher effect can exist. Their explanation relies on prompt substitution between monetary and non-monetary gold; this is hard to reconcile with Cagan's observation (1984) that under the gold standard swings in the price level lasted fifty years. And last, since by their explanation all changes in the price are just that, *not* inflation, why does the paradox show up in nominal yields?

6 We would note at this point that we do not pursue the Keynes-Wicksell explanation very much further. Just as Cagan had rejected it for the US (see note 4), we can, on exactly the same grounds, reject it for Britain. While in the short run the money multiplier in Britain was quite flexible, substantial and long-lasting changes in the broad money stock were produced not by changes in bank created money (as Wicksell required) but by changes in the monetary base. (It is worth remarking parenthetically that our confidence in this rejection is reinforced by our finding, below, of evidence consistent with another theory.)

7 Engle and Granger (1987) extend the analysis to consider vectors of variables that are $I(d)$, for which linear combinations are $I(d-b)$, in which case x is said to be *cointegrated of order d, b*. The case considered here is the most common, having $d = b = 1$.

8 In Capie, Mills and Wood (1991) the more general class of vector ARMA models were considered. No significant moving average parts were found in any of the models considered there, so here we concentrate entirely on pure (vector) autoregressions. For a textbook discussion of such classes of multivariate models, see, for example, Mills (1990a: ch. 14).

9 In interpreting these impulse response functions, one should be aware that they could be accompanied by rather large confidence intervals, the computation of which are extremely computer intensive (see Runkle, 1987). The interpretation of such intervals is, however, the subject of some debate; see Runkle (1987) and Sims (1987).

Part III

The open economy context of price and output movements 1870–1914

9 Silver, gold and the international monetary order 1851–96

P.L. COTTRELL

The purpose of this chapter is to examine the development of the international monetary arrangements behind the evolving world economy of the second half of the nineteenth century. It will attempt to map out a complementary path to that already provided by Alec Ford in the second chapter of his (1962) *Gold Standard* . . .. With very few exceptions, (de Cecco, 1974; Foreman-Peck, 1983; Kindleberger, 1984) most modern scholars of nineteenth century international monetary history have taken the post-1880 gold standard almost for granted and, so instead of asking why it emerged (unlike 'near-contemporaries' e.g. Hawtrey, 1934), have concentrated upon trying to understand how it operated. The main contention here will be that the international gold standard of the late nineteenth century was a product of problems with silver, the monetary metal before 1870 – in particular its mild appreciation relative to gold during the mid-century and, more especially, the dramatic fall in the (gold) price of silver from the early 1870s until the turn of the century. The movements in the (gold) price of silver (see table 9.1) provoked considerable contemporary debate over the international monetary order, resulting in a series of international monetary conferences from 1867. These attempted to obtain agreement amongst the major economies regarding the international monetary order and accordingly became a focus for the bimetallic agitation of the last quarter of the nineteenth century.

For a quarter of a century after Waterloo the ratio of the (gold) prices of silver and gold on the London bullion market remained remarkably steady, but from the late 1840s silver began to appreciate relatively to gold, so that after 1851, its (gold) price exceeded 61*d*. This movement in silver prices continued until 1860, with silver reaching an average (gold) price of 62 1/16*d*. during that year, and the (gold) price of silver remained above its pre-1851 level until 1873. This mild appreciation of silver was sufficient to disturb European monetary arrangements and provoked thoughts even in England of introducing a silver standard.

Table 9.1. *Gold price of silver, London, yearly average, 1851–96 per 1 oz.*
*British standard silver**

	average price, 1833 to 1850	59.6654d.	
1851	60.0625d.	1873	59.25d.
1852	61	1874	58.3125
1853	60.5	1875	56.875
1854	61.5	1876	52.75
1855	61.5	1877	54.8125
1856	61.3125	1878	52.5625
1857	61.3125	1879	51.25
1858	61.75	1880	52.25
1859	61.3125	1881	51.6875
1860	62.0625	1882	51.625
1861	61.6875	1883	50.5625
1862	60.8125	1884	50.625
1863	61.4375	1885	48.625
1864	61.375	1886	45.375
1865	61.375	1887	44.625
1866	61.0625	1888	42.875
1867	61.125	1889	42.6875
1868	60.5625	1890	47.6875
1869	60.4375	1891	45.0625
1870	60.5625	1892	39.0625
1871	60.5	1893	35.3125
1872	60.3125	1894	28.9375
		1895	29.875
		1896	30.75
	pre-1914 trough – 1902	24.0625d.	

*92.5 per cent fine.
Sources: B. P. P.: 1876: VIII, S. C. on Depreciation of Silver, Appendix 5B; 1899:
XXXI, Committee into the Indian Currency, C-9376, Appendix No. 12.

English protagonists for a silver standard were concerned about the
stability of the pound sterling. They pointed to both the distributional
effects arising from a considerable rise in prices and the likely greater
intensity of future economic crises resulting from an increased money
supply, both the product of the inflow of the 'new' gold. The main proposer
of an English silver standard was James Maclaren, who received support
from members of the Currency School, namely Cobden, Spooner and, in

France, Chevalier. Their arguments did not win the day. Those who wished to continue to adhere to gold maintained that a change of metallic standard would disturb bargains, since contracts to pay in sterling were contracts to pay in gold and 'Providence' decided whether debtors or creditors gained. Further, the adherents to gold regarded the 'new' gold as being a consequence of the previous stringency in its supply, while its inflationary effects would lightened the burden of the National Debt to the gain of the taxpayer, although to the loss of the fundholder. There was too the likelihood of an increase in the supply of silver, caused by its appreciation relative to gold. Finds had already been made in California, along with the 'new' gold, and, as well, new quicksilver (mercury) mines had been opened – mercury being required to refine silver ore (Sayers, 1930–3: 573, 579, 580, 594–9). The main effect of the mid-century appreciation of silver for England was the consolidation of the gold standard as, because of the lack of stability in gold and silver prices, the Bank of England ceased taking silver for the reserve of the Issue Department from 1848 (BPP, 1888: XLV; *Royal Commission on the Recent Changes in the relative value of previous metals*, evidence of H.H. Gibbs, q.3683).

Whereas the mild mid-century appreciation of silver only resulted primarily in academic debate in England, it did lead to both Belgium and Switzerland introducing a silver franc and gold was demonetised in Naples, the Netherlands, Spain and India. As part of its monetary reform, Belgium minted a new stock of silver coin in 1850. However this soon led to arbitrage transactions, involving 'light' French coin, with the result that 85% of the new Belgian silver coinage was exported. Further, similar, arbitrage movements occurred in the 1860s, following Italy's adoption of the French monetary standard in 1862, but at a fineness of 83.5%, not 90%, which led to the export of Italian 'light' coin to France (de Cecco, 1974: 42).

However the biggest flows of monetary metals during the mid nineteenth century consisted of the export of silver (and gold) from Europe to the East. Taking advantage of the longstanding bimetallic ratio (15.5:1) of the French mint, but now out of line with market prices, gold was shipped to France, exchanged for silver, which in turn was exported to the Orient. The effect of this exchange of metals and their international movement was to drain France of silver and make the French franc in the 1850s and 1860s *de facto* backed by gold. This was a complete reverse of the situation which had prevailed since 1803, as during the first half of the nineteenth century gold had been undervalued by the French mint ratio which had led to it being either hoarded in France or exported from France. The mid-century British export flow of gold to France reached maxima of £13.8m (1854), £14.9m (1859) and £8.46m (1866), whereas the flow of silver to 'the East' from Britain peaked in 1857 (£17.3m), 1859 (£16m) and 1862 (£10.7m). The flow of silver to India and China from the Mediterranean rose to peaks in 1857 (£20.1m), 1859 (£16.3m) and 1864 (£16.8m). According to the international accounts of one of the importers of this European 'Treasure', the inflow of gold into India rose steadily from £1.15m in 1850–1 (fiscal year) to reach a peak of £9.8m in 1864–5, whereas Indian imports of silver display far greater annual variations with major peaks in 1857–8 (£12.2m), 1859–60 (£11.1m) and 1865–6 (£18.6m) (Cottrell, 1982: 142).

The mechanism behind the mid-century 'drain' of 'Treasure' to the East has been the subject of some debate. In the early 1930s Sayers argued that it was caused by Europe's growing import surplus with the Orient which arose from differential rates of inflation leading to a relative cheapening of Eastern luxuries on Western markets (Sayers, 1930–3). However Hughes (1960) demonstrated that the (English gold) prices of silk, tea, indigo and sugar increased more than those of Western produced goods, so that there was a price inelastic demand for such Eastern imports during the 1850s. This approach can also be applied to the mid-1860s when, as a result of the Civil War, there was a price inelastic demand in Western Europe for raw cotton from Egypt and India.

The Cotton Famine induced drain of silver to the East not only affected the bimetallic currency of France but also resulted in some silver being drawn out of the German States, while silver mined in Mexico and South America was shipped directly to India. The introduction of the greenback in the United States resulted in flows of gold and silver from North America to Europe which, also in turn, were exported to the East (*Commercial History and Review of 1867*, pp. 3–4).

The Eastern Treasure drain of the mid-century had the effect in Europe of silver being replaced by the 'new' gold. It produced what contemporaries called 'the Parachute', which lessened the inflationary edge of the 'new' gold upon Western Europe so long as silver was being exported to the East, as in practice one monetary metal was replacing another. 'The Parachute' was identified by Chevalier in the contemporary debate over the inflationary effects of the 'new' gold. However, the 'new' gold did enlarge the money supplies of Britain, France and the United States which had impact upon the level of output (Martin, 1977). Terms such as 'Parachute' give the impression of a smooth transition, but this was not the case as the drain of 'Treasure' to the 'East' created difficulties for monetary management, especially by the Bank of France, resulting in four official inquiries between 1857 and 1868 (Kindleberger, 1984: 64–5). The policies, in particular the payment of a premium upon gold and from the mid-1860s sudden variations in its discount rate, adopted by the French proto-central bank (Bopp, 1952; Rist, 1970) had an effect upon the Bank of England.

Cooperation between the two banks, regarding gold and silver flows, encouraged by the Crimean War, broke down in October 1855 and a French approach to London for a joint purchase of £2–3m of bullion, made in the autumn of 1856, was declined by Threadneedle Street.[1] The resumption of the Eastern Treasure drain almost to full flood in 1860 did result in November, 1860 in the Bank of England swapping gold for silver from the Bank of France, a cooperative action assisted by the Cobden-Chevalier Treaty and the close personal relations between Governor Dobree and some of the regents of the Bank of France (Cottrell, 1982: 135–7). However, the mid-1860s boom, with the Cotton Famine, was marked by almost guerrilla warfare between the two proto-central banks. The Bank of France continued to buy gold in London at a premium and from 1864 altered its discount rate, violently and suddenly. The Bank of England was forced to counter with comparable sudden changes in Bank rate. During the period 1861 to 1867 London–Paris interest rate differentials had a strong influence upon the English demand for credit in the form of bill creations.

The intra-European arbitrage flows of silver in the 1850s and 1860s led to efforts by Belgium, a 'small' trade dependent economy, to establish a wider currency union and, in agreement with Switzerland and Italy, it was to be based upon the gold standard. However, the result of these discussions – the Latin Monetary Union of 1865 (Willis, 1968) – as a consequence of French persuasion, was bimetallic, following the Napoleonic Code of 1803. Such a surprising arrangement, given the context of silver arbitrage flows and the drain to the East which had resulted in the franc being *de facto* gold-based, has not been explained, but de Cecco has suggested that French financiers – the *haute banque* – wished to retain the advantages of bimetallism for arbitrage operations.

Although Belgian inspired, France, the dominant economy, assumed leadership of the Latin Monetary Union. Britain was invited to join the Union, or conclude arrangements for a convenient relationship between the coinage of the Union and that of Britain. These Gallic approaches were politely declined, but in 1867 Greece and the Papal States adopted currencies in line with that of the Union and Austria concluded a preliminary treaty with France, with partial adherence from 1871. In 1868 Romania joined the Latin Monetary Union and the necessary bill was introduced in the United States Congress. Canada prepared comparable legislation, but Canadian adhesion to the Union was made dependent upon the successful passage of the bill in Washington.

This interest in the Latin Monetary Union partly arose from another mid-century concern – an international coinage – as the Union involved common standard interchangeable coins. In 1850 Chevalier, although subsequently a silver protagonist, had recommended the international introduction of gold coins of identical weight and fineness. With the appreciation of silver over the decade, he was forced to modify his ideas by the somewhat awkward device of an annual fixing of a definite ratio between his 'gold international' coins and those of silver currencies. Chevalier was reflecting a consensus which had developed at the Great Exhibition of 1851 over the need for a common international system of not only weights and measures but also coins. This was debated by the International Statistical Congress at its first meeting in Brussels in 1853 and then again in Paris in 1855. At the London meeting of the Congress in 1860 an International Commission on the subject was established which reported to the Berlin meeting of 1863. Here, a resolution was adopted in favour of assimilating the coinage of different countries.

The Latin Monetary Union was a step in this direction and British reformers in the 1860s began to argue that an easy and minor alteration of the alloy in the sovereign, together with a slight reduction of gold in the dollar, would produce a uniform international gold based currency under which the pound sterling would be equivalent in gold content to either 25 francs or 5 dollars. International money was also seen as a way of preventing financial crises (Maunder, 1867). The whole matter was debated at the first International Monetary Conference held in Paris in 1867 in tandem with the Paris international exhibition. The monetary conference had been a French initiative, aimed to produce complete or partial uniformity as between the various monetary systems current in Europe and North America through an extension of the Latin Monetary Union.

The Paris conference was attended by thirty-three delegates from twenty countries; Britain being represented by Graham, the Master of the Mint, and Rivers Wilson of the Treasury. With surprising unanimity, they were able to agree to a short list of simple recommendations for an international monetary order. Despite the continuing French commitment to bimetallism, the conference came out in favour of a single gold standard. Gold coins were to have 90% fineness and be minted on the basis of 5 francs, or multiples thereof. The international coin was to be 25-franc gold piece. Only the Dutch delegates opposed these proposals for the development of an international gold standard (the Netherlands having adopted a silver standard in 1849). Although no international treaty or convention arose directly from the conference, Austria and Switzerland went as far as beginning to mint the 25 franc 'international' (*BPP* 1867–8 [4021], xxvii; *Report of the Master of the Mint and R. Wilson on the International Monetary Conference Paris, June 1867*).

The recommendations of the 1867 conference were the subject of a British Royal Commission. The members of this commission found themselves in some difficulty. This arose from what they regarded as Britain's internationalist stance and, in the economic realm, the lead that Britain had given with regard to the adoption of Free Trade, subsequently adopted in Europe, beginning with France, and reinforced by the system of European trade treaties involving most-favoured-nation clauses, of which the first had been the Cobden-Chevalier Treaty of 1860. In their evidence both W. Bagehot and W.S. Jevons favoured the introduction of an international coinage, with Bagehot commenting:

At present the accounts of the Bank of France are half useless to English bankers . . . they do not study them at all. Although everybody knows that the bullion reserve in the Bank of France is of very great importance to us, nobody looks at it, because it is in money that they do not understand. They are aware of course that they can divide by 25, and obtain the result in pounds, but they do not make such a division; it is quite out of their way. And many great changes in the French banking system, such as the recent great increase in the amount in circulation, are quite unknown in England, solely on account of the difference in the money of the two countries. (BPP, 1867–8 [4073] xxvii, Royal Commission on International Coinage, evidence of W. Bagehot, q. 1979)

The commission was persuaded but, none the less, its members could not bring themselves to recommend either the adoption of the 25-franc international gold coin, or any alteration in the fineness of the sovereign (91.6%).

The main result of the 1867 conference was the widening of the membership of the Latin Monetary Union, based upon the French bimetallic system, primarily amongst the smaller states of Europe. However, what the conference had shown was a swing in opinion amongst the community of nations from some consideration of a silver standard in the 1850s to the recommendation of the adoption of the gold standard by the late 1860s. The only exception was Austria–Hungary which went onto a sole silver standard in 1870.

That recommendation began to be put into effect during the early 1870s. On the basis of the French war indemnity, the German Empire adopted the gold standard in 1871, a process that was completed in 1873. Not all of influence in the new Germany were convinced of the wiseness of the change. Bismarck's leading ministers Rudolf von Delbrück and Otto von Camphausen had advocated the adoption of gold, but Bleichröder opposed it. He was a bimetallist and thought that adhesion to the gold standard would lead to fluctuations in the level of interest rates and, moreover, sudden changes. Bleichröder did not contemplate with equanimity the prospect of a monetary policy which accentuated both boom and slump. He continued his rearguard action throughout the 1870s, arguing that Germany would become dependent upon financial conditions in London and maintaining in 1876 that the Reichsbank's inadequate gold reserves would need to be bolstered by a loan raised in London. Apart from scoring points on technical matters, Bleichröder stressed time and time again that the gold standard would involve high interest rates, as in 1877, which would adversely affect 'our badly suffering industry' (Stern, 1980: 180–1).

Like all Cassandras, Bleichröder was to have his hour, but his opposition in the 1870s had no effect upon those who believed that the new empire needed a suitable imperial currency. Germany's adoption of the gold standard in the early 1870s had immediate repercussions in northern Europe amongst its trading neighbours. The Dutch put aside their opposition of 1867 and in 1873 the Netherlands adopted the gold standard, restricting the coinage of silver in 1875. In the mid-1870s the Scandinavian countries also moved onto the gold standard.

During the 1860s the Nordic group of nations had been considering monetary reform on the lines of the introduction of the decimal system. In the early 1870s the possible adoption of the gold standard was added to the agenda of these discussions and in 1872 a conference of Scandinavian economists established a commission to investigate the possibilities of introducing a common Nordic monetary system. The commission met in August and made its report in September 1872. This recommended the introduction of the krone, a gold-based unit of currency, composed of 100 øre, and equivalent to $\frac{1}{2}$ Danish rix-dollar, $\frac{1}{4}$ Norwegian specie dollar and one Swedish rix dollar – very close to then-prevailing exchange rates. These recommendations were accepted by the Nordic governments and in 1873 a Monetary Union was established between Denmark and Sweden, joined by Norway in 1875. The Scandinavian Monetary Union developed further in the 1880s and 1890s. In 1885 the Union changed into a system whereby gold movements as between its three proto-central banks were almost eliminated, while in 1894 the Norwegian and Swedish central banks agreed to accept each other's notes at par, an arrangement which the Danish central bank joined in 1901. These common monetary arrangements broke up from 1905 with Norway's secession from political union with Sweden (Johansen, forthcoming; Nielsen, 1917).

Germany's demonetisation of silver from 1873 was regarded by many contemporaries as one of the major factors responsible for the fall in the gold price of silver in the 1870s, a decline that was to be a continuing major feature of the last quarter of the nineteenth century. Between 1873 and 1879 Germany sold £28.35m of silver, initially at 59.3125d. per standard ounce but finally at 50d. per standard ounce. A further factor was what came to be called by silver protagonists 'the crime of 1873'. The United States Coinage

Act of 1873, largely by pardonable oversight, omitted to include the silver dollar in a measure of coinage simplification. This legislation in fact accurately reflected that during the Civil War silver coins had gone out of circulation; indeed, many had been exported to Europe, where they had been used to feed the drain of Treasure to the East. The effect of the Act was to suspend the free coinage of silver, making gold the sole legal tender for sums less than $5. The 'crime of 1873' became a rallying call of the American silver party which drew its support from the silver mining states together with the agricultural west and south. The silver question, like prohibition, was an issue between rural America and its values and interests and the industrial urban cities of the East.

The fall in the gold price of silver was the product of many influences. As English maintainers of the gold standard in the 1850s had predicted, the supply of silver had increased. This was not so much a consequence of the mid-century premium upon silver, relative to gold, but a result of the opening up of the American West by the railroad, especially the metaliferous aureole of the Rockies. During the first half of the 1850s the world production of silver had averaged 886,115 kilos per annum, of which less than 1% had been mined in the United States. By the first half of the 1870s, world silver production had risen to 1,969,425 kilos per annum of which 28.6 per cent was contributed by American mining (Robey, 1936). Further, a main consuming area of silver – India – was taking less. One estimate placed the peak in Indian imports of silver in the late 1850s at just under 10 crore Rupees; by the early 1880s Indian imports had fallen to 6 crore Rupees (although they did recover in the late 1880s). Whereas the output of silver had expanded and the demand for it had fallen back, the situation with gold was precisely the reverse. The mining of the 'new' gold had reached a peak in the late 1850s at 201,750 kilos and by the early 1880 world production had fallen to 149,137 kilos. Moreover, with post-bellum monetary reform, the United States in the late 1870s was an importer of gold from Europe, the United States Treasury accumulating gold in an anticipation of a resumption of specie payments on 1 January 1879. The world supply of gold from sources, other than the United States, had declined from £24.6m per annum average during the late 1860s to £9.6m by the early 1880s. Indian demand for this precious metal had increased from 1880 while, with the movement onto the gold standard and growing fears over a possible world shortage of gold, there was increased aggregate gold holdings by Treasuries and proto-central banks, rising from a trough of £142.5m in 1878 to £252m by 1885.

The contemporary debate over the fall in the gold price of silver became enmeshed in arguments over stocks, new additions to stocks, and changes in the use and consumption of silver. (There were parallel comparable arguments over gold.) Whatever the cause, the fall in the gold price of silver from its inception led to an immediate swamping of the mints of the bimetallic Latin Monetary Union. It exacerbated existing Gallic monetary problems, with the Bank of France having been forced to suspend specie payments as a result of the Franco–Prussian War. During 1873 France minted £6m of silver coin and Belgium £4m. This level could not be sustained and in 1874 it was decided by the Union to limit the coinage of 5-franc pieces to 60m for France, 40m for Italy, 12m for Belgium and 8m for Switzerland. This arrangement continued until November 1878 when the mints of the Union were closed to the coinage of silver, although the Bank of France resumed cash payments on 1 January 1878. To many contemporaries the closure of the mints of the Latin Monetary Union to silver was the final break in the monetary links between silver and gold, an action which threatened currency stability and price stability.

The post-1873 decline in the gold price of silver not only affected Europe and the United States but also substantial parts of the evolving world economy, especially Asia and Latin America, still primarily silver using continents. For Britain, given its growing trade with these areas, this raised substantial questions, but the most important of all was with regard to India and in particular in the 1870s remittances from the sub-continent back to London. Other British concerns regarding the effect of fall of silver upon India were to develop in the 1880s. In 1876 a Select Committee on the Depreciation of Silver and its effects upon the Anglo–Indian Exchange sat and, despite all the evidence it collected, was unable to come to any clear conclusions for future policy (*BPP*, 1876 (338) VII, *Select Committee on the price of silver and its effects in the exchange between India and England*). All it could find was six reasons why silver had begun to fall in price relative to gold and in particular silver mining in Nevada – the continuing exploitation of the Comstock lode discovered in 1859, changes in European monetary arrangements during the 1870s, and the reduction in the demand for silver imports by India. From 1878 the Government of India began to threaten that it would put India on the gold standard.

While the British government came under increasing pressure from Latin American and Indian merchants regarding the 'silver question', within the United States Congress there were comparable lobby groups, composed of representatives from the silver mining and agricultural states together with reflationists, seeking a positive remedy. In 1877 a measure for free silver coinage passed the House, was overridden by the President, but who, in turn was vetoed by the Congress, in which each state had parity of numerical representation. It reached the statute books as the Bland–Allison Act of 1878 which called for a monthly coinage of between $2m to $4m in silver, with such coins being full legal tender for any amount. Under the Act, which lasted until 1890, $380m of silver was minted.

The United States attempted to make the 'silver question' an international issue and Washington called an International Monetary Conference, which was convened in Paris in 1878, again in tandem with an international exhibition. Germany refused to attend the conference, while Goschen, the British delegate who had been chairman of the 1876 Select Committee, regarded the American proposal for a universal double monetary standard – international bimetalism – as 'a veritable utopia' (Nicholson, 1893). The English delegation as a whole pointed out that Britain would not entertain any change in its monetary arrangements. The American representatives had probably recognised this, as their immediate aim behind calling the conference was rather to reopen the mints of the Latin Monetary Union to silver. However, this came up against the opposition of the Belgian members of the conference and some resistance even from the French hosts. None the less the 1878 conference did lead to some measures sustaining and maintaining the monetary use of silver. Germany stopped selling silver, a diplomatic gesture but probably one forced by market conditions. Italy, which had had an inconvertible note issue since 1866, continued to coin silver, up to 20m francs per annum, half the rate of the 1874 to 1878 arrangements of the Latin Monetary Union.

The United States persisted in trying to obtain an international solution to the silver problem. Along with French representatives, Americans agreed in 1881 on a joint resolution which called for an international monetary convention. The necessary conference was called by France and in its deliberations the monetary use of silver was not only defended by the American participants but also by the delegates from Austria–Hungary and Russia. The British and Empire representatives were Fremantle of the Indian Mint, Sir Louis Mallet, and Reay. The conference recognised that any substantial revival of the monetary use of silver amongst the major Powers depended upon a change in attitude on the part of both Britain and Germany. The delegates decided to focus whatever pressure they could mount upon Britain and passed a resolution which called for an increase in the British monetary use of silver. This, they felt, could be achieved through the Bank of England using silver in its reserve, up to the maximum of 20% allowed by the Bank Charter Act of 1844, and by new British legislation which raised the limit upon silver being legal tender from 40s. to £5.

Lord Frederick Cavendish MP approached the Bank of England, following the conference's resolution, but received the reply that

Having laid your letter before the Court we have to inform you that it was felt that 'the Monetary question' discussed at the Conference, being one partly of abstract science, and partly of political application, did not form a legitimate subject for their discussion, or for the delivery of the judgement of the Bank in its Corporate capacity. (BoE: Letter Book 19; Grenfell and Gilliat to Lord Frederick Cavendish, 30.vi. 1881, f. 164).

Directors of the Bank had already made up their minds some years before that dealings in silver would be unwise; in February 1875, when silver had fallen to 57.5*d*., Alfred Latham, a former Governor had suggested buying silver, but this was rejected by the rest of the Court as inexpedient (Clapham, 1970: 300). The Bank was subject to other lobbying, being approached by Lowell, the American Ambassador in London, through Cavendish. Lowell was anxious that there should be no change in Indian monetary arrangements, fearful that if the rupee was no longer based on silver, as the Indian government had continually threatened since 1878, this would end any monetary role for silver. In London he wanted the Bank of England to once more hold silver in its reserve, but this approach got no further than that of Cavendish, even if it received a more direct reply.

The reappearance of silver bullion as an asset in the Issue Department . . . depend[s] entirely on the return of the mints of other countries to such rules as would ensure the certainty of conversion of Gold into Silver and Silver into Gold. (BoE, Letter Book 19, Grenfell and Gilliat to Cavendish, 30.vi.1881, f. 166. See also Dd 7.vi.1881–23.iii.1882, Court of the Directors of the Bank, 30.vi.1881.)

The Bank's stonewalling reply was felt by some to have been due to Lowell's approaches having been private, rather than on the basis of instructions from Washington. However, an 'official' inquiry from the Italian Ambassador did not lead to any movement in Threadneedle Street's stance over 'the Monetary question' (Horton, 1892). The Chancellor of the Exchequer did receive a confidential explanation of the Bank's policy regarding the holding of silver (BoE, Letter Book 19: to the Chancellor, 30.vi.1881, f. 168). Consequently, the Paris International Monetary Conference of 1881 was adjourned to April 1882 and even then it was not reopened, as it was felt by its conveners that 'conclusions were not yet sufficiently positive'.

On its own initiative the Italian government issued a set of proposals to restore some monetary use to silver, although Italian notes continued to be inconvertible. It asked the member states of the Latin Monetary Union to recommence the coining of silver francs in terms of a rate of 0.5 francs per head of population for five years. This was to be undertaken in conjunction with the United States raising the minimum monthly level of silver coinage under the 1878 legislation to $3m. Berlin was requested to continue to refrain from silver sales for a further five years and, within the German coinage, to substitute silver for gold 5-mark pieces and smaller notes. With respect to Britain and the British Empire, Rome reiterated and extended the resolutions of the 1881 conference in terms of India maintaining an unrestricted silver coinage, coupled with an increased use of silver in the United Kingdom. In particular, the Italian government not only wished to see the Bank of England holding 20% of its bullion reserve in the form of silver, but also the British legal tender limit for silver being raised not to £5 (the conference resolution), but to £20, with Britain coining £0.5m of silver annually.

Although the abortive 1881 conference led to no official action, apart from the vain attempt of the Italian government, with the continuing general fall of prices, there was a swing in British and German public opinion regarding the silver question. During 1881 and 1882, the British Bimetallic League was formed and its first office to be opened was in Manchester, a reflection of the cotton industry's emerging concerns regarding its Indian market (Green, 1988: 596). The President of the League was H.H. Gibbs of the Latin American London trading and banking house of A. Gibbs & Sons. Gibbs had been the Governor of the Bank of England during the mid-1870s and a British delegate to the International Monetary Conference of 1878. Since then he had shifted from being a monometallist to bimetallist and in 1881 he wrote the *Double Standard*, perhaps not the most effective piece of bimetallic propaganda as it contained nine succinct arguments against bimetallism, followed by an equivalent number of but only loosely established refutations.[2] Gibbs was one of the few members of 'the City' to support bimetallism and, unlike many other London bankers, he also favoured tariff reform (Daunton, 1989: 149). Although directly affected by the fall in silver through his merchant house's South American trade, Gibbs' support for bimetallism also arose from a belief that the deflation was adversely affecting producers, creators of wealth. He regarded much of 'the City' as commission earners from book-keeping, which as such were either untouched or benefited from silver's problems and the price fall through both arbitrage on exchange transactions and the real balance effect arising from being creditors. Another 'City' renegade, H.R. Grenfell, was the League's Vice-President; he was a member of the Political Economy Club from 1876 and had been the Governor of the Bank at the time of the 1881 conference and the subsequent correspondence that it generated with the Bank.[3] Like Gibbs, he, too, had moved into the bimetallic camp, becoming another 'City' heretic on the monetary question. What pushed him in this direction is unknown, but possibilities would include the copper trade's increasing dependance upon South American supplies and his own connections with the Landed Interest through being Master of the Mid-Kent Harriers. Other notable supporters were Foxwell, Fielden and Sir H. Meysey-Thomson. The League drew its grass-roots support from the agricultural interest suffering from the fall in wheat and wool prices, the Lancashire cotton industry perturbed by the growth of Indian domestic manufacturing shielded in part by the fall of the silver rupee, and Oriental and Latin American merchants who were finding increasing difficulties in exporting to silver using areas.

The fluctuations in the prices of gold and silver had affected Britain's exchanges with the East. The 'Exchange Banks' did provide a service for hedging and the Indian Exchange was also assisted by the availability of Indian Council Bills. However, the exchange markets with respect to China, Japan and also the South American silver-using countries were not so developed and the exchange as a result was subject to greater fluctuations (King, 1987: 273–8). The greater instability of the exchange was also alleged to have had the effect of discouraging British overseas investment in silver-based areas. Moreover, it was felt that the fluctuations as between gold and silver had changed trading patterns, encouraging silver-based countries to deal between themselves, so diverting trade. This was seen as a reason for both the growth of the Indian cotton industry from the mid-1870s, and its exports to elsewhere in silver-based Asia, with a consequential detrimental effect for Lancashire with respect to its major export markets of India, China, Hong Kong and Japan. The fall in the price of silver seemed also to be leading to providing a bounty on exports from silver-using countries. This was regarded as a further explanation for both Indian cotton exports and the growth of imports of wheat by Britain from India, a further thorn in the side of English southern farmers and their landlords.[4]

The concern over post-1873 fluctuations as between the prices of gold and silver went further as many argued that the fall in the gold price of silver was a cause of the general fall in (gold) prices. Here, the silver question was but a part of the broader anxiety of the late nineteenth century over deflation. It was considered that the deflation was depressive through reducing nominal profits, which because of the 'veil of money' was 'curtailing business and discouraging enterprise'. The burden of debts was increased while, as wages were sticky, they were becoming 'a large proportion of the total cost of production'.

During the long slump of the mid-1880s late Victorian concern over the state of the British economy culminated and bimetallism, with its promise of reflation, along with protectionism, appeared to many to be suitable palliatives. The 'Monetary question' was considered by the Royal Commission on the Depression of Trade and Industry but its members felt unable to pronounce on what they regarded as none the less a critical problem. They recommended a further inquiry which led to the immediate establishment of what has come to be known as the Royal Commission on Gold and Silver.

The members of the Commission contained five outright bimetallists – L. Mallet, who had attended the 1881 conference, A.J. Balfour, H. Chaplin,[5] D. Barbour,[6] and Houldsworth, representing Lancashire, against which there appeared to be, when the Commission was constituted, six avowed monometallists – Herschell,[7] Fremantle,[8] Lubbock,[9] Farrer,[10] Birch,[11] and Courtney.[12] The Commission asked 10,705 questions of 38 witnesses. Of those interviewed, nine supported the bimetallist case with the emerging economics profession represented by Professor J. Shield Nicholson of Edinburgh University (Nicholson, 1893). The pro-bimetallist witnesses broadly represented the grass roots of the faction with Robert Barclay, an exporter to India and other silver-based countries, R.B. Chapman, the former Financial Secretary to the Government of India, and S. Williamson MP, head of the Liverpool merchant house of Balfour, Williamson & Co. which traded with Chile and California. Both Gibbs and Grenfell gave evidence. Gibbs' line of argument over six sessions followed very closely the stance that he had taken in an article recently (October, 1886) published in the *Fortnightly Review*. His scheme for bimetallism was based upon the French law of 1803 in that he wanted open mints for the coinage of gold and silver, a fixed ratio as between gold and silver, and all coins to be legal tender. He was broad minded enough to acknowledge that either gold or silver could be dominant at any one time which actually was an achille's heel in his argument (*BPP*, 1888:XLV, *Royal Commission on Recent Changes in the Relative Values of Precious Metals, Evidence of H.H. Gibbs, 99–171, 3461, 3477*). Generally, the bimetallic case presented to the Commission was internally consistent, only H.L. Raphael, the bullion dealer, maintaining that British adherence to a double standard had to be contingent upon its parallel adoption by France, Germany and the United States. Marshall, the Cambridge economist, went further than the bimetallists, producing a plan for a monetary order – symmetallism – based upon a bar consisting of both silver and gold in fixed proportions. Others, who the Commission did not hear, thought of adding platinum to this bar.

The bimetallic supporters were opposed in their evidence by eight monometallists, but of whom four saw some need for change in the international monetary order. D. Watney was convinced of the alleged scarcity of gold and consequently argued for economy in its use as a monetary metal. Lord Bramwell thought he recognised that there should be larger currency groupings, whereas Thomas Comber accepted bimetallism for countries other than Britain. Amongst the monometallists J. Barr Robertson went as far as supporting the issue of inconvertible paper money. The lack of cohesion within the monometallist evidence had its effect upon the monometallist members of the Commission. With only objections from Lubbock and Birch, the monometallists within the Commission came out in favour in their *Report* (the Commission produced three) for an international agreement to coin more silver. They saw Britain's role in this as consisting of two parts: the Bank of England holding silver in the Issue Department and issuing either a fiduciary £1 note or £1 and 10s. notes backed by silver. This apparent shift in favour of an increased British monetary use of silver created alarm amongst some other monometallists, especially Giffen, who had given evidence to the Commission and had been campaigning against bimetallism since 1879 (Giffen, 1892). How the report was interpreted tended to vary with readers' monetary allegiances. Many in their passion overlooked the problem of British coinage, with perhaps more than half of the gold circulation in the mid-1880s being under the legal minimum weight. Lord Randolph Churchill, Chancellor in 1886, had produced a Treasury backed proposal for a £6m fiduciary issue of £1 notes which went into a draft bill in 1887 along with a Coinage Fund (Pressnell, 1968: 172–3). Churchill had been a bimetallist while at the India Office but developed amnesia over this former allegiance when he moved, briefly, to 11 Downing Street (Green, 1988: 588). Other politicians were to have similar lapses of memory which were to affect their autobiographies.

Bimetallists were encouraged by the Royal Commission's *Report* and an opportunity to air what they felt was their growing ascendancy was provided by a further Monetary Congress in 1889, the venue being once more Paris, the site of another French International Exhibition. The Congress was presided over by Maguin, the Vice-President of the Bank of France, and Britain, with India, was represented by a 'balanced' deputation of Grenfell, Fremantle, and Murray of the Treasury who had been secretary to the Gold and Silver Commission (Horton, 1892). The *Report* of the Commission may have also influenced Goschen, now Chancellor replacing Lord Randolph Churchill, but who had been Britain's outspoken mono-metallist representative to the 1878 international conference. In 1887 new silver coins had been minted to mark the Queen Empress's Golden Jubilee – the 4s. Double Florin, a first move to decimal coinage, and the 5s. Crown, of which two would replace the increasingly worn circulation of half-sovereigns. The new coins were not well received by the public or the banks in Scotland (Clapham, 1970: 315). In 1889, Goschen received the Silver Deputation and announced measures to encourage further the use of silver in Britain. These consisted of government industrial departments paying wages in silver, while the Treasury would meet the Bank of England's commission charge of 0.25% on the delivery of silver. To some this appeared that the government was shifting towards a bimetallist course, but actually Goschen's 1889 silver measures also produced profits which financed the much needed re-coinage of pre-Victorian gold in circulation. Goschen was the only Chancellor who had been a Bank director and he was committed to the gold standard, but saw a role for silver in facilitating what he regarded as the superior gold standard (Pressnell, 1968: 170). Following the Baring Crisis in January 1891, Goschen aired plans for a fiduciary issue of £1 and 10s. notes, but these were soon grounded by the Bank of England's long-standing opposition to the issue of small notes (Clapham, 1970: 314–15; Pressnell, 1968: 176–8). None the less, Goschen still continued to conjure with some monetary reform and restated the proposal that the Bank of England should hold 20% of the Issue Department's bullion reserve in silver.

The silver party made greater gains in the United States. As the price for their support for the Republican McKinley tariff of 1888, they obtained the Sherman Silver Purchase Act of 1890. This introduced the monthly purchase of 4.5m ounces of silver; the legislation ran until 1893, by when $500m of silver had been purchased under its provisions. Not all of the international tide was running in favour of monetary silver during the early 1890s as in 1892 Austria–Hungary adopted the gold standard, but with an inconvertible currency.

Goschen's silver measures and plans, together with the Sherman Act, encouraged the supporters of bimetallism to call yet another international monetary conference. The conference met at Brussels in 1892 but it rapidly became apparent that the delegates from Austria–Hungary, Britain, Germany, Italy, Russia, Sweden and Switzerland were now against international bimetallism. British opposition was the result of Sir William Harcourt having packed the British delegation with monometallist 'City' men to more than balance Houldsworth, the representative of Lancashire (Green, 1988: 611). As in 1881, the convention was forced to be adjourned and its organisers recognised that bimetallism would not come about by debate at such a gathering, rather a conference could only celebrate a prior agreement reached by the community of nations.

In 1893 the Sherman Act lapsed and the Indian mints were closed to the coinage of silver, sovereigns being made legal tender in India in 1899. These all seemed to be the inevitable fateful steps towards the global triumph of gold, but actually the monetary controversy in Britain reached its peak during the early 1890s. In the opening years of the decade prices tumbled rapidly, both a cyclical and secular movement. The problems of agriculture led in Britain to a further Royal Commission being appointed to investigate the industry's difficulties. That received a barrage of pro-bimetallic evidence. Lancashire too was still firmly in the bimetallic camp with the cotton industry's now acute concern for its Indian market. By the early 1890s, the Indian monetary problem, Britain's real interest in the silver question, which had been growing like a canker since the early 1870s, had reached a point where remedial action could no longer be postponed. In

1891, the Indian government for a second time in six years requested permission from London to close the mints. That the Imperial metropolis had to react was emphasised in early 1892 by both the suspension of the sale of Indian Council Bills and the introduction of an import tariff, with all the implications of the latter for Lancashire (Green, 1968: 602–3). The two mainsprings of bimetallism in Britain – corn and cotton – were now in acute tension. That they might achieve their aims seemed even more likely with Balfour going to 10 Downing Street in 1895 as Leader of the Commons under Salisbury as Prime Minister in the Lords. The monometallists in the 'City' could now not be sure whether they had exorcised the heresy of bimetallism and in 1895 formed the Gold Standard Defence Association in the offices of the London bank Glyn, Mills, led by Lubbock, Lord Farrer, H.D. Macleod, and Giffen (Gold Standard Defence Association, *The Gold Standard. A Selection from the Papers issued by the . . . Association in 1895–1898*).

However, Balfour, in the Cabinet, was not prepared to commit himself, replying to a question in the house:

I am, as I have always been, strongly in favour of an international agreement; but I have no right to pledge my colleagues on the subject, nor have I any grounds for thinking that such an agreement would at the present moment be the result of an international conference. A second abortive conference would be a serious misfortune. (Reply to a question tabled by Sir John Leng, 22.viii.1895, quoted in *The Bimetallist*, September 1895, p. 240)

The words 'at the present moment' were omitted in report of *The Times*, and that of other papers, which led to a belief that Balfour had changed his colours. With a divided Cabinet over the monetary question and a Chancellor – Hicks Beach – who had only accepted his portfolio on the condition that he would not be pressed by his ministerial colleagues on the currency, that indeed was to prove to be the case. The Tories unhitched their waggon from silver, but instead moved towards tariff reform led by Chamberlain, who had been a bimetallist.

The continuing fears of the 'City' monometallists were misplaced, although they were to be raised once more on two further occasions during the 1890s. The silver party of the Southern and Western States in America collapsed following W. Jennings Bryan's defeat in the Presidential election of 1896, during which he had campaigned for free silver coinage at the ratio of 16:1.[13] But Bryan was still felt by the White House to be a force which led during the summer of 1897 to an American monetary mission to Europe headed by Senator Wolcott. This now appears to have been a sleight of hand to take the wind totally out of Bryan's sails through transferring any blame regarding silver from Eastern yankee bankers to the even more corrupt 'Old World'. However, Wolcott did reach an agreement with the French government and his visit to London resulted in a City petition to Downing Street. While the Indian monetary question was dealt with by a series of parliamentary committees,[14] Farrer, working amongst the Whitehall mandarins and the Pall Mall clubs, ensured that India would go onto the gold standard. Only the outbreak of the Boer War, with its threat to the supply of South African gold, revived once more, albeit temporarily, the hopes of British bimetallists (Green, 1988: 604–6).

In 1896 Russia went onto the gold standard and Japan followed in 1897 (*BPP*, 1899: xxxi, Committee on Indian Currency, c.9376, Appendices). The lira finally reached metallic par in 1900, when also there was a full resumption of the gold standard by the United States, the country having been *de facto* on the standard since 1879. Most Latin American countries joined the gold standard during the decade after 1897. By the 1910s, amongst major countries only China was left on a silver standard, a complete change in the world monetary order as compared with 1870 when only Britain and Portugal had been on the gold standard.

Many commentators have stressed the diversity in the adherence of economies to the late-nineteenth-century gold standard. It was Hawtrey who first suggested that Britain and America backed onto the gold standard, almost by accident, as a result of the experience of inconvertible paper currencies during the Napoleonic and Civil Wars respectively. It could equally be argued that the experience of inconvertible silver led to much of the rest of the world backing onto the gold standard from the early 1870s. However, that reversal of the monetary order was no accident and only took place after major domestic and international debate.

The extent of the bimetallic controversy which raged from the late 1870s until the late 1890s, largely overlooked and ignored by monetary historians, was such that it severely questions, for instance, Fetter's contention that, in the case of Britain, the monetary orthodoxy of gold had been established by 1875 (Fetter, 1965). In many respects the world went unwillingly onto gold from the early 1870s with one of the major objections being the likelihood of both higher, and fluctuating, interest rates, domestic credit conditions being determined by international factors. There had been British provincial complaints on these lines from the mid-1860s, provoked, in particular, by the experience of the 1866 crisis (Persius [R. Browning], *Addenda to Pamphlet on the Currency considered with a view to the Effectual Prevention of Panics*, 1868, p. 4; Dover, 1866). An English statistical preoccupation from the 1870s was to establish the greater variability of Bank Rate as compared with discount rates on the continent. In France and Germany the proto-central banks in the late nineteenth century did hold higher reserves and, as Alec Ford has pointed out (1962: 22–4), disregarded the 'rules of the game' in order to sustain them. The continental protection of monetary reserves stemmed from many factors: a reaction to the belief that there was a shortage of gold, the weakness of the French balance of payments in the last quarter of the nineteenth century, the lack of fully developed linkages as between the proto-central bank and the domestic banking system (and the far greater importance of currency within the money supply) which would ensure that changes in interest rates had the desired effect, and the wish to maintain stable interest rates for the 'good' of domestic industry and commerce. The latter met Bleichröder's point in his arguments with Bismarck of the 1870s. These 'high' continental monetary reserves proved to be crucial for the Bank of England at times of international monetary crisis. The Bank of France lent £3m in gold at 3% during the Baring Crisis as a result of an approach by Goschen through Rothschilds (Clapham, 1970: 329–30, 336; Morgan, 1943: 222–3). The experience of the Baring Crisis also forced the Bank of England to develop the 'gold devices' to supplement the efficacy of Bank Rate, employing them in the late 1890s and early 1900s in part to shield the domestic economy against greater variations in interest rates (Sayers, 1936: ch. IV).

With Britain's dominance over the world economy and London's supremacy over international finance, bimetallists rightly recognised that their campaign would only be successful were there a change in Britain's monetary arrangements. However, Gibbs and Grenfell generally did not reflect the opinions of the 'City' which clung tenaciously to gold from the 1850s. As an international creditor, the 'City' gained from the late-nineteenth-century deflation. Other British support for bimetallism came from declining pressure groups within society. The Agricultural and Landed Interest was no longer a force in politics; it only had sufficient power to command inquiries into its problems, not remedies. Lancashire too was on the wane, though less clearly than southern landlords and their tenant farmers. Manchester had lost the major influence over international economic policy it had had during the mid-century. None the less, the climax of the bimetallic controversy in Britain in the early 1890s shows that it was 'a close run thing'. The Tory victory in the 1895 election did shake the 'City'. However, the Tories decided, wrongly, that tariff reform would win more votes in future electoral contests, whereas the British monetary and banking question after the Baring Crisis became one of reserves, domestic and international. The silver issue receded with the greater global availability of gold. The low point in world gold production was reached in 1888 and over the next decade output doubled (Cagan, 1965: 59–60, 62). Gold was discovered in the Witwatersrand in 1886 and, although the ore had a low metallic content and required deep mining, by 1888 forty-four mines were in operation producing £1.3m of gold per annum (Houghton, 1971: 13–14). It was the 'new' gold of the 1890s which led to Marshall by the end of the decade to regard gold as the natural order, thus giving up his ideas of 'symmetallism'.

Silver was displaced from the international order, although with a struggle and kicking by its supporters. None the less, silver did play a role in international dealings and have an impact upon the development of the world economy. The Orient became more important to Western Europe, especially Britain from the 1840s (Landes, 1958: 55–6), and European, largely French, silver (together with Indian opium), provided a means of settling the 'Old World's' adverse international balance with Asia. Just as the depreciation of gold over the mid-century had some positive impact upon the real level of output of the Western industrial economies, so the depreciation of silver had a comparable effect in the less developed world during the last quarter of the nineteenth century. Gauging that effect is difficult, because of other contemporary factors, in particular the inflow of Western capital and differing price trends as regards commodities. None the less, whereas the exports of gold-based underdeveloped countries grew at only 1% per annum, those of silver-based countries expanded by 4% per annum. Further, while the value of exports of many gold-based countries actually fell between the early 1870s and the mid-1890s, this was not the case with any member of the 'silver group'. There were, admittedly, considerable variations in the export experience of the silver group. The leader was Korea, opened up by Japan from 1876, whose exports expanded at 16.9% per annum between 1872–5 and 1896–9, whereas the laggard was Mauritius with export growth of only 0.3% per annum between 1872–5 and 1893–6. Contrary to Lancashire's concern, the Indian experience was not exceptional, with export growth of only 1.7% per annum. The overall Indian export performance may have been affected by commodity price trends; Indian real income per capita increased by 14.6 per cent between the 1870s and the 1890s as industrialisation got underway. Silver depreciation also certainly played a role in the emergence of Japan as the first Asian industrial power. Japanese exports increased at 5.6% per annum between the 1870s and the 1890s, while it has been estimated that Japanese real national income tripled over the same period (Nugent, 1973; Latham, 1979).

Notes

1 Bank of England Archives, London (hereafter BoE) Cou/B610: Deputy Governor's Letters, f. 152. I am grateful to the Governor and Company of the Bank of England for permission to consult the institution's archives and to the

staff of the Museum and Historical Research section, especially the late Eric Kelly, for their help and assistance.

2 Born in 1819, Gibbs was a director of the Bank of England from 1853 until 1901. He also wrote (with H.R. Grenfell) *The Bimetallic Controversy* (1886) and *Colloquy on Currency* (1893), a 144-page 'play' – a pentameron, perhaps a reflection of a classical education. He was MP for the City of London between April 1891 and July 1892, but did not use the opportunity to further the bimetallic campaign. Bimetallism infected the Gibbs family with H.C. Gibbs writing *A Bimetallic Primer*.

3 1824–1902; was MP for Stoke (1862) and Treasurer of the Political Economy Club from 1882. The Grenfell family fortune was based upon the copper trade, represented in London by Pascoe Grenfell and Sons, copper merchants. Members of the family were directors of the Bank of England almost continuously from 1830 until 1940. See Cassis (1985).

4 British imports of wheat from India began in 1872, by the early 1880s they amounted to 9.5m hundredweights per annum average (Mitchell and Deane, 1971: 101). American farmers had similar complaints regarding United States' imports of wheat from the sub-continent.

5 1840–1923; a representative of the agricultural interest. Was MP for Mid Lincolnshire 1868–1906, Chancellor of the Duchy of Lancaster 1885–6, President of the Board of Agriculture 1886–92, and President of the Local Government Board 1895–1900. Chaplin continued to campaign in the Commons for bimetallism right into the 1890s.

6 1841–1928, Barbour's special interest was India; he was a Financial Member of the Council of the Governor-General of India between 1887 and 1893 and a member of the Indian Currency Committee, 1898. He continued to write on the monetary problem with respect to India into the 1890s; see, for instance, *The National Review* (April, 1895).

7 1837–99; lawyer and MP for Durham 1874–85. Solicitor-General 1880–5, Lord High Chancellor 1886 and 1892–5.

8 1834–14; Deputy Master of the Mint 1870–94. British Official Director of the Suez Canal Co.

9 1834–1913; London banker and scientist.

10 1819–99; Free Trader and Civil Servant, beginning as Assistant Secretary to the Marine Department of the Board of Trade, 1850, and becoming Permanent Secretary to the Board of Trade.

11 Former Governor of the Bank of England. The then Governor, Mark Collet, thought it would not be proper to give evidence before the Commission. A few directors of the Bank did favour bimetallism; three senior directors gave their personal views – J.G. Hubbard, M.W. Blake and A.C. de Rothschild. See Clapham, 1970: 313–14.

12 Sitting on the Commission led Leonard Courtney, former Professor of Political Economy at University College, London, to become a protagonist for bimetallism.

13 In his 'Cross of gold campaign' when Bryan denounced the East as 'the enemy's country', he was airing a view which rural America had held since the eighteenth

century. Bryan, the rural radical and abstainer by family upbringing, was also a prohibitionist and campaigned for the drys in the 1920s. None the less, he gained his seat in Congress in 1890 with the help of Omaha liquor interests. He did not mention prohibition in his 1896 campaign and only supported openly national prohibition from 1920 once it had become clear to him that his personal presidential hopes were dashed – after the 1908 campaign (Sinclair, 1962: 147–53).

14 BPP, 1893–4: LXV, *Committee on the Indian Currency*, c. 7060 [it was chaired, like the Gold and Silver Commission, by Herschell]; 1899: xxxi, *Committee on Indian Currency*, c. 9390. In 1899 Giffen opposed a gold currency for the sub-continent, along with Indian nationalists, on the grounds that silver was the tradition and a change would cause more problems than it resolved. Marshall spoke for an Indian gold standard and one of his pupils later cut his spurs on the subject (Keynes, 1913).

10 The world food economy and pre-World War I Argentina

C. KNICK HARLEY

The world became a single market for food between the middle of the nineteenth century and the First World War. Europe constituted the centre, importing from the periphery; the frontier, where new settlement occurred in response to export opportunities, moved from the American mid-west into the Russian steppes and the high plains of North America and eventually into the Southern Hemisphere. Examination of the last frontier in Argentina clarifies the evolution of the integrated international trading economy of the late nineteenth century. Alec Ford (1962; 1965) used Argentina as a window to illuminate the operation of the gold standard and particularly the monetary interaction between Britain and the new economies of the periphery during the business cycle. A longer-run view of Argentina, focused on product markets, provides an equally useful perspective on trade expansion and specialisation in the centre and the periphery. During the late nineteenth century, the world integrated economically with central economies specialising in manufacturing and services, and frontier areas, culminating in Argentina, successively supplying world markets with grains and meat.

Two underlying forces integrated world product markets. First, transportation costs fell dramatically as new technologies of iron production and steam power were applied to railroads and ocean shipping. Second, population grew rapidly in Europe and older settled areas of the United States. The resulting higher agricultural prices on the frontier drew settlement for agricultural production to new areas while the centre increasingly specialised in manufacturing and services. Transportation costs, which were high at mid-century and then fell dramatically, imparted a particularly spatial character to the evolution of the nineteenth century world economy. Before mid-century, one integrated economy centred on the industrial areas of north-western Europe and extended into a Baltic hinterland for agricultural supply, and a second centred on the north-eastern United States and extended into the mid-west. During the balance of the century, these two economies became integrated and extended their influence beyond the Black Sea in one direction and beyond the Mississippi in the other, finally to encompass the entire globe.

For approximately a generation between 1860 and 1890, transportation improved particularly rapidly. This epoch was dominated by spatial disequilibrium created by suddenly lower transportation costs, while before and after, less spectacular expansion occurred in response to population and income growth. The era of rapid transportation improvement saw incorporation of the entire United States, the steppes on south-eastern Europe, and even significant portions of South Asia into a Europe-centred food economy. By the turn of the century, only the most remote regions in the prairies of Canada and in the Southern Hemisphere still remained to be settled and they were brought into the international system by the slower but continuing process of population growth.

The era dominated by rapid technological change in transportation possesses a particular unity. Agricultural settlement into hitherto sparsely settled regions, made attractive by low-cost transportation, put unprecedented pressure on domestic agriculture in Britain and the eastern United States. Seldom have well-established activities coming under such sustained pressure from new technology on a global scale (although British textiles earlier in the century provides some parallel). During the previous century, trade had increased dramatically as new products – sugar, tobacco and cotton – not produced in the importing region became staples. In addition, Britain's timber imports had also grown dramatically, but in response to domestic depletion and rising prices. The great late-nineteenth-century expansion of trade in agricultural commodities, in contrast, generated dramatic declines in the price of domestically-produced import-competing food in the consuming regions. This result was confined to the era of unique transportation improvement. By the interwar years, geographical expansion of agriculture was complete. Agricultural output eventually resumed its growth but now on the basis of biotechnology rather than geographic expansion and protective policies discouraged international trade in foodstuffs. By the First World War, the era of expanding trade based on the exchange of agricultural commodities for manufactured goods was coming to an end. Already, particularly in Europe, the more modern pattern of trade dominated by two way exchange of manufactured goods was emerging.

World integration reached its global limits with Argentina, Australasia and the Canadian west. Between the American Civil War and 1890, the spectacular impact of steam and iron technology radically shrunk global space but insufficiently to incorporate the most distant areas. The full inclusion of the Southern Hemisphere into the Atlantic economy, although clearly dependent on new transportation technology, particularly the technology of meat transportation, lacked the dramatic impetus from the technological revolution in transportation which had led to the spectacular character of the preceding several decades. The final stage of global integration was driven mainly by growth in population and income.

In the course of nineteenth-century international integration, capital and labour moved to increasingly distant areas to produce agricultural goods to exchange for manufactured goods. Usually the export commodities were foodstuffs, but textile raw materials were often important. The international grain market emerged first and illustrates clearly the relative impact of transportation improvement and increasing demand as underlying driving forces. Late in the century, meat joined grain as a major item in international trade – and was particularly important for Argentina. The driving forces resembled those in grain, but important differences existed. Unlike the grain trade, the organisation of the meat trade was fundamentally transformed. Transporting meat, either live, frozen or chilled, required close coordination which came to be provided by integrated meat firms.

Evolution of the grain market

The intercontinental grain trade epitomised the changes in the international economy created by iron and steam. Agricultural settlement expanded into the interior of the United States and of Southern Russia largely on the basis of the existing, but very different, agricultural techniques already in use in each region. The rapid growth and geographical extension occurred within a fundamentally unchanged framework developed by the European grain trade in earlier decades. Despite organisational improvements, such as the automatic handling of grain in bulk and the development of futures markets, the changes are well summarised as a lowering of the cost of transportation in an already sophisticated trade. International specialisation resulted from transportation improvement interacting with internationally mobile labour and capital in a world of increasing population.

The general outlines of the developments of railroads and steamships are well known, but the extent of the changes, particularly in the staple food trades, is often underestimated. The revolutionary nature of the change in the spatial features of the late nineteenth century economy is best illustrated by the contrasting trends of grain and meat (or cattle) prices in the American mid-west and Britain[1] (figure 10.1). The wedge between Chicago and British prices fell from equalling the Chicago price to relative insignificance in a half century.[2]

The grain market provides an excellent opportunity for quantitative analysis of causes and effects of underlying change because both the

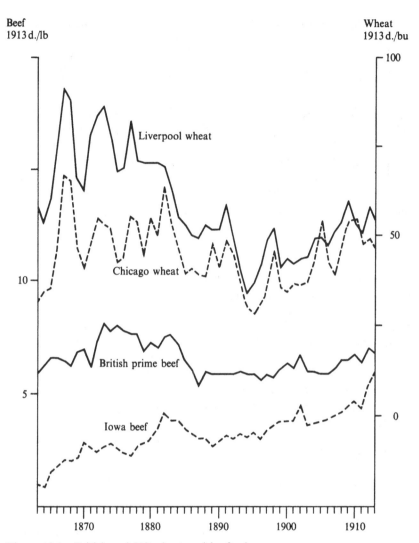

Figure 10.1   British and US wheat and beef prices.

product and the organisation were maintained unchanged over long periods. An appropriate model needs to focus on the spatial character of trade. Consider two regions separated by considerable transportation costs, the new with abundant land and access to competing factors (much by emigrating from the older areas) but little population, and the old with dense population relative to resources. New region supply and demand

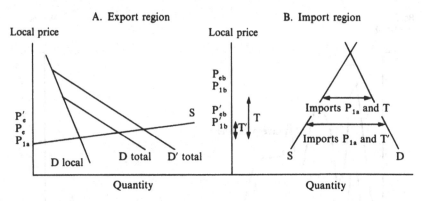

Figure 10.2   Spatial market with transportation cost.

schedules (local price of grain on the price axis) resembled region A in figure 10.2, while the old regions had schedules as in region B. Without trade, price would be high in the old region and low in the new region. The potential price differential exceeded the transportation costs between the regions (indicated as distance T in panel B), and provided incentives to trade. Trade would narrow the price differentials until an equilibrium was attained; the price in the exporting region generating excess supply equal to excess demand in the importing region generated by that price plus transportation cost. If the price difference exceeded transportation costs, traders would respond to profitable arbitrage opportunities, increase shipments and thereby narrow the price gap until the excess profits from arbitrage were eliminated. If the gap were less than transport costs, traders would cease shipment to avoid loss and the differential would increase.

Equilibrium can be found in figure 10.2 (one of several diagrams that could illustrate the same point). Transportation costs are the distance T (in panel B). For any price in the exporting region (A) there is a corresponding price in the importing region (B) equal to the price in the exporting region plus transport cost. Consider, for example, price P_{1a} which corresponds to the low non-trade price in the exporting region. That price plus transport cost equals P_{1b}. P_{1b} in the importing region is below the market clearing price in that region in the absence of trade; quantity demanded at that price exceeds quantity supplied. The difference is excess demand – the quantity the high cost region would be willing to import at price P_{1a} in the exporting region. To find equilibrium, this demand from the importer can be added to the domestic demand in the exporter to generate a total demand curve facing the exporter. Obviously there is excess demand in the exporting region at this price – supply equalled domestic demand without any export demand. A total demand curve (domestic plus export) for the exporting region can be constructed by repeating this procedure with other pairs of prices. At various prices in the exporting region, the excess demand in the importing country at that price plus transportation cost is added to the domestic demand curve. Equilibrium occurs at P_e where supply in the low cost region equals demand (domestic plus foreign excess demand at corresponding price plus transport costs).

The diagram can now be used to analyse the effect of falling transportation costs. A fall in transportation cost (from T to T') implies that a particular price in the exporting region now corresponds to a lower price in the importing region so import demand there will be greater, because local supply will be less and demand more. Consequently, at any given price, the total demand in the exporting region will have shifted out. Price will rise in the exporting region. The importing regions will also share in the decline in transportation costs through a lower price. At the higher prices in the exporting region more will be produced but less demanded, so exports must rise. The importing region will import this greater amount (since one region's exports is the other's import) only at a lower price that increases demand and lowers local supply.

Any shift of the underlying supply or demand curve will also shift equilibrium and can be incorporated in the figure in obvious ways. In fact, population increases shifting demand played a major role in late-nineteenth-century intercontinental trade expansion. The simple model can be extended to multiple supplying and demanding regions at the expense of some complication. In this case, equilibrium yields a price constellation with all trading regions' prices differing by relevant transportation costs. Equilibrium prices generate total excess demands in importing regions equal to total excess supplies in exporting regions.

The model can be used to quantify, at least approximately, the evolution of the wheat market between 1850 and the First World War. Demand was inelastic with regard to price[3] and shifted in proportion to population. Income elasticity was small enough to ignore. Research indicates that importing regions had approximately unit elastic supply. In the exporting region, supply response included the expansion of settlement in response to price and was somewhat more elastic. US experience, which is relatively well studied, provides a quantitative estimate that has been extrapolated to all regions despite obvious major differences among the exporting regions. With this specification, the effect of the change in Chicago–Liverpool wheat price differential and population growth can be analysed. The analysis is incomplete, however, because the movement of the Chicago–Liverpool price differential between the 1850s and the war, dramatic though it is, seriously understates the impact of the railways. Transportation cost between Chicago and the importing regions at mid-century would be unchanged without the railroad because most grain travelled by the Great Lakes, the Erie Canal and by sea even after the Civil War. Railroads' initial impact dramatically lowered the cost of moving wheat to Chicago from areas not adjacent to water transport.[4] So it is appropriate to calculate two equilibria with 1850 Chicago–Liverpool price differentials, one approximating the situation in the absence of railroads (which is close to the actual situation in 1850) and a second allowing for the impact of providing a complete railroad network with mid-century technology.

Analysis of change in the wheat market has been reported in detail elsewhere (Harley, 1986); results are summarised in table 10.1. The simulations take actual 1913 observations (reported in line 1) as a base and calculate equilibria with population and transportation cost changes. The values in line 2 estimate prices with prewar population but 1850 transportation technology, including a full railroad network in exporting regions. Line 3 calculates the effect of 1850 population, transportation technology and a full railroad network. The results indicate that already profitable railroad construction in 1850 would have increased frontier supply and driven down prices everywhere.[5] In grain-producing regions, both west of Chicago and in the mid west, substitution of railroad for road transportation would raise farm gate prices stimulating production even while the Chicago price fell. Line 4 estimates 1850 values in the absence of the complete railroad network; these calculated values are reassuringly close to actual values for 1850.

The distribution of the gains from transportation improvement among exporting and importing regions are the most interesting results from the simulations. Comparison of the equilibrium prices in lines 1 and 2 dramatically illustrate that, other things being equal, most of the benefits from the fall in transportation costs accrued to the consumers rather than the producers of wheat.[6] In the absence of population growth, transportation improvement would have resulted in considerably increased specialisation and increase in frontier production. In fact, however, most of the increase in production occurred in response to population growth (compare lines 2 and 3).

The gains from transportation improvement accrued principally to consumers because demand was inelastic and supply elastic.[7] Export price rose and the import price fell to absorb the fall in transportation cost. New equilibrium required that price rise in the exporters increase desired exports by the same amount the price fall in the importing region increase desired imports. Importers' demand and supply were inelastic while exporters' supply was elastic, so importers' price had to fall more than exporters' price rose.

Table 10.1 *Analysis of the world wheat market 1850–1913*

CASE	Chicago	Prices (1913 US$)		Quantities (1913 = 100)	
		New York	Britain	World	US West
1. 1913 Actual:					
	0.95	0.97	1.00	100	100
2. 1913 population, railroads, 1850 transportation cost:					
	0.90	1.55	1.85	95	77
3. 1850 population, railroads, 1850 transportation cost:					
	0.35	1.00	1.30	50	30
4. 1850 population, no railroads, 1850 transportation cost:					
	0.55	1.20	1.60	50	25

Source: Harley (1986), p. 607.

Analysis of the grain market challenges generally accepted conclusions on the impact of nineteenth-century transportation improvement. Recent work on transportation (Fogel, 1964; Williamson, 1974) has concentrated on the United States but a broader perspective is necessary. First, transportation costs are best considered as the wedge between prices in the consuming and producing region. Second, endogenous differences in movement of the price of the traded commodity in different locations must be near the center of the analysis. Robert Fogel's classic work did not examine the change in regional prices, while Jeffrey Williamson's attempt to go beyond Fogel's conclusion was seriously incomplete on the second criterion.

Contemporaries saw new technology in transportation as a distinguishing characteristic of their age. Robert Fogel, in asking the legitimate and potentially answerable question: 'what would it have cost to replace the transportation services of the US railways in 1890 with the next best alternative?' in fact, failed to address the primary issue. While it is easy to assume that the 1890 alternative was a pre-Industrial Revolution technology, Fogel's analysis makes clear this was not generally the case. The 1890 alternative to railroads in interregional trade (and in much of the intraregional as well) was water transport, which, particularly on the Mississippi River and on the Great Lakes which form Fogel's principal alternatives, had been influenced almost as strongly by iron and steam

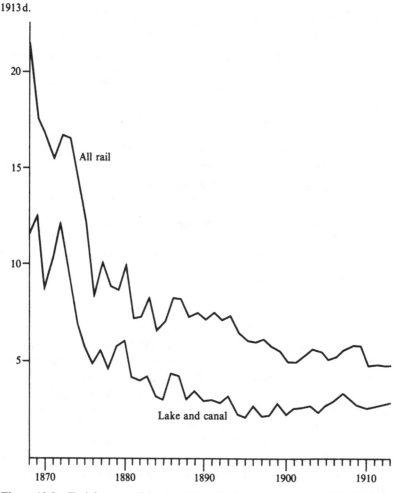

Figure 10.3   Freight rates Chicago to New York, water and rail, 1868–1913 (from US Statistical Abstract, British GNP deflator).

technology as the railroad. The first important application of steam to transportation had been on American rivers in the early nineteenth century, and improvements in the technology drove costs down dramatically through the century. Later in the century, iron and steam transformed shipping on the Great Lakes just as it did on the high seas. Between Chicago and New York both all rail, and lake and canal freights fell rapidly, although the rail series fell somewhat faster (figure 10.3), so comparison of rail and water in 1890 provides little information on the impact of transportation improvements between 1850 and the early twentieth century.[8]

Jeffrey Williamson attempted to remedy this limitation in Fogel's work in his model of the late nineteenth century American economy, by explicitly considering the effect of the decline in price differentials between the West and East. His analysis revealed substantially larger impacts for transportation improvements than had Fogel.[9] Williamson's work still falls short of adequately modelling the impact of the new technology because he assumed that the United States was small in the international economy and international price trends were exogenous. While the US alone probably had only modest impact on even the world wheat market, it is not reasonable to assume that the technological improvements in transportation had little impact. Williamson's assumption that the fall in the east coast price of agricultural commodities was exogenous led him to miss the main impact of transportation improvement.

The intercontinental meat trade

Meat was the second great intercontinental food trade of the late nineteenth century. Although Britain was the only major importer, the trade came to rival that in grain. By 1900, Britain's meat imports exceeded the value of her wheat imports by about a third. Meat exports became important later than grain and had particular impact on Southern Hemisphere exporters. Wool and hide exports had initially brought Southern Hemisphere exporters into the world market and wool remained overwhelmingly important; both Australia and Argentina began to export significant quantities of wheat in the 1880s but by 1913 refrigerated meat gained considerable importance amounting to nearly a third of Argentine export earnings and a fifth of New Zealand's. The general history of the meat trade is illustrated by Britain's extra European imports of live animals for slaughter and of refrigerated meat[10] (figure 10.4).

In broad outline the meat trade developed similarly to the grain trade. British prices declined while American producer prices rose as transportation cost fell and markets integrated (figure 10.1). There were, however, important differences in the development of trade in fresh meat – animals for slaughter and refrigerated meat – during the last quarter of the century. It is appropriate, therefore, to follow the traditional distinction between pig meat and butchers' meat, since the trade in beef and mutton evolved very differently from the trade in pig meat. Trade in pig meat was concentrated in bacon and hams. In 1900, bacon, ham and other salt pork at £17.7 million made up 92% of British pig meat imports, £13 million of this coming from North America and most of the balance from Denmark. The

Mn. cwts

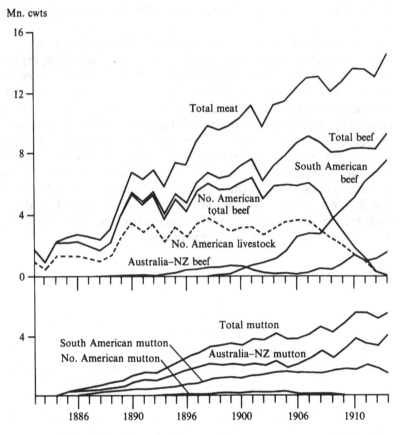

Figure 10.4   United Kingdom meat imports (for sources, see note 10 below).

United States had exported salted pork products before a large grain export trade developed. The meat, preserved by traditional methods, could be shipped without special treatment. The technology changed little over the course of the century[11] and the history of the growth of the trade closely paralleled that of grain. Increasing population stimulated demand and falling transportation costs encouraged international specialisation.

Butchers' meat, in the form of live animals, and beef and mutton entered intercontinental trade around 1880, and occasioned much more fundamental changes. Lower transportation costs and increased demand drove the developments, as they did in grain, but the impact of new technology cannot be simply summarised as much lower freight rates. New wholesale and retail distribution of fresh meat evolved with the rise of long distance trade. Regulation and technology combined to replace the age-old system of butchers purchasing live animals with a new system of centralised slaughter with dead meat moving in wholesale trade to the retail butchers. Major changes in industrial organisation accompanied the new distribution system. Large, vertically-integrated, firms developed in both meat distribution and transportation, with the American firms of Swift, Armour, and Morris emerging dominant in both exporting and importing regions. In ocean shipping, liner companies, transport of cattle and meat led to increasingly to liner dominance of world shipping.

The British meat market underwent fundamental change stimulated, in large part, by the growth of meat imports.[12] Prior to mid-century most meat found its way to the retail butcher on its own legs. By mid-century, railways and steam ships had taken over the long distance movement of cattle and a considerable wholesale trade in dead meat had developed within London. After mid-century, animal imports from the Continent, mainly shipped from ports in the Low Countries, joined the cattle from Ireland and Scotland that had long been part of the industrial areas' meat supply. Foreign, and Irish and Scots animals, like domestic cattle, were generally sold live to butchers. By the early 1870s some experimental shipments of American cattle were made to Britain and these animals, too, entered the British cattle trade.

Reaction to the outbreak of cattle plague in 1865, the first in the century (Perren, 1978: 106–14), fundamentally altered the British meat trade. The disease was conclusively traced to cattle arriving from Continental Europe. It had spread through Britain by intermediation of the live cattle markets where diseased imported cattle came in contact with British cattle. Disease then spread farther with further marketing of infected cattle. The losses of British cattle were extensive. British authorities reacted by introducing regulations to control animal diseases. Cattle imported from areas in which disease was prevalent were confined to quarantined areas in the ports of import and had to be slaughtered within ten days of landing. Imports were prohibited altogether from areas where disease was judged to be a major problem.

The initial regulations were directed towards animals from continental Europe and provided some assistance to the development of the North American trade. It would, however, be misleading to attribute much of the long term rise in the North Atlantic live cattle trade to the health restrictions on the imports of European cattle, although a considerable short term advantage arose from the total prohibition of German and Belgian cattle imposed on 1 January 1879 under the Contagious Diseases (Animals) Act of 1878. Other European cattle were allowed for port slaughter. Initially free import of US and Canadian cattle was permitted, but for American cattle the advantage was negligible since the Privy Council almost immediately (from 3 March 1879) included the United States among the 'scheduled countries' whose cattle were allowed only for port slaughter. Canadian cattle, remaining free to enter British markets until 1892, undoubtedly attained some advantage that Canadian authorities protected with careful quarantine measures in North America. None the less, the histories of the Canadian and United States trade were broadly similar.

The North Atlantic beef trade consisted of nearly equal quantities of meat shipped as live cattle and as refrigerated meat, with live cattle making up a slight majority of shipments. This coexistence requires brief comment. Refrigerated meat was considerably cheaper to ship but savings were offset by higher prices for meat from live cattle[13] (see figure 10.5) (Perren, 1978: 160). Ocean shipment of cattle became integrated into the general cargo trade on the North Atlantic but refrigerated meat did not, despite experiments with refrigerated space on cargo liners. Refrigerated meat was carried in the special circumstances that transatlantic passenger trade presented to American exporters. Passenger liner companies to New York (in contrast to passenger lines to Montreal) decided that the carriage of live cattle along with passengers reduced the vessels' attractiveness to passengers so much as to be unprofitable. The refrigerated meat trade, however, provided an unobjectionable cargo of considerable value even at freights below those attractive to cargo liners (Harley, 1989).

Trade in frozen meat developed after the mid-1880s, almost exclusively from very distant areas in the Southern Hemisphere – New Zealand, Australia, and the Argentine – and rapidly grew to considerable importance (Critchell and Raymond, 1912; Perren, 1978: ch. 10). Freezing, made possible by new technology of mechanical refrigeration, adapted the meat trade for great distances. From Australian and New Zealand ports, where the voyage of first-class steamships took approximately two months, a trade in live animals never developed despite the low animal prices in Australasia. The voyage to the Argentine was considerably shorter – it took just under a month's steaming to get from the Plate to Northern European ports – and during the 1890s a considerable trade in live cattle from Argentina developed, reaching a peak of 89,000 animals in 1898. This trade came to an abrupt end in 1900 when the British Privy Council imposed a total ban on Argentine cattle in response to foot and mouth disease. This ban remained in force, with a brief exception in 1903, and forced Argentina to export dead meat exclusively.

Early refrigeration was unable to maintain the narrow range of temperatures required to keep meat chilled through tropical waters but could preserve frozen meat. This was of relatively little consequence to

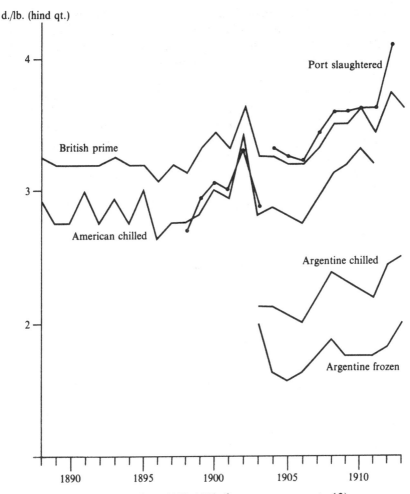

Figure 10.5 British beef prices, 1888–1913 (for sources, see note 13).

Australasian shippers, since the length of the voyage exceeded the period for which chilled meat could be kept. The need to rely on frozen transport also had little consequence for trade in mutton and lamb since these carcasses froze more effectively and with less quality loss than did beef. The frozen mutton trade grew rapidly. New Zealand started exporting about 1884; two years later, Argentine shippers started at slightly lower levels and Australia began a more sporadic and smaller trade (Perren, 1978: 214). The trade grew to more than 250,000 tons annually in the immediate prewar years and consisted of nearly half of Britain's mutton supply.

A frozen beef trade from the Southern Hemisphere developed at the same time but more slowly and erratically, hindered by the deterioration in the quality of beef from freezing (see the price data in figure 10.5). Until prohibited, the trade in live cattle provided a more attractive alternative for Argentina. In 1898, Argentina exported 89,000 live cattle worth £1.3 million to Britain but only 150,000 hundredweight of frozen beef worth £150,000. Prohibition of cattle imports in 1900 revolutionised the Argentine trade; 772,000 cwt. of frozen beef worth £1.2 million were imported in 1901 and the trade grew rapidly thereafter. Australasian shipment of frozen beef developed before the Argentine trade but by the turn of the century were irregular and quickly fell to a secondary position.

Improved refrigeration technology in the early twentieth century finally permitted the shipment of higher value chilled beef from Argentina and frozen beef shipments declined. Unofficial figures show Argentine chilled beef appearing on the British market around the turn of the century and its shipments increasing rapidly. In 1909 (the first year chilled and frozen are shown separately in the official statistics) the value of British imports of Argentine chilled and frozen beef was practically identical; by 1913, the value of chilled beef imports was nearly twice the value of frozen.

Industrial organisational consequences of the meat trade

The intercontinental trade in animals, the advent of statutorily mandated port slaughter and the trade in refrigerated meat radically altered business organisation, in both the meat trade itself and the shipping industry associated with it. Fresh meat distribution networks required dedicated skills and physical assets with few alternative uses. As Oliver Williamson (1985) has pointed out, transaction specific assets present coordination difficulties with small firms at various stages of production and distribution and invite hierarchical arrangement. In the meat trade, integrated firms replaced the small firms that had concentrated on individual stages of production and distribution. Contracting problems of asset specificity do not, however, always lead to integrated firms; sometimes long-term contractual relationships emerge between firms. Such long-term contracting developed between the meat firms and the ocean liner companies and with railroad companies within the exporting regions in the late nineteenth century. In ocean shipping, these contracts, combined with the technological conditions of cattle and meat transportation, increased the role of the liners in carriage generally.

The international trade in meat initially involved the shipment of live cattle and only modestly altered condition of distribution. As larger numbers of cattle moved longer distances, logistics of moving and caring for the cattle in transit become more complex and urgent, leading to greater organisation of the trade. Without advanced planning, shipping space and fodder could not be obtained from local sources as simply as they had previously. Coordination failures were potentially more serious than previously, but live cattle could be relatively easily cared for if unforeseen events developed, and little new specific capital was needed. Relatively small firms could still compete effectively.

Statutory port slaughter greatly increased the urgency of coordination by eliminating the leeway of coping with coordination failure by simply feeding cattle for a few days. Meat imports were no longer (relatively) non-perishable cattle but now highly perishable meat whose distribution required transaction-specific organisation and physical assets. Most obviously, adequate and reliable transportation and storage in England had to be arranged. Rather less obviously, aggregate supplies had to be coordinated to avoid gluts and shortages. The same coordination and distribution needs were even more pressing in the refrigerated meat trade, since American-killed meat reached Britain after a substantial part of its storage life expired.

Under these conditions, vertically integrated firms came to dominate the meat trade. In the 1880s, leading firms that were developing the dead meat trade in the United States – Armour, Swift and Morris – developed substantial interests in the transatlantic beef and cattle trade and quickly came to handle most meat and cattle shipments. In the 1890s, they established British subsidiaries to handle meat distribution and by the early years of this century they had moved extensively into wholesale distribution not only in London and Liverpool but in provincial centres as well (Perren, 1978: 164–6). The large firms grew, both in America and in international trade, primarily by providing reliable transportation and distribution during the relatively short period in which dead meat could be marketed. Large integrated firms proved to have an advantage over fragmented firms at various stages because they could coordinate the specialised equipment and organisation required for handling the perishable product (Yeager, 1981: ch. III).

Special requirements of the meat trade also altered ocean transportation. Because of interrelatedness within shipping technology, the impact of cattle and meat shipments was greater than might be supposed. Beef imports, both live cattle, which remained the most important source of imports, and dead meat provided challenges to ocean shipping. Shippers of cattle and meat depended on regularly available shipping space to enable them to provide regular supply. Shipping companies, for their part, provided specially built vessels for the carriage of cattle and expensive insulated hold space and refrigeration machinery for meat. Both shipper and carrier had commitments whose value depended on continued performance by the other. Asset specificity, although inviting hierarchical organisation, did not lead to integration of transportation capacity into the meat firms because ocean shipping is extremely capital intensive, and meat and cattle never exhausted the capacity of the vessels in which it was carried. Transactions between the meat companies and the shipowners were structured between independent firms, with provisions to protect the transaction specific assets of each. Contracts of considerable duration for fixed amount of shipping space per week became the standard transaction. The meat company agreed to pay for space that the liner company guaranteed to provide, whether used or not. At a minimum these contracts ran for several months; in the North Atlantic, annual contracts seem to have been most common. In the Argentine after the turn of the century, the contracts were of even longer duration, with three-year contracts common. These longer contracts probably reflected the even greater commitments and difficulty of arranging alternatives that both the shipping firms and the packers faced in Argentina.

Cattle and meat contracts played an important role in increasing the importance of large ship-owning firms in late nineteenth century ocean shipping (Harley, 1989). Long-term contracting in the meat trade required liner organisation with substantial fleets of vessels; cattle and meat contracts also committed ships to regular liner sailings. The cattle and meat, however, never filled the vessels on which they were carried. Consequently these liners, already committed to the trade, bid vigorously for the other available cargo. By the end of the 1880s on the North Atlantic, the capacity of liner companies – particularly those engaged in the cattle trade – had become so great that they could carry all the other American exports to the principal liner ports. Liners bidding for cargoes drove freight rates below rates tramp steamers would accept. By this process, the live and fresh meat trade altered the transportation conditions on grain and provisions from America.

Argentina and the international economy

Westward expansion of the United States was the most important manifestation of international integration. The growth of the American economy, however, was turbulent and confusing and the forces of integration are difficult to disentangle in the emergence of a great economic and political power. Consequently examination of the small late-coming economies, Argentina, Canada and Australasia, helps clarify the history of nineteenth century integration. Of these economies, Argentina's history illuminates the expansion of the international economy more closely than the others.

Canada is often linked with Argentina as a prime example of the final integration of the world economy but the comparison is misleading. Certainly, the great grain potential of the Western Prairies was exploited in the decade before the war and Canada at last shared in the frontier expansion that the United States had enjoyed for generations. The impact of the 'wheat boom' on Canada should not, however, be overemphasised; even in 1920, there were more farmers in Ontario than in all the Prairies. Equally, Canadian farmers had long exported cattle; since the 1880s, the trade had been more important relative to the size of the economy even than in the United States. Between 1886 and 1890, for example, Britain imported about 400,000 cattle from Canada, over a quarter of all the cattle imported from North America. Canada was not a new entrant into the international food economy at the end of the century.

The Australasian colonies more closely parallel Argentina, but Australia was beset by persistent problems of drought while New Zealand concentrated heavily on frozen mutton. Argentina, deeply involved in both grain and meat, best illustrates the 'closing of the frontier' on a global scale. Argentina began to enter the international economy in the 1880s, but only during and after the Boer War did integration become pervasive.

Transportation improvement and demand shifts in response to population and income together drove integration of the world economy but their respective importance varied from time to time. Transportation improvements dominated expansion from 1860 to 1890 but were largely spent by the end of the 1880s. The transportation revolution incorporated most, but not quite all, of the globe into a single market. The final inclusion of the Southern Hemisphere exporters was accomplished by growing demand.

The great impact of steam and iron on transportation costs occurred rather later than a simple chronology of invention leads us to believe. The textbook innovation in iron production and steam power occurred in the eighteenth century, but railroads and steamships cheapened transportation after the American Civil War.[14] When the transportation revolution came, it came very fast, at least as timed by a clock of population growth and migration, the other driving forces of international integration. The convergence of the price of American spring wheat in Chicago and Liverpool illustrates the process (see figure 10.1). The differential equalled the Chicago prices in the mid 1850s but had fallen to only just over 20% of the Chicago price by the early 1880s (Harley, 1980: 220). By the end of the 1880s, the great technological improvements were complete and transportation costs fell more slowly.

While transport improved most rapidly, interregional integration and specialisation lagged behind opportunities. Expansion of frontier agriculture involved settlement, infrastructure creation, and farm-making, all of which took time. As a result, agricultural prices remained high and frontier opportunities attractive until about 1890 when settlement finally exhausted the opportunities opened by transportation. The extent of the lag and opportunities varied. A wide gap opened during the American Civil War that the great postwar boom nearly eliminated but a gap widened again in the late 1870s. Unexploited new opportunities gave particular force to the American boom after the Civil War and to the subsequent boom of the 1880s; both exploited opportunities for settlement and specialisation created by the great transportation innovations. After 1890, transportation technology improved much more slowly, and in addition, transportation costs had fallen to a point where further reductions had small impact. Consequently, slower moving forces of population and income growth dominated the integration of the remaining export economies.

Slower underlying change, combined with some over-optimism in the 1880s boom, explain the periphery difficulties in the 1890s. Recovery was slow by the standards of the recent past. Strong external impetus to development finally came to Argentina in the years before the war, not as part of a world-wide disequilibrium as occurred in the previous generation, but because relatively modest changes in the big economies, particularly in the United States, had a magnified impact on the modest remaining margin of expansion.

Before the 1880s, Argentina's modest export economy had rested mainly on hides obtained from the vast herds of feral cattle, escaped descendants of early colonial stock, that roamed the Pampas wild. Both domestic and international stimuli to integration into the world food economy arose in the 1880s. Domestically, the era opened with the successful conclusion of General Julio Roca's 'Conquest of the Desert' in 1879 which ended Indian threat to European exploitation of the Pampas. Newly available land, attractive with existing transportation technology, drew international resources (railroad investment and immigration) into the Pampas for grain production. By the middle of the 1880s, refrigeration technology also attracted capital, most of it British, into the first 'frigorificos' to provide frozen mutton for the British market. Early in the 1890s shipments of live cattle to the British market began. Argentina's initial era came to a dramatic close with the Baring Crisis in 1890–1. The crisis, like the expansion, resulted from a complicated mixture of domestic and international influences. On one hand, international commodity prices had fallen to long run equilibrium levels consistent with the transportation technology and may even have been driven somewhat lower by investments predicated on the higher prices that had prevailed earlier in the decade. Low commodity prices and an Argentine infrastructure with excess capacity made additional investment unattractive to the international community. At the same time the situation was greatly worsened by the unsustainable banking innovations that had been undertaken for primarily domestic reasons in the late 1880s.

The 1890s were a difficult period for Argentina. Net immigration nearly ceased and railroad building was severely limited. Despite falling prices and lack of prosperity, trade volumes grew rapidly during the decade as farmers, railroads and frigorificos all accepted lower returns on costs previously sunk. Grain exports grew from very modest levels to nearly 2 million tons a year by the middle of the decade before falling back. More spectacularly the exports of frozen mutton more than doubled during the decade and the exports of live cattle to Britain increased to nearly 90,000 head in 1898. By the years immediately before the Boer War, British animal and meat imports from Argentina considerably exceeded grain imports, although the relative trend importance of grain and meat is hard to judge because of the volatility of grain exports (figure 10.6).

The Boer War (1899–1902) brought temporary resurgence to Argentina (Hanson, 1938: ch. V). British military demand for meat in South Africa provided a substantial boon to the Argentine meat export economy and attracted investment into new freezing capacity in the Plate. Expansion of freezing capacity was also stimulated, in a more negative way, of course, by the exclusion of live Argentine cattle from the British market in 1901. Prosperity, however, was temporary, and the new ventures into frigorificos proved unprofitable following the end of the South African War. None the less, the trade in frozen beef grew rapidly. By 1901 British imports were 772,000 tons of frozen beef; a more than 50% increase over the meat on the nearly 90,000 live cattle of the late 1890s.

Trend developments eventually replaced the temporary impetus of the Boer War. After a brief setback, Argentine exports grew dramatically during the last years before the war, attracting new investment and immigration. British food prices illustrate the new character of the immediate prewar period. From the 1870s until the 1890s, improvements in transportation technology dominated and British prices fell while prices rose in export regions. In the decade before the War, however, British and export prices rose together. Increased demand had replaced cheaper transport as the primary driving force.

A striking feature of the immediate pre-war years when Argentina became an important exporter was the disappearance of the United States as a leading food exporter. The sudden end of American food exports is astonishing unless we realise that a microcosm of the world economy existed within the United States. The West was an important part of the periphery, a major food exporter; but the East was a central industrial region that imported food and had a geographical first claim on western food. This had been the case throughout the century and remained

Mn. 1913 £

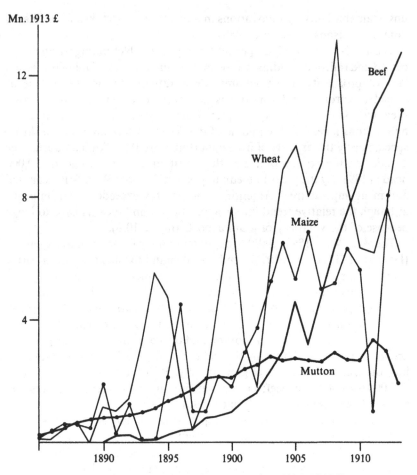

Figure 10.6   Principal British imports from Argentina, 1895–1913 (for sources, see note 13).

unaltered, but the net balance changed. American wheat exports dropped from an annual average of 22 million quarters in the late 1890s to 14 million just before the war and by then almost all the grain leaving the country came from the Pacific Coast; the interior surplus fed the industrial East. A similar development occurred in meat. North American cattle imported into Britain declined from a peak of about 550,000 head in the first years of the century to only 12,000 in 1913 and chilled beef declined from a peak of over 3 million hundredweight to only 1,000 hundredweight in 1913. Growing population and the extension of arable farming into the range cattle land of the west eliminated the US meat surplus.

American meat export decline coincided with the appearance of technology that permitted export of chilled beef from Argentina. British imports of Argentine beef expanded from about a million hundredweight at the turn of the century to nearly 3 million hundredweight in 1912, largely replacing North American exports of the previous decade (see figure 10.4). Frozen beef from Australia and to a lesser extent New Zealand also expanded rapidly to provide an additional million or million and a half hundredweight by the outbreak of the war. Despite concern in America that the export decline was the result of competitive pressure from the Southern Hemisphere, informed contemporaries concluded that causation, in fact, went the other way. American cattle prices rose, gradually after 1906 then rapidly after 1909, mirroring the fall in exports. Western American supply of beef had fallen while American population growth continued (Clemen, 1923:437; Edminster, 1926: ch. III). American demand exhausted domestic supplies; prices rose and Argentine sources seized a profitable opportunity.

Argentina responded with a great growth spurt. Railway mileage doubled between the turn of the century and the War, immigration and foreign borrowing resumed on a large scale after 1904 (Hanson, 1938: ch. VI). The export stimulus led to general growth in Argentina. Historians' long-run verdict on this period has been mixed, however, primarily because the institutional arrangements that accompanied the export boom have been seen as counterproductive in the long run. Meat exports were concentrated in the hands of a few principal shippers. Furthermore, the meat trade and the meat exporters developed connections with the landowning elite in Argentina and the economic power and class structure that arose has frequently been noted as a structural weakness that plagued Argentina later in the twentieth century (Smith, 1969: ch. II).

It is beyond the purpose of this essay to assess the long-run implications for Argentina of the organisation of early twentieth century expansion. It is, however, appropriate to place some, at least, of those institutions within the context of the late nineteenth century international food economy. The North Atlantic meat trade, in particular, provides insights into the origins and economic strength of the large meat exporting firms. Large firms had earlier come to dominate the meat trade in the North Atlantic and extension of that role to the Argentine meat trade is hardly surprising. The frozen meat trade required specific investments at various geographic locations: freezing plants in Argentina, cold storage at British ports, coordinated distribution within Britain. The transactions-specific assets in the distribution chain presented debilities to market transactions between independent firms at various stages. Consequently a small number of integrated firms, initially British, such as James Nelson and Sons Ltd., dominated the Argentine meat exports from the beginning. Five companies began in the mid-1880 of which only three survived into the 1890s. Four additional firms were established during the Boer War boom.

The structure changed in detail but not in essence after 1907. The major American meat firms entered the Argentine market as chilled beef trade became more important. Swift purchased the predominantly English La Plata Cold Storage in 1907. This integrated Argentine refrigeration capacity with Swift's British distribution network for chilled beef. In 1909, the other American firms entered Argentina. A combine of Swift, Armour and Morris purchased a plant at La Blanca that had been set up by Argentine producer interests. For the remaining years before the war the trade was in the hands of seven firms, the largest two American owned and the remainder with British and Argentine interests. The dynamics of changing market share are somewhat unclear during this period (Hanson, 1932: ch. V). Collusive oligopolistic agreements can be documented and the firms were undoubtedly engaged in strategic behaviour. The Americans certainly both benefited from and contributed to the rapid increase in the share of the higher quality chilled beef in the trade. By 1906, just before Swift's entry, chilled beef's share was just over a third; by 1913, the chilled had grown enormously to 5.2 million hundredweight while the frozen had fallen to 1.9 million. The American firms had over half the Argentine meat trade by the eve of the war, and some 60% of chilled beef exports, benefiting from their relevant previous experience and facilities (Hanson, 1932: 171).

Conclusion

In a little over half a century before the First World War, the market for first grain and then meat became a single global entity. Integration was brought about by the combined effects of technological improvement in transportation and of population growth in old industrial centers. Argentina entered the world food market at the last stage of the process. Argentina's entry, although part of a general process, differed significantly from earlier expansion, particularly in the United States, because the spectacular transportation cost reductions of the 1870s and 1880s were not duplicated during the generation before the war. Argentina's boom awaited population growth that increased European demand and nearly eliminated the food surplus of the United States.

Considerable research already exists on the grain market but meat, although nearly as important, is relatively poorly studied. Meat exports became important later than grain and were central in the integration of the Southern Hemisphere food exporting economies. The international trade in meat also introduced institutional changes in the organisation of exports. Demand growth, advances in the technology of refrigeration, and British regulation underlay the growth of trade refrigerated meat which became Argentina's primary export. Perishability of the meat led to the organisation of the trade around large integrated firms able to coordinate from slaughter to retail outlet. These firms originated in North America and spread to both Europe and South America. It is likely that in Argentina they possessed more market and political power than they had in the larger and much more diversified American economy where they originated.

Notes

1 The wheat prices are from Harley (1980). British meat prices are from Sauerback continued in the *Journal of the Royal Statistical Society*. Iowa prices are farm prices for beef cattle from Strand (1942), p. 936 converted to meat prices on the assumption that 55% of the weight is meat. All prices have been deflated by a British GNP deflator (Deane, 1968: 104–5; Feinstein, 1972: T 132).

2 To be sure, other organisational changes beyond the direct prices of transportation accompanied transportation improvements and contributed to the narrowing of the price gap.

3 A value of −0.3 is used in the calculations.

4 See Fogel (1964), ch. 3 and Fishlow (1965), ch. 2.

5 Obviously the exact figures in this calculation, even more than the others, cannot be taken literally. In particular, in this simulation the Chicago price is driven below those actually observed and the assumed supply elasticity may not be relevant in those ranges.

6 A similar result arises from a comparison of 1850 populations with 1850 and 1913 transportation costs.

7 The effect of the different elasticities of response are reinforced by the additive nature of transportation costs. Thus, if the effects of the fall in transportation costs were split evenly between exporting and importing regions, the percentage rise in price in the exporting region would be greater than the percentage fall in the importing region because export price was below the import price by the amount of transportation cost.

8 Fogel (1979) is, in fact, very clear on this point.

9 Williamson's particular calculations seem, however, to have been seriously flawed. See Khan (1986).

10 The data come mainly from Perren (1978), pp. 131, 164, 170, 213–14. Meat imports prior to 1890 and Argentine chilled beef after 1908 come from the British Annual Statement of Trade. Meat and live animals have been aggregated following the proceedure in Hooker (1909), pp. 320–1.

11 The seasonality of the business altered as refrigerated packing houses allowed the curing and packing process to be carried out year around, beginning in the 1870s. There were also issues of quality, relating primarily to the high proportion of fat on American swine, that underwent some change.

12 The discussion that follows depends heavily on the excellent account in Perren (1978).

13 The price data for domestic meat is the Sauerbeck series. Port slaughtered American meat prices come from the annual agricultural statistics in the British Parliamentary Papers. This series has a break in 1903. Evidence suggests that the gap shown after 1903 also existed earlier. Other prices come from W. Weddel and Company's *Annual Report of the Frozen Meat Trade.* The British and the port slaughtered series represent thè price for meat from an entire animal while other prices are for hind quarters. Hind quarters sold for about 1d. per pound more than fore quarters so the British slaughtered prices are about $\frac{1}{2}$d. low relative to other prices. Consequently the quotations for British beef and port slaughtered beef have been increased by $\frac{1}{2}$d. in figure 10.5.

14 For a discussion of the impact technologies on transportation, see Fishlow (1966) and Harley (1988).

Part IV

The macroeconomy in the interwar years

11 Institutional rigidity in the British labour market, 1870–1939: a comparative perspective

MARK THOMAS

Despite the common experience of large-scale unemployment in the inter-war period, we find the two decades in many ways very different from each other and linked by huge depression of a world-wide order. (Alec Ford, 1984: p. 6)

Although the focus of economic historians of inter-war Britain has traditionally fallen onto the troubles of the 1930s, in many respects it is the previous decade that is the more puzzling. This is especially true of the behaviour of the labour market, and, in particular, in terms of unemployment rates – the conventional barometer of economic health. In a recent review of the comparative macroeconomic performance of industrialised nations, Newell and Symons (1988) observe that on average unemployment rates were 2.8 times as high in the 1930s as in the 1920s. In Britain, however, the comparable figure was considerably lower, at 1.4. The primary reason for the shallowness of the depression lies, of course, in the obdurately high level of joblessness in the 1920s. The statistics of the unemployment insurance scheme provide an average figure for the 1920s of 11.2% – a level of industrial unemployment matched only by the Scandinavian countries. Indeed, if we apply Maddison's (1964) revisions of the industrial series to produce economy-wide estimates, Britain stands alone.[1]

The issue of why unemployment rates were so high in Britain, both historically and comparatively, was a major research agenda for political economists in the 1920s. It is worth reminding ourselves that the issue did not arise with Keynes, and that his 'orthodox' and 'classical' economists were far from deaf to the severity of the problem. Pigou, Clay, and Cannan busied themselves throughout the twenties searching for the sources of persistently high unemployment. They concentrated attention on the operation of the labour market, and in particular on the institutional arrangements that prevented market clearing. With the onset of the Great Depression, and with the rise of the Keynesian paradigm, that perspective appeared to lose its relevance. The peculiarities of the British labour market mattered less when all countries suffered from the same disease. Unemployment became a problem of the macroeconomy, rather than the labour market. And, to a very large extent, that is where it has remained.

For Alec Ford and his generation of economic historians, the 1920s and 1930s were very different decades. Yet their way of approaching them was very similar. The emphasis was on macroeconomic disequilibrium – especially that linked to the international economy, through the decline in the great staples, the destruction of overseas assets, and the folly of the return to gold in the twenties, and the collapse of international markets and the intensification of beggar-thy-neighbour policies in the thirties. There is little in the Keynesian explanations of this generation of the sort of local conditions that were emphasised by contemporaries. In particular, there is almost no discussion of the impact of institutional rigidities on unemployment in the 1920s. The balance of thought has shifted considerably in the past decade, with the so-called supply-side revolution in macroeconomics. The first sign of this change among historians of interwar Britain came with the publication of Benjamin and Kochin's famous paper linking high unemployment to generous unemployment benefits.[2] The renaissance of classical thinking about the interwar economy has perhaps matured most fully in the work of Kent Matthews (1986). Yet, even here, there is surprisingly little attention paid to the structure and organisation of the labour market – especially to the themes explored by the earlier generation of classical theorists.[3]

The purpose of this chapter is to return to this earlier tradition. What were the developments in the British labour market between 1913 and 1921 that contemporaries considered responsible for its weak performance in the 1920s? How far were such developments peculiar to Britain? And to what extent should we attribute the high unemployment of the 1920s and the slow recovery of the 1930s to institutional rigidities? Finally, how should we characterise the labour market of the day in the light of the answers to such questions? Is Ford correct in seeing the sticky behaviour of money wage rates as 'fitt[ing] in well with the choice of a Keynesian style of approach' to interwar unemployment? (1984: 9). Or is another perspective more appropriate?

The institutional revolution in the British labour market 1880–1938

In the post-war period . . . there is strong reason to believe, that, partly through direct State action, and partly through the added strength given to workpeople's organisations engaged in wage bargaining by the development of unemployment insurance, wage-rates have, over a wide area, been set at a level which is too high . . .

and that the very large percentage of unemployment which has prevailed during the whole of the last six years is due in considerable measure to this new factor in our economic life. (Pigou, 1927b: 355)

The dominant representation of the classical-Keynesian debate over unemployment in undergraduate texts focuses on the competing claims of real and nominal wage rigidity in the interwar labour market. Although this is clearly too simplistic an interpretation of either position,[4] it is nevertheless true (Casson, 1983) that real wage rigidity was a major source of disgruntlement for the generation of economists before the *General Theory* – for Pigou, Clay and Cannan, as well as Hutt, Hicks and Beveridge (the first in proto-Austrian phase, the others before conversion to Keynesian thinking). For these men, the central clue to the intractability of interwar unemployment was to be found in the performance of the real wage relative to productivity. Clay (1929b: 339) estimated that real wages increased by 12% between 1907 and 1924, despite stagnant labour productivity. Bowley's figures were even more startling – full-time real earnings were 13% higher in December 1924 than in July 1914, and rose a further 6% by December 1929.[5] This, despite rates of unemployment that never fell below 8.7% between 1921 and 1929.[6] For theorists who believed, with Hicks, that 'the theory of the determination of wages in a free market is simply a special case of the general theory of value' in which prices and quantities are set by the forces of supply and demand (1932: 1),[7] this was only possible if there was some obstacle to arbitrage.[8] The real wage in the 1920s showed no signs of falling to accommodate the pressure of unemployment. Why not? The answer the pre-Keynesian provided was rooted in certain institutional peculiarities of postwar Britain.

Three aspects of the British labour market of the mid-1920s seemed pertinent. Firstly, the level of unemployment was unprecedented in recent historical terms. The trade union records showed an average (annual) unemployment rate between 1860 and 1914 of 4.5%, much below the average of 12.4% for 1921–9. Secondly, as noted above, British unemployment was considerably higher even than in the war-ravaged countries of Western Europe. Thirdly, unemployment was maldistributed within the British economy, being highest in the export-based staples, and lowest in those industries sheltered from foreign competition. The common denominator to these problems, apparently *sui generis* to 1920s Britain, was an institutional revolution in the labour market whose roots lay deep in the nineteenth century, which had gained momentum in the decade before the Great War, and which reached full maturity in the early twenties – the process of collective bargaining.

The leading players in the spread of collective bargaining were the trade unions, the government, and the employers (individually and through associations). According to Clay, 'organized labour had been fighting [for collective bargaining] for over a century' (1929: 177). The spread of unionism, especially in the phase of New Unionism after 1889, was largely predicated on the perceived success of collective negotiation for better pay and working conditions.[9] The extension of union membership (which doubled between 1900 and 1914, and again between 1914 and 1920) clearly involved more workers in this process. By 1920, over half the eligible industrial workforce belonged to a trade union.

The revolution in bargaining was not simply one of numbers. There was also a significant change in the mechanism of negotiation. Hicks (1930: 25) identified three stages in the evolution of collective bargaining: from the local negotiations of the mid nineteenth century, which were gradually formalised as the century wore on, through the 'establishment of rudimentary forms of general negotiations' in the wake of the formation of employers' associations after 1880, which were used mainly as a type of court of appeal from the localities, to the final phase of central bodies determining negotiating postures and strategies. None of this would have been possible without the generally hospitable environment provided by both employers and government (Geary, 1989; McKibbon, 1984). The rise of employers' associations after the 1880s (there were almost 1,500 such organisations by 1914) helped to rationalise the system (Garside and Gospel, 1982). The final phase in the establishment of formal bargaining arrangements was largely a wartime and postwar phenomenon, associated particularly with the Whitley Reports (1917–18) and the establishment of Joint Industrial Councils.[10] Clay's comments on the Whitley reports are revealing:

even in 1914 [the method of collective bargaining] had occupied the whole field in perhaps no industry, and in most industries occupied only a center surrounded by a ragged edge of unorganised bargaining. The fifty or sixty Joint Industrial Councils that survive represent a big extension of organised and systematic negotiation into territory formerly governed by intermittent and haphazard meetings. They have effected a considerable standardization of terms of employment and codification of agreements and customs, and so fixed, as it were, a habit of collective bargaining, which the war had encouraged, just before the post-war depression came to discourage it. (1929a: 176)

By 1925, there were an estimated three million workers covered by Joint Industrial Councils (Richardson, 1933: 118). The trend towards central coordination of bargaining between unions and employers perhaps reached its apogee in the 1920s when the Turner-Mond talks spawned a permanent National Industrial Council, composed of representatives of the TUC, the FBI and the National Confederation of Employers' Organisations, to discuss matters of significant industrial importance, and to monitor industrial conciliation (Chang, 1936: 210–11).

Moreover, collective bargaining was 'constitutionalised' by public decree (Clay, 1929b: 325). The core of the government's role was the construction of what Chang (1936: 16) referred to as 'the two principal institutions . . . of the British framework of industrial peace, namely, the system of social security and the complete recognition of trade unionism'. The latter was probably inevitable from the moment that the franchise was extended to the industrial working class in 1867. The traditionally pivotal pieces of legislation are the Trade Disputes Act,.1906, which counteracted the notorious Taff Vale judgement, and the Trade Union Act, 1913, which went half-way to doing the same for the Osborne Case. Clay (1929a: 186) perceived these decisions, along with the insertion of the Fair Wages Clause (which required employers to pay rates of wages and observe conditions of labour not less favourable than those commonly found in the local district) into public contracts as 'consistent with this reliance on, and encourage-ment of, collective bargaining' by the state. To the pre-Keynesian, however, it was the system of social security that was 'more significant in principle than [the] extension' of trade unionism (Clay, 1929b: 323).

The first stage in the public regulation of labour markets was the Trade Board system, introduced in 1909 in belated response to the discovery of the evils of sweating in the late 1880s and its increased publicity with the work of the Anti-Sweating League and the indefatigable Webbs. The original terms of the 1909 Act specified minimum wages in four industries (tailoring, paper-box making, machine-made lace finishing, and chain making),[11] but also laid down machinery for dealing with other industries in which 'exceptionally low wages' were the norm. By 1916, there were thirteen Trade Boards in place, setting minimum wages for about half a million workers.[12] Two years later, an amending Trade Boards Act was passed, 'to provide statutory wage-fixing machinery in trades where self-organisation of employers and of workers had . . . failed to render voluntary collective agreements effective throughout the trade' (Sells, 1939: 29–30). The state had taken on the burden of regulating wages and working conditions in 'orphan' industries that lacked adequate employee protection. By 1921, there were 63 Trade Boards in place, with responsibility for 3 million workers (International Labour Office, 1939, p. 104). Thereafter, the scope of the Boards diminished: by 1925, the coverage of the system had shrunk by 50% (Ministry of Labour, 1926a), and by 1935, although 47 Boards remained in existence, they covered only 1,136,000 workers (International Labour Office, 1939: 105). This gradual decline was to a limited extent countered by the passage of the Agricultural Wages (Regulation) Act in 1924, and the establishment of special boards in coal, cotton, and road haulage in the mid-1930s. And, even if their overall scope was declining, the minimum wage regulations none the less conferred added legitimacy to the principles of collective bargaining, as well as providing mechanisms for legal enforcement to supplement the industrial code of strike and lock-out.

By 1929, according to Clay's estimates (1929b: 324), as much as 60% of the British labour force (excluding domestic servants) was covered by collective agreements. But the consequences of rigid wage rates did not follow automatically – 'Has the extension of collective bargaining destroyed [the] plasticity [of the prewar labour market], this automatic adaptation of wage-rates to opportunities of employment?' Clay answered in the positive, but denied that it was inevitably so. 'The mere substitution of regular for informal discussion does not by itself make it more or less difficult to adjust wage-rates to varying conditions. The change is one of procedure only', he suggested (1929: 333). Wages were not entirely rigid in the 1920s; indeed, wage-changes were more frequent, and, because of the extension of national agreements, more extensive than before 1914. Yet, despite this increase in activity, unemployment remained. How could this apparent paradox be explained?

The solution was to be found in society's changing attitudes towards unemployment, its costs and consequences. For one, the spread of unemployment insurance enabled unions to be more aggressive, without bearing the consequences of the increased unemployment for which they were primarily responsible (Isles, 1934: 196). With the safety-net of generous benefits (now paid out of state rather than union funds), union members were less likely to rebel against their leadership if increased wages created unemployment (Clay, 1929b: 335). According to Clay, 'this comparative disregard of unemployment in wage determinations is as distinctive a change from prewar practice as the extension of collective bargaining, and much more significant for the problem' of wage rigidity (1929b: 336).[13] The onset of an insurance scheme, indeed, signalled to workers a change in the state's attitude towards wages as well as unemployment. Pigou, in his testimony to the Macmillan Committee, argued that 'resistances are very much strengthened by the general public sense since the war that you do not want to cut down people's wages . . . [t]here is a general feeling that this is the last thing that you would like to do if you can help it' (Pigou, 1931, quoted in Casson, 1983: 51). Moreover, the insurance scheme was expensive, and its costs bore primarily upon business. Clay posited that 'the burden upon the export industries of insurance contributions and [local] rates is a serious handicap in their endeavour to recover their pre-war trade', and a significant cause of the reduced competitiveness of British industries in international markets, the weakness of the overseas accounts, and the dismal level of unemployment in the staples (Clay, 1929a: 129–32, quotation from p. 132). The modern focus on the supply-creating effects of a high benefit–wage ratio, familiar from Benjamin and Kochin's provocative essay (1979), was relatively rarely argued at the time. There were exceptions – Cannan was certainly aware of the problem of subsidised search (1930: 46–7), as were Cassell (Corbett, 1990), Rueff (Benjamin and Kochin, 1979: 468ff.), and even Keynes (Beenstock and Warburton, 1986a: 2). However, most contemporary economists would have rejected the extreme argument associated with Benjamin and Kochin – that unemployment was little more than a statistical artefact created by the generosity of state hand-outs. Pigou, for one, emphasised the welfare costs of high and persistent unemployment (1927a: 220–1), and considered it to be fundamentally a problem visited upon those out of work by the intransigence of the employed (1927b: 359, 366).

The rise of collective bargaining altered attitudes in other directions as well. Clay suggested that 'non-economic factors' were introduced into wage bargaining with the spread of organised, widely publicised negotiations. He bemoaned the 'appeal to social and ethical standards of "fair" and "living" wages, to pseudo-principles such as the sanctity of pre-war *real* wages, to the unpopularity of reducing rates of wages of the lower-paid workers, none of which have any bearing on the capacity of industry to pay wages and provide employment' (Clay, 1929b: 334–5). One particular concern of contemporaries was the increase in cost-of-living consciousness which grew out of the impact of wartime inflation on real earnings. Cost-of-living bonuses had become institutionalised in labour contracts as early as 1915 and were sufficiently widely applied that workers fully expected their continuation after the war. Public opinion clearly leaned in that direction, as evidenced by the passage of the Wages (Temporary Regulation) Act of 1918 which forbade employers from paying lower rates than those prevailing on Armistice Day, without application to an Interim Court of Arbitration (Wright, 1984: 159). The first application of an automatic process of adjusting wages rates to price movements took place in 1917; thereafter 'the arrangement commended itself to other trades and its use spread rapidly during the brief post-war boom' (Pool, 1938: 256). By 1922, some three million workers were covered by cost-of-living sliding scale agreements. Although the adherence to such rules rapidly fell away after 1925, the consensus among political economists was that the increased awareness of cost-of-living considerations was permanent. It became one more element in the institutional revolution that bedevilled the efficient operation of the labour market.

Evaluating the institutional revolution

Tarling and Wilkinson (1982: 22–3) conclude in their survey of the rise of collective bargaining that 'the importance of incorporating an analysis of the institutional development into the discussion of the trends of money wages and prices is that it underlines how profoundly social and political are the forces influencing the level and changes of real and money wages'. Such a warning is clearly appropriate. The structure of the market place needs to be understood if the relative strengths of market signals are to be evaluated. This is not, however, a recipe for nihilism. It is perfectly possible to try to determine how much influence the relevant institutions had on wage and employment outcomes in the interwar labour market.

I shall approach the question in two parts. Firstly, through an *a priori* evaluation of institutional structures, involving both historical and international comparisons of the inter-war system of industrial relations. Then, through an *ex post* evaluation, by assessing the extent of (real and nominal) wage rigidity. Both of these issues are in preparation for the ultimate question – whether we should view the interwar labour market through the same Keynesian eyes as Alec Ford.

Dorothy Sells, in her study of the spread of industrial democracy in Britain, estimated that 11 million out of 15 million workers were 'covered by some definite form of wage-fixing machinery' in 1937 (1939: 49). This represents three quarters of the industrial and agricultural workforce (and 56% of employed civilian workers), and compares to Clay's figure of 60% (43% of employed civilians) in 1929. There are, however, reasons to believe that it is too high – Sells cobbled together her figure from a motley collection of sources for various years between 1920 and 1937. A more probable figure for 1937 is 8.7 million, around 44% of the total workforce.[14] And this proportion no doubt varied somewhat during the interwar years. It was highest in 1920 (at close to 9 million, about half the civilian workforce), when union density was at its peak, and probably reached its nadir in 1933 (at 7 million, or 36%). Nevertheless, it remains certain that collective bargaining *did* involve many more workers than before the war. The estimated workforce covered by agreements in 1910 was 2.4 million (Board of Trade, 1910).

These proportions were high relative to previous experience, but they were not peculiar to the interwar period. Flanders (1964: 285–6) notes that collective bargaining agreements (voluntary and statutory) covered between 80 and 90% of the labour force during 1946–50. To borrow Metcalf *et al.*'s (1982) critique of Benjamin and Kochin, a similar institutional regime did not produce similar results in the postwar period.[15] We need to look beyond the raw numbers and determine how structured bargaining altered the wage-employment nexus between the wars. For this, it is necessary to go behind the aggregates – to inspect the content of bargaining arrangements. The collective agreements in place in 1910 fell into three categories – sliding scale arrangements, piece price lists, and working agreements of other types. There were no cost-of-living agreements cited in the Board of Trade study. Of the 1,696 agreements recorded, only thirty operated on selling-price sliding scales (covering 57,500 workers), and over half of these involved only one firm. Piece lists were clearly common in a wide range of industries – from shipbuilding and metal manufactures, to tailoring and dock labour. The 1,103 working agreements cited in the report included 801 wage lists for construction work, drawn up on a town-by-town basis. Unfortunately, there is no report of such scope and detail available for the interwar period. The Ministry of Labour did occasionally publish details on the use of sliding scales (cost-of-living and selling-price) in industry, and in 1934 published the first (and only) volume of a comprehensive survey of collective agreements.[16] These are fortunately sufficient to gauge the structure of collective agreements and examine their implications for wage flexibility.

In his detailed analysis of industrial wage bargaining in 1930s Britain, A.G. Pool (1938) focused on three major types of automatic adjustment to market conditions – proceeds-sharing, cost-of-living sliding scales, and selling-price sliding scales. At no time during the interwar period, however, did these dominate wage-setting. Proceeds-sharing was limited to one industry (coal-mining), and selling-price scales to one group of industries (iron and steel and some allied sectors). Only the cost-of-living scales were broadly applied in the interwar period and their numerical importance was restricted to 1921–5 (see table 11.1). At no time did such procedures involve more than 25% of the workforce.[17] The majority of workers had their wages regulated by open bargaining, either collective or individual.

Nevertheless, the application of automatic cost-of-living arrangements, in particular, has entered the folk-lore of the interwar labour market. This is largely because of their presumed effectiveness during the deflation of 1921–3. Prices and wages both fell sharply in this episode (by about 16% and 11% a year respectively). This, it has been argued, demonstrated the effectiveness of formal indexation arrangements, while at the same time ensuring their immediate demise, by destroying workers' taste for them. However, as Broadberry (1986: 89) has noted, fewer than 20% of aggregate wage reductions in 1922 came from COLA (cost-of-living adjustment) clauses, and only 11% in 1921. Selling-price sliding scales, which accounted for 56% of wage cuts in 1921, were much the more important. Moreover, COLAs did not deliver as much flexibility as many of their advocates suggested. To begin with, most incorporated wage floors (usually related to

Table 11.1. *Collective bargaining agreements in force 1920–1938*

	Workers covered by Cost-of-Living agreements	Workers covered by Selling price agreements
December 1920	1.25m	
August 1921	2.75m	
July 1922	3.00m	
July 1925	2.50m	0.22m
December 1930	1.25m*	
July 1933	1.25m*	0.16m*

Note: *Since many agreements were terminated during the depression, either because the scheme had been suspended or because the average wage had fallen below the lower limit of the original agreement, the figure for the coverage of cost-of-living scales in 1930 and 1933, and for selling-price agreements in 1933, are seriously overstated. The true figures, according to the Ministry of Labour were c. one million in 1930 (PRO, LAB 41/83, p. 231), and between 750,000 and a million in 1933 (1933a: 238), for the cost-of-living scales. No revised figure was given for the selling-price scales.

wages in force in July 1914 plus a percentage), below which the scales ceased to operate. Few involved full indexation, in which wages moved fully with prices, and many imposed adjustment asymmetries, in which wages moved in line with rising prices, but incompletely with price declines.[18] Similar limitations applied to the proceeds-sharing arrangements in coal-mining. The procedure here, as embodied in national agreements in 1921 and 1924, was that miners and owners would divide the surplus (defined as total revenues less standard wages and other production costs, and standard profits equal to 17% of standard wages) on an 83 : 17 basis.[19] Wages could not, however, fall below the stipulated standard.

The folk-lore looks distinctly tattered. Thus, Broadberry (1986: 86–91), argues that the rapid fall in wages between 1921 and 1923 had less to do with the application of COLAs in wage contracts than with the actions and attitudes of union leaders. The strong correlation between union density and the path of nominal wages is noted to support this hypothesis, along with Ernest Bevin's testimony to the Macmillan Committee in which he stated that the unions were prepared to accept a significant fall in nominal wages during the early 1920s as an antidote to wartime inflation, but not

Table 11.2. *Changes in wage rates 1920–38*

	Approximate number of separate individuals reported as affected by:		Estimated weekly amount of changes in rates of wages		Estimated net weekly increase (+) or decrease (−) in rates of wages of all workers affected
	Net increases	Net decreases	Increases	Decreases	
1920	7,867,000	500	4,793,200[a]	180[a]	+4,793,020
1921	78,000	7,244,000	13,600[a]	6,074,600[a]	−6,061,000
1922	73,700	7,633,000	11,450[a]	4,221,500[a]	−4,210,050
1923	1,202,000	3,079,000	454,000[b]	763,000[b]	− 317,000
1924	3,019,000	481,500	880,000[b]	330,500[b]	+ 553,900
1925	873,000	851,000	146,300[b]	226,100[b]	− 78,100
1926	420,000	740,000	207,800	158,500	+ 49,300
1927	282,000	1,855,000	125,100	482,900	− 357,800
1928	217,000	1,615,000	41,000	183,000	− 142,000
1929	142,000	917,000	48,400	127,200	− 78,800
1930	768,000	1,100,000	92,400	149,000	− 56,600
1931	47,000	3,010,000	16,400	417,550	− 401,150
1932	33,500	1,949,000	11,900	261,100	− 249,200
1933	179,500	894,000	40,000	105,250	− 65,250
1934	1,344,000	85,500	111,700	20,200	+ 91,500
1935	2,366,500	49,600	210,700	21,000	+ 192,100
1936	4,062,400	800	512,250	19,350	+ 492,900
1937	5,161,200	4,400	909,500	122,600	+ 786,900
1938	2,381,000	322,200	388,000	144,700	+ 243,300

Notes: Columns 1, 2: There were in addition a number of workers who received both wage rate increases and decreases in any given year. Columns 3, 4: These figures, unless otherwise noted, refer to the gross, rather than net, effect of wage changes. Column 5: This figure provides the net effect of wage rate increases and declines in any given year.
[a]These figures refer to net increases and decreases respectively.
[b]These figures were preliminary; they were later amended to take account of further information. In these cases, the net increase figure (col. 5) is the corrected figure.
Source: Ministry of Labour (1925a–40a).

Table 11.3. *Sources of official wage changes 1922–38*

	COLAs	Selling price	Concili- ation	Arbit- ration	Direct negoti- ation	JICs	Trade boards
1922	18.8	19.1	7.7	0.9	42.2	7.8	3.4
1923	16.3	49.3	1.8	5.5	12.8	7.0	7.4
1924	13.7	55.2	2.3	10.9	12.4	5.3	0.1
1925	28.9	36.6	1.4	2.8	10.3	13.1	6.5
1926	34.0	14.8	0.3	1.4	48.1	0.7	0.7
1927	23.2	53.4	1.1	1.0	20.1	0.1	0.9
1928	33.7	4.0	7.9	19.0	32.2	2.0	1.3
1929	40.4	8.9	0.6	37.2	10.7	0.9	1.2
1930	44.1	8.8	2.5	0.5	41.5	0.9	2.3
1931	22.1	5.2	19.1	9.6	39.2	2.8	2.0
1932	23.5	5.8	1.4	21.1	24.7	21.6	1.9
1933	57.0	14.7	2.9	0.9	15.4	0.9	8.2
1934	19.4	11.1	6.1	10.3	31.1	21.1	0.8
1935	13.2	4.4	23.7	2.8	49.4	5.7	0.9
1936	4.6	8.7	13.6	0.3	60.7	11.2	1.0
1937	9.9	31.6	7.1	0.2	32.7	9.3	5.1
1938	16.8	46.2	10.0	0.5	20.1	3.0	3.6

Note: Calculated as the proportion of the aggregate amount of wage changes (increases and decreases) accounted for by each method.
Source: Ministry of Labour (1923a–40a).

beyond certain limits.[20] The evidence does not, however, entirely support Broadberry's claim, since COLAs dominated reported wage changes in the late 1920s and into the 1930s, at a time when their quantitative significance had fallen away. What is going on here?

Tables 11.2 and 11.3 set out the information processed and recorded annually by the Ministry of Labour on wage changes in British industry. Note the striking proportion of wage changes accounted for by COLAs in 1928–30, when they were responsible for over 40% of wage reductions, despite involving less than 7% of the employed workforce (PRO, LAB 41/83) – and in 1933, when COLAs covered only 0.75 million workers (about 4% of the labour force), yet accounted for 57% of all wage cuts. COLAs, far from becoming marginalised, appear to be rising in significance. And, when the proportion of wage changes originating in automatic

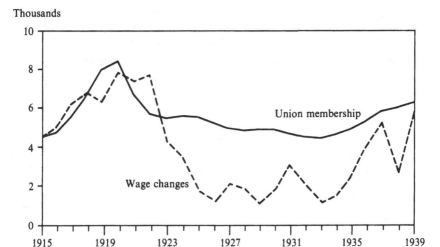

Figure 11.1   The official reporting of wage-rate changes, and the level of unionisation in the British labour market, 1915–39.

selling-price and proceeds-sharing arrangements is figured in, the sense that formal institutional agreements dominated wage bargaining becomes even stronger. How can this paradox be explained?

I believe that the collapse of union membership after 1920 holds the key. However, in contrast with Broadberry, I would not emphasise the link between union density and falling money-wages in some sort of cooperative game between workers, employers and government. Rather, the link that I wish to establish is purely statistical – between union density and the number of wage changes reported to the Ministry of Labour. In figure 11.1, I have plotted the number of wage changes against Bain and Price's measure of union density. A strong, positive, if non-linear relationship emerges (the simple correlation of the two variables is 0.709).[21] When the Ministry of Labour reported the wage change figures, they were careful to point out that they represented 'in the main those arranged between *organised* groups of employers and workpeople, and that many changes among unorganised workers, especially those affecting only employees of single firms' are excluded (Ministry of Labour, 1940a: 104, emphasis added). Institutionalised wage-setting mechanisms (via sliding scales, as well as through arbitration and conciliation, all of which involved union participation) continued to be included in the Ministry's reports, but fewer and fewer workers were covered by them. A rising proportion of workers were excluded from the official returns. The figures in table 11.2 are quite likely to underestimate total wage changes in the British labour market throughout the 1920s and 1930s, especially those arranged through direct negotiation. It follows that wages may have been considerably more flexible than the standard data suggest.[22] The Ministry of Labour data may have caused contemporaries to exaggerate wage rigidity; they certainly place too much emphasis on institutionalised forms of wage-setting. We need to shift focus from COLAs and union monopoly models of wage bargaining and pay attention instead to the determinants of wages in direct negotiations.

What were the mechanisms of wage-setting in direct negotiations between workers and firms? One way to approach this question is to utilise formal bargaining theory. The focus here is on successful bargaining, in which agreement is reached without conflict or external arbitration. The key result in understanding the outcome of a bargaining process, in which the relative strengths of the parties involved are crucial, is due to Nash (1950; 1953). The Nash solution (see Harsanyi, 1988), which developed out of the application of game theory to Zeuthen's insight that relative risk-aversion is the key to understanding the process of negotiation, is that the agreement point between two parties (say, a union and a firm) will maximise:

$$r = (u_1 - c_1)^a (u_2 - c_2)^b, \tag{1}$$

known as the Nash product, subject to the solution falling within the feasible set of opportunities, and to the condition that each party's utility under agreement (u_1, u_2) will be greater or equal to the utility under conflict (c_1, c_2); the parameters, a and b, measure the relative bargaining strength of the two parties.[23] The Nash solution can be applied to the process of collective bargaining, by recognising the gains to be made for each party if agreement is reached, and the opportunity costs if it is not (Carruth and Oswald, 1989; Nickell, 1990). The standard assumption is that firms aim to maximise profits, and unions (or workers) to maximise the wage. These are irreconcilable aims – higher wages mean lower profits (although, of course, higher profits need not mean lower wages, at least over the longer run). However, unless they are reconciled, firms will make no profits and workers will be on the dole. This leads to a Nash solution of the form:

$$\text{Max. } (w - \bar{w})\pi(w), \tag{2}$$

where w is the negotiated wage, $\bar{w}$ is the stop wage, and $\pi(w)$ is the profit function of the firm. The first order conditions from this equation are

$$\pi(w) + (w - \bar{w})\pi'(w) = 0. \tag{3}$$

Applying the standard duality result, whereby employment, n, is equal to $-\pi'(w)$ this can be rewritten as (see Carruth and Oswald, 1989: 8),

$$w = \bar{w} + \frac{\pi(w)}{n}. \tag{4}$$

Translated into words, the bargained wage is equal to the sum of the stop wage and profits per employee.

Two significant implications follow. Firstly, any wage equations predicated on bargains between workers and firms should include a profits term. This need not be a measure of true profits, but rather of *known* profits. Secondly, equation (4) provides a justification for including a benefit measure in any empirical wage equation. On the first point, Carruth and Oswald have found a significant role for average profits in wage equations for the period, 1956–83, suggesting that '*ceteris paribus*, real wage-levels were 5–13% higher in the later 1980s due solely to the prosperity of British industry' (1989: 132–57, quotation from p. 152). It would be very interesting to see if this result holds also for the interwar period.

If almost no attention has been paid to profits as an explicandum of wage behaviour in interwar Britain, the same can by no means be said about benefits. The literature which grew from Benjamin and Kochin's original article is voluminous. There is no need to rehearse the debate in all its fractiousness (a comprehensive, if incisive, review may be found in Hatton, 1986). Suffice it to say that few observers now accept the Benjamin–Kochin interpretation in its simple form. Matthews, although accepting that benefits mattered in this period, dismisses Benjamin and Kochin by noting that 'research on the interwar labour market calls for sound theoretical specification and reasonable empirical estimates' (1986: 40), virtues that were evidently lacking in the original model. Matthews is in fact one of the few macroeconomic modellers to see a significant role for benefits in the determination of unemployment. In his rational expectations model of the interwar economy, he finds a short-run elasticity of unemployment to (unanticipated) movements in real benefit of 0.08, rising to 0.27 in five years, and 0.37 after a decade (1986: 186). To put this in perspective, note that weighted benefits[24] increased (in real terms) by 17% between 1924 and 1929, another 8% from 1929–32, and another 5% from 1932–7. It turns out that the cumulative effect of rising benefit scales between 1924 and 1932 accounts for almost all of registered unemployment in 1937 by this model. However, few macroeconomists would place this much emphasis on the benefit system.[25] Thus, the most recent investigation of this problem, Dimsdale *et al.* (1989), finds a distinctly limited role for benefits – estimating that the rising replacement ratio[26] pushed unemployment up by 1% (out of a total increase of 12%) between 1929 and 1932, and by an additional percentage point between 1932 and 1937. Their conclusion is supported by the limited microeconomic evidence we have from the period, as reported in Eichengreen (1986). There is evidently still some room for debate over the role of benefits in interwar Britain, but the balance of opinion appears to provide it with at most a minor role.[27]

The British labour market in (some) international perspective

If we turn to international comparisons, it soon becomes clear that Britain was less of an outlier in industrial relations than contemporaries believed (or at least argued). In terms of the degree of union participation in the labour market, the level of centralised employee organisation, and the articulation of state goals in public policy, Britain shared common characteristics with a number of other countries in this period. Moreover, collective bargaining was well established overseas as well, and revealed many similar features to the British structure of industrial relations and wage bargaining. The review that follows is necessarily tentative, and makes no pretence to completeness. Nevertheless, the evidence is, I think, sufficiently compelling to destroy the illusion of British exceptionalism. And if the British style of wage determination was no different from that in place in other countries, does it seem reasonable to argue that collective bargaining was at the root of Britain's high and persistent unemployment rate?

I begin with the basic components of industrial relations – unions and employers.

The main trends in union membership across countries are presented in table 11.4. Britain was evidently far from being the most unionised society in the West after 1900. In 1910, of the eight countries covered by the Bain–Price data, Australia, Germany and Denmark had higher densities (according to 1913 evidence of International Federation of Trade Unions, Britain's density also ranked below Belgium, Holland, Sweden, Norway and the US). By 1920, with the rapid wartime growth of union membership in Britain, only Germany had a higher density. But, by the late-1920s, Britain ranked below Sweden, Australia, Denmark and Germany.

The aggregate figures may, of course, be misleading. The form and style of unionism matter also. We need to know more about the distribution of union activity across industrial sectors; to know more about the relative size of unions; to know more about their strategies; to know whether unions were typically organised on a local, regional, or national basis; to know whether they operated in an environment where confrontation or cooperation was the dominant reaction from employers and the state. Certainly the evidence on such complexities is even more fragmentary – we should recognise too that unionism was in process throughout this period and that generalisations based on one period may not apply to another.

Table 11.4. *Comparative trade union densities 1895–1940* (%)

	Australia	Canada	Denmark	Germany	Norway	Sweden	UK	USA
1895	5.4			2.5		1.2	9.9	3.0
1900	9.0			5.7	3.4	4.8	12.7	5.5
1905	na			10.2	na	7.6	11.9	10.5
1910	21.0		15.3	18.1	7.6	8.3	14.6	9.0
1913	31.2		na	21.3	na	9.4	23.1	10.3
1920	42.2	15.0	35.1	52.6	20.4	27.7	45.2	16.7
1925	42.1	na	na	29.0	na	28.7	30.1	10.4
1930	43.5	13.5	32.0	33.7	18.3	36.0	25.4	8.9
1935	36.1	na	na	na	na	40.7	24.9	9.1
1940	40.4	18.3	42.4	na	>34.3	54.0	33.1	16.4

Note: Densities calculated as total union membership as percentage of total eligible workforce.
Source: Bain and Price (1980: tables 2.1, 3.1, 5.1, 6.1, 7.1, 10.1).

Nevertheless, it seems safe to conclude that Britain's union profile should not be moved from the mainstream to an extreme by added information about its structural composition relative to others,[28] its level of organisation,[29] or its scale. On the matter of strategy, and without descending into caricature, we might best characterise the attitudes of British unions to industrial capitalism as accommodating, those in France as antagonistic to the point of destructiveness, and those in Germany as divided (from an early stage) between unions founded on the principles of Marx and Lasselles and bent on class confrontation, and the more liberal Hirsch-Duncker and Catholic unions, whose accommodationist strategy ultimately prevailed.[30] And the Scandinavian union movement, especially in Sweden, by and large followed a similar line as the British of compromise and cooperation.

The most obvious symptom of union strategy (and employer resistance) is strike behaviour. The pattern of strikes in a number of Western economies between 1895 and 1940 is given in figure 11.2, which reproduces the number of man-days lost per 100,000 non-agricultural wage-earners (Flora, 1987: 681–7). This reveals a remarkable uniformity across countries, not only during the famous strike waves, but at other times also. The correlation between the strike activity rate in the UK and other countries is 0.84 (excluding the war years and 1926). Superficially, Britain's strike

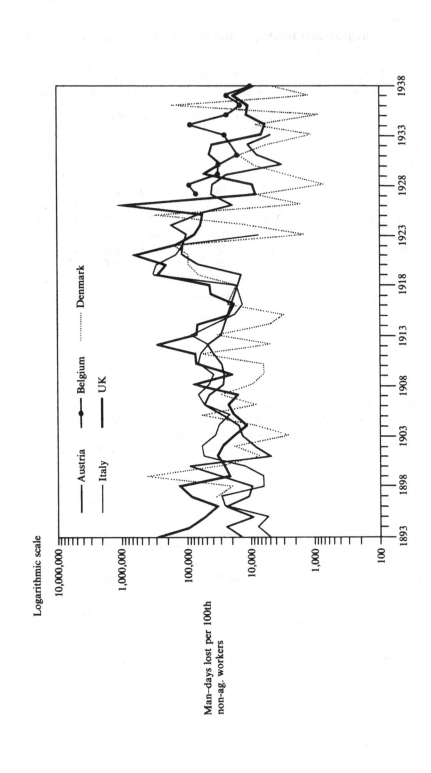

Logarithmic scale

Man–days lost per 100th
non-ag. workers

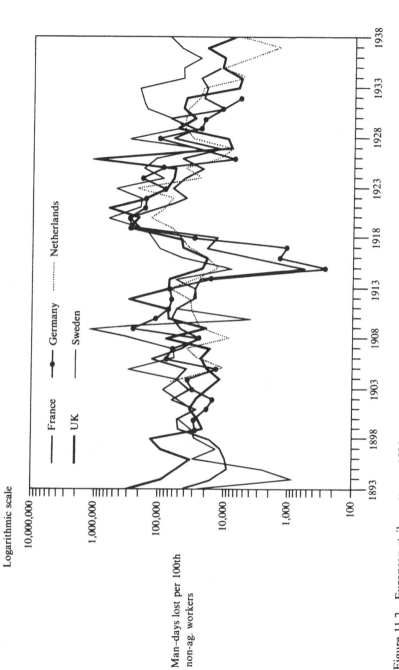

Figure 11.2 European strike patterns, 1893–1938.

record conforms to a general European pattern. However, some scepticism is appropriate.

According to the leading authorities on historical strike behaviour, the 'normal' profile of the British case is the product of two characteristics that were clearly aberrant as European strikes in this period went – a relatively low incidence of strikes, coupled with a remarkably high degree of coverage on the average (Shorter and Tilly, 1974: 320ff). The number of strikes per million workers averaged only 0.38 per annum between 1900 and 1929, compared to an unweighted average of 0.77 for twelve European and North American countries for much the same period (with a range of 0.53 to 1.8).[31] Strikes may have been only half as frequent in Britain, but they were comparatively large affairs. The average number of strikers per dispute for the twelve countries surveyed was 312, while for Britain it was 1,100.

However, we should not make too much of these differences. The statistics on size illustrate tellingly the dangers of arguing from averages. Thus, for example, the average size of strikes in Britain between 1892 and 1900 was 317, close to the European average as a whole. Indeed, to a significant degree, the very high figure of 1,100 is due to three unrepresentative periods of industrial activity – 1911–13, 1919–21, and especially 1926. If we exclude these years, and the period of DORA (1915–18), during which strikes were illegal, the average intensity of strikes falls from 1,100 to 450, a number similar to the US, Belgium, Spain and Norway, hardly bastions of centralised trade union activity. Moreover, since the average number of workers involved may represent the degree of large-scale production in a society, we have to be cautious even here. Indeed, if Britain was different from its Western counterparts, it was in the relative paucity of strikes, which fits the accommodationist view of industrial relations, rather than in the dominance by a few union giants, a perspective that exaggerates union aggression.[32]

Strikes are not, of course, merely the product of union aggression. Employers also play a role in precipitating conflict. In the institutional theory of strike behaviour, most closely associated with Arthur Ross (see, for example, Ross and Irwin, 1951; Ross and Hartman, 1960), the factors that make it more likely that conflict will degenerate into a strike rather than being settled by negotiation include the resistance of employers to unions and to the principle of collective bargaining, single- rather than multi-firm bargaining, and the absence of a government sympathetic to workers' interests.[33] Thus, Ross finds that Sweden, with a long tradition of social democratic governments, centralised unions, and cooperative employers, was marked by lower strike activity between 1927 and 1940 than the US or Canada, societies in which employers were hostile and governments at best indifferent to union activity, and where centralised unions had limited adherence. Britain and Australia fell somewhere between these extremes, with less centralised union systems than Sweden, and a stronger tradition of social democracy than in North America. This analysis, which may be seen as a forerunner of the corporatist literature of the 1980s (of which more below), directs our attention towards collective bargaining as the arena in which the tensions between employers and workers are worked out.

International evidence on collective bargaining before 1940 is both fragmentary and poorly integrated. Different countries collected different statistics to highlight particular aspects of their system of industrial relations. Despite this statistical chaos, some points emerge forcefully. The first is that it is quite incorrect to claim that 'in no other European country [than Britain] had anything resembling a system of collective bargaining come into existence before 1914' (Geary, 1989: 4). In Scandinavian countries in particular, coordinated negotiations were well established before 1914. The rapid growth of unions in Denmark and Sweden led, in both cases, to confrontation with the employers followed by compromise. The 'September Agreement' of 1899 in Denmark and the 'December Compromise' of 1906 in Sweden marked the early maturity of industrial relations, with full recognition of the rights of employers' and workers' associations in negotiations. By 1913, almost 40% of the industrial labour force in Sweden (227,000) were covered by collective agreements (Germany, 1913: 164*), a significant proportion of which were district or national in scope. Germany was another country where the practice of employer–union negotiations over wages, hours and working conditions was well established before the First World War. Almost 2 million workers were covered by collective agreements in 1914 (Reich, 1938: 66); this represents some 16% of the industrial workforce, compared to a density of closer to 25% in Britain in 1910. No doubt the figure would have been larger but for the utter refusal of coal-mine owners to participate in any cooperative system.[34] And, no doubt, there was a core of German industrialists who clung to traditional authoritarianism. Such patriarchal tendencies were well represented by the Centralverband der Deutschen Industrie, one of the leading Trade Associations, which considered 'collective agreements between organisations of employers and of trade unions' to be 'extremely dangerous for German industry and its continued development' (quoted in Berghahn and Karsten, 1987: 146–7). Nevertheless, over 160,000 enterprises participated in agreements in 1913, many of them as part of associations. And more than half of the workers involved were covered by national or district agreements. Elsewhere on the continent, however, organisation was rudimentary. According to figures produced by the German Arbeitsministerium, there were 115,000 and

23,000 (about 3% of their respective workforces) included in agreements in Austria and the Netherlands in 1911. Nor did collective bargaining develop very far in France before 1913. However, looking further afield, there were some stirrings in the US labour market from as early as the 1890s (Bonnett, 1956: 350ff, 413ff).

As in Britain, it was the impact of the war that transformed collective bargaining, and for much the same reasons of maintaining worker stability, morale, and of coordinating the war effort in a period of scarce (skilled) labour, and, after the end of war, of rebuilding the civilian economy and smoothing the transfer of demobilised troops into the labour force.[35] This was especially the case in Germany where, under the benificent eye of a republican government publicly committed to industrial democracy, the number of wage-earners covered by agreements climbed to 6 million in January 1920, 8.6 million in 1921, and 12.3 million at the start of 1923 (Reich, 1938: 108).[36] The 1923 figure represents close to 45% of the total German labour force (the proportion in Britain in 1923 was probably much the same). With hyperinflation and industrial dislocation, coverage fell away somewhat. Yet, by 1931, the final year for which figures were presented before the Nazis outlawed the union movement, there were over 12 million workers covered by agreements.[37] The extent of collective bargaining elsewhere is illustrated by the figures presented in table 11.5. To add to the catalogue, it was reported in 1921, that 'as a consequence of the rapid growth of organization of labor in Italy collective bargaining seems to have become the universal method . . . for fixing wage and working conditions' (US, 1921: 160); almost 30% of Czech industrial workers were covered by collective agreements in 1925 (United States, 1925: 25). Evidence also suggests that collective agreements multiplied in scale and scope in the US in the immediate postwar period (Carr, 1925).[38]

However, it is not enough just to cite the large number of collective agreements in force outside of Britain. Clay and Pigou would also want to know the form that negotiations took. Were employers' associations compliant or aggressive in the defence of their interests? Were negotiations carried out at the level of the individual firm or on a more centralised plane? Did the central government influence negotiations directly or indirectly through regulations such as minimum wage laws? Was cost-of-living consciousness as entrenched as they believed it to be in Britain? It is not possible to be completely certain on all these issues, given the paucity of information, but some useful observations can be made.

A distinction needs to be made when discussing the structure of bargaining arrangements, that between administrative and geographical scope. Clearly, for there to be national bargaining, more than one firm needs to be involved in negotiations. But not all multi-firm deals are

Table 11.5. *Collective agreements in force 1927–34*

		Agreements in force	Establishments covered	Workers covered	Proportion of total workforce (%)
Australia	1927	744			
	1933	653			
Austria	1927	2,737	147,596	1,007,723	32.2
	1930	2,259	219,246	824,568	26.2
	1933	1,660	174,067	489,480	15.5
Germany	1927	7,490	807,300	10,970,120	34.2
	1931		804,788	12,006,255	37.2
Netherlands	1927	894	16,976	267,791	8.8
	1930	1,546	23,528	385,972	12.1
	1934	1,132	25,431	258,185	7.6
Norway	1927	846		122,536	10.8
	1930	1,629		159,651	13.7
	1934	2,534		203,502	16.4
Sweden	1927	2,960	16,502	494,625	17.7
	1930	4,422	20,185	580,931	20.1
	1934	6,288	25,864	674,700	22.4

Note: Swedish data refer to employers covered, rather than establishments.
Source: International Labour Office (1936: 276, table I); Mitchell (1975: table C1).

national, or even regional, in coverage. Multi-firm bargaining was the primary form in Britain from the late nineteenth century, even before collective agreements moved from the local to the national stage. Employers' associations also existed in many European countries, as well as the US, before 1914. However, in many cases their operation was limited. Thus, in Italy, the Confederazione italiana dell'industria was founded in 1910 as a trade association, and had no power to negotiate labour contracts (Treu and Martinelli, 1984: 265), while the Association of Dutch Employers was formed in 1899 to lobby government on the proposed workmen's compensation law (van Voorden, 1984). Only in countries in which unionisation threatened the perceived collective interests of employers were associations formed to deal with labour questions. This is true of Australia (e.g. the Master Builders' Federation of 1890), Sweden (the Swedish Employers' Confederation-SAF-formed in 1902, four years after the Confederation of Swedish Trade Unions, and in the year of a general strike), France (in the wake of the Waldeck–Rousseau Act of 1884 which legitimised union activity), the US (in its early phase in response to the Knights of Labor, later in reaction to the growth of AFL unionism), and Germany (with the late creation of the Vereinigung deutscher Arbeitgeber-verbände in 1913, a perfect example of the reluctance of many employers to sacrifice individual control over wage-setting, despite a long history of co-operation in other areas).[39] After the First World War, multi-employer bargaining became more widespread. Thus, by 1931, only 4.4% of German workers were covered by single-employer contracts, compared with 30% in 1914 (Reich, 1938: 109; Ministry of Labour, 1922a: 326). Only in the US (and perhaps Canada) did single-employer bargaining continue to dominate in the inter-war period. Moreover, and in significant contrast to the British situation, multi-employer negotiations had the power of law (and Labour Courts) behind them. In Britain, such arrangements were 'gentlemen's agreements'; in France, Italy, Germany, Sweden, and so on, they were legally enforceable contracts, and employers could be taken to court if they did not uphold the collective agreement (Sisson, 1987: 14; International Labour Office, 1938). The sanctity of state approval was undoubtedly a two-edged sword as far as labour market efficiency was concerned – it gave associations more power to coerce their member firms, but it also reduced the potential flexibility of companies to monitor and adjust arrangements to local conditions.

The rise of multi-employer associations was certainly conducive to centralised bargaining. However, associations could be organised on a regional rather than a national basis. Was the transition towards national agreements that we found in Britain between 1910 and 1924 common to other countries? Certainly, the German evidence suggests it. There was a clear shift towards a national scope between 1914 and 1921 (from 5.6 to 21.6% of all workers covered); this trend was reversed through the first half of the twenties (falling to 12.6% of workers by January 1925), but by 1931 over 26% of workers were covered by economy-wide agreements.[40] District agreements also became more significant over time (rising from 46% of worker coverage in 1914 to 56% in 1921 and 77% in 1925), leaving fewer and fewer workers in local and single employer negotiations (49% in 1914 dropping to 9.9% by 1931).[41] Unfortunately, data are not as forthcoming for other countries. However, descriptive evidence suggests a strong degree of centralisation in the Scandinavian countries (especially in Denmark), while the Fascist labour law of April 1926 recognised for each branch of economic activity, only one representative of labour and capital in negotiations (van Aarsten, 1939: 213–14). In France and Belgium, in contrast, it was not until the crises of 1936 that collective agreements were restructured on a national basis (International Labour Office, 1936: 84–6).

Up to then, only isolated industries (such as printing in France) had participated in national negotiations. Likewise, the New Deal proved a turning point in the structure of collective bargaining in the US, not least because of its impact on the growth of unionism. Ross (1948: 55–6) identified the newer CIO unions (especially those experiencing rapid growth after 1934) as embracing the concept of centralised negotiations, in contrast to the old-line AFL unions which preferred to deal at the local level.[42]

Our knowledge of the rules that governed collective agreements outside Britain is sketchy. But some similarities to the British system are worth noting. Firstly, as Pool observes,

in other countries the history of cost-of-living sliding scales has been broadly similar [to Britain]. They were the product of war and post-war inflation, attaining their greatest popularity when currency depreciation was most severe . . . [w]ith the stabilisation of currencies the need for sliding scales became less urgent . . . [and they] have become restricted to a very small part of the industrial field. (1938: 257–8)

Certainly, formal adjustment procedures were well established in a wide array of countries in 1921 (including Australia, Austria, Belgium, New Zealand, Poland and Sweden). It is hard to believe, given the focus on automatic price adjustments and given successive periods of inflation and deflation in many of the continental economies, that cost-of-living consciousness was any less well established in Europe than in Britain.

The evidence on labour market structures is important to putting Britain in wider perspective, to be sure, but we should remember that Clay and Pigou placed greater emphasis on attitudes than on institutions in explaining the reduced plasticity of wages to unemployment in the 1920s. Although it is difficult to be absolutely certain about societal attitudes towards bargaining and unemployment in any country, the available evidence is consistent with the overall picture of British conformity. Certainly there was a widespread commitment in most overseas countries to a system of minimum wage regulations and 'fair wage' clauses (International Labour Office, 1939). This in turn reflected a measure of governmental interest and involvement in the labour market that was comparable to the British case. Indeed, the Scandinavian countries, with their prewar tradition of coordinated industrial relations, and Weimar Germany, with a republican state committed to using the law to underwrite labour contracts and formalise collective bargaining, perhaps went further than Britain in the centralised structural organisation of the labour market. This comports with the developing social democratic tenor of public policy in these countries, reflected also in their commitment to social insurance programmes more broadly. Unemployment insurance was not introduced into Sweden until 1934, and then only on a relatively small scale. In contrast, the German social insurance programme was the precursor to the British system, and it too has come under criticism for underwriting voluntary unemployment. Recent work by David Corbett (1990), however, provides little support for this hypothesis.

To return to another theme much emphasised by pre-Keynesian analysts, there is little support for the view that social insurance contributions were a major source of uncompetitiveness for British industry. In relative terms, indeed, employers' contributions were lower in Britain than in most continental states. As a proportion of wages in the coal industry, for example, insurance contributions rose from 4 to 5.3% between 1925 and 1929 in Britain; these figures were considerably lower than in Germany (11.9% in 1929), Czechoslovakia (9.2%), Holland and Poland (9.5%), or France (7.2%). Only Belgium among major coal exporters paid lower insurance (International Labour Office, 1931: 88). What identified Britain as a poor competitor in international markets was high unit labour costs (50% higher than in the Ruhr in 1925). Given the emphasis on wage rigidity, it is instructive to note that by 1929 unit labour costs in British coal-mining were on a par with every continental economy west of the Elbe, having fallen by 26% in four years.

What conclusions may be drawn from this brief overview? Firstly, to reiterate, there is little evidence that Britain was an outlier in the structural organisation of the labour market in our period. Contemporaries who found something unique and disturbing about collective bargaining and the principles of industrial security were tied too firmly to Little Englander prejudices. Secondly, the material cited here resonates with the recent literature on corporatism and labour market outcomes. The corporatist model asserts that the more centralised are a country's labour market institutions, the better able it is to react sensibly and efficiently to macroeconomic shocks (Bruno and Sachs, 1985). Employee bargaining strength is reduced and union accountability is heightened in an exhaustively centralised system of wage-setting. However, the shift from firm to industry level negotiations lowers labour demand elasticities, thereby reducing the employment effects of any shock, while also increasing upward pressure on wages (Nickell, 1990: 416). The latter point suggests a revision of the basic model (Calmfors and Driffill, 1988; Freeman, 1988), in which there is a U-shaped relationship between the degree of corporatism (or centralisation) and economic performance – countries that are either completely decentralised (e.g. the contemporary US) or completely centralised (e.g. Austria) will outperform countries that are somewhat centralised (e.g. Britain).[43] If we accept the logic of this model,[44] interwar Britain might have been better off had it been a fully corporatist state, rather than the curious mixture of central regulation and private initiative that still exists today. Support for this argument may be derived from the work of Gregory, Ho, McDermott and Hagan, which found the highly-centralised labour market of Australia, with its wage tribunals and entrenched trade unions, performed at least as well during the 1930s as 'the comparatively free labour market of the US' (1988: 423). The irony of this result for the classicals' position needs no emphasis.

How rigid were real wages in interwar Britain?

The pre-Keynesians did not think the institutional innovations of the 1920s intrinsically harmful. Rather their condemnation of the form and format of collective bargaining was contingent on the poor performance of labour market aggregates. Had unemployment remained at the 1920 level (3.2%) throughout the decade, the institutional critique would never have been so well worked out. The major premise of the classical position was that real wage rigidity accounted for the intransigence of unemployment (and the competitive weakness of the British export economy); the identification of bargaining institutions was merely the minor premise. In contrast to the scepticism evinced above, there is considerable empirical evidence that real wages were relatively rigid in the interwar period.

It is possible to identify three separate hypotheses regarding wage flexibility in the pre-Keynesian model. The first is that real wages were relatively inflexible to levels of unemployment. The second is that real wage behaviour was asymmetric to changes in unemployment. The third is that money wages were relatively flexible to changes in (consumer) prices. I shall focus on each of these in turn.

The evidence for the first hypothesis is compelling. The weak perform-ance of the Sargan real wage equation in the interwar period is a standard, often replicated result. Among recent work, Newell & Symons (1988: 82) find almost no feedback from unemployment to real wages over 1923–38. Similarly, Dimsdale, Nickell and Horsewood (1989) find only a small, albeit well-defined, role for unemployment in real wage setting in their quarterly model of the labour market between 1925 and 1939. The excep-tion to this general rule is provided by Hatton (1988), who posits that the adjustment of real wages to macroeconomic disequilibrium was more rapid in the interwar period (1923–38) than either before 1913 or since 1945. This result is, however, derived from Sach's real wage gap model, which is not well motivated theoretically or empirically.[45] Moreover, it provides an incomplete test of the classical hypothesis, since it focuses on real wage responsiveness to perturbations around the starting point (1923), rather than to deviations from full employment equilibrium.[46]

The second pre-Keynesian hypothesis was well stated by Pigou in his evidence to the Macmillan Committee (Casson, 1983: 52). Pigou and his peers believed that real rigidity of wages was asymmetric – that excess demand would drive wages up with only a small time-lag, whereas excess supply would have very little effect. Following the analysis of Beckerman and Jenkinson (1986), I tested this hypothesis by regressing the change in the wage against measures of excess supply and excess demand in the labour market. The independent variables used were the residuals from Broadberry's (1983) aggregate equations derived from a disequilibrium model of labour supply and demand. After first differencing the series to achieve stationarity, and using the real wage (normalised by Feinstein's (1972) GDP deflator), the results (using OLS, and with t-statistics in parentheses) were as follows:

$$drw = 0.7971 + 0.4371 \text{ laged} - 0.0156 \text{ lages} \qquad (5)$$
$$(7.506) \quad (5.296) \qquad (-0.310)$$
$$F = 25.44; \; r^2 = 0.777,$$

where laged and lages are the one-period lagged versions of the excess demand and excess supply variables (both reduced by e^{-3}). The predicted asymmetry is confirmed – real wages are insensitive to excess supply, but react strongly to excess demand conditions. The policy implications of this result are discussed below.

As a test of the third pre-Keynesian hypothesis, namely the flexibility of money wages to price changes, I ran a variant of the previous regression, in which the dependent variable was the change in the nominal wage, and in which a price variable (in this case, the change in the retail price index over the previous period, lagdp) appeared on the right-hand side. The result here (again OLS) is again instructive:

$$dw = 150.600 + 0.0419 \text{ lagdp} + 0.0846 \text{ laged} - 0.0021 \text{ lages} \qquad (6)$$
$$(8.27) \quad (0.419) \qquad (5.744) \qquad (-0.237)$$
$$F = 20.91; \; r^2 = 0.810.$$

The asymmetry results of the previous equation are repeated.[47] However, there is no support for the price flexibility hypothesis – the coefficient on retail price movements is insignificant, statistically and empirically. This result reinforces the general finding of nominal inertia in wage setting in interwar labour models (Broadberry, 1986: 95; Matthews, 1986: 54; Dimsdale et al., 1989: 286; and, in particular, Crafts, 1989: 250).

What can be made of these results? It is clear that the classicals' position was in some respects entirely appropriate. Real wages were relatively inflexible to unemployment levels, and tended to respond more to positive than to negative shocks. Against this, their emphasis on cost-of-living consciousness as a primary factor in wage-setting seems misplaced. The empirical evidence supports an interpretation in which agents were as slow to respond to price movements as to changes in the real economy. The interwar labour market was, in a wide range of respects, characterised by inflexibility and inertia.

But this evidence only goes part-way to justify the pre-Keynesian interpretation of the 1920s. The very fact of rigid real wages does not lead inevitably to rigid institutions as the *explicandum superiorum* of poor labour market performance. The asymmetry in real wage responsiveness likewise is consistent with a number of other approaches, which are consonant with the practices of the modern labour market, but which do not depend on the institutional detail of the pre-Keynesian interpretation. In particular, it meets the predictions of both efficiency wage models – which build on the notion that wages are used primarily as a screening device for productivity – and insider–outsider theory – the argument that those out of work cannot and do not compete equally with those with jobs.[48]

The efficiency wage models propose that employers change wages in order to attract new workers of a given quality, or to encourage their current workforce to try harder. Underemployment equilibrium will result in this case when firms decide that lowering wages will tend to reduce productivity (and thus profits) more than it will cut costs (and raise profits). The insider–outsider model also builds on the notion of firm-specific human capital, and, in particular, on the realisation that hiring and firing workers carries significant costs for employers (whether due to the expense of training replacements, or to productivity losses after selective dismissal). In the version of this theory advanced by Lindbeck and Snower (1988), the employment pool divides into three groups – the insiders (those with current jobs), the entrants (those being currently hired), and outsiders (those without a job). The essence of the theory is that outsiders do not compete with insiders in setting wages. The insiders earn economic rent, according to the leverage gained from the costs of turnover to the firm, and this rent appears as a wage above marginal productivity, conventionally defined. Wages are rigid downwards because employers perceive the costs of replacing insiders as greater than any wage gains that they might achieve. When dismissal is inevitable (and turnover in this model is dominated by reductions in labour demand, not by the search for better workers), the theory predicts that the most recent hirings will be the first to go (the inverse seniority rule, or LIFO process). This is largely because these workers (entrants) have yet to build up the firm-specific capital which makes them especially valuable (and, thereafter, an insider). The model would also predict increasing disparities between real wages and productivity in the aggregate economy (as Clay (1929b) described), if the proportion of insiders increases (especially in this period with the gradual decasualisation of the labour market), and if the rent of each insider grows over time (as turnover costs rise). Wages are the result of a bargaining process between employers and firms, with each party aware of the special status of the insiders.

Both of these models provide alternative explanations for asymmetric nominal wage rigidity. Are they viable alternatives to the institutional arguments rehearsed by Clay and Pigou? I would argue that the insider–outsider theory offers a fruitful way of looking at the interwar labour market. The efficiency-wage model appears to have less relevance, unless it can be shown (and I doubt that it can), that employers were systematically (and increasingly) ill-informed about their workers' productivity, and that firms believed that they could manipulate their employees' work effort by offering higher wages. The insider–outsider model does, however, fit neatly with recent evidence, notably Crafts' finding of a differential wage effect from long-term and short-run unemployment. Crafts found that the growing proportion of the unemployed who were out of work for over a year (outsiders) had little or no influence on (nominal) wage bargaining for the employed (insiders).[49]

The insider–outsider model can, moreover, be understood as an aspect of the well-worn structural-regional characterisation of interwar unemployment.[50] Those workers who lost jobs in the traditional staple industries (coal, shipbuilding, iron and steel, textiles), especially those with well-developed, industry-specific skills, took on the character of outsiders to the vibrant sectors of the labour market, such as services, light engineering, and vehicles.[51] It is no accident that most of the long-term unemployed (57% in 1936) came from the staple sectors. These workers were unlikely to find work in either their own trades or elsewhere. They had very low reemployment probabilities from the very moment of dismissal, joining an extremely long queue at the exchanges, made up of individuals with distressingly similar career histories (Thomas, 1988: 134–5). They simply did not compete with those already in work and, moreover, they were not seen by employers as good prospects. As Heim (1984) has noted, when the light industries of the south-east expanded their workforce in the 1930s, they looked not to dispossessed male workers, but to women and youths who could be trained easily, and who had no background of 'bad' working habits. Only a few youngsters from the staples managed to gain entry into the new positions. If we add to the long-term unemployed the large number of youths whose total experience in the labour market of the 1920s and 1930s was a series of blind-alley jobs (and who can be viewed as eternal entrants, carrying no power in wage setting), we can see that the segmentation of the labour force between insiders and outsiders is a potentially powerful mechanism for understanding wage rigidity.

Moreover, it is tempting, given the regional specificity of the staple sectors, to see the regional problem as a geographical extension of the insider–outsider model, in which the labour market in Outer Britain had almost no influence on wages in Inner Britain. Such a suggestion strikes a chord with Thomas and Stoney's analysis of wage-setting (1972), in which they found that, had regional unemployment rates been equalised at the national average, wage rates would have fallen at 4.3% a year between 1925 and 1938, rather than rising slowly.

Restrictive institutions are thus clearly not the only way to explain rigid nominal wages. In an era when unions were declining in influence, and when collective bargaining arrangements provided a means for coordinated responses to labour market conditions, they may not even be the most likely. The insider–outsider model, which depends not on formal institutions, but on the (similar) behaviour of individual firms, provides an integrated, persuasive explanation for wage rigidity.

The most damaging criticism of the pre-Keynesian perspective on the working of the interwar labour market relates not, however, to the misplaced emphasis on institutions. It lies rather in the false notion that bargaining between workers and employers determines *real* wages. Only nominal wages are open to negotiation; the prices which convert nominal to real wages are set by broader macroeconomic (or international) forces. Therefore, to understand the relationship between unemployment and wages, we have to look beyond the labour market and analyse the process of price-setting as well. The pre-Keynesian emphasis on real wages is also misplaced; indeed, as I discuss in the next section, there may not even be a systematic relation between levels of employment and the (*ex post*) real wage.

Keynes and the classics

In his explanation of unemployment, Keynes, in contrast to his predecessors, spent little time discussing the role of unions and collective bargaining. The one reference in the *General Theory* to bargaining is in chapter 2, in which Keynes explains how Pigou and others could treat the unemployed millions of the 1920s and early 1930s as 'voluntary' (1936: 7–8). Not that Keynes would have denied that unions and government-mandated minimum wages contributed to wage rigidity. The apparent lack of interest in the bargaining process was motivated rather by his belief that other issues more clearly delineated his differences with orthodox thinking.

The 'more fundamental objections . . . flow from our disputing the assumption that the general level of real wages is directly determined by the character of the wage bargain. *In assuming that the wage bargain determines the real wage the classical school have slipped in an illicit assumption* . . . We shall endeavour to show that primarily it is certain other forces which determine the general level of real wages' (1936: 13, emphasis added).[52] There are three dimensions to Keynes' objection. The first is the empirical observation that it was money rather than real wages that were sticky 'during the decade 1924–1934' (1936: 276).[53] The second involves the policy prescription, developed in chapter 19, that the 'money-wage level . . . be maintained as stable as possible, at any rate in the short period' (1936: 270),[54] a proposition that emerges from Keynes' conviction that a flexible wage policy has considerably greater welfare costs than a flexible monetary policy. From our perspective, however, the most significant of Keynes' arguments is that real wages are set by prices as well as wages; thus, since bargaining can only influence the latter, it is impossible for workers to determine the real wage, even if they wanted to (1936: 13). Prices are an *ex post* factor in wage bargaining; moreover, the process of negotiating a money wage involves the balancing of the firm's (product-price) real wage target with the employee's (consumption-price) real wage target.[55] Since output prices are determined in the goods market, while it is money wages that are determined in the labour market, it makes little sense to blame *real* wage rigidity on the bargaining process.[56] 'It is certain other forces which determine the general level of real wages' (1936: 13) – notably whatever determines the price level. By distinguishing between nominal wage bargaining and real wage outcomes, Keynes was effectively rejecting the entire analytical apparatus of Pigou and Clay, with its focus on the labour market in isolation, positing in its stead a general (macroeconomic) equilibrium approach.

In the *General Theory*, Keynes was content to retain the traditional Marshallian analysis of price setting, with its emphasis on atomistic firms in a competitive marketplace. The emphasis on sticky money wages and rapid adjustment of prices generated the famous debate with Dunlop (1938), Tarshis (1939) and Richardson (1939), in which Keynes' surmise that 'the change in real wages associated with a change in money-wages . . . is almost always in the opposite direction' was challenged. The data, both British and American, suggested that real wages moved pro-cyclically – that prices were in fact less flexible than wages. Keynes' response (1939) was to drop the Marshallian analysis, and to offer in its place a model of normal cost pricing, in which firms set prices as a mark-up over costs. This fits well with Hall and Hitch's investigation (1939) of actual pricing behaviour, which ridiculed the notion of businessmen calculating marginal revenues and costs, as well as with Kalecki's theoretical analysis (1938) of the relationship between a firm's mark-up and the degree of competition in its market. Keynes suggested that cost-plus pricing fit better with his own analysis (allowing one 'to simplify considerably the more complicated version of. . . my "General Theory"') than did the 'traditional conclusion'.[57]

The implications of different pricing regimes for the analysis of real wages and unemployment may be illustrated with the aid of a simple macro-economic model, derived by Nickell (1988). The model is composed of three equations, determining demand, prices and wages respectively. The level of aggregate demand is determined by monetary factors (represented by the level of real money balances) and exogenous real demand variables (such as fiscal stance):

$$y = a_0 + a_1(m-p) + a_2x^d, \tag{7}$$

where m is the money stock, p is the price level and x^d is the vector of real demand variables. This equation may be viewed as the reduced form of a standard IS–LM model, in which the parameter, a_1, captures the interest elasticity of money demand and also the impact of interest rates on demand for output, via income and wealth effects. Prices in this model are determined as a mark-up on costs (wages and import prices), in which the mark-up is influenced by the level of output and the extent of nominal inertia (as proxied by the divergence between actual and expected prices):

$$p = u_0 + u_1w + u_2p_m + (1 - u_1 - u_2)p^e + u_3y, \tag{8}$$

where w is the nominal wage, p_m is the price of imports, and p^e is the level of expected prices. Wages in turn are determined by a bargaining process, influenced by current and expected domestic prices, the level of economic activity and the level of import prices (working through their impact on firm profits):

$$w = v_0 + v_1p + v_2p^e - (v_1 + v_2 - 1)p_m + v_3y + z, \tag{9}$$

in which z represents wage pressure variables, such as union power and the level of benefits. With suitable manipulation, these equations can be transformed to provide a consistent and fully specified model in which wages, prices and output are determined by the exogenous elements of the system.

Demand: $\qquad y = a_0 + a_1(m-p) + a_2x^d$ (10)

Price setting: $p - w = b_0 - b_1(p-p^e) + b_2y + b_3p_m$ (11)

Wage setting: $w - p = c_0 - c_1(p-p^e) + c_2y - c_3p_m + z,$ (12)

where p_m is the real price of imports. For convenience, prices are here presented as a mark-up over wages, and the wage equation is depicted in real wage terms. The model does, however, retain the more realistic assumption that wage bargains are about nominal wages, and that prices

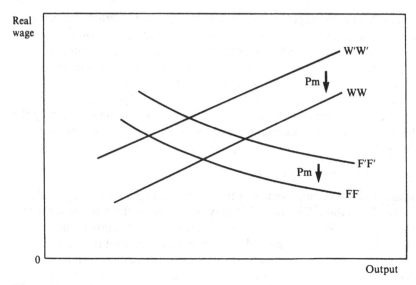

Figure 11.3   The equilibrium labour market model.

reflect the overall cost pattern. Nominal inertia in wage and price determination are captured by the parameters, b_1 and c_1.

Figure 11.3 captures the spirit of this model, by placing the price and wage setting equations in output and real wage space. The target real wage, WW, derived from (12) responds positively to changes in real output. The feasible real wage (FF) is derived by inverting the price setting equation, such that feasible real wages are a decreasing function of economic activity. Equilibrium is determined by the resolution of the two sides of the bargaining process. Figure 11.3 depicts a no-surprise equilibrium, in which prices match expectations for both parties in the wage bargain. It is notable that demand variables play no role in determining equilibrium in this model. A demand shock can temporarily lower output and employment, but, in the absence of supply reactions, recovery will bring the economy back to full employment equilibrium. This reflects the natural rate properties of the model, in which exogenous supply side factors – which include not only wage pressure variables but also the behaviour of import prices – alone establish the long-run level of output.[58] Changes in these variables will tend to shift the target and feasible wage functions. Thus, greater wage pressure will force WW up, reducing output and increasing wages in equilibrium. A fall in the relative price of imports will cut firms' costs (moving FF outwards), while encouraging greater wage pressure from workers (thus, pushing WW up). Real wages will tend to rise, while the precise impact on domestic output will be contingent on the elasticity of wage and price setting to the change in relative prices.[59] But, in this case, real wages are not the source of the shock, but rather the means by which it is transmitted to the labour market.

Thus, wage pressures are not the only possible source of an increase in the real wage, nor indeed of a negative relation between real wage and output (employment) changes from one equilibrium to another. Moreover, under certain circumstances, added wage pressure may have no impact on the real wage whatsoever. This will happen if the feasible real wage is invariant to output (b_2 is zero), and if price expectations are fully realised (or if b_1 is zero). In this case, FF will be fixed, and any increase in the target wage will translate automatically into a fall in output and employment. This would be the case if prices were set solely on a normal cost basis, in which the mark-up of prices is a constant mark-up over wages. There is no necessary *ex post* relationship between real wage behaviour and changes in labour market institutions.

The point is made more forcefully when we move from comparative statistics to an analysis of the economy's behaviour between equilibria. The economy may be derailed by a supply shock from the cost side (a change in z or p_m), or by an exogenous shock to demand from the real or money sector (via a change in x^d or m). What will be the path of the real wage in the wake of such a shock? In the characterisation of atomistic firms and an imperfect labour market that was common both to pre-Keynesians and the *General Theory*, such that nominal wages are sticky and output prices are fully flexible, an adverse shock will always cause the real wage to rise as output (and employment) falls, regardless of its origin.[60] It is thus impossible to determine whether unemployment is classical (supply-led) or Keynesian (demand-led) from data on the cyclical behaviour of real wages. The debates[61] over the elasticity of employment to own-product real wages become irrelevant; a negative relationship between real wages and employment cannot alone prove or disprove the pre-Keynesian case (*pace* Casson).

Once the competitive assumption of fully flexible prices is dropped, even the standard *ex post* relationship between real wages and the level of economic activity falls by the wayside. The real wage can rise, fall, or stay the same in the wake of a demand or a supply shock, depending on the particular responsiveness of wages and prices to changes in nominal and real variables. Thus, if prices are set on a normal cost basis and are more inertial than nominal wages, real wages will fall in the wake of an adverse demand shock, even as employment is falling. The reaction of the real wage to an adverse supply shock is likewise contingent. In the immediate aftermath of the shock, real wages will almost always rise.[62] However, the subsequent path of real wages and output is dependent on price and wage setting behaviour. The trend in output (i.e. the depth of the recession) will depend on the full extent of nominal inertia (in both wage and price setting) and the combined elasticity of wages and prices to movements in real economic activity. The behaviour of the real wage is determined primarily by price-setting behaviour. If there is considerable inertia in price setting, real wages are likely to be falling throughout much of the recession. The unravelling of the pre-Keynesian analysis is complete. A supply shock need not create a continuous process of rising real wages and falling output; when unemployment is accompanied by higher real wages this is no sure sign that a supply shock is responsible; supply shocks can be attributed to factors beyond the labour market.

As in so much of economics, however, the resolution of the debate between Keynes and Pigou rests on statistical evidence. This is also true of a number of other core differences between the two camps beyond the origin of interwar unemployment, such as the speed of recovery, and whether recovery could be aided by centralised macroeconomic policies, and, if so, of what sort. The focal questions can only be resolved by empirical investigation: Was unemployment created by institutional forces, which raised the target wage above feasible levels, pricing British producers out of world markets and advantaging overseas competitors at home? Or did institutional problems tend rather to reduce the responsiveness of the domestic economy to other exogenous forces? In more modern terms, was unemployment caused by a supply or demand shock?[63] How rapid was the process of equilibriation (and, for recent historians, what was its source)? And was a policy of fiscal expansion sensible given the underlying supply structure of the economy?

In their application of the Nickell model to interwar Britain, Dimsdale *et al.* (1989) find that the behaviour of prices, wages and output during the period 1929–37 is consistent with a major demand shock accompanied by a large fall in the real price of imports. Import prices fell by 36% between 1929 and 1933, while the price of domestic output (the GDP deflator) fell by 7.5%. The drop in real import prices placed upward pressure on the real wage (see figure 11.3), which more than compensated for the deflationary impact of the demand shock. Thus, falling output and employment was accompanied by rising real wages. However, in this analysis, the causal direction was not, as in the pre-Keynesian model, or as in the recent work of Capie, Griffiths & Beenstock (1984), from real wages to unemployment, but from exogenous international factors to the real wage. Similarly, during recovery, real import prices rose by over ten per cent, creating an inward shift in FF (in figure 11.3), its downward impact on real wages reinforced by a downward shift in WW. The fall in real wages during recovery is, again, linked to terms of trade effects, rather than to the easing of institutional forces in the labour market.

Even if institutional forces were not the source of the disequilibrating shock to the economy after 1929, institutions nevertheless do matter, because they shape the responsiveness of the economy to any macro-economic disturbance. However, it is not just the institutions of the labour market that count. Labour market outcomes also depend crucially on the structures of the product market, and the behaviour of firms, as producers as well as employers. In the case of an adverse demand shock, for example, the depth of the resulting downturn will be greater the more product markets are imperfect and the more rigid are product, as well as labour, markets to changes in prices and output.[64] The path of the real wage will depend on the relative levels of inertia in wage and price determination. If prices exhibit more nominal inertia than wages, and if prices adjust more grudgingly than wages to declining activity, then the real wage will fall. This requires that b_1 in equation 11 is large and b_2 is zero, as would be the case with rigid normal cost pricing, in which firms do not change their mark-up in response to changing demand conditions, in an imperfectly competitive market characterised by high transaction costs of changing prices. There is considerable supporting evidence for this interpretation for interwar Britain.[65] The polling data of Hall and Hitch have been supplemented by more rigorous econometric modelling of the aggregate price equation. Thus, Broadberry (1986: 96) finds that in equilibrium, the GDP deflator is a weighted average of wage and import costs,[66] with no independent role for demand variables. This result was replicated by Dimsdale et al. in their quarterly model of the interwar economy, which also found nominal wages to be somewhat responsive to changes in economic activity (a result reproduced in Crafts, 1989),[67] while prices were apparently more inertial than wages. The competitive goods market that underpinned pre-Keynesian theory lacks empirical justification.

Conclusions

Ironically, even if Keynes was right to focus attention on the behaviour of demand, and to reject simplistic associations between real wages and employment as evidence of a supply based explanation of Britain's economic problem in the 1930s, a number of the very questions that we began with remain. Did the institutions of the British economy create more vulnerabilities to shocks than in other modern economies? Did the British economy become more vulnerable over time as institutions matured? It is not necessary to believe that the problems of the British economy were supply determined to find institutions culpable. Nor is it necessary to share the pre-Keynesian perspective in identifying the institutions that mattered, or the way in which they influenced labour market (and macroeconomic) outcomes. I have already suggested that bargaining arrangements were little different in Britain from many other countries. However, other supply-side features also matter. These not only include benefits, insurance contributions and employment taxes. They also include less formal structures in the labour market, notably the balance of power and authority between those currently employed and those out of work, as well as the emerging institutional structures of the product market, including those subsumed under the general rubric of the corporate economy – larger firms practising oligopolistic pricing, collusion and cooperation, and greater coordination of industry and government, via tariffs, rationalisation programmes and rearmament. And there is good reason to believe that the importance of both these elements was increasing during the 1920s. The British economy was bombarded by adverse shocks early in that decade – supply-side rearrangements such as the substantial decline in hours in 1920–1, as well as a series of demand shocks emanating from the international economy. These undoubtedly set in play a number of forces which may well have increased the sclerosis of the British economy – both by increasing the demand for institutional restraints to protect vulnerable sectors of the economy (reflected in the merger and Trust movements as well as in the spread of Trade Boards) and by redistributing market power within the economy. The latter point returns to the insider–outsider theory discussed earlier. There are good reasons to believe that the power of insiders was higher in 1929 than in 1913 – technological change increased the importance of human capital and skill hoarding to firms; there was substantial decasualisation of the labour force; the loss of staple markets after the First World War was concentrated in a few small areas; the collapse of the coal strike and the return to gold further intensified the decline of key industries in depressed regions; the failure of local economies to recover may well have fuelled skill deterioration and worker discouragement among the unemployed, increasing the relative power of the insiders and reducing the pressure of unemployment on wage rates. We would therefore anticipate greater real rigidity of nominal wages in 1929 than in 1913, as well as greater price inertia in the wake of the demise of atomistic competition in a wide array of British industries. In one sense, then, the pre-Keynesians were precisely right. The 1920s was a period of increased inflexibility of markets, conditioning the relatively poor performance of the British economy. Nevertheless, in order to understand fully the sources and implications of these developments, we need to look beyond the narrow issues discussed by Pigou and Clay, and, indeed, to undertake international comparisons on a broader canvas than attempted in this essay. Alec Ford was right, indeed, to suggest that the 1920s and 1930s were very different decades. It is likely, however, that they differed in more dimensions than even he imagined, and that the supply-side changes in the one intensified the problems raised by demand-side developments in the other.

Notes

1 Maddison produces a figure for Britain of 6.8%, compared to unemployment rates of below 5% for all other countries covered. Of particular relevance is the collapse of the Scandinavian figures – from 18.7 to 4.5% in the case of Denmark, and 14.2 to 3.4% for Sweden. Note that Maddison's revisions have come under fire from Eichengreen and Hatton (1988: 9–10) for reasons (associated especially with ignoring underemployment in agriculture) that may well bias downwards the Scandinavian series relative to the British estimate.

2 This was also a theme of Clay and Pigou, although the emphasis then was on the impact of higher social insurance costs on the hiring practices of employers, rather than the effects of benefits on job search by workers.

3 Matthews does devote four pages (pp. 35–8) to a discussion of the classicals' position, derived largely from the work of Casson (1983). However, his macroeconomic model owes little to their institutional concerns. The key administrative feature of his model is the insurance scheme, but in a form that owes more to Benjamin and Kochin than to Clay or Pigou.

4 And is just downright misleading a reading of what is important in the General Theory.

5 Casson incorrectly refers to this as an increase in 'the real wage' (1983: 180). However, the Ministry of Labour statistics, as summarised by Richardson (1933: 19), indicate that average real wages were 'only about 3 per cent above the level of July 1914' over the whole of the 1920s. By 1929, whereas money wage rates were $c.$ 72.5% higher than in August 1914, real wages had increased by about 7.5%.

6 I quote the rate of unemployment among insured workers, since pre-Keynesian theorists did not have access to more recent revised estimates of 'actual' employment.

7 And assuming an orthodox downward-sloping demand curve.

8 'The implication is that such unemployment as exists at any time is due wholly to the fact that changes in demand conditions are continually taking place and that frictional resistances prevent the appropriate wage adjustments from being made instantaneously' (Pigou, 1933: 252).

9 Note, however, Boyer's recent work on 'what unions did' before 1914, which emphasises the role of unions as provident societies, as well as centralised bargaining agencies. See also, Webb and Webb (1897), pp. 152ff., and Johnson (1985), pp. 75–80.

10 The JICs were established with equal representation of management and labour 'for the purpose of regular consultation and co-operation' on 'matters affecting

the progress and well-being of the trade, from the point of view of all those engaged in it' (Liberal Industrial Inquiry, 1928: 172).

11 The conditions in the first of these having been publicised by Beatrice Potter, and in the latter by John Burnett, twenty years previously.

12 This figure includes those covered by the five Irish Boards.

13 The same sort of argument may be found in Pigou (1927b: 339), and Richardson (1933: 30).

14 The major difference between Sells' figure and my own rests on her use of the number of wage changes recorded in 1920 as an estimate of the volume of workers covered by voluntary agreements throughout the interwar period. I prefer to use the number of union members as a proxy for voluntary coverage. A close examination of the annual series of wage changes recorded in the *Ministry of Labour Gazette* reveals a very close correlation with union membership. This suggests two things: firstly, that the recorded number of wage changes is likely to be an underestimate of its true figure, as union density fell after 1920; secondly, that voluntary agreements were unlikely to have remained stable in scope throughout 1920–38.

15 One feasible response to this observation is, of course, that prices rose after 1945, and that downward wage rigidity was never tested.

16 A number of other volumes were envisioned, but were never published. However, drafts of them are available in the Public Record Office, under the class list LAB41.

17 At the peak of the COL sliding scale arrangements (July 1922), the three approaches probably accounted for half of workers covered by collective agreements.

18 One example is the bleaching and dyeing industry, in which the elasticity of wages with respect to price increases was 1, and with respect to price declines, only 0.8426.

19 As Pool observes, there was some variation between districts (1938: 208–9).

20 Certainly this argument has more merit than Casson's bold assertion that COLAs were 'short-lived because during the . . . deflation there was pressure to abandon indexation from the same people who had demanded it earlier' (1983: 184). The problem with this interpretation lies in the timing of both the rise and fall of COL indexation. The majority of sliding scales were introduced into contracts after deflation took hold (60% between January 1920 and July 1922), while they were not abandoned in large numbers until after 1925.

21 I tested the relationship by regressing the number of individuals affected by wage changes against a number of variables, including the logarithm of union density (lnu), the size of the working population, unemployment, inflation, and dummy variables to capture the effects of war (1 if 1915–18, 0 otherwise), and COLAs (1 in 1921–25, 0.5 in 1920 and 1926–29, 0.25 otherwise). A standard result was (t-statistics in parentheses):

$$\text{Number} = -68148.4 + 8281.1\,\text{lnu} + 2291.3\,\text{War} + 941.3\,\text{Cola}$$
$$(-4.351) \quad (4.489) \quad\quad (2.490) \quad\quad (0.835)$$
$$r^2 = 0.580;\ F = 12.063;$$
$$DW = 1.173.$$

No other variables were statistically significant in other variants of this regression.

22 This theme is explored in greater depth in a companion paper, entitled 'How flexible were wages in interwar Britain?' (Thomas, 1991).

23 Note that this axiomatic result can also be replicated with a strategic process. See, Binmore, Rubinstein & Wolinsky (1986).

24 Benefits weighted according to the family circumstances of recipients.

25 One evident problem with Matthews is that he uses the benefit level for a man with a wife and 2 children – the same variable as Benjamin and Kochin. This is clearly an inappropriate characterisation of the family structure of most benefit recipients. Experiments with other models show how sensitive results are to the modelling of this variable.

26 The ratio of unemployment benefits to the average wage.

27 Other papers that play down the role of benefits include Hatton (1983), Broadberry (1983), Crafts (1987), and Dimsdale (1984). The other recent contribution that concurs with Matthews on the importance of benefits to the path of unemployment is Beenstock and Warburton (1986a), which emphasises less the role of rising benefit levels as the greater ease of access after 1929.

28 British unionism was largely industrial in scope. Agriculture, distribution, government and the professions (excepting health care) were relative back waters of union development. But this structure was widely the case, as figures for the US, Sweden and Canada make clear. The density of unionism in manufacturing, mining, construction and transportation was $c.$ 21% in 1911 in Britain, 42% in 1921, and 26% in 1931. The pertinent figures for the US are 23% (1920), 14% (1930), and 36% (1939), and for Sweden, 17% (1911), 46% (1921), 66% (1931) (calculated from Bain and Price, 1980). These figures are consistent with Britain lying somewhere in the middle of union densities of Western economies.

29 According to the report of International Federation of Trade Unions (1913), Italy was the only country before the First World War where local unions were quantitatively more significant than central unions. Moreover, the qualitative evidence suggests that the gradual transformation of unions to national agendas on work and wages was common to most Western countries. In some cases, notably in Scandinavia, the process of centralisation pre-dated the British – in 1913, 70% of workers covered fell under national agreements. In Australia, Canada, and the United States unionism did not move to a national basis; but even here the trend was away from local negotiations towards regional bargaining.

30 This division ignores the 'yellow' company unions, developed by employers such as Krupps to defuse the union movement, which were more representative of the strategy of capital than of labour.

31 Data are not available for precisely the same time period for all of the countries involved. The average is calculated from data for Belgium, 1901–29, Canada, 1901–29, Denmark, 1900–29, Finland, 1907–29, France, 1900–29, Germany, 1900–29, Holland, 1901–29, Italy, 1900–23, Norway, 1903–29, Spain, 1910–29, Sweden, 1903–29, and the United States, 1900–29 (Shorter & Tilly, 1974: 333).

32 It is also worth noting that the sources of strikes are very similar in Britain as

elsewhere. Between 1910 and 1924, 66% of British stoppages were over wages, a proportion very close to that in Canada, Finland, Italy, Japan, Spain, Sweden and the US. Only Australia and New Zealand, with their centralised wage setting machinery, had lower proportions (International Labour Office, 1927: 94).

33 Other factors cited by Ross and Irwin (1951: 336–8) include the absence of a closed shop, the existence of leadership disputes within a union, and jurisdictional conflict of unions cometing for the same labour force.

34 There were 77 German miners covered by collective agreements in 1912, compared to 900,000 in Britain (1910). If the coal workers are removed from the British list of collective agreements, the proportion of the industrial workforce covered falls to 17%, almost identical to the German figure in 1913.

35 In the case of Germany, the threat of armed revolution was another spur to cooperation between employers' associations and organised labour. The conclusion of the Stinnes–Legien agreement (whereby unions were recognised, and company unions disbanded) and the establishment of the Zentralarbeitsgemeinschaft (which offered a bilateral, non-state solution to industrial problems) in October–November, 1918, are testimony to the pressure of events in the wake of German defeat.

36 These figures exclude Angestellten (salaried employees), who numbered about one million in 1921 and twice as many two years later.

37 Reich, in his excellent review of German industrial relations under Weimar, notes that these figures underestimate the impact of collective bargaining on wage-setting in the labour market (1938: 89). The operation of the Allgemeinverbindlichkeit system, whereby collective agreements were automatically taken to apply to *all* firms in a given district or locality, ensured a degree of universality unknown in the British system. Thus, in 1927, a further five million workers were incorporated in agreements to which they were not signatories.

38 One exception worth noting is France, where 'the movement to regulate employment relations by collective agreements has made less progress . . . than in many other countries' (United States, 1935a: 959). In 1933, only 7.5% of industrial workers were party to collective agreements.

39 A number of smaller associations had been founded during the earlier strike wave of the late 1880s (Kruger, 1926: 319).

40 Figures are from various supplements to the *Reichsarbeitsblatt* issued by the Arbeitsministerium. The details on Tarifvertrage were collected for 31 December for years before 1923 and for 1 January thereafter. To escape confusion, all years are quoted as though the figures refer to 1 January.

41 Note, however, that company agreements accounted for 43% of contracts in both 1922 and 1931. The average number of workers per company contract was 142 in 1931, compared to 1,386 for all agreements.

42 In 1935, over 75% of bargaining arrangements in the US involved single firms (United States, 1935b: 1,445).

43 Note also that the form of the shock – whether supply or demand – matters. This may resolve the apparent contradiction of the Pigou-Clay position by Bruno and Sachs.

44 Note, however, that there remains considerable controversy over the merits (and even the *modus operandi*) of the corporatist model. See, for example, the contrasting results of Alogoskoufis and Manning (1988) and Jackman *et al.* (as reported in Nickell, 1990).

45 For a detailed critique of real wage-gap models, see Thomas (1990).

46 One of the underlying assumptions of the real wage-gap approach is that the labour market is in equilibrium at the starting point of the analysis. It manifestly was not in 1923 – indeed, the dramatic increase in the labour share across the war, coupled with the historically high level of unemployment, suggests this most strongly. The real wage increase between 1913 and 1923 does not appear to have been warranted by changes in productivity or the terms of trade. Thus, Clay (1929a: 339) noted that real wages rose by 12% between 1907 and 1924, while labour productivity stagnated, revealing considerable 'maladjustment' in the wage-structure in the early 1920s. When measured against a full employment standard, the speed of adjustment was slower and insufficient. Unemployment was intransigent, and real wages remained buoyant. Hatton reconciles the result of more rapid wage adjustments with the fact of high interwar unemployment by suggesting that 'the permanent upward shift in the wage share of national income [from *c.* 53% in 1913 to *c.* 62% in 1923] appears to have imposed a profit squeeze which exacerbated unemployment' (1988: 83). Unfortunately, this conclusion reveals a common problem of data selection in interwar labour market model-building. Hatton uses Feinstein's labour share estimate (which is estimated as the ratio of the wage and salary bill to GDP), which he then models as the product of employment and the wage rate divided by GDP. The wage rate is not the appropriate variable here; it is a severely biased proxy for the movement of average wages and salaries in this period. Indeed, Bowley's Law, that the share of *wages* in national income remained constant between 1880 and 1938, is largely verified by the evidence – it experienced no large-scale jump between 1913 and 1923. Thus, the application of the real wage gap analysis to Britain over 1900–40 is likely to find no evidence of excess real wages. For a fuller explanation, see Thomas (1991).

47 Note that neither lages nor laged was normalised in this regression.

48 I do not discuss implicit contract models here. They too can explain rigid wages, but have no place for involuntary unemployment. See Hart and Holmstrom (1986) and Worrall (1989) for further treatment.

49 The predicted net effect of a 1% increase in long-term unemployment is to *raise* wages by 0.2%. The result is consistent with Nickell's work with wage equations for the 1980s.

50 And, is moreover, consistent with Clay's version of the 1920s.

51 To a certain extent, they also took on the mantle of outsiders in their own industries. This was especially true of older workers, dismissed less because of the application of FIFO policies (though these may have existed in sectors where productivity was known to decline after a certain age), but because entire firms closed down. Note, however, that wages did fall a good distance in many of the staples – by 17% in iron and steel (1927–32), 24% in cotton (1927–31), 16% in coal (1927–32), 18% in woollens (1928–34), 15% in coke (1927–32) – in a

period when overall wage rates fell by little more than 5%.

52 Keynes adds in chapter 19, Appendix A, 'in particular the relation between the schedule of the marginal efficiency of capital and the rate of interest' (1936: 278).

53 Keynes did not offer this merely as an analytical convenience. There are hints throughout the *General Theory* that money wage stickiness is a product of the macroeconomic system as Keynes understood it. For a speculative assessment, see Chick (1983).

54 'Provided that equilibrium with the rest of the world can be secured by means of fluctuating exchanges' (1936: 270).

55 Note that there is almost nothing in the empirical evidence, either quantitative or qualitative, to suggest that real wages were the target variable in most negotiations. There were a number of sectors in which sliding-scale arrangements based on the selling price of the final product meant real wage bargaining *de facto*. Cost-of-living adjustment clauses in 1920–2 may have operated similarly; but after 1923 they were slowly falling away, at a time, moreover, when there were significant divergences in the behaviour of producers' and consumers' prices. The weak performance of both retail prices and the GDP deflator in nominal wage equations emphasises that the real wage was *not* the key bargaining variable.

56 Or, of course, to argue that flexible wages can ensure full employment (1936: ch. 19, esp. pp. 260–7).

57 Although Keynes was not disposed to accept Dunlop's or Tarshis' results.

58 To place the model in more familiar unemployment–real wage space, the production function may be invoked. In this case, the target and feasible real wage equations will be inverted, such that there is a negative relationship between higher wage bids and unemployment, while the feasible real wage increases in unemployment. The natural rate of unemployment is determined by the matching of feasible and target wages. See Layard (1986: 34ff).

59 If b_3 is less than c_3, then output will tend to fall as import prices decline. See Dimsdale *et al.* (1989).

60 Let the supply shock originate in increased union power, which puts (successful) upward pressure on nominal (and real) wages; employment drops as firms move along their labour demand functions. This is the standard story. In the case of an adverse demand shock in a competitive product market with sticky wages, prices will fall below their expected level, causing firms to reduce output and real wages to rise. The outcome is the same, although the causal mechanism is very different.

61 For example, that between Beenstock, Capie and Griffiths (1984), Dimsdale (1984) and Beenstock & Warburton (1986b).

62 The exception being the case in which the mark-up of prices over costs is a rigid constant, invariant to changes in the level of activity, such that the price increase will precisely consume the nominal wage gain.

63 Or, more accurately, perhaps, was unemployment caused by a process of continuous supply shocks emanating from the revolution in labour market institutions, or from a series of demand shocks, the most serious being the collapse of world markets in 1929–32?

64 In the case of a supply shock, however, wage and price stickiness will tend to dampen down the resulting fluctuations.

65 Although not unanimous. In their econometric review of wage-setting in fourteen countries, Newell & Symons (1988: 81–4) found 'no sign of nominal rigidity' in the determination of real wages in Britain, in contrast to the ruling experience in western labour markets. Their index of nominal wage rigidity (for which the UK and US indices scored close to zero; other figures range from 1.2 for Sweden and 1.4 for Germany, to around 3 for Denmark, Czechoslovakia and Belgium) is the long-run inflation parameter from a standard real wage equation. However, the absence of trend productivity or non-wage supply side variables (such as the level of benefits and employment taxes) may suggest misspecification of their equation.

66 The weights being 0.67 and 0.33 respectively.

67 In contrast to Broadberry (1986: 95), who concludes that unemployment exerted no significant downward pressure on nominal wages in the short-run, and Matthews (1986: 54), whose rational expectations model generates an appropriately signed but statistically insignificant coefficient on unemployment.

12 Employment and wages in the interwar period: the case of the staple industries

IAN GAZELEY and PATRICIA G. RICE

Introduction

The relative fortunes of the staple industries between the wars are central to the debate concerning Britain's economic performance during this period. For many contemporaries, the performance of the staples was the appropriate barometer by which to judge the overall performance of the economy, as Allen has commented:

It is not surprising that observers tended to base their generalisations concerning British Industry on data drawn from the great trades. With their rise and expansion Britain had become rich and powerful. . . . For these reasons it became usual to regard the state of the staple industries as indicative of the economic condition of Great Britain as a whole. (Allen, 1970: 18)

The six major staple industries (cotton textiles, wool and worsted, coal-mining, ship-building and ship-repair, mechanical engineering and iron and steel – henceforth referred to as S6) dominated the Victorian economy, and gave rise to the popular image of Britain as the 'workshop of the world'. In 1913, coal, iron and steel, textiles, machinery, cutlery, tools and hardware produced some two-thirds of manufactured exports; the cotton industry alone accounted for 31% of manufactured exports. At the time of the 1907 census of production, 30.8% of the coal industry's production was exported, 31.6% in the case of iron and steel and 83.6% in the cotton industry.

In contrast to the late Victorian and Edwardian period, during the interwar years 'the world's workshop [was] on short-time' (Mowat, 1968: 259). The economic performance of the staple industries during this period is characterised by relatively low levels of output and high unemployment – linked in most cases to a collapse of their export markets. This reversal in the fortunes of the staple industries and the associated high levels of unemployment of the interwar period has been the subject of much enquiry in recent economic history. However it is potentially misleading to regard the staple industries as a homogenous group whose long-term decline gave rise to the high average unemployment rates of the interwar years. As we show in this paper, there are marked differences in the performance of individual staple industries during the interwar period. Furthermore, while it may be true for the textile sector that the 1920s signalled the start of a decline from which the industry never recovered, such a description is less appropriate for the ship-building industry where the sharp fluctuations in output and employment of the interwar years was succeeded by a period of relatively strong performance following the Second World War.

In this chapter, we focus on the behaviour of employment in the major staple industries during the inter-war period. For this purpose, we have compiled new quarterly data series on employment, wages, raw material prices and output prices for a number of key industries including coal-mining, ship-building, cotton, and wool and worsted. We examine the pattern of employment and prices over the period 1924 to 1938 as revealed by this new data set, drawing comparisons with previously available data for this period.

A major advantage of disaggregate quarterly data on employment, wages and prices is that it allows the estimation of models of employment at the industry level. To date, the empirical modelling of (un)employment during the interwar period has relied extensively on aggregate data for the economy as a whole. By their very nature such studies can tell us nothing about the diversity of experience among individual industries. In the fifth section of the chapter, we present a simple dynamic model of employment determination at the industry level. The estimates of wage and price elasticities of employment obtained from this model using the new quarterly data series are presented in the final section and compared with estimates from previous studies for the interwar and postwar periods.

Employment in the staple industries

Table 12.1 outlines the behaviour of employment in the major staple industries over the period 1920 to 1938 using annual estimates of the number of wage and salaried employees from Chapman and Knight (1954). This table illustrates clearly the extent to which employment losses during the great depression were concentrated within the traditional staple industries. Between 1929 and 1932, total civilian employment fell by some 770,000 of which 670,000, or 87%, were employed in the so-called 'staple' industries (S6). Employment within this group fell by some 26% over this period, as compared with a loss of just 7% in the 'non-staple' manufacturing industries, and an employment increase of 2% in the non-manufactur-

Table 12.1. *Numbers in employment 1920–38*

Year	Coal-mining	Ship-building	Cotton	Wool & worsted	Staples S6	Manuf. & mining	Non-manuf.	All industries
1920	1083.0	282.3	533.7	274.5	3597.4	7871.8	9106.7	16978
1921	840.0	211.8	410.0	224.3	2471.4	6051.7	8647.4	14699
1922	971.0	168.3	525.6	296.2	2658.9	6438.0	8484.8	14923
1923	1084.0	136.5	493.1	300.0	2826.7	6766.0	8519.6	15286
1924	1056.8	155.1	504.6	295.0	2835.8	6876.0	8639.9	15516
1925	936.0	137.5	541.6	251.6	2677.6	6789.5	8896.6	15686
1926	562.0	116.0	485.5	258.1	2142.0	6229.5	9023.3	15253
1927	833.3	142.1	535.2	276.1	2653.8	6927.7	9315.0	16243
1928	768.3	136.6	509.0	258.0	2519.7	6858.3	9473.1	16331
1929	812.5	139.2	480.2	261.1	2554.3	6980.2	9639.3	16620
1930	766.0	123.3	366.0	214.6	2232.8	6491.2	9749.1	16240
1931	689.2	76.8	334.3	215.1	1950.0	6003.3	9775.1	15788
1932	630.0	61.1	364.2	234.1	1884.2	6012.4	9838.1	15850
1933	613.3	61.0	390.9	250.7	1959.7	6239.5	10021.9	16261
1934	643.5	74.7	377.2	241.9	2075.7	6549.1	10272.0	16821
1935	644.0	85.0	364.9	246.6	2124.1	6705.5	10469.6	17175
1936	655.0	105.7	372.4	256.4	2272.5	7071.8	10728.3	17800
1937	705.6	121.5	377.5	251.7	2442.4	7468.3	11013.5	18482
1938	674.0	129.1	301.6	220.7	2299.0	7330.7	11116.9	18448

ing sector. However, within the 'staple' group itself, the experience was equally diverse. For example, in the wool and worsted industry, employment fell by 18% between 1929 and 1930 and then quickly recovered, while in ship-building, employment declined steadily from 1929 to 1933, reaching just 44% of its 1929 level.

To date, Chapman and Knight (1954) has been the main source of data for empirical studies of employment in individual industries during the interwar years (for example Hatton (1981)). An obvious drawback of this data is that it provides only annual observations. Furthermore, the series are derived by interpolation of Census of Production data for the years 1924, 1930 and 1935; interpolation between these dates being based on the Ministry of Labour data on unemployment among insured workers. An alternative source of data is Beck (1951) which provides information on the number of insured workers in employment for some thirty industries derived from Ministry of Labour data, but unfortunately these series are for the period 1927 to 1938 only.

For the purposes of this study, we derived quarterly series for the number of insured workers in employment for the key staple industries based on information published in the Ministry of Labour Gazettes (MLG) for the period. The Ministry of Labour provides monthly data on the number of insured workers registering as unemployed in the UK on an industry group basis for most of the manufacturing sector. In addition, it provides information on the total number of insured workers, employed and unemployed, in each industry at July of each year. Linear interpolation is used to derive a monthly series for the number of insured workers from the annual data. From this is subtracted the number of insured workers registered as unemployed to obtain a series for employment of insured workers in each of ship-building and ship-repair, cotton spinning and wool and worsted. While, it is the case that the MLG publishes this information for the whole period 1920 to 1938, changes in the industrial classification used mean that, for most industries, a consistent data series is available only from 1924 onwards.

An important limitation of this data is that it refers to insured workers only and the coverage of the unemployment insurance scheme changes considerably during the interwar period. However, in the case of the 'staple' industries considered in this study this is not a problem since coverage under the scheme did not change significantly after 1924.

In addition to the information relating to the employment of insured workers, the MLG provides survey data relating to employment in 'principal industries' including ship-building, cotton and wool and wor- sted. This data is based upon information provided by employers and is available on a regional basis. Unfortunately, for many of the industries, the sample of participating firms is small and is not representative of the industry as a whole. Moreover, the coverage of the survey changed significantly in 1926, and several industries are excluded thereafter. However, this survey data is a valuable supplement to the insured employment data discussed above, and in some cases, notably ship- building, it does enable employment to be analysed on a regional basis.

Finally, in addition to the staple industries listed above, we consider the coal-mining industry. In this case, detailed information on output, employment and earnings by region is included in the reports of the Secretary of Mines, and is published in the Ministry of Labour Gazettes from 1922 onwards. From this source, we have compiled a quarterly series for employment in coal-mining based on the number of manshifts employed during the quarter.

The quarterly series for employment are shown in figures 12.1a–d, and these highlight some important differences in the experience of the four staple industries considered. The employment series for coal-mining displays considerably more volatility than that for the other industries, as is to be expected given that employment here is measured in terms of the number of manshifts worked rather than simply the number of persons employed. The underlying trend in coal-mining employment is declining sharply following the strike of 1926. There are some signs of a recovery from 1934, but employment in the late 1930s remains considerably below its pre-1926 levels. On the basis of this series, the 'great depression' appears to have had relatively little impact on employment in coal-mining, in so far as the rate of decline in employment between 1929 and 1933 is of the same order of magnitude as occurred between 1926 and 1929.

In certain respects, the experience of the two textile industries is not dissimilar to that of coal-mining, although the underlying downward trend in employment is much less pronounced, particularly in the case of cotton spinning. The downturns in employment following the 'crash' of 1929, while significant, are not exceptional in the context of the period as a whole. Within cotton spinning, employment falls by some 16% between 1929.4 and 1930.3, after which it recovers quickly, and apart from a brief setback in mid-1932, employment over the period 1932 to 1937 is on average higher than in the late 1920s. In wool and worsted, employment falls rather more slowly after 1929, bottoming out in 1931.3 at 75% of its 1929.4 level, but here too, employment quickly regains its 1929 levels, and remains there until the downturn of 1937.

In the case of the ship-building and ship-repair industry, a very different picture emerges. Here, the magnitude of the fluctuations in employment are much greater and the period of the cycles, longer than observed elsewhere. Between 1924 and 1930, employment in ship-building experiences two pronounced cyclical fluctuations around a relatively constant underlying trend. Following the 'crash' of 1929, employment in ship-building falls sharply and continues to decline through to the beginning of 1933, when it stands at just 40% of its level of 1929.4. From 1933 onwards, employment grows steadily, but by the end of 1938, it is still significantly below its 1929 levels.

In order to better understand, the sources of these movements in employment, we need to look at the behaviour of not only labour costs, but also raw material prices and output prices over the same period. In the next section of the chapter, we examine the quarterly data series for wages and prices.

Figure 12.1   Employment in four staple industries, 1922–40.

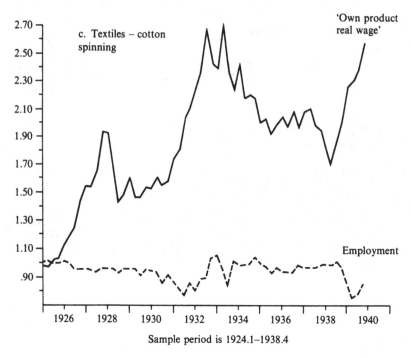

c. Textiles – cotton spinning

'Own product real wage'

Employment

Sample period is 1924.1–1938.4

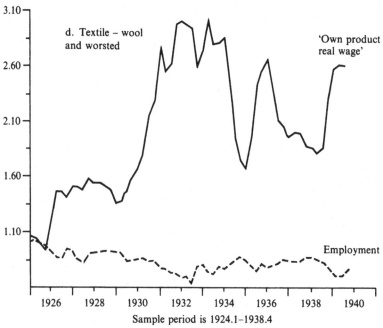

d. Textile – wool and worsted

'Own product real wage'

Employment

Sample period is 1924.1–1938.4

Labour costs and prices

Wages

In general, quarterly data on wage movements in individual industries during the interwar period is not readily available. From 1924 onwards, the Ministry of Labour publishes a quarterly index of aggregate wages based on wage rates in thirty-two industries, but the disaggregate data from which this index is compiled is not published. To date, our knowledge of the behaviour of wages and earnings in individual industries over this period is derived largely from the annual wage indices published by Bowley (1947), and by Ramsbottom (1935; 1938; 1939).

As far as the coal-mining industry is concerned, a reliable quarterly series for earnings may be readily compiled from information on average earnings-per-manshift contained in the reports of the Secretary of Mines. Furthermore, in the case of cotton spinning, Jewkes and Gray (1935) provide a quarterly series for average wage rates and average earnings between 1920 and 1933. This series may be extended to 1938 using the information on average earnings provided by employers under the Ministry of Labour's monthly survey of wages and employment in principal industries. *A priori*, one might expect this estimate of average wages to be biased given the over-representation of large employers in the sample. However, for the period 1920 to 1933, we find a high degree of correlation between the index of average wages in cotton spinning derived from the Ministry of Labour survey data and that published by Jewkes and Gray.

For the two remaining industries, ship-building and ship-repair and wool and worsted, it is necessary to return to the raw data on wage rates in principal occupations and industries published monthly in the Ministry of Labour Gazette (MLG) under the heading 'Changes in Rates of Wages and Hours of Labour'. The information in these tables is based upon returns from employers or trades unions where wage rates are fixed either by collective agreements, or by statutory orders under the provisions of the Trade Boards Acts. The tables are extremely detailed providing informa-tion on changes in wage rates disaggregated by occupation, industry and region. Where necessary and practicable, the information reported in the MLG has been supplemented by information contained in the reports/ journals of employers federations and other secondary sources.

In general during this period, wage structures in the traditional staple industries were significantly more complex than those which prevailed in the newer industries, and this is well illustrated by the ship-building and ship-repair industry. During the First World War, increases in basic rates of pay for both time and piece workers were granted in the form of lump-sum and percentage additions to base rates; reflecting in part the increase in retail prices that occurred during the war. In the immediate postwar period, the industry maintained these arrangements, although part of the wartime increases (percentage additions to basic rates) were integrated into new occupational base rates at the end of 1919 and beginning of 1920. This occurred at the same time as the industry moved towards a shorter working week for time workers. As prices declined in the latter half of 1920, employers successfully reduced wages via reductions in wartime bonus. By 1924, the majority of adult male workers in the industry had all of the wartime additions to their base-rates withdrawn. Between 1924 and the introduction of a National Uniform Wage agreement in 1930, some of these bonuses were reinstated.

To compile a quarterly index of average wages in the industry for this period, we have used data on changes in wage rates for members of eleven occupations employed by firms within the Ship-building Employers Federation on the north-east coast. This region accounted for roughly 42% of merchant shipbuilding output between 1924 and 1938, and a considerable proportion of naval building during the interwar period. In 1936, 55 of the total of 360 shipbuilding firms in Britain belonged to the Ship-building Employers Federation, but of these, the 34 largest firms accounted for 60% of employment in the industry. To a very large extent, *changes* in wage rates within the industry were governed by the outcome of negotiations between the relevant trades unions and the Ship-building Employers Federation, although the *level* of wages paid in particular occupations may have varied across yards in different regions. Thus, in any given month, the level of the wage rate for a rivetter employed on the Clyde may differ from that for one employed in the Belfast yards, but the monthly changes in wage rates are identical for all yards owned by firms within the Federation. Hence, the data series for the north-east provides a good indicator of the monthly movement of wages across the ship-building industry.

For the ship-repair industry, the index of wages is based on changes in wage rates for eighteen occupations (thirteen skilled and five other) in the Bristol Channel and South Wales yards, which along with those located along the Thames and the Mersey, specialised in ship-repair. Unlike the ship-building industry, ship-repair did not operate national collective agreements rather firms within a region jointly bargained on a local basis with the relevant Trades Unions. As a result, the wage series complied for the Bristol and South Wales area is not necessarily a good guide to wage movements elsewhere in the other important centres. That said, wage rates in the ship-repair sector tend to be more stable than those in ship-building.

The wage structure within the wool and worsted industry is equally complex. The widespread existence of sliding-scale agreements imply that even the construction of the wage indices for individual occupations is a complex process. Each occupation has a different base rate and therefore is affected differently by changes in the 'cost-of-living' segment of the wage which depends on the base rate. Our series is based upon monthly movements in wage rates paid to male and female time-rate workers in twenty-two occupations within the Yorkshire wool and worsted Industry, which accounts for 88% of employment within the industry in 1931.

In general, the information reported in the MLG relates to changes in wage rates in a given month, and only rarely does it provide data on the level of wage rates. Hence in compiling series for wage rates, we have used the MLG data on changes in wage rates in conjunction with benchmark estimates of the level of wage rates from other sources. The accuracy of the wage series may be assessed by comparing our estimates with the figures reported in the Ministry of Labour's 1929 survey of wages which provides point estimates of wage rates in the week ending 31 August 1929 for a wide range of occupations by town and county. In the majority of occupations considered, the estimate of wage rates derived from the MLG data is within 2d. of the figure reported in the Ministry of Labour survey. For the wool and worsted and ship-building industries, point estimates of wages puiblished in the reports of the Committee on Trade and Industry (Balfour Committee 1926–8) provide an additional means of checking the accuracy of the new series.

Given the monthly wage series for the individual occupations within each industry, a series for average wages in the industry as a whole is compiled by taking a weighted average across occupations and regions. The choice of weights is restricted by the fact that detailed information on employment by occupation and region is available *only* for the census years 1921 and 1931. In view of this, we took as weights the number employed in each occupational group in April 1931 as reported in the 1931 population census, as follows:

$$W_i = \sum_j w_{ij} n_{ij}^o / \sum_j w_{ij}^o n_{ij}^o$$

where w_{ij} is the wage of the jth occupational group in the ith industry in the current period; n_{ij}^o is the employment of the jth occupational group in the ith industry in April 1931, the base period and w_{ij}^o is the wage of the jth occupational group in the ith industry in April 1931. Unfortunately, the occupational classification adopted in the 1931 census does not always conform to the occupational listing used by the MLG for reporting wage changes. In a number of cases, we have had to take unweighted averages of wage rates across groups of occupations to arrive at an occupational classification that conforms to the 1931 census. For example in the case of the wool and worsted industry, the MLG provides us with wage rate data for twenty-two separate occupations, but the census only distinguishes twelve occupational categories.

It is of interest to compare these new series for wages within specific industries with those of Bowley and Ramsbottom. For this purpose, the monthly wage series derived from the MLG data have been averaged to provide an annual series and the results reported in table 12.2. In the case of ship-building, the most notable difference between the alternative series is that the new series, unlike that both of Bowley and of Ramsbottom, shows no evidence of a decline in nominal wages during the period of the 'great depression'. Moreover, the new series suggest that nominal wages grew much faster after 1935 than implied by the two alternatives. For the wool and worsted industry, the differences between the series are less marked. The overall decline in nominal wages during the period 1929 and 1933 is of a similar order of magnitude for all three series, although the timing of the decreases differs somewhat.

Given the limited information available on the methods used by Bowley and Ramsbottom to compile their series, it is difficult to pinpoint the source of the differences between the series. To some extent, they arise from differences in the methods of aggregation used, and in particular differences in the weights attached to the wage rates of individual occupations in deriving an industry average. Furthermore, an important contributory factor is differences in occupational coverage across the three series, with the new series including a much wider range of occupations than that of Bowley or Ramsbottom.

Finally, it is clear from table 12.2 that the picture which emerges from examining annual observations on wages differs markedly depending on whether one bases the annual figure on a particular monthly observation (for example, December as in the case of the Ramsbottom series) or on a twelve-monthly average. This is most apparent during periods when wages are changing rapidly as in the 1920/2 depression. This serves to emphasise the importance of using observations of greater frequency, either monthly or quarterly, to examine movements of employment wages and prices during the interwar period.

Materials and output prices

By comparison with the wage data, information on commodity prices during the interwar period is readily available from a number of sources, notably the *Board of Trade Journal* and *The Economist*. Hence, compiling appropriate quarterly price indices is a relatively straightforward task, the basic features of which are outlined below.

Table 12.2. *Index of average wages 1920–38*

Year	Gazeley/ Rice MLG series annual av. (1924 = 100)	Gazeley/ Rice MLG series Dec. values (1924 = 100)	Ramsbottom Dec. values (1924 = 100)	Bowley Sept. Values (1924 = 100)
	Ship-building and ship-repair			
1920	173	177	175	
1921	169	152		
1922	119	99	101	
1923	95	96		
1924	100	105	106	100
1925	106	105		100
1926	106	105	106	100
1927	106	105		100
1928	109	110	108	100
1929	111	110		100
1930	116	115	110	100
1931	116	115		100
1932	116	115	108	92
1933	116	115		92
1934	116	115	108	92
1935	116	115	108	92
1936	120	119	112	96
1937	128	130	121	104
1938	135	134	125	108
	Wool and worsted			
1920	140	166	162	163
1921	133	119		118
1922	105	100	100	100
1923	100	100		100
1924	100	100	100	100
1925	100	100		100
1926	100	100	100	100
1927	100	100		100
1928	100	100	100	100
1929	100	100		100
1930	94	91	91	91
1931	88	80		85
1932	80	80	84	82
1933	80	80		80
1934	80	80	82	80
1935	81	80	82	80
1936	88	87	89	80
1937	88	88	89	87
1938	88	88	89	87

For the two textile industries, cotton spinning and wool and worsted, the most important of the non-labour inputs are the raw materials – raw cotton and raw wool. Throughout the interwar period *The Economist* provides weekly information on the wholesale prices of a variety of raw cottons and raw wools, and this forms the basis of the quarterly data series used in this study. From the same source, we obtain data on the price of cotton yarns, the output of the cotton spinning industry. Obtaining a consistent price series for the output of the wool and worsted industry is somewhat more problematic because information on the price of woollen yarns and cloth is not available on a regular basis prior to 1930. As a proxy, we adopt an index of the price of wool tops, an intermediate product; this price being very highly correlated with that of woollen yarns from 1930 onwards.

For the coal-mining industry, singling out a material input for consideration is less straightforward. However, rather than neglect non-labour inputs altogether, a general price index for miscellaneous material inputs based on the Board of Trade's wholesale price index for iron and steel, and that for other metals (excluding coal) is considered. The quarterly index of coal prices is compiled from information on the wholesale price of various types of coal published weekly in *The Economist*.

Finally as far as the ship-building industry is concerned, the most important of its material inputs is steel, and once again we use information on the wholesale price of steel contained in *The Economist* to compile a quarterly price index for the period. Given the heterogenous nature of the product and the practise of tendering for contracts, measuring the price of the output of the ship-building industry presents more of a problem. In the event, the information available for this period is very limited, and as a proxy for the output price we are restricted to using the market value of a 'ready' steamer as compiled by the trade journal *Fairplay*.

Figures 12.2a to 12.2b depict the quarterly series for labour costs, raw materials price and output price for each of the staple industries. The series for labour costs is derived by adding to the figure for average wages an estimate of the average contribution per worker paid by employers for unemployment and health insurance. This estimate is a weighted average of the scale rates of contribution, taking as weights the proportion of each age/gender group in the industrial labour force as recorded in the 1931 Census of Population.

A striking feature of these price indices is the degree of rigidity evident in nominal labour costs relative to the price series. This is most apparent in ship-building and wool and worsted where the measure of average labour costs is based on wage rates prevailing in the industry. For coal mining and cotton spinning, labour costs are measured in terms of earnings and consequently reflect movements in overtime hours worked and bonus

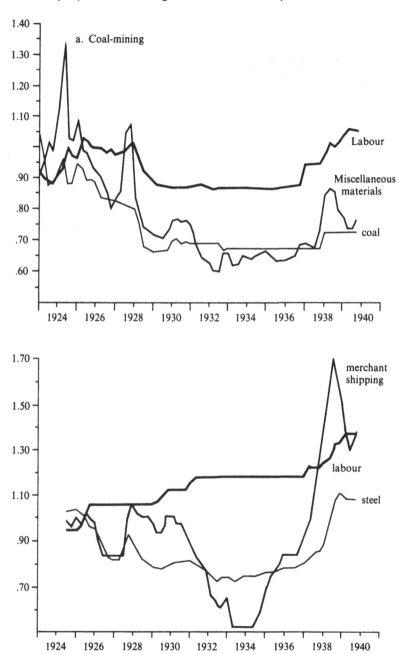

Figure 12.2   Labour costs, raw materials price, and output price for four staple industries, 1922–40.

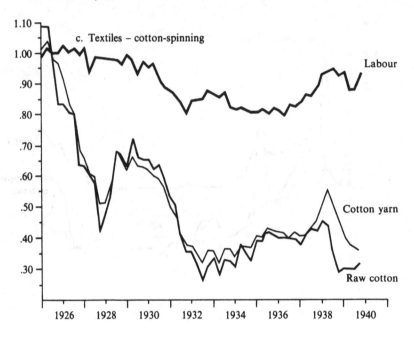

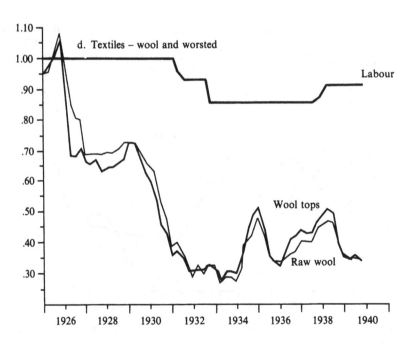

payments, even so the index of labour costs tends to be far more stable than those of raw material or output prices.

In general during the interwar period, material prices and output prices move together. This is seen clearly in cotton spinning and wool and worsted, where the two series track each other closely, but the relationship holds also, albeit less strongly, in the coal-mining industry. In ship-building too, the price of steel and the price of merchant shipping tend to move in the same direction, but the latter is far more volatile, particularly after 1928, and as a result the price of materials relative to output rose sharply between 1929 and 1932.

As a first step in the analysis of the behaviour of employment in the staple industries, we examine the relationship between employment and the 'own product' real wage, as depicted in figures 12.1a–d. These graphs illustrate a strong inverse relationship between employment and the 'own product' real wage throughout the period under consideration. This relationship is apparent in each of the industries studied, but is most striking in the ship-building and ship-repair industry where peaks in the real wage are matched almost exactly by troughs in employment. Interestingly, the relationship appears to break down in 1937 when employment continues to grow despite a sharp increase in the real wage. A priori, we assume that this reflects the effects of the substantial increase in the naval ship-building programme which occurred at this time.

On the face of it, figures 12.1 and 12.2 provide clear evidence in support of the hypothesis that the substantial increases in unemployment that occurred in the manufacturing sector in the early 1930s were the result of a sharp increase in the real wage arising from nominal wage rigidity in the face of falling output prices. Moreover, the growth in employment after 1933 may be traced to falls in the real wage as output prices recovered. In the words of Beenstock et al. (1984), 'Both the recession and the recovery were largely instigated by real wage developments which were concentrated in the manufacturing and industrial sectors' (p. 68). But such analysis is by its very nature superficial, and to analyse the relationship between labour costs, price and employment in greater detail, we turn now to the issue of estimating models of employment determination.

Modelling employment

In this particular piece of econometric analysis, we have chosen to focus on the characteristics of the relationship between labour costs, price and employment within the 'staple' industries and in particular to assess the responsiveness of employment to changes in the 'own product' real wage. In order to do this, we have chosen to abstract from the process of wage and price determination during this period, and assume that the firms within the industry take wages and prices as given when determining their desired level of employment. Clearly, the assumption of price-taking behaviour is more appropriate for some of the industries considered than for others. However, our strategy in this paper is to adopt the same relatively simple model of employment determination for all industries thereby allowing direct comparisons between them to be made.

More formally, the basic model of employment determination adopted in this study is one in which employment decisions are made by profit-maximising firms facing given prices for their output and for their inputs of labour and raw materials, together with a fixed stock of capital. In general, decisions about the level of employment in any period must be made before prices are known, although it may be assumed that information regarding the level of capital stock is available. Thus, it is assumed that firms choose the planned level of employment in any period to maximise expected profits conditional on expected prices and the amount of capital available. Given expected prices p^e for output, w^e for labour and p_m^e for materials, and a stock of capital k, the (restricted) profit function, $\pi(p^e, w^e, p_m^e, k, t)$, represents the maximum net revenue the producer can expect in period t, where π is (positively) linearly homogeneous and convex in prices for each k and t. By Hotelling's lemma, the firm's profit maximising level of employment is given by (minus) the first-order partial derivative of the restricted profit function with respect to the expected price of labour, w^e.

It is common in studies of this type to adopt a log-linear functional form for the employment function (for example Hatton (1981)), but in so doing, restrictions are imposed *a priori* on the nature of the underlying technology. To avoid placing unwarranted restrictions on the technology, we require a flexible functional form for $\pi(.)$; namely a functional form with sufficient free parameters to provide a second-order approximation to any arbitrary, twice differentiable function with the appropriate theoretical homogeneity and curvature properties. A number of alternative flexible functional forms have been employed in previous studies of demand, and our choice is based largely on pragmatic considerations of ease of estimation. The functional form adopted is the biquadratic form due to Diewert (1985), and given this form for the (restricted) profit function, the optimal level of employment of labour, n^*, in period t is given by

$$n^* = \alpha_0 + \alpha_1(w^e/p^e) + \alpha_2(p_m^e/p^e) + \alpha_3 k + \alpha_4 t + \alpha_5 k^2 + \alpha_6 t^2 + \alpha_7 kt. \quad (1)$$

For a more detailed discussion of the properties of the biquadratic (restricted) profit function, the reader is referred to the technical appendix to this paper.

The estimation approach adopted in this study is that which is commonly referred to as 'general to specific'; namely starting from a very general estimating equation, we arrive at a preferred parsimonious specification through a sequence of nested hypothesis tests. The initial specification allows for the fact that actual employment may not adjust to its profit-maximising level in a single time period through the inclusion of eight lagged values of the dependent variable. While the expected price variables in equation (1) are proxied by an eight-period distributed lag on past prices. Finally, in addition to the price and quantity variables identified in equation (1), the general estimating equation includes a set of seasonal dummies (sdi) and also, where appropriate, a set of dummy variables (d26i) to allow for the effects of the General Strike of 1926. Thus the general estimating equation corresponding to the employment function (1) is as follows

$$n_t = \beta_0 + \sum_{j=1}^{8} \delta_j n_{t-j} + \beta_{10}(w/p)_{t-1} + \sum_{j=1}^{7} \beta_{1j}\Delta(w/p)_{t-j}$$

$$+ \beta_{20}(p_m/p)_{t-1} + \sum_{j=1}^{7} \beta_{2j}\Delta(p_m/p)_{t-j}$$

$$+ \beta_3 k_t + \beta_4 t + \beta_5 k_t^2 + \beta_6 t^2 + \beta_7(k_t t) + \gamma_i sdi + \eta_i d26i + \varepsilon_t \qquad (2)$$

where the ε_t are assumed to be identically independently normally distributed random variables with mean 0 and variance σ^2. The model as specified is estimated by OLS for the period 1926.1 to 1938.4 in the case of the cotton-spinning, wool and worsted and shipbuilding industries. For coal-mining, the sample period for estimation is January 1924 to April 1938, omitting February 1926 to April 1928 because of the absence of employment and price data for the period of the General Strike.

Results

The OLS parameter estimates for the preferred specification of the employment equation together with their (asymptotic) 't' statistics are reported in table 12.3. In the case of ship-building and ship-repair, two sets of estimates are reported; one being based on insured employment in the UK as a whole, and the other, on employment in the northern counties yards only. As well as parameter estimates, table 12.3 gives a goodness-of-fit measure in the form of the 'corrected R-squared' statistics, plus test statistics for serial correlation and parameter stability. In each case, the preferred specification shows no evidence of first or fourth order serial correlation or of parameter instability.

Table 12.3. *Estimates of the parameters of the 'biquadratic' form of employment function*

(i) Coal mining

Dependant variable: n = manshifts worked during quarter (millions of 1924 pounds sterling).

n_{-1}	0.2569	(1.9575)
n_{-2}	0.4195	(2.6909)
n_{-5}	−0.2623	(2.2617)
n_{-6}	−0.4090	(−2.5521)
$(w/p)_{-1}$	−6.9985	(−2.0467)
$\Delta(w/p)_{-3}$	11.440	(3.4630)
$\Delta(w/p)_{-4}$	12.168	(2.7880)
$\Delta(w/p)_{-5}$	22.421	(4.6009)
$\Delta(w/p)_{-6}$	21.290	(4.1024)
$\Delta(w/p)_{-7}$	13.544	(3.2739)
$(p_m/p)_{-1}$	18.210	(6.2105)
$\Delta(p_m/p)_{-1}$	−12.702	(−2.7511)
$\Delta(p_m/p)_{-2}$	−11.876	(−3.0943)
$\Delta(p_m/p)_{-3}$	−19.609	(−4.7520)
$\Delta(p_m/p)_{-4}$	−7.5413	(−2.0596)
$\Delta(p_m/p)_{-5}$	−7.8166	(−1.9538)
$\Delta(p_m/p)_{-6}$	−13.368	(−3.2082)
$\Delta(p_m/p)_{-7}$	−12.067	(−3.3141)
k	−76.201	(−4.1716)
k^2	0.2243	(4.2065)
t	−39.270	(−4.1078)
t^2	0.0618	(4.3554)
kt	0.2277	(4.0322)
sd3	−1.1809	(−2.2564)
Const.	6509.000	(4.1736)
R^2		0.9847

LM test for serial correlation:
First order: $F(1,19) = 1.7983$
Fourth order: $F(4,16) = 0.5136$
Chow test for parameter stability:
Break at 1934.4: $F(16,8) = 0.7087$
Break at 1925.4: $F(9,15) = 1.7509$
Sample period: 1924.1 to 1938.4 (excluding 1926.2 to 1928.4)

Table 12.3. (*cont.*)

(ii) Ship-building and ship-repair

Dependent variable: n = average number of persons employed during quarter (millions of 1924 pounds sterling).

	(a) UK 'Insured employment'		(b) North-east yards 'insured employment'	
n_{-1}	1.3342	(9.3355)	1.1681	(9.7542)
n_{-2}	−0.8169	(−3.9505)	−0.5598	(−5.3835)
n_{-3}	0.372	(1.8331)	—	
n_{-4}	−0.2784	(−2.2922)	—	
n_{-6}	—		−0.2138	(−2.2919)
n_{-7}	—		0.1528	(1.7994)
$(w/p)_{-1}$	−0.2115	(−4.2046)	−0.1103	(−4.6596)
$\Delta(w/p)_{-1}$	0.1148	(2.4645)	0.0789	(3.3536)
$\Delta(w/p)_{-2}$	0.0813	(2.1929)	0.0331	(1.8260)
$\Delta(w/p)_{-4}$	—		0.0127	(2.6678)
$\Delta(w/p)_{-5}$	0.1132	(3.7091)	0.0364	(2.3457)
$\Delta(w/p)_{-6}$	0.0207	(2.1685)	—	
$(p_m/p)_{-1}$	0.2108	(3.7269)	0.1139	(4.1154)
$\Delta(p_m/p)_{-1}$	−0.1437	(−2.6527)	−0.0920	(−3.3292)
$\Delta(p_m/p)_{-2}$	−0.0876	(−1.9345)	−0.0420	(−1.8768)
$\Delta(p_m/p)_{-4}$	0.0429	(3.4799)	—	
$\Delta(p_m/p)_{-5}$	−0.1124	(−2.8537)	−0.0267	(−1.3759)
$\Delta(p_m/p)_{-6}$	—		0.0128	(1.9998)
t	0.0029	(2.4066)	0.0031	(4.3020)
t^2	−0.254E−4	(−2.44684)	−0.272E−4	(−4.2781)
sd1	0.0071	(2.3885)	0.0056	(3.4784)
const.	0.1159	(2.5403)	−0.0186	(−1.0228)
R^2	0.9891		0.9731	

LM test for serial correlation:
First order: $F(1,31) = 0.2562$ $F(1,31) = 0.7264$
Fourth order: $F(4,28) = 0.5033$ $F(4,28) = 0.7603$
Chow test for parameter stability:
Break at 1934.4: $F(16,20) = 0.3954$ $F(16,20) = 0.2754$
Sample period: 1925.3 to 1938.4.

Table 12.3. (*cont.*)

(iii) Textiles

Dependant variable: n = average number of persons employed during quarter (millions of 1924 pounds sterling).

	(a) Cotton spinning		(b) Wool and worsted	
n_{-1}	0.3546	(2.8894)	0.5918	(5.7488)
n_{-3}	−0.7037	(−4.8902)		
n_{-4}	0.2267	(1.3115)		
n_{-5}	−0.3769	(−2.6690)	−0.5048	(−2.7481)
$(w/p)_{-1}$	−0.0378	(−2.3904)		
$\Delta(w/p)_{-1}$	−0.0365	(−2.4340)		
$\Delta(w/p)_{-2}$				
$(w/p)_{-3}$			−0.0648	(−2.6143)
$\Delta(w/p)_{-3}$	−0.0302	(−2.3059)	0.0797	(3.1709)
$\Delta(w/p)_{-4}$			0.0101	(3.7055)
$\Delta(w/p)_{-5}$			0.0373	(1.9971)
$\Delta(w/p)_{-7}$	−0.0285	(−2.1984)		
$(p_m/p)_{-1}$			−0.7542	(−5.5937)
$\Delta(p_m/p)_{-1}$			0.4287	(3.6386)
$\Delta(p_m/p)_{-2}$			0.3832	(4.2365)
$\Delta(p_m/p)_{-3}$			0.2239	(3.0282)
$(p_m/p)_{-5}$	−0.0582	(−1.6973)		
$\Delta(p_m/p)_{-6}$	−0.0715	(−1.9678)		
k	3.6765	(4.1239)	0.3641	(2.1581)
k^2	−0.0104	(−4.1296)	−0.0028	(−2.1246)
t	5.6050	(4.1245)		
t^2	−0.2418	(−4.1312)	0.0001	(3.1317)
kt	−0.0317	(−4.1330)	−0.0003	(−3.6817)
sd1	−0.0175	(3.1032)	−0.0135	(−1.3258)
sd2	−0.0245	(−4.3566)	−0.0149	(−1.5535)
sd3	−0.0117	(−1.9230)	−0.0271	(−3.3302)
d262	−0.0191	(−1.4011)	−0.0759	(−2.9289)
d263	−0.0275	(−2.1037)	−0.0607	(−2.1620)
d264	−0.0232	(−1.7730)	−0.0493	(−1.9755)
const.	−324.280	(−4.1127)	−9.6936	(−1.8471)
R^2		0.8330		0.8830

LM test for serial correlation:
First order: $F(1,28) = 0.028$ $F(1,29) = 0.2161$
Fourth order: $F(4,25) = 0.1602$ $F(4,26) = 1.9180$
Chow test for parameter stability:
Break at 1934.4: $F(16,14) = 1.9087$ $F(16,15) = 1.4750$
Sample period: 1926.1 to 1938.4

Before considering the estimated price effects in detail, a number of other aspects of these employment equations are worth noting. Starting first with the estimated effects on employment outside of the coal-mining industry of the 'general strike' of 1926. Within the textile industries of cotton spinning and wool and worsted, employment is found to be significantly lower in the second, third and fourth quarters of 1926 than otherwise would have been the case. However, we find no evidence of significant effects on the level of employment in ship-building. These results are broadly consistent with the reports in the Ministry of Labour Gazettes of the period. These drew attention to the exceptionally sharp increase in unemployment in the textile sector in May 1926, and the abnormally high levels of employment that persisted throughout the year (Ministry of Labour Gazette, 1927). A similar pattern is not observed in the ship-building industry. Here, unemployment was somewhat higher than average, but the seasonal variation followed that of previous years.

In general both the first and second order terms in k, the capital stock variable and t, the time trend, are found to be statistically significant. The exception to this is ship-building where the estimated parameters for the terms in the capital stock variable are not statistically significant. This may be due to the fact that the only available constant-price capital stock series for ship-building relates to the gross stock, whereas for the other industries a net measure may be used. In the event, the time trend appears to serve as a proxy for capital in this case.

In order to examine the effects of changes in prices on employment, it is more informative to consider the short-run and long-run elasticities of demand implied by the estimated parameters, and these are given in table 12.4. In considering these elasticities, it must be remembered that since output is not exogenously determined in this model, change in input prices give rise to scale effects as well as substitution effects on the level of employment.

In general terms, these estimated elasticities are consistent with *a priori* expectations. The estimated wage elasticities, both short-run and long-run, are negative in all cases. As regards the elasticities with respect to material prices, we find that in the two textile industries, labour and the raw material are complements in the sense that an increase in the price of the raw material, all other prices remaining constant, reduces employment. Rather surprisingly, this does not appear to be true of the relationship between employment in ship-building and the price of steel. Instead, increases in steel prices are positively correlated with employment in the short and long run, suggesting that the two inputs are substitutes. Similarly, within the coal-mining industry, labour and material inputs appear to be substitutes in production. In this case, this may reflect the fact that the index of material

Table 12.4. *Estimates of labour demand elasticities*

Elasticity of demand wrt the price of	Mean value	Standard deviation	Minimum value	Maximum value
(i) Coal mining				
(a) labour				
short-run	−0.3192	0.0647	−0.4172	−0.1610
long-run	−0.3209	0.0651	−0.4194	−0.1618
(b) materials				
short-run	0.2152	0.0334	0.1277	0.2716
long-run	0.7149	0.1109	0.4243	0.9024
(c) output				
short-run	0.1041	0.0355	0.0247	0.1683
long-run	−0.3941	0.0550	−0.5318	−0.2612
(ii) Ship-building: UK				
(a) labour				
short-run	−0.9374	0.6117	−2.4307	−0.3580
long-run	−5.2684	3.4383	−13.6620	−2.0124
(b) materials				
short-run	0.5284	0.3345	0.2087	1.3504
long-run	4.7017	1.6856	10.9080	
(c) output				
short-run	0.4090	0.2776	0.1494	1.0802
long-run	1.0007	0.7422	0.2341	2.7534
(iii) Ship-building: North-east yards				
(a) labour				
short-run	−0.9548	0.7557	−3.0516	−0.3078
long-run	−7.4250	5.8764	−23.731	−2.3936
(b) materials				
short-run	0.5406	0.4185	0.1888	1.7076
long-run	6.2150	4.8116	2.1707	19.6320
(c) output				
short-run	0.4142	0.3373	0.1171	1.3340
long-run	1.2100	1.0705	0.1804	4.0995
(iv) Cotton spinning				
(a) labour				
short-run	−0.4495	0.0881	−0.6874	−0.3185
long-run	−0.1524	0.0298	−0.2340	−0.1080
(b) materials				
short-run	0.0000	0.0000	0.0000	0.0000
long-run	−0.1134	0.0142	−0.1523	−0.0800

Table 12.4. (*cont.*)

Elasticity of demand wrt the price of	Mean value	Standard deviation	Minimum value	Maximum value
(c) output				
short-run	0.4495	0.0881	0.3185	0.6874
long-run	0.2657	0.0312	0.2106	0.3512
(v) Wool and worsted				
(a) labour				
short-run	0.0000	0.0000	0.0000	0.0000
long-run	−0.2788	0.0083	−0.4888	−0.1543
(b) materials				
short-run	−0.5865	0.0044	−0.7915	−0.4861
long-run	−1.4884	0.0284	−2.0087	−1.2334
(c) output				
short-run	0.5865	0.0044	0.4861	0.7915
long-run	1.7672	0.0571	1.4481	2.4975

prices used, being based on the prices of iron, steel and other metals, is acting as a proxy for the price of plant and equipment.

Finally, the estimated elasticities with respect to the output price are positive in general; the one exception being in coal-mining. Here, an expansion of output in response to an increase in the output price leads to a relatively small increase in employment in the short-run, but in the long run, it would appear that material inputs are substituted for labour to the extent that employment declines.

It is of interest to compare these results with those of other studies of the period. Estimates of elasticities of employment on an industry-by-industry basis are few and far between. Hatton (1981) used annual data on employment from Chapman and Knight (1953) together with the Ramsbottom wage series to estimate employment functions by sector for the period 1921 to 1938. The limitations of this annual data set have been discussed already in the second and third sections of the paper, added to which the relatively small number of observations restricts the specification of the dynamics of the model. In addition, labour is the only input considered explicitly in the Hatton study, although a time trend is included as a proxy for the capital stock, and the failure to consider non-labour inputs may be expected to bias parameter estimates. Of the industry groups considered by Hatton, those that correspond most closely to the staple industries included in the present study are textiles (cotton spinning, cotton weaving and wool and worsted), ship-building (including ship-repair and marine engineering) and mining and quarrying. For the last two of these, Hatton obtains a very poor fit, and none of the estimated parameters is found to be statistically significant. In the case of the textile group, the specification performs much better, and the estimated long-run elasticity with respect to the wage is −0.25, which is of the same order of magnitude as the mean elasticities for cotton spinning and wool and worsted reported in Table 12.4.

Using the same annual data set, Casson (1983) estimated employment functions for five industries for the period 1920 to 1938, including ship-building. Like Hatton, Casson adopted a log-linear functional form including the own-product real wage, together with current and lagged output and a time trend as explanatory variables. In general, the estimated wage elasticities from this study are poorly determined. Moreover, evidence of parameter instability and persistent serial correlation suggest that the model is mis-specified.

Estimates of elasticities of employment based on aggregate data for the UK economy are more numerous. Hatton (1987) reports an estimated long-run wage elasticity of −0.57 for the economy as a whole based on the Ministry of Labour Gazette quarterly data series for the period 1924.4 to 1939.2. Using essentially the same data set, but a different model specification, Dimsdale, Nickell and Horsewood (1989) obtain an estimate of −0.26 for the aggregate long-run wage elasticity.

One of the most noticeable features of these results is the far greater magnitude of the estimated elasticities for ship-building than for the other industries considered. This is true for the whole of the sample period, but is particularly marked during the period of the Great Depression. In the light of the relative magnitudes of the fluctuations in employment and 'own product' real wage depicted in figures 12.1a–d, this is not altogether surprising. On the one hand, the fluctuations in the employment series are far greater in ship-building than in the other industries. At the same time, the observed variation in the 'own product' real wage is considerably less than in the two textile industries.

In assessing the reliability of these estimates, it should be noted that the extent to which the available employment series accurately reflect variations in the labour input differs across the industries considered. Most notably, systematic short-time working in the form of restrictions on the number of hours worked per week occurred in the textile industries at intervals throughout the period 1924 to 1938. These changes in the labour input arising from changes in hours of work are not reflected in the estimates of the number of insured workers employed. Consequently the responsiveness of labour demand within these industries to changes in wages tends to be underestimated.

A more important qualification to be borne in mind is that the model adopted in this paper assumes that all changes in market conditions are fully reflected in price changes. If product markets are imperfectly competitive then this is not the case, and demand elasticities estimated from the model will tend to be biased upwards. To address these questions, it is necessary to model explicitly the product market for each industry and it is on this issue that future work is to focus.

Appendix 1 Data

Employment, n

(i) *Coal-mining*
The number of manshifts employed during the quarter as published in the *Ministry of Mines Reports*. (Millions of 1924 pounds sterling).

(ii) *Ship-building*
(a) The average number of insured persons employed in UK shipyards over the quarter (millions of 1924 pounds sterling). (b) The average number of insured persons employed in the Northern counties shipyards (millions of 1924 pounds sterling).

A monthly series for the number of insured workers in the industry is derived by linear interpolation from the annual estimates published in the *Ministry of Labour Gazette* (MLG). The number of insured workers registered as unemployed reported in the *MLG*, 'Employment in Principal Industries – the Ship-building Trades' is subtracted from the estimate of the insured labour force to obtain an estimate of insured employment. Monthly observations are averaged to obtain a quarterly series.

(iii) *Cotton spinning*
The average number of insured workers employed in cotton spinning over the quarter (millions of 1924 pounds sterling).

From July 1932, annual data on the insured labour force in cotton preparation and spinning is published in the *Ministry of Labour Gazette* (MLG). A monthly series for the insured labour force is derived by linear interpolation from the annual estimates. Monthly estimates of insured employment are obtained by subtracting from the estimate of the insured labour force, the number of insured workers who are unemployed as published in the MLG. Using monthly data for the period July 1932 and December 1938, insured employment is regressed on the figure for employment in cotton spinning reported in the MLG survey, 'Employment in principal Industries in the UK'. The results of this regression are used to obtain estimates of insured employment in cotton spinning from the MLG survey data for the period January 1924 to June 1932. The monthly figures so derived are averaged to obtain a quarterly series for insured employment.

(iv) *Wool and worsted*
Average number of insured persons employed over the quarter (millions of 1924 pounds sterling).

A monthly series for the insured labour force is derived by linear interpolation from the annual estimates published in the MLG. Monthly estimates of employment among the insured labour force are obtained by subtracting from the estimates of the insured labour force, the number of insured workers registered as unemployed. Monthly observations are averaged to obtain a quarterly series.

Price of labour, w

(i) *Coal-mining*
Index of average earnings per manshift plus an estimate of the employers' average contribution per manshift for unemployment and health insurance (average 1924 = 100).

The figure for average earnings per manshift is taken from the *Ministry of Mines Reports*. The estimate of the average weekly insurance contribution per worker is obtained from the scale rates of contributions (*19th Abstract of Labour Statistics, 1928, Cmnd 3140*, and the *22nd Abstract statistics 1936/37, Cmnd 5556*) takaing as weights the proportion of each age/gender group in the labour force in 1931 as reported in the *1931 Population Census*. This is divided by the average number of shifts worked per week in each quarter to obtain the series for average insurance contribution per manshift.

(ii) *Ship-building*
Index of average weekly wage rate per worker plus employers' average weekly contribution for health and unemployment insurance (average 1924 = 100).

Monthly data series on average wage rates by occupation for time workers in Federated (north-east coast) yards is compiled from data given in the *MLG*, 'Principal Changes in Wage Rates', using benchmark estimates for January 1920 from Dougan, D., *The History of North-East Ship-building*. The monthly data is aggregated across occupations taking as weights the occupational composition of employment in 1931 as reported in the *1931 Population Census*. To the estimates of average wages is added an estimate of the employers' average weekly insurance contribution computed on the same basis as for coal-mining.

(iii) Cotton spinning
Index of average weekly earnings per worker plus employers' average weekly contribution per worker for unemployment and health insurance (average 1924 = 100).

For the period 1924 to 1933, the quarterly series for earnings in cotton spinning is taken from Jewkes and Gray. From 1934 onwards, average earnings in cotton spinning are estimated from the data on the total wage bill and the number of workers employed reported in the *MLG*, 'Employment in Principal Industries'. To the estimates for average earnings is added an estimate of the employers' average weekly insurance contribution computed on the same basis as for coal-mining.

(iv) Wool and worsted
Index of the average weekly wage rate per worker plus the employers' average weekly contribution per worker for health and unemployment insurance (average 1924 = 100).

The average weekly wage rate is compiled from monthly data on wage rates in twelve occupational groups in the wool and worsted industry in Yorkshire published in the *MLG*, with weights based on the occupational composition of employment in 1931 as reported in the *1931 Population Census*. To the average wage rate is added an estimate of the employers' average weekly insurance contribution computed as for coal-mining.

Price of material inputs, p_m^*

(i) Coal-mining
Index of the price of miscellaneous material inputs (average 1924 = 100).

Quarterly series derived from Feinstein's annual price index for unspecified plant and machinery (Feinstein, C., *Domestic Capital Formation in the U.K. 1920–1938*) by interpolation using the Board of Trade wholesale price index for Iron and Steel and Other metals (*Board of Trade Journal*, various issues).

(ii) Ship-building
Index of the price of steel (average 1924 = 100).

Quarterly series compiled from monthly data on the wholesale price of heavy steel rails (*The Economist*, various issues).

(iii) Cotton spinning
Index of the price of raw cotton (average 1924 = 100).

Quarterly series compiled from monthly observations on the price of 'American middling' (*The Economist*, various issues).

(iv) Wool and worsted
Index of the price of raw wool (average 1924 = 100).

Quarterly series compiled from monthly observations on the price of 'Queensland scoured super combing' (*The Economist*, various issues).

Price of output, p

(i) Coal-mining
Index of the wholesale price of coal (average 1924 = 100).

Quarterly series compiled from monthly observations on the price of Cardiff Best Admiralty coal (*The Economist*, various issues).

(ii) Ship-building
Index of the price of merchant ships (average 1924 = 100).

Quarterly series for the market value of a ready steamer of 7,500 tons deadweight as compiled by 'Fairplay' (*The Economist*, 'The Economic and Commercial History of . . .', Supplement to mid-Feb. edition 1924–38).

(iii) Cotton spinning
Index of the wholesale price of cotton yarn (average 1924 = 100).

Quarterly series compiled from monthly observations on the price of '32's twist' yarn (*The Economist*, various issues).

(iv) Wool and worsted
Index of the price of wool tops (average 1924 = 100).

Quarterly series compiled from monthly observations on the price of '64s average tops' (*The Economist*, various issues).

Capital stock, k

(i) Coal-mining
Depreciated value of mineworks, buildings and structures at constant 1930 prices derived by linear interpolation from annual estimates in Feinstein, C., *Domestic Capital Formation in the U.K. 1920–1938* (millions of 1930 pounds sterling).

(ii) Ship-building
First-cost value of all fixed assets at constant 1930 prices derived by linear interpolation from the annual series in Feinstein, *Domestic Capital* (millions of 1930 pounds sterling).

(iii) Cotton spinning
Depreciated value of all fixed assets at constant 1930 price derived by linear interpolation from annual estimates in Feinstein, *Domestic Capital* (millions of 1930 pounds sterling).

(iv) Wool and worsted
Depreciated value of all fixed assets at constant 1930 prices derived by linear interpolation from annual series in Feinstein, *Domestic Capital*.

Appendix 2 Technical

In general, if p is a given vector of prices for the n variable inputs/outputs and k is the fixed capital stock then the (normalised) biquadratic form for the restricted profit function is given by

$$\pi(p,k,t) = \Sigma a_i p_i + (\Sigma a_{i1} p_i)k + (\Sigma a_{i2} p_i)t$$
$$+ (\tfrac{1}{2}\Sigma\Sigma b_{ih} p_i p_h (p_n)^{-1}) + (\tfrac{1}{2}\Sigma\alpha_{1i} p_i)d_{11}k^2$$
$$+ (\tfrac{1}{2}\Sigma\alpha_{2i} p_i)d_{22}t^2 + (\Sigma\alpha_{3i} p_i)d_{12}kt$$

where the parameters satisfy the symmetry conditions $b_{ih} = b_{hi}$ for $1 < i < h < n-1$.

The parameters α_{1i}, α_{2i} and α_{3i} are known non-negative numbers not all equal to zero, and as proposed in Diewert (1985), they take the following values:

$$\alpha_{1i} = \alpha_{2i} = \alpha_{3i} = 1/p_i^1 \text{ for } i = 1, \ldots, n-1 \text{ and } \alpha_{1n} = \alpha_{2n} = \alpha_{3n} = 0$$

where p_i^1 is the price of the variable output/input i in period 1.

The biquadratic function defined above is a flexible functional form for the restricted profit function for any given α_1, α_2 and $\alpha_3 > O_n$. It satisfies the linear homogeneity in prices property. Furthermore, if the $(n-1) \times (n-1)$ symmetric matrix of parameters $B \equiv [b_{ih}]$ is positive semi-definite then the biquadratic restricted profit function satisfies the convexity in prices property globally.

It should be noted that the price p_n enters the biquadratic profit function asymmetrically with the other prices. Different choices for the numeraire good implies a different functional form for the cost function and while all these functional forms are flexible, they may fit the data rather differently.

By Hotelling's lemma, the first order partial derivative of the restricted profit function with respect to the price p_i is equal to the net supply function, $x_i^*(p,k,t)$, for the ith output/input ($x_i^* > 0$ if the ith good is an output, $x_i^* < 0$ if the ith good is an input).

$$x_i^*(p,k,t) = a_i + a_{i1}k + a_{i2}t + \Sigma b_{ih} p_h (p_n)^{-1} + (\tfrac{1}{2}\alpha_{1i}d_{11})k^2 + (\tfrac{1}{2}\alpha_{2i}d_{22})t^2 + (\alpha_{3i}d_{12})kt$$

13 The gold standard between the wars

JOHN REDMOND

The interwar years represent one of the most complete and controversial periods of international currency experience: complete in the sense that they contain sub-periods in which the whole range of exchange rate regimes were operative and controversial in that it is possible to interpret the experience as supportive of either fixed or floating exchange rates. To add to this richness there are numerous related side issues including the operation of the (then) newly created exchange stabilisation funds and the need for and nature (or, perhaps better, lack) of central bank cooperation. These years can be roughly divided into three sub-periods: floating exchange rates (1918–25), the restored international gold standard (1925–31) and a period of managed floating (1931–9), during which the remnants of the gold standard gradually disappeared.

The focus of this chapter is the restored gold standard and, inevitably, it shall concentrate on the 1925–31 period and the events leading up to the return to gold in Britain, since no international gold standard can be said to have existed in the absence of sterling, although some attention will obviously also have to be paid to the gradual fading away of what remained of the gold standard system after 1931. There are five sections: a background section which briefly examines the operation of the pre-World War I system, the war years and the 1918–25 period, an examination of the debate surrounding the British return to gold, the experience of the restored gold standard and why it failed (1925–31), the 1930s which includes the final disintegration of the gold standard, the adoption of managed floating and the Tripartite Agreement and, finally, some conclusions concerning the interwar period in general and the workings of the interwar gold standard in particular.

Some background: the 1880s to 1925

Any attempt to understand the post-World War I restoration of the gold standard has to begin by examining how the pre-1914 gold standard was

346

supposed to and, indeed, widely perceived to have worked (and why) and how it actually did work (and why).[1] We might speak here of the myth of the (automatic) price-specie-flow mechanism whereby a country with a balance of payments deficit would have to pay for it by losing gold which would cause its money supply to fall thereby inducing a fall in prices and an increase in competitiveness leading to balance of payments equilibrium; this process would be simultaneously reinforced by rising prices in the rest of the world due to a gain of gold. It is now quite clear that the pre-WWI gold standard did not work in this simple way – there were other important channels of adjustment[2] and the relatively easy adjustment at the centre was frequently at the expense of the periphery and, to the extent that peripheral countries (in Latin America, for example) preferred to abandon the gold standard rather than to accept (downward) adjustment, then the gold standard did not work in the nineteenth century.[3] However, the view from the centre was rather different.

It is also clear that the period immediately before 1914 was unique in international monetary history – in terms of favourable circumstances[4] and dominance by a single, supremely strong (or at least widely believed to be) centre in London. In a sense, this coincidence of favourable conditions in the world economy with the operation of the gold standard contained the seeds of the interwar monetary problems because whilst the relationship was perceived (correctly) to be a causal one (in part) the causation was interpreted (wrongly) to have run from the latter to the former. Armed with this distorted view of the pre-1914 gold standard, policy makers (and, indeed, virtually everyone else) were anxious to restore it as soon as possible after the war. In fact the commitment to do so was undertaken in Britain before the war actually ended. The Interim Report of the Cunliffe Committee provided an unequivocal definition of postwar British monetary policy in 1918: 'In our opinion it is imperative that after the war the conditions necessary to the maintenance of an effective gold standard should be restored without delay.'[5] In short, a return to gold as soon as possible; moreover, the rest of the world (or at least the parts that mattered) concurred with this view.

The onset of war effectively brought the international gold standard to an end in July 1914. After some initial confusion most countries settled for retaining the gold standard in principle whilst abandoning it in practice. Exchange rates stayed close to par – for example, sterling was pegged at $4.76 (approximately 2% below par) in January 1916 and many other currencies were still close to par at the end of the war (Brown, Jnr, 1940: I, 70) – and the gold losses that would have inevitably been set in motion by the inflationary war financing of the belligerents were prevented by a combination of patriotism, wartime conditions and various technical and administrative devices. However, it was obvious that this could not last. The war had wrought many changes in the international economy and had accelerated some existing trends. The external positions of the belligerents had changed considerably and international finance was now complicated by the question of war debts and reparations. Whilst it was to be some time before it was realised and accepted, it is clear that the 'pre-war monetary system based on the gold standard was another casualty of the Great War' (Kunz, 1987: 8).

The most concrete manifestation of this was the domestic inflation experienced by most countries stemming from the expediencies adopted to finance their war effort. With the exception of the USA (which restored the gold standard in June 1919) no country was in a position to return to gold at the old parity and, indeed, few were prepared to contemplate a return at any parity immediately after the war. Even the 'soundest' of countries had resorted to inflationary financing and in some cases wartime finances were appallingly run.[6] The culmination of all this was, of course, the great inflations of the early 1920s, particularly that of Germany. However, the effect of this was not to caution against any ill-conceived attempt to restore the gold standard but rather to reinforce the general determination to do so. In fact, the early 1920s were largely interpreted as a period of exchange rate disorder and contain one of Nurkse's examples of interwar exchange rate instability due to destabilising speculation – the French franc, 1922–6. Whether such a characterisation of the franc in particular and of the period in general is appropriate has been widely questioned since[7] but, at the time, the inflation and, in the case of the French, the associated irresponsible monetary policy ('Germany will pay') was effectively blamed on fluctuating exchange rates and not vice versa.

The general conclusion drawn – which was to hamper Keynes in his efforts to prevent sterling's return to gold at the old parity – was that 'managed' currencies were unstable and inflationary. The resolve to return to the more orderly prewar world of fixed exchange rates was thus strengthened by the experience of not being on gold and was confirmed at international conferences at Brussels (1920) and Genoa (1922). It is true that at Genoa some concessions were made to reality in that the possibility of some countries not returning to gold at their prewar parity and the need to economise on the use of gold with a gold exchange standard were admitted. However, the decision to hold a conference of central bankers to discuss such matters was never implemented in spite of the Bank of England's efforts to do so and this failure set the scene for the uncoordinated return to gold that was to follow and, indeed, reflected the more general failure of the Genoa Conference.[8] This ramshackle restoration of the gold standard began with that of the Swedes (at the prewar parity) in

April 1924 and they were soon followed by those of some fifty other countries of which the most important were the French and the British. It is to the latter that we now turn.

The British return to gold, 1925

No survey of the interwar gold standard would be complete without an examination of the debate which has surrounded this controversial decision both then and since. This is necessary because the gold standard could not truly be described as international without the adherence of sterling and useful because the British debate sheds light on most, if not all, of the important issues. It should, of course, be made clear from the onset that the commitment to return to gold at the prewar parity was undertaken blindly, almost as an act of faith: it was 'an instinctive reaction . . . [based on a view of the] . . . gold standard as a symbol of past economic glories and . . . a desire to turn the clock back to a time when Britain played a dominant role in international trade and finance' (Cairncross & Eichengreen, 1983: 29). However, although the policy was mistaken, it was based on an illusion not only widely believed within Britain but shared with much of the rest of the world. Britain was not alone in restoring the old parity and frequently where this was not possible and stabilisation had to be undertaken at a lower parity there was a feeling of disappointment, even failure, as was very much the case in France.[9]

Moreover, there has been a tendency to give Keynes' voice greater weight than it deserved.[10] His propensity to shift ground[11] (although understandable in the context of his efforts to exert maximum pressure on decision makers and to rescue what he increasingly saw as a lost cause), his initial espousal of an extreme and politically unacceptable alternative (a 'managed' currency),[12] his errors of judgement and the fact that his most stinging attack on the return to gold came after the event (Keynes, 1925) all contributed to his failure to convince Churchill of the wrongness of the policy. It is now clear that Keynes did have ample opportunity to influence policy decisions – his was not the voice of truth, ignored and left in the wilderness, as the original conventional interpretation of events implied. It was simply that he was in a very small minority and that Churchill did not find his arguments sufficiently convincing. Keynes was even present at the dinner party at which the final decision was sealed.[13] The travails of Keynes contrast sharply with the position of Montagu Norman, Governor of the Bank of England, who found Churchill 'in the receptive and responsive mood of a backward pupil who was willing to be taught'[14] and with most of England on his side he was always going to win the argument.

In fact, the main argument was never really about whether or not Britain should restore the gold standard. There were two separate issues: the important question of 'when' which brought into play the substantial number of people who opposed deflation but accepted the principle of a return to gold at the old parity (and, consequently, felt some unease about the timing of the return) and the much less important (in this context) and less contentious question of 'whether' which was taken up by the (very) few who, because of the deflation, opposed the return itself. (It is interesting to note that the possibility of restoring the gold standard at a new lower parity was not championed extensively by anyone in particular and, indeed, received very little consideration until after the event.) In the case of the outright opposition to the restoration of the gold standard Keynes did stand more or less alone by 1925; he had received some support from the press (Henderson and Lord Beaverbrook), a few members of Parliament, the Federation of British Industry (but only briefly in 1920–2) and, most importantly, McKenna, a former Chancellor and then Chairman of the Midland Bank but, in early 1925, even McKenna was moved to announce that 'as long as nine out of ten people think the Gold Standard is the best, then it is the best'.[15] This brings us to the crux of the matter: alternatives to the restoration of the gold standard were not seriously considered.

However, there was not inconsiderable opposition to deflation, although this became increasingly muted as 1925 approached and its proponents gradually convinced themselves that the return to gold was in the long-term interests of the country – it is important to realise that, following the events in central Europe in the early 1920s, inflation was as much feared as deflation – and that sterling was sufficiently near par to make the required adjustment trivial and/or the necessary adjustment could be achieved by changes elsewhere (a rise in American prices). Those who opposed the return to gold itself were clearly also in the 'anti-deflation' camp but so too was Hawtrey, an influential Treasury official, who took part in 'Mr. Churchill's Exercise' (see Moggridge, 1972: 64–73) in early 1925 in which he continued to express his fears about the consequences of deflation (Moggridge, 1972: 71–3). Meanwhile, the Federation of British Industry, whilst abandoning its tendency to be hostile towards the restoration of the gold standard, remained concerned about the effects of deflation until the very end and gave only a lukewarm reception to the decision to return in 1925. Obviously, the trade unions and the Labour Movement in general were also concerned about deflation (although a Labour Government in power proved to be as committed to returning to gold as any other). Nor were Norman and the Bank of England unaware of the internal conse-quences of their policy.[16] They simply believed that the benefits of their objective were worth the sacrifice and whether the jibe that 'the sacrifice and the medicine were to be the lot of the miners and shipbuilders, the entrepreneurs and the unemployed . . . [whilst] . . . the speakers using the high moral tone . . . would be among the small number of beneficiaries' (Pollard, 1979: 18) is justified (even though true) is perhaps debatable.

Ultimately, the importance of deflation is dependent on the degree to which sterling was overvalued in 1925 (and remained so thereafter) and this indeed has become the central question. Whilst the conventional wisdom has been to side with Keynes – and his 10% overvaluation thesis has been widely (if wrongly) accepted – there has always been an undercurrent of opinion which has disputed this including Gregory (1926), Cassel (1926), Walter (1951), Sayers (1960) and, most recently, Matthews (1986; 1989). The contemporary debate centred on two elements: firstly, the choice between wholesale and retail prices which crystallised in the shape of the Bradbury Committee's assertion that the pound was overvalued by as little as 1.5% (based on wholesale prices) and Keynes' contention of a 10% overvaluation (based on retail prices); and secondly, the choice of retail price index with Gregory criticising Keynes' use of the price index of a single state (Massachusetts) to measure the American price level, claiming that the use of the more general US Bureau of Labour retail price index indicated no overvaluation at all.[17]

The first question is largely a theoretical one and cannot be resolved here[18] whilst the second is a matter of opinion although it is difficult not to be more sympathetic to Gregory's view. A more general conclusion would be to interpret these differences as indicative of the general confusion. Indeed, the range of contemporary opinion is interesting to say the least with Governor Strong (of the Federal Reserve Bank of New York) and the Federation of British Industry apparently concurring that sterling was overvalued by 10% in mid-1924 which was also the view held by *The Times* in early 1925[19] whilst, conversely, Cassel, the main populariser of the purchasing power parity hypothesis, argued that the pound was under-valued in the second half of 1925 by up to 6%.[20] Perhaps Norman's self-confessed confusion with and distrust of such calculations[21] was not an unreasonable contemporary conclusion to draw – although it does lead rather too conveniently to the view that if you have no reliable means with which to calculate the equilibrium value of sterling then you may as well restore the prewar parity.

However, perhaps a more constructive approach is to seek safety in numbers and this is done by Redmond (1984) who calculates a whole range of purchasing power parities based on a range of different price indices (Redmond, 1984: table 1, p. 524). Unfortunately, this exercise is somewhat inconclusive since it finds a positive correlation between the extent to which nontraded goods dominate the chosen price indices and the degree of overvaluation. Nevertheless, the results are highly suggestive in that they indicate a range of possibilities from a 4% undervaluation to a 14% overvaluation which, taken in conjunction with the argument that structural (non-price) changes since 1914 had depressed sterling's equilibrium value, supports the view that the pound was, at best, approaching equilibrium against the dollar in 1925 but was more likely overvalued (although it is difficult to specify by how much). But this is only part of the story: in particular it takes no account of the well-known undervaluations of the French and Belgians or of Poland[22] or, indeed, the apparent overvaluations of Italy,[23] the British Dominions (Presnell, 1978: 80) and of Sweden, Denmark and Norway[24] and the uncertain position of Germany.[25] This requires a multilateral test of purchasing power parity and Redmond (1984) goes on to provide this, again using a range of price indices and the results are unambiguous: in 1925 the pound was overvalued by between 5% and 25% (Redmond, 1984: table 3, p. 529).

Finally, reference must be made to the recent contributions by Matthews (1986: 1989) which differ from both the conventional route and the conventional conclusion in that use is made of a supply-side model of exchange rate determination to generate the conclusion that the pound was not overvalued in 1925. Whilst this is novel, it also has problems. Matthews' criticisms of empirical testing of the purchasing power parity hypothesis are well made but, although his own model is more sophisticated, it is far from clear that it is any less deficient; he himself concedes that it is controversial and not without fault and acceptance of his conclusions rests on acceptance of his methodology (Matthews, 1989: 95–6). Moreover, his main results relate only to the pound–dollar exchange rate and given the ambiguity generated by purchasing power parity calculations of this relationship (described above) they are not entirely surprising. Finally, his efforts to undermine the importance of the French franc's undervaluation and his attempts to apply his model multilaterally are unconvincing (Matthews, 1989: 92–5).

The assertion of Matthews and others that sterling was not overvalued in 1925 would be much more convincing if there were some evidence to suggest that Britain was forced off gold in 1931 by peculiar circumstances and that its underlying position was basically sound. In fact, Kunz (1987) does argue precisely this – that 'the pound might have remained on the gold standard throughout the interwar period (and with it many other currencies) . . . had Britain not been dealt, within a three week period, a powerful triple blow' (Kunz, 1987: 5) (consisting of the German banking collapse and the reports of the Macmillan and May Committees). Eichengreen also implies this possibility when he uses a simulation exercise to try and determine whether the loss of gold in the third quarter of 1931 was due to balance of payments weakness associated with long term factors which would eventually have forced sterling off gold anyway or to 'an unfortunate . . . consequence of the unanticipated financial and political developments of the summer of 1931' (Cairncross and Eichengreen, 1983: 74). Since his simulations suggest the latter then they are implicitly supportive of the view that the pound would not have been forced off gold under normal circumstances. However, Eichengreen, himself, ends by stressing his model's restrictive assumptions and this argument is generally unconvincing: the high levels of unemployment in Britain in the late 1920s and the tendency towards a flagging pound and gold losses are clear signs of an overvalued currency and contrast sharply with the boom in France associated with the undervalued franc (Kemp, 1971: 84–6). This shifts the focus back to the argument that the war had brought fundamental changes which made the restoration of the pre-war parity a flawed and ill-conceived policy. If this is the case then we do not, in fact, need purchasing power parity calculations to show that the pound was overvalued in 1925 since one of the deficiencies of such calculations is that they cannot take account of such structural (non-price) changes.

So far we have been very critical of the return to gold but, whilst the criticism is largely deserved, this is not to say that the harsher versions of the story – that it was a bankers' policy designed to serve the interests of the City of London and operated by a selfish Bank of England and its 'rake' (Pollard, 1970: 21) of a Governor – are justified. Norman and the Bank of England were not unaware of the domestic impact of their policies and, indeed, frequently refrained from raising Bank rate in the late 1920s because of domestic concerns. More generally, they saw the return to gold at the prewar parity as a sound policy for the country as a whole. Indeed, the return to gold has been construed as an export (and hence employment) policy: the export trades were depressed partly because of the adverse effects of currency disorganisation on the volume of world trade; the greatest contribution that Britain could make to the stimulation of trade was to take the lead and return to gold as soon as possible, preferably at the old rate since this would maximise credibility.[26] It remains true that the pound was overvalued in 1925 and that the return to gold was a fundamentally misconceived policy. However, it is equally true that policy makers were not really in a position to take any other decision – opinion was overwhelmingly in favour of the policy and no credible alternative ever received any substantial support; moreover, at the time, it appeared to be a rational policy – if this was to be the 'greatest mistake' of Churchill's life then he could scarcely have known it at the time. More fundamentally, there is much to be said for the argument that 'the battle for Britain's gold standard had to be fought and lost before its raison d'etre could be transformed from an assumption to a debatable issue' (Kunz, 1987: 190). In short, it was an experience that we had to go through in order to move on to something else.

The international gold standard: restored and lost 1925–31

Clearly, the path back to gold had not been easy for Britain which restored its prewar parity in April 1925 with the aid of an American credit, the use of Bank rate, an embargo on foreign loans (which was not lifted until November) and upward speculative pressure on sterling in anticipation of the return to gold. This struggle was to continue and to get worse with major exchange rate crises in 1927, 1929 and, finally, in 1931.[27] The problems in 1927 were partially domestic in origin: the industrial troubles of 1926 led to a reduction in exports and also in confidence which caused an outflow of short term capital. However, possibly more important were external forces in the shape of a gold outflow to France following *de facto* stabilisation of the franc in 1926. The situation was only rescued after dire warnings had been given by Norman to the French which resulted in a change in their policy. After a period of respite in the first half of 1928 a heavy drain of French balances from London began in the summer. The effect of the American stock market boom then began to come increasingly into play as the pressure on sterling reached its height in 1929 before being fortuitously relieved by the Wall Street Crash which coincided with an increase in Bank rate. This was then followed by what now appears to have been the calm before the storm which lasted for approximately a year (October 1929–October 1930) during which time the spot pound was often at a premium against the dollar, Bank rate was progressively reduced and the Bank of England gained gold.

The British return to gold marked the beginning of a head-long rush back to the gold standard. Some countries also restored thier prewar parities (the British Dominions, Switzerland, Holland, Denmark, Norway, Sweden, Japan and Argentina) whilst some stabilised at devalued levels (France, Belgium, Italy, Portugal, Finland, Czechoslovakia, Yugoslavia, Greece, Bulgaria, Rumania, Estonia, Latvia and Chile) and others were compelled to adopt new currencies, having experienced hyperinflation (Austria, Hungary, Poland, Germany and Russia). The most important of these stabilisations was undoubtedly that of France which stabilised *de facto* in 1926 and *de jure* in 1928 at an undervalued level, following a period of great financial difficulty; indeed, Britain's return to gold in April coincided with the resignation of a French Government in the face of a crisis which it could not resolve (a rather frequent occurrence in the interwar years). In view of 'the almost pathological addiction to monetary stability and orthodoxy which prevailed in France . . . to the virtual exclusion of all other considerations' (Kemp, 1971: 82) it is clear, with hindsight, that it was almost certainly to France's advantage in the 1920s that the prewar parity had become well beyond redemption since the undervalued exchange rate contributed a great deal to French prosperity (although, of course, France was to reap the harvest of this addiction to financial orthodoxy in the 1930s). However, even as the French enjoyed their boom, sterling was not the only currency experiencing difficulties and cracks were beginning to appear in the restored international gold standard well before sterling's demise in September 1931.

The first casualties were several of the British Dominions and a number of Latin American countries. Canada was the very first – having only rejoined the gold standard in July 1926 'by spring 1929 at the latest Canada had made an early and unadmitted departure from gold' (Drummond, 1981: 57). In Australia and New Zealand the collapse in world commodity prices caused balance of payments crises which forced devaluations in March and April 1930, respectively. The Latin American exodus began with Uruguay (April), Argentina (November) and Brazil (December) in 1929 who were followed by Venezuela (September 1930) and Mexico (August 1931). However, the international gold standard came effectively to its rather dramatic end when Britain left in September 1931. This episode is well documented[28] – and only a brief summary need be given here. The banking crisis began in Austria and then Germany in May–June (and there were parallel problems in Hungary and Rumania) with the collapse of a major bank in each country. The German difficulties were particularly unfortunate for Britain as they led to the freezing of £70 million of British short-term credits in Germany. The collapse of the Danatbank also coincided precisely (13 July) with the publication of the Macmillan Committee Report which highlighted the substantial excess of British short-term liabilities over assets.[29] In itself this was not unusual for a world banking centre but coming at a time when many of these assets were becoming immobilised on the continent the effect on confidence was dramatic and the crisis spread to Britain.

On 31 July the publication of the May Report made matters even worse: it expressed concern over the British budget deficit (and proposed expenditure cuts); on the continent budget deficits meant inflation and currency depreciation and so this gave a further shock to confidence. The Government tried to agree expenditure cuts in August but was forced to resign when unable to do so to be replaced by the first National Government whilst credits were negotiated from the US and France to support the pound which were virtually exhausted within the month. The pressure on sterling continued in September and efforts to obtain further credits were unsuccessful. There was an element of farce on 15 September when 'unrest' in the Navy over pay cuts was widely reported abroad as the 'Invergordon mutiny'. This was followed by a final massive loss of reserves on the 18th and 19th, and Britain formally suspended the gold standard on 21 September. By the end of the year Sweden, Denmark, Norway, Eire, Austria, Portugal, Finland, Egypt, India, British Malaya, Palestine, Bolivia, Salvador and Japan had also left the gold standard to add to the earlier defectors (and the sterling area had been created). All that remained were France and the gold bloc, the USA and various minor countries, and the international currency system had entered a period of fragmentation from which it was only superficially rescued by the Tripartite Agreement in 1936.

Why was Britain forced off gold in 1931 and why did the interwar gold standard fail? In view of the fact that Britain was the lynchpin of the system (or at least widely perceived to be so) then these two questions are inextricably linked, so much so that they can be taken together. The immediate cause of Britain leaving gold is clear enough: a series of runs on the pound caused by exceptional circumstances which eventually created irresistible pressure for depreciation. However, this only reflected a deeper malaise. Unfortunately, the explanations for the breakdown of the gold standard are numerous, highly inter-related and, to a large extent, as awash with myths as the interpretations of the pre-1914 system on which the postwar return to gold was based. Indeed, Eichengreen, presents a list of the main explanations which he then goes on to demolish on the grounds that they relate to factors which were, in reality, much the same during both the pre- and post-World War I gold standards (Eichengreen, 1985a: 21-3) (although this is possibly only partially valid since, in some cases, it is a matter of degree in that the same tendencies may have existed in both periods but may have been stronger post-war than pre-war). In fact, the causes of the breakdown of the interwar gold standard can be broadly categorised as stemming from two sources: differences in the pre- and postwar gold standards in themselves and differences in the pre- and postwar economic conditions in which they operated. The various explanations are overlapping, not mutually exclusive and include all of Eichengreen's list.

The principal difference between pre- and postwar systems was allegedly that the latter was a gold *exchange* standard; this was an attempt to economise on the use of gold and had been officially sanctioned at Genoa. However, it transpires that reserve currencies were also widely used prewar and, indeed, the ratio of official foreign exchange reserves to gold was much the same in 1925 as it was in 1913[30] although the important differences may well have been qualitative and psychological rather than quantitative. The use of reserve currencies was much more visible in the 1920s because of

Genoa and also because it represented an important aspect in many of the League of Nation's financial reconstruction schemes whereby all reserves could be held in the form of reserve currencies which were convertible to gold.[31] It was also embraced with widely differing degrees of enthusiasm reflecting the variability of the motives for adopting a gold exchange standard; specifically, there were always doubts about its permanence in some countries (Yeager, 1976: 331) and membership was felt to undermine a country's prestige in some quarters:

It is largely for this reason that the countries whose balances were in absolute amount the most important – including, for instance, France, Germany, Italy and Poland – did not regard their own use of the gold exchange standard as anything but a transitory expedient. (League of Nations, 1944: 42).

Furthermore, there is no doubt that the gold exchange standard became increasingly less popular as the 1920s progressed and came to be regarded by some as a 'British fad'[32] designed to make it easier for Britain to restore and maintain the gold standard.

Linked to the use of reserve currencies is the question as to whether there was a shortage of gold in the 1920s. The use of the former would seem to suggest that there was and, indeed, (along with French restraint) that it allowed this shortage to be concealed until 1928. Whether there was an overall shortage of international liquidity in general is perhaps more doubtful (Moggridge, 1989: 291–3) but what does seem clear is that liquidity and, in particular, gold were badly distributed and became even more so after the French began to accumulate gold on a large scale from 1928 (Moggridge, 1989: 294). This maldistribution of gold was partly due to a much wider problem: the large number of under- and overvaluations in the 1920s. The gradual growth of the gold standard in the prewar era encouraged equilibrium rates and contrasts sharply with the rush back to gold in the mid-1920s during which only minimal attention seems to have been paid to the actual rates. A final issue is that of sterilisation – failure to follow the 'rules of the game'. This has received considerable attention and it seems likely that the 'rules' were substantially ignored by everyone.[33] Contemporary opinion singled out America for particular criticism but this view has now been softened considerably (Drummond, 1987: 36–7) and France has become recognised as the worst culprit (see, e.g. Moggridge, 1989: 286). However, it is usually pointed out that sterilisation was equally common before 1914 with the implication that failure to follow the 'rules of the game' can therefore be blamed for the failure of the interwar gold standard (e.g. Foreman–Peck, 1983: 241). This does not necessarily follow: before World War I, in the face of generally favourable conditions and with the possibility of pushing adjustment out to the periphery the major countries at or near the centre could ignore the 'rule of the game' but in the changed conditions of the 1920s such 'selfish' behaviour would inevitably have an adverse impact on the workings of the system.

These 'changed conditions' constitute the other group of explanations for the collapse of the interwar gold standard. The war itself led to major changes in many countries' balance of payments: trade patterns were disrupted and many of the changes became permanent whilst invisible account positions were irrevocably altered – in particular, the invisible earnings of Britain, France and Germany were sharply reduced and those of the US increased. The war also created the new complications of international debt and reparations which, although their full economic impact was never realised because they were largely unpaid, they did bedevil the international financial system with a certain political instability. Another important postwar change concerned the position of London. In the first place, Britain had become a considerable net debtor on the short-term capital account and, to make matters worse, its debits tended to be with stronger countries (like the US) and its credits with weaker countries (like Germany). It was the revelation of this by the Macmillan Committee which set off the final run on sterling but this changed circumstance of London was a potential source of weakness throughout the 1920s. Secondly, and more fundamentally, in the prewar system London was the unchallenged centre in which there was supreme confidence and, indeed, sterling was considered 'as good as gold'. However, the war weakened London and strengthened New York but not, apparently, sufficiently for it to play London's prewar role and 'an uneasy and half-realized dyarchy was created' which became even worse when, 'in the later twenties, the remarkable strength of the French franc introduced a third element into the central core of the . . . system'.[34] This created problems: firstly, there was now a new possibility of instability due to erratic movements of funds between two (or three) competing centres (League of Nations, 1944: 46); secondly, neither New York nor Paris proved to be either willing or able to fulfil London's role of using its current account surplus to fund long-term investment, a process which had underpinned the prewar gold standard.

Turning directly to adjustment, it has been argued that the wage and price flexibility of the prewar years and the early 1920s had been replaced by downward rigidity in the late 1920s (see, e.g. Scammell, 1965: 116–17). However, this has been questioned: it is not clear that wages were particularly flexible pre-1914 and the 1920–2 period (during which wages fell by 40% in both the UK and the US) was a product of the carry over of peculiar war-time agreements (Eichengreen, 1985a: 23). Nevertheless, it remains true that prices and wages were less flexibile by the late 1920s due partly to increasingly protected domestic markets and to the growth of cartels. Moreover, it is also true that a substantial amount of very rapid downward adjustment was required post-1925 which was never the case pre-1914 which was 'an era of swift industrial expansion . . . [when] adjustment of the gold standard type could be achieved without deflationary effects' (Scammell, 1965: 117). Consequently, it may well be the case that wage and price inflexibility did, in some sense, play a role in the collapse of the gold standard in a world in which other avenues of adjustment were closed.

The final change in the post-World War I situation was in the 'attitudes and expectations of investors' (Eichengreen, 1985a: 24). Having dismissed the other explanations, Eichengreen reaches this view: there was no longer the same confidence that had prevailed before the war largely because of correct perceptions that 'policymakers' commitment to defend the gold reserve and gold parity was increasingly tempered by other . . . [internal] . . . considerations' (Eichengreen, 1985a: 24). Such constraints imposed by internal considerations 'jammed' the gold standard adjustment mechanism (Moggridge, 1989: 288, and see also 277–8) and this was widely known. It was also true of most countries and, allied with many of the factors already described, clearly undermined confidence. Furthermore, many countries did not have much faith in the permanence of the system and, in particular, 'France was a reluctant member of the gold exchange system; she regarded her partial adhesion to it as an essentially temporary makeshift and . . . The fate of the gold exchange standard was sealed when France decided in 1928 to take nothing but gold in settlement of the enormous surplus . . . from the current balance of payments' (League of Nations, 1944: 39). The reasons for the collapse of the interwar gold standard can be summarised quite briefly: differences between the postwar and actual prewar systems were of limited importance but the differences between the former and the idealised prewar gold standard were substantial and were important. The two other key factors were the changed underlying economic circumstances, particularly, the position of London, and lack of confidence in the system.

The 1930s: the final disintegration of the gold standard and the Tripartite Agreement

Britain's defection in 1931 signalled the end of the international gold standard. Pressure now shifted to Scandinavia – and currencies there and elsewhere followed the pound off gold – and then to the US which was sufficiently strong to withstand it. Britain was able to introduce a policy of cheap money but continued adherence to the gold standard was to cause great difficulties on the continent where some countries were to experience broadly similar problems to those of Britain in the late 1920s. The gold standard did not disappear overnight but faded away and the desire for international cooperation remained strong in many quarters. There were two other developments particularly associated with Britain: the creation of exchange stabilisation funds, of which the Bank of England's was the first, which allegedly engaged in competitive depreciation and the creation of the sterling area. The latter was unplanned and consisted of some twenty countries (although the exact membership was variable) which, because of colonial and/or trading links, chose to peg their currencies to the pound and hold most or all of their reserves in sterling. Whilst this development was not unwelcome in Britain, efforts within the Empire – at the Ottawa Conference, for example – to establish a concerted exchange rate policy were firmly resisted (in keeping with the general reluctance to commit the pound in any way which was also apparent during the negotiations of the Tripartite Agreement).

The next phase of the disintegration of the gold standard began in 1933. The American devaluation has been characterised as the only clear-cut competitive devaluation of the 1930s (Moggridge, 1989: 307; see also Eichengreen and Sachs, 1985: 930). However, there seems to be some conflict as to whether the US left gold deliberately or was forced to leave: 'Unlike Great Britain, the United States had not been driven off the gold standard.'[35] 'Like Britain in 1931, the United States had been forced off gold . . .' (Drummond, 1987: 47). In fact, this disagreement is resolved by differentiating between internal and external factors. The dollar was not forced off gold by the latter – there was no balance of payments pressure since the current account was in surplus and the net short-term capital position was in the Americans' favour and the external capital flight was minimal and largely reflected fears of a deliberate departure from the gold standard anyway – but the technicalities of the American gold standard meant that the dollar was forced off by the former: most American gold was not 'free' but was used to back the paper currency and in March 1933 the Federal Reserve Bank of New York ran out of 'free' gold. The source of the problem was internal in that it was a domestic gold drain stemming from successive banking crises which caused the dollar to leave gold but the decision was unforced in that it represented a deliberate choice of policy to deal with the banking crisis.

Roosevelt took office at the height of the third (and final) banking crisis and immediately imposed a partial embargo on gold exports which was made complete and permanent on 20 April, 1933; America had left the gold standard. He then embarked on a policy of buying gold to push up its (dollar) price (depreciate the dollar) in an attempt to raise internal (American) prices and facilitate recovery. However dubious the merits of

this policy the effect on the foreign exchanges was clear enough: by January
1934 the dollar had depreciated to 59.06% of its old parity at which point it
was stabilised. This second phase of the disintegration of the gold standard
was completed by more rapid depreciations in Latin America (of currencies
which were linked to the dollar) and South Africa also decided to leave gold
and join the sterling area around this time. Finally, an important casualty
of the American policy was the World Economic Conference of June/July
1933 which some participants sought to use as a vehicle to restore an
international monetary standard. This was 'torpedoed' by the infamous
message from Roosevelt which indicated that America was not interested in
such a thing. In fact, in some ways, it is the collapse of the World Economic
Conference that ought more properly to be regarded as the end of the
interwar gold standard rather than Britain's leaving in 1931.

At the conference those countries which still maintained freely convertible currencies (France, Belgium, Holland, Italy, Poland and Switzerland)
formed the gold bloc but their position was essentially untenable and the
final drama of the gold standard was played out in 1934–6. This marks the
third phase of the disintegration. The only available policy for the gold bloc
was deflation and this was pursued with vigour and, in France, it led to a
procession of governments and ministers reminiscent of the early 1920s.
The Economist was moved to comment:

A political wit once remarked that in France the Budget is always on the way to
being balanced, and that in the political sphere, France is generally in a state of
crisis, with occasional lapses into stable government.[36]

The first victim was Belgium which, in the face of high unemployment,
capital flight[37] and the collapse of international trade on which the Belgian
economy was so dependent, devalued in March 1935 by 28%.[38] This
redoubled the pressure on the rest of the gold bloc which, by now,
effectively consisted only of France, Holland and Switzerland since Italy
and Poland had turned to exchange controls. Despite the intermittent gold
flight and the dire state of the domestic economy the French sought to
pursue their financial orthodoxy to the limit until eventually, in 1936, the
population had had enough and elected a Socialist government (under
Blum) committed to reflation. This was clearly incompatible with their
electoral promise not to devalue and the question now became how they
could devalue in such a way as to be internally acceptable (for domestic
political reasons) and externally acceptable (in order not to provoke
retaliatory British and American devaluations).

In fact, there had been a movement towards some form of international
monetary cooperation and intermittent negotiations ever since the Americans had stabilised the dollar in early 1934. The French now proposed
nothing less than a return to a fixed franc-dollar-pound relationship.

However, this proved to be totally unacceptable to both the Americans, who simply wanted to avoid further competitive depreciations, and the British who were loathe to peg sterling to anything and wished to maintain their freedom of action. What actually emerged was so much watered down that it has been described (with some justification) as 'a declaration in favour of the international economic equivalent of motherhood' (Clarke, 1977: 38). In fact, it was not an agreement at all but simply three separate (identical) declarations which implied very little real commitment (other than to allow the French to devalue without retaliation). In September 1936 the French did this and were soon followed by Holland and Switzerland, thereby bringing the interwar gold standard to an end. Up to the war there was substantial day to day consultation over exchange rates but Britain, France and the US basically continued to manage their currencies as they wished and the Tripartite Agreement is probably best described as having 'brought a shadow of international monetary cooperation but not its substance' (Drummond, 1981: 223). Thus, the interwar years closed with a return to some semblance of monetary order but the world had to wait until after another war before an international monetary system comparable to the gold standard could be created.

Conclusions

The experience of the interwar gold standard has been widely used for the purpose of drawing 'lessons'. In the long run, it may well emerge that the principal lesson to be drawn in that it is essential that the correct lesson is the one actually drawn. What is particularly depressing in this respect is that history shows a tendency to repeat itself: the lessons drawn by the League of Nations (1944), and many others, have been as fundamentally wrong as those drawn from the experience of the pre-World War I gold standard in the early 1920s. However, it is nevertheless appropriate to end with several general comments about the interwar period, some of which may be construed as 'lessons', others as merely observations. One controversial area, not directly related to the gold standard, is the question of competitive depreciation in the 1930s. Whilst the American devaluation of 1933–4 seems clearly to have been of this nature, there is some disagreement as to whether or not the British EEA engaged in this practice.[39] The conclusion that the EEA 'may have come close to the line' (Moggridge, 1989: 307), is perhaps the best characterisation of its activities and the extent to which it crossed the line then becomes a matter of judgement.

One notable outcome of the period was the decline in the power of the Bank of England or, more precisely, a shift of power from the Bank to government. It is perhaps a supreme irony that a policy designed to restore the power of the Bank of England and the City of London (the return to gold) ultimately had the effect of undermining that power even further: by 1931 the control of sterling and the associated policy instruments had clearly passed away from the Bank. The reason for this shift partly reflects the growing appreciation of potential clashes between internal and external policy objectives (which had, in fact, severely impeded the Bank's room for manoeuvre in the late 1920s (see Kunz, 1987: 18)). It was no longer possible or desirable to let the Bank continue to manage the pound independently whether this was through an 'automatic' gold standard mechanism or not. Indeed, recognition of the need to take internal balance considerations into account together with the creation of exchange equalisation funds represents the end of the myth of 'automatic' adjustment and a formal shift towards discretionary adjustment (with the discretion firmly in the hands of governments and not central banks). Moreover, this need to give priority to domestic issues lies at the root of the failures in international cooperation which are taken up below.[40]

Another controversial area of the interwar years concerns the relationship between the gold standard and the general health of the economy. There seems little doubt that the three waves of gold standard disintegration in 1931, 1933–4 and 1935–6 had liberating effects on the economies concerned and stimulated recovery; this was particularly true in the British case where leaving gold (and refusing to fix sterling to anything thereafter) allowed the introduction of a cheap money policy. It should therefore follow that maintaining the gold standard frequently contributed to recession and depression (with the obvious exception of the undervalued franc in the late 1920s which had the opposite effect). However, this has been disputed: it has been suggested that the French recession in the 1930s was mainly due to a 'deeper underlying malaise' (Kemp, 1971: 98), and, also, the argument that the pound was not overvalued in 1925–31 clearly implies that the British return to gold did not contribute to the recession of the late 1920s; indeed, the most recent assertion that sterling was not overvalued makes this very point (Matthews, 1986: 572). Nevertheless, it is clear that a lower exchange rate would often have been beneficial[41] and consequently that, at the very least, adherence to the gold standard at the rates chosen was very unhelpful to (amongst others) the British economy in the 1920s and, ultimately, to the French economy in the 1930s.

Perhaps the most controversial issue of the period relates to what the interwar currency experience implies about the comparative merits of fixed and floating exchange rates. The cases for both sides have been forcefully argued.[42] However, it is becoming increasingly apparent that exchange rates in the 1930s were as stable as in the 1920s (and actually more so than in the 1970s).[43] Furthermore, insofar as the 1920s gold standard engendered exchange stability it did so in a temporary artificial way which simply shifted the instability elsewhere and at the cost of excessive instability when it was abandoned; this was clearly the case with the pound, the dollar and the franc. What was required was not simply fixed exchange rates but stable *equilibrium* exchange rates and, whilst to some extent the pre-World War I gold standard provided the latter, the post-World War I gold standard only provided the former.

In fact, it is probably true that the interwar period can tell us little about the merits of fixed and floating exchange rates because there was never a properly functioning gold standard and free floating exchange rates were never really given a chance as even the most well-known advocate of the 'fixed exchange rates are best' school concedes: *'freely* fluctuating exchanges were far from common . . . changes were usually controlled. For considerable periods at a time, rates were "pegged" or kept within certain limits of variation' (League of Nations, 1944: 8–9, and see also 122, 211). What the interwar currency experience would seem to suggest is that governments interfere with exchange rates at their peril and that exchange rate instability between the wars was not due to destabilising private speculation (the League of Nations (1944) view) but to government interference. Moreover this interference was haphazard, uncoordinated and, to some extent, selfish – there was no organisation, no order and no one was 'in charge' (Drummond, 1987: 52). It therefore follows that if governments are to interfere then they should cooperate.

This is particularly true in an era when power is passing from one centre to another during which cooperation becomes highly desirable if not essential. In the 1920s some effort was made in this direction – the Genoa Conference shows an awareness of the need for cooperation even if the actual outcome was disappointing – and there was, of course, a close relationship between Governor Norman of the Bank of England and Governor Strong of the Federal Reserve – so much so that Hoover, then Secretary of Commerce, was moved to call Strong a 'mental annex' of Europe when he lowered interest rates to help his European friends thereby (allegedly) sowing the seeds of the boom that culminated in the Wall Street Crash (Kunz, 1987: 18) However, the relationship between the Banks of England and France was rather less warm (e.g. see Kunz, 1987: 18) and US–UK cooperation also weakened after 1928 when Strong was replaced by Harrison, and the Americans became increasingly concerned with internal problems. Finally, the interwar gold standard itself was obviously a non-cooperative venture in practice: there was no coordination of choice of parity (with disastrous results), gold was unevenly distributed (Eichengreen, 1985b: 140–1), there was no suitable centre and sterilisation ensured that the 'automatic' adjustment mechanism could not work, thereby creating a critical void in the system.

In the 1930s, interwar economic cooperation reached its nadir with the collapse of the World Economic conference in 1933. The 1936 Tripartite Agreement represented only a slight improvement – it was insubstantial and the major countries continued to go their own way with regard to the management of their currencies. There was only rudimentary coordination which was not to become fully fledged until Bretton Woods. To make matters worse there were clearly instances of aggressively uncooperative behaviour in the shape of the American devaluation of 1933–4 and, to the extent that this interpretation is acceptable, the holding down of sterling by the EEA. Even the cooperation that did occur was either based on simultaneous national decisions which gave the appearance of cooperation when there was none (the sterling area) (Drummond, 1981: 9–10) or on a combination of excessive monetary orthodoxy and ignorance (the gold bloc).[44]

In general terms, the costs of this non-cooperative behaviour are clear enough from a simple examination of the economic history of the period. However, a more rigorous approach and more specific 'costing' are provided by Eichengreen (1985b) who develops a formal model which clearly shows that lack of cooperation created a deflationary bias in the international economic system which could have been partially eliminated if any country had been willing or able to take on a leadership role but completely eliminated if there had been full cooperation (Eichengreen, 1985b: 162–3). Broadberry (1989) takes up the same issue and, in effect, presents a kind of prisoners' dilemma whereby coordinated expansion would benefit everyone but isolated individual expansion would benefit others at the expense of the expanding country and so no one pursues expansionary policies. Perhaps the lack of international economic cooperation and coordination is the main unifying theme which links the experience of the early 1920s, the interwar gold standard and the 1930s. Perhaps also, that the lessons of the interwar international monetary experience lie less in the kind of exchange regime to which it apparently (or allegedly) gives support and more in the way in which it shows that international cooperation is essential if whatever system chosen is to be successfully implemented.

Notes

1 A related question is when. Although it is clear that the movement towards an international gold standard began to gain momentum in the 1870s, it is difficult to be precise about the date from which the system became fully operative. The earliest acceptable date is probably 1880 but J.B. Condliffe, *The Commerce of Nations* (1950), p. 362 and Yeager (1976), p. 299 suggest as late as 1897. At any rate, the operation of the prewar international gold standard was obviously a much shorter episode in international monetary history than is often implied.

2 A useful summary (with references) is provided by Eichengreen (1985a), pp. 9–12.

3 See, for example, Ford (1962), ch. 8 and Triffin (1985).

4 These included a tendency towards equilibrium exchange rates because the system had evolved gradually, a ready supply of gold, rising world prices after 1896 (which converted deflationary adjustments into slightly less reflationary adjustments), relative calm in the world in general in the shape of an absence of major wars and social and political upheaval and (possibly) greater flexibility of prices and wages (compared to after 1918).

5 Cunliffe Committee, *First Interim Report*, 15 August 1918, paragraph 47.

6 For example, this accusation is directed at the French by Kemp (1971), p. 83.

7 It has now become almost a textbook view that the speculation associated with the franc in the early 1920s was more stabilising than destabilising in that 'speculators' were merely correctly anticipating the consequences of French monetary policy. See, for example, Yeager (1976), pp. 328–9 and Foreman-Peck (1983), p. 231. This interpretation is largely confirmed in B.J. Eichengreen 'Did Speculation Destabilise the French Franc in the 1920s?' *Explorations in Economic History* (1982). More general support for the hypothesis that exchange rates were relatively orderly in this period (in the sense of being determined by economic fundamentals) is to be found in J.H. Hodgson, 'An Analysis of Floating Exchange Rates: the Pound–Dollar Rate, 1919–25, *Southern Economic Journal*, 1972, and L.B. Thomas, 'Behaviour of Flexible Exchange Rates: Additional Tests from the Post-World War I Episode, *Southern Economic Journal*, 1973.

8 The conference was very ambitious but the three main protagonists could effectively not even agree on the agenda. British suggestions that the US should forego some of its war debt claims led ultimately to the Americans not even attending whilst the French were largely concerned with enforcing their claim for reparations. The conference resolutions were 'anodyne and . . . without force or effect' (Drummond, 1987: 31).

9 Yeager (1976), p. 329, observes that at the time of the *de jure* stabilisation of the franc in 1928, 'Even Premier Poincare continued to harbor the quixotic feeling that national honor called for a return to pre-war par'. See also, Brown Jnr. (1940), pp. 458–9.

10 P.J. Grigg, Churchill's Private Secretary, refers to 'the still small voice of Keynes' (Grigg, 1948: 182).

11 'Certainly Keynes was a man of changing, if not short, views' (Griggs, 1948: 183).

12 J.M. Keynes, *A Tract on Monetary Reform* (1923). More generally, C.P. Kindleberger, *The World in Depression, 1929-39* (1973), p. 47 quotes an American view of the debate: 'Keynes was pretty generally regarded as an extremist'.

13 This is described in Grigg (1948), pp. 182-4.

14 A. Boyle, *Montagu Norman*, (1976), p. 179. This may represent the exaggerated view of one of Norman's biographers but Norman's role remains crucial, so much so that *The Economist* (2 May, 1925, p. 846) was moved to describe the return to gold as 'the crowning achievement of Mr. Montagu Norman'.

15 Chairman's speech, Annual Meeting of the shareholders of the Midland Bank, 25 January 1925 (reported in Grigg, 1948: 184).

16 Indeed, by 1927, 'it was clear that the Bank of England was unwilling to sacrifice British industry on the altar of the gold standard' (Cairncross and Eichengreen, 1983: 46) and, by 1929, 'there is no question that the Governor . . . [of the Bank of England] . . . felt debarred from the unrestricted use of this device [i.e. Bank rate]' (Kunz, 1987: 18).

17 T.E. Gregory, *The First Year of the Gold Standard* (1926), pp. 49–56.

18 A useful survey of this and the other problems associated with purchasing power parity calculations is provided by L.H. Officer, 'The Purchasing Power Parity Theory of Exchange Rates: A Review Article', *IMF Staff Papers*, 1976.

19 Strong Papers, Letter to Mellon, 27 May 1924, *FBI Bulletin*, 15 July 1924, and *The Times*, 26 January 1925, City Notes, p. 20, respectively.

20 *The Times*, 9 February 1926, Annual Financial and Commercial Review of 1925, p. ii.

21 Norman's evidence to the (Bradbury) Committee on Currency, 24 June, quoted in Moggridge (1972), p. 89.

22 T.E. Gregory, *The Gold Standard and Its Future*, 1932, p. 43.

23 D.H. Aldcroft, *The European Economy, 1914-70*, 1978, p. 170, and Drummond (1987), p. 36.

24 D.H. Aldcroft, *From Versailles to Wall Street, 1919-29*, 1977, p. 170.

25 According to Moggridge (1989), the war-time changes and the experience of the early 1920s 'make it almost impossible to assess the appropriateness of Germany's exchange rate . . . at stabilisation' (p. 277), although clearly there is no presumption that it was the equilibrium one.

26 This view is forcefully put by Sayers (1960), pp. 89–92. See also G. Cassel, *The Downfall of the Gold Standard*, 1936, p. 40, and Cairncross and Eichengreen (1983), pp. 29–30.

27 The rest of this paragraph draws heavily on Cairncross and Eichengreen (1983), pp. 44–50.

28 See, for example, Cairncross and Eichengreen (1983), pp. 52–72; Drummond (1987), pp. 39–44; Kunz (1987); pp. 29–146 and Yeager (1976), pp. 339–44.

29 Rather ironically the Macmillan Report argued that the figures on net short term liabilities were actually 'reassuring' because they showed a decreasing trend in short term liabilities since 1928.

30 P.H. Lindert, *Key Currencies and Gold, 1900–1913*, 1969, chs. 1, 2.

31 This was the case for the schemes for Austria, Hungary, Greece, Bulgaria and Estonia. Italy also chose to do this whilst others went part of the way (Moggridge, 1989: 289).

32 Royal Institute of International Affairs, *The International Gold Problem*, 1931, p. 91.

33 See, for example, Foreman-Peck (1983), pp. 241–3; League of Nations (1944), pp. 68–88; Moggridge (1989), pp. 279–86; and Yeager (1976), pp. 332–4.

34 A.C.L. Day, *The Future of Sterling*, 1954, p. 31.

35 Yeager (1976), p. 350. See also *The Economist*, 31 January, 1934, p. 70 and *Lloyds Bank Review*, March 1933, p. 106.

36 *The Economist*, 2 December 1933, p. 1056. In fact, there were nineteen different administrations in France between September 1931 and December 1938.

37 According to the *Wall Street Journal* of 26 March 1935, as reported in H.L. Shepherd, *The Monetary Experience of Belgium, 1931–36*, (1936), at the height of the crisis planeloads of Belgian currency were being flown out of the country to be sold for whatever they could fetch.

38 This was followed in May 1935 by a 42% devaluation by a minor adherent to the gold bloc (Danzig).

39 Cairncross and Eichengreen (1983), p. 89 claim that it did whilst Drummond (1981), pp. 201 and 256 claims it did not. One of the most authoritative sources – S. Howson, *Sterling's Managed Float: The Operations of the Exchange Equalisation Account, 1932–39*, (1980) – would seem to tend towards the latter view when she argues that the EEA would not have violated the IMF's principles, adopted in the late 1970s (p. 98).

40 It was the inward shift in the focus of American policy in 1928 that effectively marked the end of interwar international economic cooperation. See Clarke (1967), p. 220.

41 Despite his earlier argument, this is conceded by Kemp (1971), p. 90, and this specific point is also made in the case of Britain by Moggridge (1972), pp. 111–12.

42 See, for example, League of Nations (1944) for the fixed rate case and Yeager (1976) for the floating rate case.

43 See, for example, Drummond (1981), pp. 253–4, and Foreman-Peck (1983), p. 255.

44 An 'unbelievable ignorance of economic questions' in France is noted by T. Kemp, *The French Franc, 1919–1939*, 1972, p. 103, and the same point is made by A. Sauvy, 'The Economic Crisis of the 1930s in France, *Journal of Contemporary History*, 1969, p. 33.

14 Purchasing power parity and controls during the 1930s

STEPHEN N. BROADBERRY and

MARK P. TAYLOR

Introduction

In its simplest form, purchasing power parity (PPP) states that the exchange rate should be equal to the ratio of the foreign to the domestic price level. It has natural intuitive appeal as a long-run equilibrium relationship. The central notion underlying PPP is that deviations from the parity represent profitable arbitrage opportunities, which if exploited, will tend to bring about PPP.

Recent work by Engle and Granger (1987), Johansen (1988) and others has established the statistical notion of cointegration of time series, which corresponds to the theoretical notion of a long-run equilibrium relationship. Taylor (1988) has applied this methodology to the floating exchange rate regime since 1973, while Taylor and McMahon (1988) examine the floating rate regime of the 1920s. The evidence is favourable to long-run PPP during the 1920s, but unfavourable during the 1970s and 1980s. These results are in line with many other studies of these two periods (see, for example, Frenkel, 1978, 1981).

Curiously, the floating exchange rate regime of the 1930s has received little attention.[1] This period is of particular interest because of the widespread adoption of protective controls, exchange rate management and exchange control, which may be expected to interfere with the arbitrage necessary for PPP. In a recent study, however, Broadberry (1987) found that long-run PPP held for the sterling dollar rate during the 1930s. Broadberry used the dynamic modelling error correction framework of Hendry (1983) and others, pioneered in an exchange rate context by Edison (1981). In this paper we examine long-run PPP during the 1930s using the cointegration framework. We examine four major currencies: the US dollar, sterling, the French franc and the German Reichsmark. Some interesting results emerge. First, no exchange rate involving the Reichsmark exhibits PPP. We attribute this to the scale of control of German foreign trade during the Nazi period. Secondly, however, the results for the US dollar, sterling and the French franc are broadly supportive of long-run PPP if allowance is made for tariffs and asymmetric price responses. Thus only very drastic controls prevented PPP through arbitrage in the 1930s.

In addition, we provide some evidence on the arbitrage mechanism, using Granger causality tests. The direction of causality between the exchange rate and price varied with the exchange rate regime, which is consistent with adjustment to PPP through both commodity and asset markets. These findings are broadly in line with the results of Frenkel (1978) for the 1920s.

Controls in the international economy of the 1930s

Introduction

As Frenkel (1978) notes, the doctrine of purchasing power parity has its origins in the writings of John Wheatley and David Ricardo. The basic idea is that the exchange rate between two currencies should equal the ratio of prices in the two countries.

A revival of interest in the doctrine during the 1920s highlighted differences of interpretation. For those who emphasised commodity arbitrage, prices were seen as adjusting to changes in exchange rates as international trade occurred in response to excess supplies and demands of commodities (Angell, 1922; Ohlin, 1967). For others, emphasising asset markets, exchange rates were seen as adjusting to changes in the price level, which were often seen as having monetary origins (Cassel, 1921; 1928).

As Frenkel (1978) notes, however, it is possible to see both exchange rates and prices as moving in response to other exogenous forces, with arbitrage occurring in commodity and asset markets. Thus it will be helpful to consider barriers to arbitrage, which may be expected to have impeded the attainment of PPP during the 1930s.

Protection

The interwar period saw a sharp rise in the degree of protection, which we may expect to have interfered with commodity arbitrage. In the US, the Fordney-McCumber duties of 1922 reversed the reductions of the Underwood-Simmons Tarrif Act of 1913 and raised tariffs back to their previously high levels. Humphrey (1955) reports average rates of duties rising from 27 to 39% on dutiable imports, and from 9 to 14% on total imports. As Falkus (1971) notes, however, the US was virtually self-sufficient in both industrial and primary goods so that the Fordney-McCumber duties could only have had a limited impact on the world economy.[2] Their 'psychological' or 'strategic' impact is often stressed, nevertheless, since the US was the world's largest creditor nation, had a healthy current account surplus and large gold reserves.[3]

Again, the psychological or strategic impact of the 1930 Smoot-Hawley Tarrif is often stressed. Originating as a measure to protect agriculture, congressional pressure ensured that it spread to cover other primary products and manufactures. According to Humphrey (1955) the average rates of duties rose from 39 to 53% on dutiable imports and from 14 to 18% on total imports. Kindleberger (1987) sees the Tariff as important because it signalled that the US would not take on one of the key responsibilities of world leadership, to maintain a relatively open market for distress goods (Kindleberger, 1987: 291–2).

In Britain, the continuation after the war of the supposedly temporary McKenna Duties of 1915 and the Safeguarding of Industry Act cannot be seen as very major deviations from a general policy of free trade. Only a small number of items were covered, and rates were generally low (Capie, 1983: 40–1). However, the Abnormal Importations Act of 1931 and the Import Duties Act of 1932 saw the introduction of a general tariff on manufactures. Nominal rates of protection were generally 20 or $33\frac{1}{3}$%. In addition, some quotas were also imposed, notably in iron and steel and agriculture. Thus during the 1930s substantial protection covered British imports of industrial and agricultural products. This growth of protection was accompanied by an extension of the principle of Imperial Preference, and the growth of bilateral agreements in place of the 'most-favoured-nation' principle (Capie, 1983: 43–4).

French tariff levels during the 1920s were lower than before the First World War, according to the estimates of Liepmann (1938). French agriculture and industry enjoyed a highly competitive position during the 1920s due to the policy of under-valuation of the franc. With the deterioration in France's trading position during the Great Depression from 1929, however, France followed other countries in resorting to protectionist measures. Owing to the fact that many of the tariffs had been consolidated in commercial treaties which could not be quickly altered, however, much of the increase in protection took the form of import quotas. In 1933 existing quotas were reduced to 25% of their previous amount and the other 75% used as bargaining counters (Arudt, 1944: 137).

For Germany, the estimates of Liepmann (1938) suggest an increase in the level of tariffs during the 1920s over the 1913 level, although more so for industrial than agricultural products. During the Great Depression from 1929, however, agricultural tariffs rose more sharply than industrial tariffs, which were held back by commercial treaties (as in the case of France).

During the period of Nazi rule from 1933, foreign trade was administered through a system of exchange control, which we discuss below.

Exchange rate management

Another well-known feature of the interwar period was the manipulation of currencies, which we may expect to have distorted the relationship between exchange rates and relative prices. After a period of relatively clean floating during the early 1920s, the mid-1920s saw the restoration of the gold exchange standard. The US remained on gold during and after the First World War, while Britain returned to gold at the prewar parity in 1925. It is generally argued on the basis of PPP calculations that this overvalued the pound (Moggridge, 1972; Broadberry, 1986).

By contrast, the French franc was stabilised on gold in 1926 at a much depreciated parity, which undervalued the franc and gave French industry a competitive advantage (Tsiang, 1959). In Germany, stabilisation on gold was secured with the introduction of the Reichsmark in 1924, although monetary stability had been effectively restored in 1923 with the introduction of the Rentenmark to replace the Mark, which had become worthless in the face of a dramatic hyperinflation. Given the scale of the hyperinflation, PPP calculations have not been attempted for Germany (Hardach, 1980: 28–9).

The 1920s were thus characterised by stabilisation of exchange rates at inappropriate levels. Nurkse (1944) argues that when the restored gold standard broke down with the financial crisis of 1931, it was followed by a cycle of competitive depreciation. In September 1931 during a financial crisis originating in Austria, there was a run on the pound and Britain was forced off the gold standard (Kindleberger, 1987: 154–8). The pound initially depreciated substantially against the US dollar, the French franc and the Reichsmark, which all remained tied to gold. However, in April 1933 the US broke the link with gold, and after a short period of experimentation with gold prices, the dollar was stabilised against gold at a lower parity in February 1934 (Kindleberger, 1987: 475–81).

The French franc remained tied to gold until September 1936 when, accompanied by the Tripartite Monetary Agreement, there was a devaluation of the franc (Sayers, 1976: 475–81). Initially, the franc was pegged at a new lower rate against the pound, but from March 1937 to May 1938 there was a period of floating during which there was little support of the franc by the French Exchange Fund (Sayers, 1976: 481–3).

In Germany, although there was some talk of devaluation during the crisis of 1931, fear of inflation effectively ruled out such a policy, and the Reichsmark remained tied to gold throughout the 1930s (Kindleberger,

1987: 151–3). However, the system of exchange control and bilateral clearing agreements, which we examine below, meant that the overvalued official exchange rate was increasingly remote from reality.

During the 1930s, then, the operation of the British Exchange Equalisation Account, the American Stabilisation Fund and the French Exchange Fund acted to interfere with market rates of exchange. Cooperation between central banks was generally rather weak, with each country pursuing its perceived national interest (Clarke, 1967, 1973, 1977; Broadberry, 1989).

Exchange control

German international economic policy during the 1930s was rather different from that of the other three major Western economies. Forced, by capital flight and fear of devaluation, to introduce the first measures of exchange control in 1931, Germany ended up pursuing a policy of bilateralism (Arndt, 1944: ch. 7). Faced initially by a run on the Reichsmark in 1931, the scale of the problem meant that exchange control could not be limited to capital exports. This was particularly true once the Nazis had embarked on a policy of reflation.

In November 1931 the system of foreign exchange rationing allocated to accredited importers a proportion of the amount used by each firm during a base period. The quotas were then gradually reduced until in 1934 the Reichsbank was reduced to a system of day-to-day allotments based on the intake of foreign exchange (Arndt, 1944: 181–5). In September 1934 under the New Plan, foreign exchange certificates had to be obtained from one of twenty-seven Import Control Boards, which thus ensured complete state control of German foreign trade.

Lack of foreign exchange had driven German importers to arrange barter deals with export firms during 1932–3, and this was generalised from 1933 with the 'Aski' accounts (Auslander-Sonder Konten fur Inlandszahlungen), opened with German banks in favour of foreign exporters. These acted like constantly renewed private deals and greatly extended the scope of barter trading. However, the overvaluation of the mark led to an excess supply of Aski marks, which could only be disposed of at a discount. The government tried to limit this effective devaluation by only allowing the use of depreciated rates on 'additional' exports, which could not be sold at the official exchange rate. However, this created definitional problems and the growth of restrictions to counter evasion.[4]

The Aski system was increasingly replaced by clearing agreements, concluded bilaterally between Germany and her trading partners. Importers paid for goods in domestic currency to a clearing agency, from which exporters to the other country were paid, also in domestic currency. This system had the advantage that it could be easily extended to include all types of international transactions, such as debt payments, as well as commercial transactions (Arndt, 1944: 187).

In trade with Britain and the US, with which Germany had no clearing agreements, the problem of the overvalued mark had to be tackled with export subsidies. Between Germany and France, trade occurred through a clearing agreement (Arndt, 1944: 190–2).

Purchasing power parity as an equilibrium condition

The simplest form of PPP requires that the nominal exchange rate should be equal to the ratio of the foreign to the domestic price level. Writing e_t for the logarithm of the nominal exchange rate (defined as the foreign currency price of a unit of domestic currency) at time t and p_t for the logarithm of the foreign to domestic price ratio, we require:

$$e_t = p_t \tag{1}$$

The (logarithm of the) real exchange rate (c_t) is defined as:

$$c_t \equiv e_t - p_t \tag{2}$$

Thus long-run PPP requires that in the long run:

$$c_t = 0 \tag{3}$$

For this to be the case, c_t must be a (zero-mean) stationary process.

Taylor (1987) suggests a slightly less stringent test for long-run PPP, testing for stationarity of the process:

$$g_t = e_t - \alpha p_t \tag{4}$$

Comparing (4) with (1), the only difference is that we allow the scalar α in (4) to deviate from unity. If g_t is a zero-mean stationary process, then in long-run equilibrium the nominal exchange rate will be proportional to relative prices, but a one percent increase in domestic relative to foreign prices will lead to an α percent long run depreciation of the exchange rate, where α is not necessarily unity. Clearly, that g_t be a stationary process is a necessary condition for c_t to be stationary, so that failure to find a stationary g_t for some α is itself a rejection of long-run PPP. Some motivation for allowing α to differ from unity can be derived by examining a simple model of protection.

Suppose that η_t measures the German price of tradeable goods, η_t^* the US price of tradeables, and that e_t is measured as dollars per mark (all variables in logarithms). Suppose also that tariffs effectively raise tradeables prices by a factor of $\tau(>1)$. Consider then exchange rates, e_t^1 and e_t^2:

$$e_t^1 = \eta_t^* - \tau\eta_t \tag{5}$$

$$e_t^2 = \tau\eta_t^* - \eta_t \tag{6}$$

If $e_t < e_t^1$ then there will be profitable commodity arbitrage opportunities available by importing German goods into the US. Conversely, if $e_t > e_t^2$, profitable commodity arbitrage involves importing US tradeables into Germany. In long run equilibrium, it seems reasonable to suppose that e_t will be given by the arithmetic mean of e_t^1 and e_t^2. Hence we have from (5) and (6):

$$e_t = \alpha(\eta_t^* - \eta_t) \tag{7}$$

where

$$\alpha = (\tau + 1)/2$$

Hence one way of interpreting equation (4) is to assume the presence of tariffs.

The implication of the above analysis is that long run proportionality between the exchange rate and relative prices may not be strictly one-to-one, and hence that considering:

$$e_t = \alpha p_t \tag{8}$$

As a long-run equilibrium condition, where perhaps $\alpha \neq 1$, is an interesting exercise.

Finally, it may be inappropriate to impose symmetry. Broadberry (1987) found that the sterling dollar exchange rate behaved asymmetrically in response to changes in price in Britain and America during the period when Britain had abandoned the gold standard but the United States remained on gold. Hence we also examine the long-run relationship

$$e_t = \alpha_1\eta_t^* - \alpha_2\eta_t \tag{9}$$

where, as before, η_t and η_t^* are the domestic and foreign price levels (measured in logarithms). Such a model would also follow from relaxing the constraint that the tariff rates in (5) and (6) are the same.

Cointegration and PPP

Following Engle and Granger (1987) cointegration of a pair of variables may be defined as follows. A series x_t which has a stationary, invertible, non-deterministic ARMA representation after differencing d times is integrated of order d, denoted $x_t \sim I(d)$. Thus a series which is integrated of order zero, $I(0)$, is itself stationary, while the simplest example of an $I(1)$ series is a random walk. For a pair of variables to be cointegrated, a necessary (but not sufficient) condition is that they be integrated of the same order. If both x_t and y_t are $I(d)$ then the linear combination:

$$z_t = x_t - \alpha y_t \tag{10}$$

will generally also be $I(d)$. However, if there exists a constant scalar α such that $z_t \sim I(d-b)$, $b > 0$, x_t and y_t are said to be cointegrated of order (d,b), denoted $(x_t, y_t)' \sim CI(d,b)$. An important case of this, and the one we are most concerned with in this paper, is where x_t and y_t are both $I(1)$ and $z_t \sim I(0)$. For then, although x_t and y_t may each have infinite variance, the linear combination z_t is stationary. If economic theory suggests a long run relationship:

$$x_t - \alpha y_t = 0 \tag{11}$$

then the statistical relationship (10) is clearly of some interest, since unless z_t is $I(0)$, x_t and y_t will tend to drift apart without bound. Hence cointegration of a pair of variables is at least a necessary condition for them to have a stable long-run (linear) relationship.

Engle and Granger (1987) outline several methods for testing for cointegration, of which we shall make use of only one or two. It is first of all necessary to have a test for whether a series is $I(0)$. Granger and Engle suggest the use of a test based on the work of Fuller (1976) and Dickey and Fuller (1979; 1981). To test the hypothesis:

$$H_0: x_t \sim I(1) \tag{12}$$

the following ordinary least squares (OLS) regression is run:

$$\Delta x_t = \beta x_{t-1} + \gamma_0 + u_t \tag{13}$$

where u_t is approximately white noise. The test statistic is the standard 't-ratio' for the estimate of β, and the rejection region consists of (absolutely) large, negative values. The t-ratio will not in fact have a t-distribution under the null, because of the infinite variance of x_t, but Fuller (1976) reports approximate critical values for this statistic calculated by Monte Carlo methods. These values are -3.51, -2.89 and -2.58 for nominal test sizes of 1, 5 and 10 per cent respectively, and a sample size of 100 observations.[5]

Some motivation for this test can be obtained by considering the first-order autoregressive representation of x_t:

$$x_t = \lambda_0 + \lambda_1 x_{t-1} + u_t \tag{14}$$

If $\lambda_1 = 1$ then x_t has a unit root, indeed x_t follows a random walk, is non-stationary and can drift without bound. On the other hand, if $\lambda_1 < 1$, x_t is a stationary process. Equation (14) can be reparameterised as

$$\Delta x_t = \lambda_0 + (\lambda_1 - 1)x_{t-1} + u_t \tag{15}$$

which is of the form (13). Testing for a unit root requires $\lambda_1 = 1$ in (15) or $\beta < 0$ in (13). The series is stationary if $\lambda_1 < 1$ in (15) or if $\beta < 0$ in (13). Thus a statistically significant negative β in (13) would lead us to reject the null hypothesis that $x_t \sim I(1)$. This is the Dickey-Fuller test (DF) reported in the results.

If u_t in (13) is serially correlated, then lags of the dependent variable must be added to make the disturbance white noise. Thus the following OLS regression is run

$$\Delta x_t = \beta x_{t-1} + \sum_{i=1}^{n} \gamma_i \Delta x_{t-1} + \gamma_0 + u_t \tag{16}$$

where n is chosen so that the disturbance u_t is approximately white noise. Again, the test statistic is the standard t-ratio for β and again the rejection region consists of (absolutely) large negative values. This is the augmented Dickey-Fuller test (ADF) reported in the results.

Having tested the hypothesis that the two variables in question are I(1), we can then proceed to examine the hypothesis that they are cointegrated. One method of doing so is to form the 'cointegrating regression':

$$x_t = \delta + \alpha y_t + z_t \tag{17}$$

and to test whether the 'cointegrating residual', z_t appears to be I(0). An obvious way to proceed is to subject the residuals from (17) to a test for a unit root as outlined above. It turns out, however, that one cannot use the critical values tabulated by Fuller (1976) to test for a unit root in the residuals from the cointegrating regression. The reason for this is that OLS chooses α to minimise the residual variance, so that we might expect to reject the null hypothesis of I(1) residuals more often than suggested by the nominal test size, so that the critical values have to be raised in order to correct the test bias. Engle and Granger (1987) have tabulated critical values for tests of this kind on the cointegrating residuals, generated by Monte Carlo methods. If it is unnecessary to add any lagged differences into the auxiliary regression in order to induce a white noise disturbance (i.e. $n = 0$ in (16), so that (16) collapses to (13)), then under the null hypothesis the variable in question follows a random walk, and the 't-ratio' of the lagged level (the 'Dickey-Fuller statistic') has approximate critical values of -4.07, -3.37 and -3.03 for nominal test sizes of 1, 5 and 10 per cent respectively, with a sample size of 100 observations. If it is necessary to add one or more lagged first difference into the auxiliary regression in order to induce an approximately white noise disturbance, then the 't-ratio' of the lagged level (the 'augmented Dickey-Fuller statistic') has approximate critical values of -3.77, -3.17 and -2.84 for nominal test sizes of 1, 5 and 10 per cent and a sample size of 100 observations.

The test procedures applied below, then, are as follows. We first test the hypothesis that the (logarithms of the) nominal exchange rate and the ratio of price indices are I(1) series. If we cannot reject this hypothesis, we can go on to test for cointegration by testing the residuals from the cointegrating regressions to see if they appear to be I(0). Only if we can reject the hypothesis that the cointegrating residuals are I(1) can we claim to have found cointegration, and hence a form of long-run PPP.

The next step is to relax the condition of symmetry. Here, we test the degree of integration of the individual price series, before forming the more general cointegrating regression:

$$x_t = \delta + \alpha_1 y_{1t} + \alpha_2 y_{2t} + z_t \tag{18}$$

Again, the cointegrating residual z_t can be tested for a unit root to establish cointegration, and appropriate critical values for the test statistics have been provided by Engle and Yoo (1987).

Additional problems are, however, encountered when testing for cointegration among more than two variables. In particular, for N I(1) variables, it is statistically possible for there to be $N-1$ distinct cointegrating linear combinations. This leads us naturally to consider the methods recently advanced by Johansen (1988). The Johansen procedure allows maximum likelihood estimation of the full set of possible cointegrating vectors and a test of their statistical significance. In addition, the technique allows tests of simple linear restrictions on the cointegrating parameters, such as symmetry and proportionality.

Data

Data on exchange rates and relative prices are taken from League of Nations, Statistical Yearbook (various issues). The data were collected on a monthly basis from January 1930 to August 1939 and are in the form of index numbers using the average of 1929 as the base of 100. All data are unadjusted for seasonality. In the regressions, a log-linear specification has been used.

We can be confident that the exchange rate data were accurately recorded. However, we can be less confident about the price data.[6] The League of Nations published more than one price series for some countries. Generally, a wholesale price index is available, but for the UK and the US we also have cost of living (COL) indices. As Frenkel (1978) notes, economists favouring the commodity arbitrage interpretation of PPP have preferred to use wholesale price indices, which include mainly internationally traded commodities. Economists favouring the asset market interpretation of PPP have tended to prefer COL indices, which cover items not internationally traded. In fact, we find no evidence of a long-run relationship between the exchange rate and relative COL indices for the US and UK, so that most of the results in this paper are for wholesale price indices.

Exchange rates and relative wholesale prices are plotted over time in figures 14.1 and 14.2. It is clear from figure 14.1 that any exchange rate involving the Reichsmark will not exhibit long-run PPP. The series do not come anywhere near converging in the long-run. In fact, it is not difficult to explain this divergence, since we know that the German economy was subject to severe controls under the Nazi regime from 1933. Hence, arbitrage through international trade was effectively curbed.

However, for the exchange rates involving the US dollar, sterling and the French franc, long run PPP seems at least a possibility. In figure 14.2, although there is substantial short-run divergence between exchange rates and relative prices, the series converge in the long run.

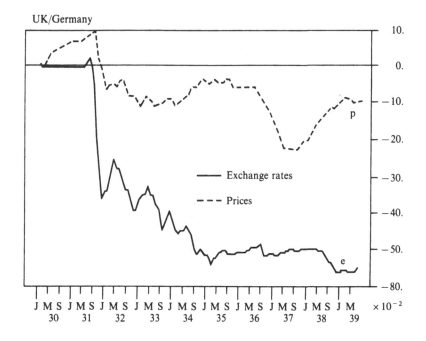

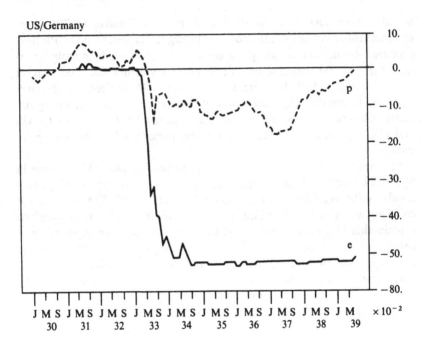

US/Germany

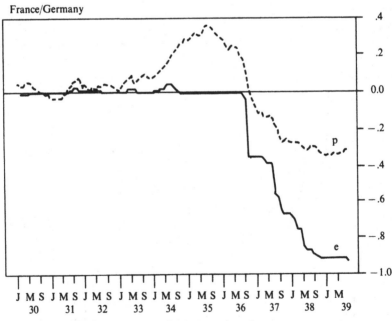

France/Germany

Figure 14.1   Exchange rates and relative prices, I.

US/France

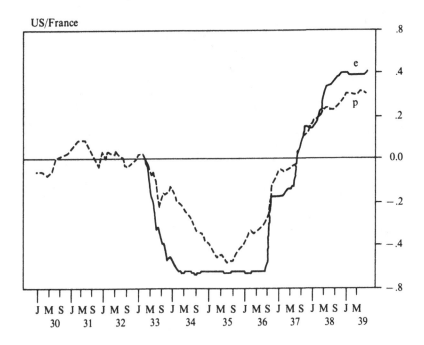

UK/France

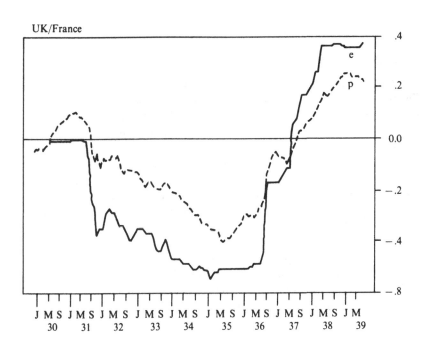

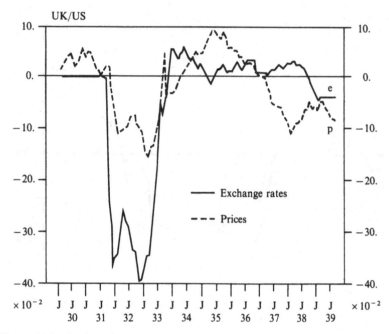

Figure 14.2   Exchange rates and relative price, II.

Cointegration results

Our first task is to test for a unit root in the nominal exchange rate series. The tests reported in table 14.1 indicate that for all exchange rates the null hypothesis that the series are I(1) cannot be rejected, while the null hypothesis that the first differences of the exchange rates are I(1) can be rejected. Thus we can conclude that the exchange rates are indeed I(1).

In table 14.2 we perform similar tests for the relative price series. The null hypothesis that relative prices are I(1) cannot be rejected, while the null hypothesis that relative price changes are I(1) can be rejected. Thus relative prices are I(1), and we have shown that exchange rates and relative prices are integrated of the same order.

In table 14.3 we test for a unit root in the real exchange rate series. We cannot reject the null hypothesis that the real exchange rates are I(1). Thus in this simple form, long-run PPP fails for all currencies.

We then move on to provide some further testing for weaker forms of long-run PPP, as outlined in the second section above. Allowing for tariffs,

Table 14.1. *Tests for a unit root in the nominal exchange rate*

	Levels		First differences	
	DF	ADF	DF	ADF
Sterling–mark		−1.922		−6.671*
Dollar–mark		−1.437		−3.504*
Franc–mark	−1.445		−9.494*	
Sterling–dollar		−1.930		−5.072*
Sterling–franc		−0.109	−8.232*	
Dollar–franc		−0.413		−5.289*

Notes: for tables 14.1, 14.2, 14.3, 14.5, 14.8:
[a]The null hypothesis is that the series in question is I(1). The approximate critical value at the 5% level is −2.89, with rejection region $\{\theta \mid \theta < -2.89\}$, and at the 10% level the critical value is −2.58.
*Denotes significance at the 5% level.
+ Denotes significance at the 10% level.
DF and ADF stand for Dickey-Fuller statistic and Augmented Dickey-Fuller Statistic respectively.

Table 14.2. *Tests for a unit root in relative prices*[a]

	Levels		First differences	
	DF	ADF	DF	ADF
Germany–UK		−1.394	−7.548*	
Germany–US	−1.199		−9.655*	
Germany–France		0.653		−4.462*
US–UK	−1.339		−9.828*	
France–UK		−0.626		−4.847*
France–US		−0.417		−5.208*

See notes to table 14.1.

Table 14.3. *Tests for a unit root in the real exchange rate*

	Levels	
	DF	ADF
Sterling–mark		−2.063
Dollar–mark		−1.212
Franc–mark	−0.131	
Sterling–dollar		−2.070
Sterling–franc	−0.857	
Dollar – franc	−1.652	

See notes to table 14.1.

we run the cointegrating regressions:

$$e_t = \alpha + \beta p_t + z_t \tag{19}$$

The results are reported in table 14.4.[7] Note that the coefficient β is in all cases greater than unity (the strictest form of long-run PPP requires $\beta = 1$).[8] We test for the weaker form of long-run PPP by testing for a unit root in the cointegrating residuals z_t from (19). We see that the null hypothesis of a unit root can only be rejected for the dollar–franc rate. Thus we find some evidence for long-run PPP for the dollar–franc rate.

The next step is to see if relaxation of symmetry makes the results more favourable to long run PPP. This is of some interest, since Broadberry (1987) notes the importance of asymmetry in the responsiveness of the sterling–dollar rate to price changes in Britain and America while the latter adhered to the gold standard during 1931–3. In table 14.5 we test for a unit root in the individual country price series and price change series. A unit root in the price series can only be rejected for Germany, while a unit root in the price change series can be rejected for all the other countries. Hence, we can conclude that, with the exception of Germany, the individual country price series are I(1). The cointegrating regressions with symmetry not imposed are:

$$e_t = \alpha + \beta_1 \eta_t^* + \beta_2 \eta_t + z_t \tag{20}$$

The results are reported in table 14.6. The coefficients β_1 and β_2 have very different (absolute) magnitudes for the sterling–dollar rate, as we would expect, and also for the sterling–franc rate. Testing the cointegrating

Table 14.4. *Cointegrating regressions and tests for cointegration*

$$e_t = \alpha + \beta p_t + z_t$$

	α	β	R^2	DW	DF	ADF
Sterling–mark	−0.244	1.907	0.60	0.04		−2.559
Dollar–mark	−0.174	2.914	0.74	0.17	−1.830	
Franc–mark	−0.220	1.487	0.75	0.04	−0.812	
Sterling–dollar	−0.029	1.240	0.38	0.10		−1.953
Sterling–franc	−0.047	1.575	0.90	0.13	−2.070	
Dollar–franc	−0.037	1.350	0.92	0.23		−3.574*

Notes: Approximate critical values for the Dickey–Fuller statistic (DF) are −3.37 at the 5% level with rejection region $\{DF \mid DF < -3.37\}$ and −3.03 at the 10% level. Approximate critical values for the Augmented Dickey–Fuller statistic (ADF) are −3.17 with rejection region $\{ADF \mid ADF < -3.17\}$ and −2.84 at the 10% level. Approximate critical value for the Durbin-Watson statistic (DW) is 0.386 at the 5% level, with rejection region $\{DW \mid DW > 0.386\}$. In all cases the null hypothesis is that the residuals (z_t) are I(1).

Table 14.5. *Tests for a unit root in the price series*

	Levels	First differences	
	ADF	DF	ADF
UK	−1.667	−6.498[+]	
US	−1.934	−7.820[+]	
France	−0.679		−4.252[+]
Germany	−3.367[+]		−0.187

See notes to table 14.1.

residuals from (20) for a unit root, we see that the null hypothesis of a unit root can be rejected for the sterling–dollar rate at the 10% level. Thus allowing for asymmetry, we find some evidence for long-run PPP for the sterling–dollar rate.[9]

As suggested by the evidence of figure 14.1, then, we find no evidence of long run PPP for any exchange rate involving the German Reichsmark.

Table 14.6. *Cointegrating regressions and tests for cointegration allowing for asymmetry*

$$e_t = \alpha + \beta_1 \eta_t^* + \beta_2 \eta_t + z_t$$

	α	β_1	β_2	R^2	DW	DF	ADF
Sterling–mark	−3.387	2.303	−1.583	0.68	0.05		−1.693
Dollar–mark	−1.770	3.226	−2.859	0.75	0.17	−1.614	
Franc–mark	−1.575	1.827	−1.514	0.76	0.04	−0.820	
Sterling–dollar	−3.568	1.339	−0.535	0.66	0.19		−3.411[+]
Sterling–franc	−4.170	1.390	−0.457	0.95	0.27		−2.935
Dollar–franc	−0.829	1.359	−1.179	0.93	0.23		−2.753

Note: Approximate critical values for the Dickey-Fuller statistic (DF) are −3.93 at the 5% level with rejection region $\{DF \mid DF < -3.93\}$ and −3.59 at the 10% level. Approximate critical values for the Augmented Dickey-Fuller statistic (ADF) are −3.62 at the 5% level with rejection region $\{ADF \mid ADF < -3.62\}$ and −3.32 at the 10% level. Approximate critical value for the Durbin-Watson statistic (DW) is 0.386 at the 5% level, with rejection region $\{DW \mid DW > 0.386\}$. In all cases the null hypothesis is that the residuals (z_t) are I(1).

Again, as suggested by figure 14.2, the results are more favourable to long-run PPP for the other three countries. Allowing for protection, long-run PPP is supported for the dollar–franc rate. Long-run PPP is also supported for the sterling–dollar rate allowing for asymmetry.

In table 4.7, we report results of the Johansen procedure for maximum likelihood estimation of the cointegrating vectors. The likelihood ratio (LR) tests for the number of cointegrating vectors indicate that we can reject the null hypothesis of no cointegrating vectors (r = 0) for all cross rates at the 5% level. In addition we can reject the null hypothesis of at most one cointegrating vector for the sterling–mark, sterling–franc and dollar–franc rates at the 5% level, and at the 10% level for the other cross rates. Since the null hypothesis of at most two cointegrating vectors cannot be rejected for any exchange rate, we can conclude that for all exchange rates there is at least one cointegrating vector, and for some exchange rates two.

In addition, it is possible to test formally for symmetry $(\beta_1 = -\beta_2)$ and for symmetry plus proportionality $(\beta_1 = -\beta_2 = 1)$. It was not possible to reject symmetry for the dollar–franc rate, which is in line with our earlier findings. However, proportionality plus symmetry could be rejected for the

Table 14.7. *Johansen maximum likelihood cointegration estimation results*

$$e_t = \alpha + \beta_1 \eta_t^* + \beta_2 \eta_t + z_t$$

(i) Tests for number of significant cointegrating vectors (r)

	$LR_0(r=0)$	$LR_1(r\leq 1)$	$LR_2(r\leq 2)$
Sterling–mark	34.762*	13.283*	3.802
Dollar–mark	31.608*	10.433$^+$	1.827
Franc–mark	29.034*	11.617$^+$	0.927
Sterling–dollar	40.046*	10.671$^+$	2.538
Sterling–franc	36.989*	12.570*	1.859
Dollar–franc	41.493*	18.504*	3.382

(ii) Tests for symmetry and proportionality

	$LR_s(\beta_1 = -\beta_2)$	$LR_p(\beta_1 = -\beta_2 = 1)$
Sterling–mark	13.538*	—
Dollar–mark	2.743$^+$	6.088*
Franc–mark	0.149	14.370*
Sterling–dollar	20.726*	—
Sterling–franc	21.734*	—
Dollar–franc	0.080	9.705*

(ii) Estimated cointegrating vectors

	β_1	β_2
Sterling–mark	8.401	−3.765
Dollar–mark	0.919	−0.219
Franc–mark	1.560	−1.917
Sterling–dollar	1.313	−0.150
Sterling–franc	1.068	−1.971
Dollar–franc	1.316	−1.340

Notes:
(i) The approximate 5% critical values for LR_0, LR_1 and LR_2 are 23.8, 12.0 and 4.2 respectively, while the corresponding 10% critical values are 21.2, 10.3 and 2.9 respectively (Johansen, 1988).
(ii) LR_s and LR_p are asymptotically central chi-square variates with r and 2r degrees of freedom respectively, where r is the number of significant cointegrating vectors (Johansen, 1988).

Table 14.8. *Tests for a unit root in the COL series*

	Levels ADF	First differences ADF	Second differences ADF
UK	−1.788	−1.926	−10.995*
US	−2.677+	−4.030*	

See notes to table 4.1.

dollar–franc rate. Similarly for the franc–mark rate, symmetry could not be rejected, although symmetry plus proportionality was rejected.

Thus our results using the Johansen procedure broadly confirm our findings from OLS estimates of the cointegrating regressions. However, we note that whereas for exchange rates involving the mark, OLS estimation clearly rejects the possibility of PPP, the Johansen procedure gives much less clear-cut results. Indeed, we are unable to reject symmetry for the franc–mark rate.

Finally, we note that we can reject PPP using cost-of-living indices for the UK and US. We see in table 14.8 that while the UK COL index is I(2), the US COL index is I(1) or I(0).

Arbitrage and Granger causality

So far we have said little about the way in which arbitrage occurred so as to bring about the long-run relationship between the exchange rate and relative prices implied by purchasing power parity. Arbitrage could occur through commodity markets, with prices adjusting to exchange rates, or through foreign exchange markets, with exchange rates adjusting to prices. Since the period under consideration covers a mixture of exchange rate regimes, it is instructive to consider the direction of causality.

To test for the direction of causality, we employ Granger causality tests using a trivariate vector autoregression (VAR) in exchange rates, domestic and foreign prices, with a constant and lag length of twelve months. The F-tests reported in tables 14.9 and 14.10 are for the exclusion from the VAR of current and lagged values of the independent variable indicated. An F-statistic above the critical value implies rejection of the null hypothesis that the indicated variable does not Granger cause the dependent variable.

Results for the full sample are reported in table 14.9. We find several cases of the exchange rate Granger-causing prices, but no case of prices

Table 14.9. *Granger causality tests, full sample period*

Dependent variable	F-test for hypothesis that indicated variable does not Granger-cause the dependent variable		
	e(£/RM)	p(UK)	p(GE)
e(£/RM)	—	1.21	1.65
p(UK)	1.80	—	1.58
p(GE)	3.61*	2.44*	—
	e($/RM)	p(US)	p(GE)
e($/RM)	—	1.57	1.79
p(US)	5.50*	—	1.69
p(GE)	1.76	1.97*	—
	e(FF/RM)	p(FR)	p(GE)
e(FF/RM)	—	1.39	0.20
p(FR)	1.09	—	1.41
p(GE)	0.58	1.20	—
	e(£/$)	p(UK)	p(US)
e(£/$)	—	1.49	0.81
p(UK)	0.71	—	0.78
p(US)	4.14*	1.58	—
	e(£/FF)	p(UK)	p(FR)
e(£/FF)	—	1.22	0.67
p(UK)	2.33*	—	1.77
p(FR)	1.61	1.57	—
	e($/FF)	p(US)	p(FR)
e($/FF)	—	0.76	1.10
p(US)	1.79	—	1.79
p(FR)	0.79	0.50	—

Note: Critical value at the 5% level is 1.92, with rejection region $\{\theta \mid \theta > 1.92\}$.

Granger-causing the exchange rate. However, in table 14.10 we report results for sub-periods determined by changes in exchange rate regimes. Sterling was floated against gold in September 1931, while the dollar was floated and restabilised against gold in April 1933 and February 1934 respectively. The franc was floated against gold in September 1936, which was also the occasion of the Tripartite Monetary Agreement between Britain, the US and France, which brought about greater exchange rate stability.[10]

Table 14.10. *Granger causality tests, sub-periods*

Sample period	Dependent variable	F-test for hypothesis that indicated variable does not Granger-cause the dependent variable		

		e(£/RM)	p(UK)	p(GE)
1931,9–1939,8	e(£/RM)	—	1.99*	4.24*
	p(UK)	1.80	—	2.13*
	p(GE)	3.38*	2.50	—

		e($/RM)	p(US)	p(GE)
1933,3–1939,8	e($/RM)	—	2.88*	5.16*
	p(US)	4.19*	—	1.91
	p(GE)	1.68	2.65*	—

		e($RM)	p(US)	p(GE)
1934,2–1939,8	e($/RM)	—	1.36	1.99
	p(US)	0.36	—	0.86
	p(GE)	1.08	1.40	—

		e(FF/RM)	p(FR)	p(GE)
1931,1–1936,8	e(FF/RM)	—	1.41	1.28
	p(FR)	2.17	—	1.29
	p(GE)	1.49	0.50	—

		e(£/$)	p(UK)	p(US)
1931,9–1939,8	e(£/$)	—	1.54	0.84
	p(UK)	1.15	—	0.95
	p(US)	4.68*	1.78	—

		e(£/$)	p(UK)	p(US)
1933,4–1939,8	e(£/$)	—	1.59	0.59
	p(UK)	0.82	—	0.92
	p(US)	3.65*	1.05	—

		e(£/$)	p(UK)	p(US)
1934,2–1939,8	e(£/$)	—	1.06	1.12
	p(UK)	0.62	—	1.47
	p(US)	0.82	0.53	—

		e(£/FF)	p(UK)	p(FR)
1931,1–1936,8	e(£/FF)	—	1.58	0.99
	p(UK)	2.74*	—	2.44*
	p(FR)	2.66*	1.56	—

Table 14.10. (*cont.*)

Sample period	Dependent variable	F-test for hypothesis that indicated variable does not Granger-cause the dependent variable		
		e(£/FF)	p(UK)	p(FR)
1931,9–1939,8	e(£/FF)	—	1.16	0.63
	p(UK)	2.35*	—	1.96*
	p(FR)	1.53	1.61	—
		e($/FF)	p(US)	p(FR)
1933,4–1939,8	e($/FF)	—	0.62	1.20
	p(US)	1.80	—	2.27*
	p(FR)	0.64	0.65	—
		e($/FF)	p(US)	p(FR)
1934,2–1939,8	e($/FF)	—	1.26	1.73
	p(US)	1.74	—	1.50
	p(FR)	0.49	0.59	—
		e($/FF)	p(US)	p(FR)
1931,1–1936,8	e($/FF)	—	1.60	0.63
	p(US)	9.84*	—	1.31
	p(FR)	1.64	0.98	—

Note: Rejection regions at the 5% level are as follows:
1931,1–1939,8 $\{\theta \mid \theta > 1.92\}$
1933,4–1939,8 $\{\theta \mid \theta > 2.12\}$
1934,2–1939,8 $\{\theta \mid \theta > 2.36\}$
1931,1–1936,8 $\{\theta \mid \theta > 2.32\}$
1931,9–1939,8 $\{\theta \mid \theta > 1.96\}$

Excluding the period before the sterling float, we find evidence for causality running from prices to the pound–mark exchange rate. Similarly, excluding the period before the dollar float, we find evidence for causality running from prices to the dollar–mark exchange rate. This causality disappears if the period of the dollar float is excluded, however. There is no evidence of causality between prices and the franc–mark exchange rate.

For the pound–dollar rate, the finding that the exchange rate Granger-caused US prices is seen to be dependent on the period of the dollar float.

For the pound–franc rate, causality runs only from the exchange rate to prices and not vice-versa, irrespective of period. For the dollar–franc rate, there is evidence of causality running from the exchange rate to US prices, but only prior to the Tripartite Monetary Agreement.

To sum up on Granger causality, the direction of causality generally appears to run from the exchange rate to prices, although there is some evidence of reverse causation from prices to the exchange rate during periods of relatively free floating. These results are thus consistent with Frenkel's (1978) eclectic interpretation, with adjustment to PPP occurring through commodity and asset markets.

Some implications

The impact of German controls

We have already noted the firm rejection of PPP for exchange rates involving the Reichsmark. This illustrates the importance of controls in preventing the arbitrage necessary to bring about PPP. We have already seen in the second section how the introduction of exchange controls on capital transactions spread to current commercial transactions, which in turn led to the development of barter trade, generalised to the Aski system and eventually to bilateral clearing arrangements.

Note, however, that the way in which commodity arbitrage was impeded differed between the countries in our sample. In German trade with France, a clearing agreement was reached, while with Britain and the US, no such agreements were concluded. In these cases, adjustment was distorted through German export subsidies.

Asymmetry and the pound-dollar rate

We have seen that for the pound–dollar rate there is evidence of a weaker form of PPP allowing for asymmetry in the responsiveness of the exchange rate to price changes in Britain and America. In Broadberry (1987) this asymmetry is investigated further, and is found to be limited to the period between September 1931 when Britain left the gold standard and April 1933 when the US devalued against gold.

Broadberry tests for symmetry using regressions of the form:

$$e_t = \alpha + \sum_{i=1}^{n} \beta_i \eta^*_{t-1} + \sum_{i=1}^{n} \gamma_i \eta_{t-1} \tag{21}$$

Symmetry is accepted if $\beta_i = -\gamma_i$ for $i = 1, \ldots, n$. Symmetry can be rejected for the period during which Britain was off gold, but the US remained on gold. The coefficients on the UK price terms are larger in absolute value than those on the US price terms, suggesting that exchange markets viewed UK price changes more seriously than US price changes, since the latter could not be sustained as long as the US dollar was tied to gold. Once both countries had left the gold standard, however, symmetry was restored.

Broadberry tests for PPP by running regressions with an error-correction specification:

$$\Delta e_t = \beta_0 + \beta_1 \Delta p_t - \beta_2 (e_{t-1} - p_{t-1}) + \beta_3 p_{t-1} \qquad (22)$$

and testing for $\beta_3 = 0$. This then implies a long-run steady state solution (when $\Delta e = \Delta p = 0$) of:

$$e = \alpha p \qquad (23)$$

where $\alpha = \beta_0/\beta_2$. This is equivalent to our version of weak PPP with tariffs, as in equation (19). This approach also allows a test of short-run PPP, which requires $\beta_1 = 1$. For the pound–dollar rate during the 1930s, long-run PPP was not rejected, but short-run PPP was rejected.

Protection and PPP

We have already seen that drastic controls prevented the operation of arbitrage necessary to bring about PPP between Germany and the other countries in our sample. Nevertheless, there is still some evidence in favour of a weak form of PPP between Britain, America and France. This is at first sight surprising, given the rise of controls, particularly protection, in all countries, documented in the second section above.

This suggests that PPP was indeed a strong force at work in the interwar world economy, and could only be prevented from operating by the imposition of drastic controls. Thus although tariffs might have intervened to prevent proportionality, arbitrage still operated to bring about a weaker form of PPP, as suggested in the model of the third section.

Conclusion

In this chapter we test the purchasing power parity hypothesis as a long-run equilibrium condition, allowing for protection, and without imposing symmetry of responses to prices. Our methodology involves testing for the cointegration of time series in exchange rates and relative prices.

Our tests are conducted using monthly seasonally adjusted data on nominal exchange rates and relative wholesale prices for Britain, America, France and Germany. No exchange rate involving the German Reichsmark exhibits PPP, due to the importance of bilateralism in German trade during the 1930s. However, the results for the other three countries are more favourable for long-run PPP. Allowing for tariffs the dollar–franc rate conforms to long-run PPP, while allowing for asymmetry, the sterling–dollar rate exhibits long-run PPP.

On the issue of causality, we generally find exchange rates causing prices rather than vice versa, except during periods of relatively free-floating exchange rates, when prices Granger-caused exchange rates. These results are consistent with adjustment to PPP through both commodity and asset markets.

Notes

1 The only econometric study is that of Whitaker and Hudgins (1977).

2 Note that Falkus almost appears to deny the principle of comparative advantage by arguing that the rest of the world had nothing to offer America.

3 Fearon (1987), p. 84. Note that the historian's rather loose term 'psychological impact' can be given a more precise meaning by seeing the US as the first player in a tariff game. Hence, our preferences for the term 'strategic impact'.

4 Arndt (1944), p. 186. See also Sweezy (1941), pp. 119–20 for a detailed description of the workings of barter deals.

5 Fuller (1976), p. 373. Note that Fuller (1976) does not distinguish between the Dickey-Fuller and augmented Dickey-Fuller tests (see below), and these critical values were in fact generated for the first-order case. However, Fuller (ibid.) does provide a large sample argument to support the use of these tables for the higher order case, and this seems to be borne out in Taylor (1986), which reports critical values for a second order model (generated by Monte Carlo methods) which are very close to those reported by Fuller.

6 All of the test procedures outlined and applied in this paper are robust to the presence of measurement error, so long as the errors are I(0), which seems a reasonable assumption. See Engle and Granger (1987).

7 Tests carried out on the reverse regression, i.e. prices regressed on exchange rates, yielded qualitatively identical results, as would be expected. See Engle and Granger (1987).

8 No standard errors are reported in table 14.4 since these are invalid when the regression variables are non-stationary. Stock (1985) shows that ordinary least squares (OLS) provides an extremely efficient ('super-consistent') estimate of the cointegrating vector, with a variance $0(T^{-2})$, as opposed to the usual case of $0(T^{-1})$ when the variables are cointegrated. Since OLS minimises the residual (which will be theoretically infinite for values of the parameters which do not

cointegrate the variables) this result is intuitive. This effect also obviates the need to consider the 'correct' direction of regression, since it will tend to swamp any simultaneity bias. See Engle and Granger (1987). Stock (1985) also shows that the OLS estimator will have an $O(T^{-1})$ bias when the variables are cointegrated, although Banerjee *et al.* (1986) find (in Monte Carlo experiments) that this bias can often be substantial in finite samples. They suggest using the R^2 from the cointegrating regression as an indicator of the reliability of the estimate.

9 The critical values for the trivariate case are reported in Engle and Yoo (1987).

10 For a discussion of exchange rate regimes changes during the 1930s, see Broadberry (1989).

References

Aldcroft, D.H. (1970), *The Inter-War Economy: Britain 1919–1939* (London: Batsford).

Aldcroft, D.H. and Fearon, P. (1972), 'Introduction', in D.H. Aldcroft and P. Fearon (eds.), *British Economic Fluctuations, 1790–1939* (London: Macmillan), 1–73.

Allen, R.G.D. (1971), *British Industries and Their Organisation* (London: Longman).

Alogoskoufis, C.S. and Manning, A. (1988), 'On the Persistence of Unemployment', *Economic Policy*, 7, 2–43.

Alogoskoufis, G. and Smith, R. (1991), 'On Error Correction Models: Specification, Interpretation, Estimation', *Journal of Economic Surveys*, 5(1), 97–128.

Angell, J.W. (1922), 'International Trade under Inconvertible Paper', *Quarterly Journal of Economics*, 36(2), 309–412.

(1926), *The Theory of International Prices* (Cambridge, MA: Harvard University Press).

Arndt, H.W. (1944), *The Economic Lessons of the Nineteen-Thirties* (Oxford: Oxford University Press for the Royal Institute of Economic Affairs).

Artis, M.J., Baldon-Hovell, R., Karakitsos, E. and Dwolatsky, B. (1984), 'The Effects of Economic Policy 1979–1982', *National Institute Economic Review*, 108, 54–67.

Artis, M.J. and Currie, D.A. (1981), 'Monetary Targets and the Exchange Rate: A Case for Conditional Targets', in W.A. Eltis and P.J.N. Sinclair (eds), *The Money Supply and the Exchange Rate* (Oxford: Clarendon Press), 176–200.

Artis, M.J. and Green, C.J. (1982), 'Using the Treasury Model to Measure the Impact of Fiscal Policy, 1974–79', in M.J. Artis *et al.* (eds), *Demand Management, Supply Constraints and Inflation* (Manchester: Manchester University Press), 30–47.

Bain, G.S. and Price, R. (1980), *Profiles of Union Growth* (Oxford: Basil Blackwell).

Balke, N.S. and Gordon, R.J. (1989), 'The Estimation of Prewar Gross National Product Methodology and New Evidence', *Journal of Political Economy*, 97(1), 38–92.

Banerjee, A., Dolado, J.J., Hendry, D.F. and Smith, G.W. (1986), 'Exploring Equilibrium Relationships in Econometrics Through Static Models: Some

Monte Carlo Evidence', *Oxford Bulletin of Economics and Statistics*, 48(3), 253–77.

Barrell, R.J. (1989), 'Manufacturing Export Prices for the G7', *National Institute Economic Review*, 128, 90–1.

Barro, R.J. (1979), 'Money and the Price Level Under the Gold Standard', *Economic Journal*, 89, 13–33.

(1984), *Macroeconomics* (New York: John Wiley).

Barro, R.J. and Gordon, D.A. (1983), 'A Positive Theory of Monetary Policy in a Natural-Rate Model', *Journal of Political Theory*, 91(4), 589–610.

Barsky, R.B. (1987), 'The Fisher Hypothesis and the Forecastability and Persistence of Inflation', *Journal of Monetary Economics*, 19, 3–24.

Barsky, R.B. and DeLong, B. (1988), 'Forecasting Pre-World War I Inflation: The Fisher Effect Revisited', NBER Working Paper No. 2784.

Barsky, R.B. and Summers, L.H. (1988), 'Gibson's Paradox and the Gold Standard', *Journal of Political Economy*, 96(3), 528–50.

Beck, G.M. (1951), *A Survey of British Employment and Unemployment 1927–45* (Oxford University: Institute of Statistics and Economics).

Beckerman, W. and Jenkinson, T. (1986), 'How Rigid Are Real Wages Anyway?', in W. Beckerman (ed.), *Wage Rigidity and Unemployment* (Baltimore: Johns Hopkins University Press), 21–42.

Beenstock, M., Capie, F. and Griffiths, B. (1984), 'Economic Recovery in the United Kingdom in the 1930s', *Bank of England Panel Paper*, 23, 57–85.

Beenstock, M. and Warburton, P. (1986a), 'The Market for Labour in Interwar Britain', *Centre for Economic Policy Research*, Discussion Paper 105 (April).

(1986b), 'Wages and Unemployment in Interwar Britain', *Explorations in Economic History*, 23(2), 153–72.

Benjamin, D. and Kochin, L. (1979), 'Searching for an Explanation of Unemployment in Interwar Britain', *Journal of Political Economy*, 87(3), 441–70.

Benjamin, D. and Kochin, L.A. (1984), 'War, Prices and Interest Rates: A Martial Solution to Gibson's Paradox', in M.D. Bordo and A.J. Schwartz (eds.), *A Retrospective on the Classical Gold Standard, 1821–1931* (Chicago: University of Chicago Press for NBER), 587–607.

Berghahn, V.R. and Karsten, D. (1987), *Industrial Relations in West Germany* (Oxford: Berg).

Bernanke, B. (1986), 'Alternative Explanations of the Money-Income Correlation', *Carnegie-Rochester Conference Series on Public Policy*, 25, 49–100.

Bessler, D.A. (1984), 'Additional Evidence on Money and Prices: US Data 1870–1913', *Explorations in Economic History*, 21(2), 97–127.

Beveridge, S. and Nelson, C.R. (1981), 'A New Approach to Decomposition of Economic Time Series into Permanent and Transitory Components with Particular Attention to Measurement of the "Business Cycle"', *Journal of Monetary Economics*, 7(2), 151–74.

Binmore, K., Rubinstein, A. and Wolinsky, A. (1986), 'The Nash Bargaining Model in Economic Modelling', *Rand Journal of Economics*, 17(2), 176–88.

Blake, N. (1988), 'The Causes of Long Term Price Movements 1870–1913', unpublished DPhil dissertation, University of York.

Blanchard, O. and Watson, M.W. (1986), 'Are Business Cycles All Alike?', in R. Gordon (ed.), *The American Business Cycle* (Chicago: NBER and Chicago Press), 123–82.

Bloomfield, A.I. (1959), *Monetary Policy Under the International Gold Standard* (New York: Federal Reserve Bank).

(1963), 'Short-term Capital Movements Under the Pre-1914 Gold Standard', *Princeton Studies in International Finance*, No. 11 (Princeton: Princeton University Press).

(1968), 'Patterns of Fluctuations in International Investment Before 1914', *Princeton Studies in International Finance*, No. 21 (Princeton: Princeton University Press).

Board of Trade (1910), *Report on Collective Agreements Between Employers and Workpeople in the United Kingdom*, Cd.5366 (London: HMSO).

Bonnett, C.E. (1956), *History of Employers' Associations in the United States* (New York: Vantage Press).

Booth, A. (1987), 'Britain in the 1930s: A Managed Economy?', *Economic History Review*, 40(4), 499–522.

Bopp, K. (1951–2), 'Bank of France: Brief Survey of Instruments, 1880–1914', *American Journal of Economics and Sociology*, 11, 229–44.

Bordo, M.D. (1981), 'The Classical Gold Standard: Some Lessons for Today', *Federal Reserve Bank of St Louis, Monthly Review*, 63(5), 1–17.

(1984), 'The Gold Standard: The Traditional Approach', in M.D. Bordo and A.J. Schwartz (eds), *A Retrospective on the Classical Gold Standard, 1821–1931* (Chicago: National Bureau of Economic Research), 23–113.

(1986a), 'Explorations in Monetary History: A Survey of the Literature', *Explorations in Economic History*, 23, 339–415.

(1986b), 'Financial Crises, Banking Crises, Stock Market Crashes and the Money Supply: Some International Evidence, 1870–1933', in F. Capie and G. Wood (eds), *Financial Crises and the World Banking System* (London: Macmillan), 190–248.

Bordo, M.D. and Schwartz, A.J. (1980), 'Money and Prices in the Nineteenth Century: An Old Debate Rejoined', *Journal of Economic History*, 40(1), 61–7.

(1981), 'Money and Prices in the Nineteenth Century: Was Thomas Tooke Right?', *Explorations in Economic History*, 18(2), 97–127.

Bordo, M. and Ellson, R. (1985), 'A Model of the Classical Gold Standard with Depletion', *Journal of Monetary Economics*, 16(1), 109–20.

Bordo, M. and Kydland, F. (1989), 'The Gold Standard as a Rule', unpublished manuscript.

Bowley, A.L. (1921), *Prices and Wages in the United Kingdom, 1914–1920* (Oxford).

(1929), 'A New Index Number of Wages', *London and Cambridge Economic Service*, special memorandum, XXVIII.

(1937), *Wages and Income in the United Kingdom Since 1860* (Cambridge: Cambridge University Press).

(1947), 'Wages, Earnings and Hours Worked, 1914–47', *London and Cambridge Economic Service*, special memorandum, L.

(1952), 'Index-Number of Wages and Cost of Living', *Journal of the Royal Statistical Society*, 115, A, Part IV, 500–6.

Box, G.E.P. and Jenkins, G.M. (1976), *Time Series Analysis: Forecasting and Control*, (San Francisco: Holden-Day), revised edition.

Broadberry, S.N. (1983), 'Unemployment in Interwar Britain: A Disequilibrium Approach', *Oxford Economic Papers*, 35(4), 463–85.

(1986), *The British Economy Between the Wars: A Macroeconomic Survey* (Oxford: Basil Blackwell).

(1986), 'Aggregate Supply in Interwar Britain', *Economic Journal*, 96(2), 467–81.

(1987), 'Purchasing Power Parity and the Pound Dollar Rate in the 1930s', *Economica*, 54(1), 69–78.

(1989), 'Monetary Interdependence and Deflation in Britain and the United States Between the Wars', in M. Miller, B. Eichengreen and R. Portes (eds), *Blueprints for Exchange Rate Management* (London: Academic Press), 47–69.

Brown, Jnr W.A. (1940), *The International Gold Standard Reinterpreted*, (New York: National Bureau of Economic Research).

Bruno, M. and Sachs, J.D. (1985), *Economics of Worldwide Stagflation* (Cambridge, MA: Harvard University Press).

Bulkley, G. and Tonks, I. (1989), 'Are UK Stock Prices Excessively Volatile? Trading Rules and Variance Bound Tests', *Economic Journal*, 99(4), 1083–98.

Burns, A.F. and Mitchell, W.C. (1946), *Measuring Business Cycles* (New York: NBER).

Buxton, N.K. and Aldcroft, D.H. (1979), *British Industry Between the Wars* (London: Scholar Press).

Cagan, P. (1965), *Determinants and Effects of Changes in the Stock of Money 1875–1960* (New York: Columbia University Press for NBER).

(1972), *The Channels of Monetary Effects on Interest Rates* (New York: NBER).

(1984), 'Mr Gibson's Paradox: Was It There?', in M.D. Bordo and A.J. Schwartz (eds), *A Retrospective on the Classical Gold Standard, 1821–1931* (Chicago: University of Chicago Press for NBER), 604–10.

Cairncross, A.K. (1953), *Home and Foreign Investment, 1870–1913* (Cambridge: Cambridge University Press).

Cairncross, A.K. and Eichengreen, B.J. (1983), *Sterling in Decline*, (Oxford: Blackwell).

Cairns, J.E. (1874), *Essays in Political Economy, Theoretical and Applied* (London: Macmillan), 8th edition.

Callahan, C. (1984), 'Movements in Aggregate Price Uncertainty in the United States', unpublished, University of North Carolina.

Calmfors, L. and Driffill, J. (1988), 'Bargaining Structure, Corporatism and Macroeconomic Performance', *Economic Policy*, 6, 14–61.

Calomiris, C.W. and Hubbard, R.G. (1987), 'International Adjustment under the Classical Gold Standard: Evidence for the US and Britain, 1879–1914', NBER Working Paper No. 2206, Cambridge, MA.

Campbell, J.Y. and Mankiw, N.G. (1987), 'Permanent and Transitory Components in Macroeconomic Fluctuations', *American Economic Review*, Papers and Proceedings, 77, 111–17.

(1987), 'Are Output Fluctuations Transitory?', *Quarterly Journal of Economics*, 102(4), 857–80.

(1989), 'International Evidence on the Persistence of Economic Fluctuations', *Journal of Monetary Economics*, 23(3), 319–33.

Cannan, E. (1930), 'The Problem of Unemployment', *Economic Journal*, 40(1), 45–55.

Capie, F. (1983), *Depression and Protectionism: Britain Between the Wars* (London: Allen and Unwin).

Capie, F. and Rodrik-Bali, G. (1983), 'Monetary Growth and Determinants in Britain, 1870–1913', *Monetary History Discussion Paper Series*, Centre for Banking and International Finance, City University, April.

Capie, F.H. and Webber, A. (1985), *A Monetary History of the United Kingdom, Volume 1: Data, Sources, Methods* (London: George Allen and Unwin).

Capie, F. and Wood, G.E. (1986), *Financial Crises and the World Banking System* (London: Macmillan).

Capie, F.H., Mills, T.C. and Wood, G.E. (1991), 'Money, Interest Rates, and the Great Depression: Britain From 1870 to 1913', in J. Foreman-Peck (ed.), *Reinterpreting the Victorian Economy: Essays in Quantitative Economic History 1860–1914* (Cambridge: Cambridge University Press).

Carr, E. (1925), *The Use of Cost-of-Living Figures in Wage Adjustments*, US Bureau of Labor Statistics, Bulletin 369 (Washington D.C.: Government Printing Office).

Carruth, A.A. and Oswald, A.J. (1989), *Pay Determination and Industrial Prosperity* (Oxford: Clarendon Press).

Cassel, G. (1921), *The World's Monetary Problems* (London: Constable).

(1928), *Postwar Monetary Stabilisation* (New York: Columbia University Press).

Cassis, Y. (1985), 'Bankers in English Society in the Late Nineteenth Century', *Economic History Review*, 2nd series, 38, 210–90.

Casson, M. (1983), *Economics of Unemployment: An Historical Perspective* (Oxford: Martin Robertson).

Chapman, A.L. and Knight, R. (1953), *Wages and Salaries in the United Kingdom 1920–38* (Cambridge: Cambridge University Press).

Chang, D. (1936), *British Methods of Industrial Peace* (New York: Columbia University Press).

Chick, V. (1983), *Macroeconomics After Keynes* (Oxford: Philip Allan).

Clapham, Sir J. (1970), *The Bank of England*, Vol. 2 (Cambridge: Cambridge University Press).

Clark, P.K. (1987), 'The Cyclical Component of US Economic Activity', *Quarterly Journal of Economics*, 102(4), 797–814.

Clark, T.A. (1984), 'Violations of the Gold Points, 1890–1914', *Journal of Political Economy*, 92(5), 791–823.

Clarke, S.V.O. (1967), *Central Bank Cooperation 1924–31* (New York: Federal Reserve Board).

(1973), 'The Reconstruction of the International Monetary System: The Attempts of 1922 and 1933', *Princeton Studies in International Finance*, No. 33.

(1977), 'Exchange Rate Stabilisation in the mid-1930s: Negotiating the Tripartite Agreement', *Princeton Studies in International Finance*, No. 41.

Clay, H. (1929a), *The Problem of Industrial Relations* (London: Macmillan).

(1929b), 'The Public Regulation of Wages in Great Britain', *Economic Journal*, 39(3), 323–43.

Clemen, R.A. (1923), *American Livestock and Meat Industry* (New York: The Ronald Press Co.).

Cochrane, J.H. (1988), 'How Big is the Random Walk in GDP?', *Journal of Political Economy*, 96(5), 893–920.

Collins, M. (1987), 'The Banking Crisis of 1878', University of Leeds Discussion Paper Series A 87/9.

(1988), 'English Banks and Business Cycles, 1848–80', in P. Cottrell and D. Moggridge (eds), *Money and Power*, (London: Macmillan), 1–39.

(1988), *Money and Banking in the United Kingdom: A History* (London: Croom Helm).

Commercial History and Review of 1867, supplement to *The Economist*, 14 March 1868, 3–4.

Committee on Industry and Trade (1928), *Survey of Metal Industries*, Vol. IV (London: HMSO).

Cooley, T.F. and LeRoy, S.F. (1985), Atheoretical Macroeconomics: A Critique', *Journal of Monetary Economics*, 16(3), 283–308.

Cooper, R. (1982), 'The Gold Standard: Historical Facts and Future Prospects', *Brookings Papers on Economic Activity*, 1, 1–45.

Coppock, D.J. (1961), 'The Causes of the Great Depression', *Manchester School*, 29(3), 205–32.

Corbett, D. (1990), 'Unemployment Insurance and Induced Search in Interwar Germany', in E. Aerts and B. Eichengreen (eds), *Unemployment and Underemployment in Historical Perspective* (Leuven: International Economic History Association), 76–87.

Cottrell, P. (1982), 'London, Paris and Silver, 1848–1867', in A. Slaven and D.H. Aldcroft (eds), *Business, Banking and Urban History* (Edinburgh: John Donald), 142.

Cottrell, P. and Moggridge, D. (1988), *Money and Power* (London: Macmillan).

Crafts, N.F.R. (1979), 'Victorian Britain Did Fail', *Economic History Review*, 32(4), 533–7.

(1987), 'Long-Term Unemployment in Britain in the 1930s', *Economic History Review*, 40(3), 418–32.

(1989), 'Long-Term Unemployment and the Wage Equation in Britain, 1925–1939', *Economica*, 56(2), 247–54.

Crafts, N.F.R., Leybourne, S.J. and Mills, T.C. (1989a), 'The Climacteric in Late Victorian Britain and France: A Reappraisal of the Evidence', *Journal of Applied Econometrics*, 4(2), 103–17.

(1989b), 'Trends and Cycles in British Industrial Production, 1700–1913', *Journal of the Royal Statistical Society*, Series A, 152(1), 43–60.

(1990), 'Measurement of Trend Growth in European Industrial Output Before

1914: Methodological Issues and New Estimates', *Explorations in Economic History*, 27(4), 442–67.

(1991), 'Economic Growth in Nineteenth Century Britain: Comparisons with Europe in the Context of Gerschenkron's Hypotheses', in R. Sylla and G. Toniolo (eds), *Patterns of European Industrialization in the XIX Century*, forthcoming (Oxford: Oxford University Press), 109–52.

Critchell, J.T. and Raymond, J. (1912), *A History of the Frozen Meat Trade* (London: Constable & Co. Ltd.).

Darby, M.R., Lothian, J.R., with Gandolfi, A.E., Schwartz, A.J. and Stockman, A.C. (1983), *The International Transmission of Inflation* (Chicago: National Bureau of Economic Research).

Daunton, M. (1989), ' "Gentlemanly Capitalism" and British Industry 1820–1914', *Past and Present*, 122, 119–58.

Davidson, J.E.H., Hendry, D.F., Srba, F. and Yeo, S. (1978), 'Econometric Modelling of the Aggregate Time-Series Relationship Between Consumers' Expenditure and Income in the United Kingdom', *Economic Journal*, 88(352), 661–92.

Deane, P. (1968), 'New Estimates of Gross National Product for the United Kingdom, 1830–1914', *Review of Income and Wealth*, 14(2), 95–112.

De Cecco, M. (1974), *Money and Empire: The International Gold Standard* (London: Blackwell).

Dick, T. and Floyd, J. (1988), 'Canada and the Gold Standard, 1880–1914', unpublished manuscript.

Dickey, D.A. and Fuller, W.A. (1979), 'Distribution of the Estimators for Autoregressive Time Series with a Unit Root', *Journal of the American Statistical Association*, 74(366), 427–31.

(1981), 'Likelihood Ratio Tests for Autoregressive Time Series with a Unit Root', *Econometrica*, 49(5), 1057–72.

Diewert, W.E. (1985), 'The Measurement of the Economic Benefits of Infrastructure Services', *University of British Columbia Discussion Paper*, No. 85-11.

Diewert, W.E. and Wales, T. (1987), 'Flexible Functional Forms and Global Curvature Conditions', *Econometrica*, 55(1), 43–68.

Dimsdale, N.H. (1981), 'British Monetary Policy and the Exchange Rate 1920–38', in W.A. Eltis and P.J.N. Sinclair (eds), *The Money Supply and the Exchange Rate* (Oxford: Clarendon Press), 306–49.

(1984), 'Employment and Real Wages in the Interwar Period', *National Institute Economic Review*, 110, 94–102.

(1990), 'Money, Interest and Cycles in Britain Since 1830', in A.S. Courakis and C. Goodhart (eds), *The Monetary Economics of Sir John Hicks* (Oxford: Clarendon Press).

Dimsdale, N.H., Nickell, S. and Horsewood, N. (1989), 'Real Wages and Unemployment in Britain During the 1930s', *Economic Journal*, 99(2), 271–92.

Dolado, J.J., Jenkinson, T. and Sosvilla-Rivero, S. (1990), 'Cointegration and Unit Roots', *Journal of Economic Surveys*, 4(3), 249–73.

Dornbusch, R. (1980), *Open Economy Macroeconomics* (New York: Basic Books).

(1988), *Exchange Rates and Inflation* (Cambridge, MA: MIT Press).

Dornbusch, R. and Jaffee, D. (1978), 'Purchasing Power Parity and Exchange Rate Problems: Introduction', *Journal of International Economics*, 8(2), 157–61.

Dornbusch, R. and Frenkel, J. (1984), 'The Gold Standard and the Bank of England in the Crisis of 1847', in M. Bordo and A. Schwartz (eds), *A Retrospective on the Classical Gold Standard, 1821–1931* (Chicago: University of Chicago Press), 233–65.

Dougan, D. (1968), *The History of North East Shipbuilding* (London: George Allen and Unwin).

Dover, R. (1866), *The Cause of Monetary Panics in England and the Remedy* (London).

Drummond, I.M. (1981), *The Floating Pound and the Sterling Area, 1931–1939* (Cambridge: Cambridge University Press).

(1987), *The Gold Standard and the International Monetary System, 1900–1939* (London: Macmillan Education Ltd.).

Dunlop, J.T. (1938), 'The Movement of Real and Money Wage Rates', *Economic Journal*, 48(3), 413–34.

Durlauf, S.N. and Phillips, P.C.B. (1988), 'Trends Versus Random Walks in Time Series Analysis', *Econometrica*, 56(6), 1333–54.

Dutton, J. (1984), 'The Bank of England and the Rules of the Game under the International Gold Standard: New Evidence', in M.D. Bordo and A.J. Schwartz (eds), *A Retrospective on the Classical Gold Standard, 1821–1931* (Chicago: University of Chicago Press), 173–95.

Dwyer, G. (1985), 'Money, Income and Prices in the United Kingdom 1870–1913', *Economic Inquiry*, 23, 415–35.

Easton, S.T. (1984), 'Real Output and the Gold Standard Years, 1830–1913', in M.D. Bordo and A.J. Schwartz (eds), *A Retrospective on the Classical Gold Standard, 1821–1931* (Chicago: National Bureau of Economic Research), 513–38.

Edelstein, M. (1982), *Overseas Investment in the Age of High Imperialism* (London: Methuen).

Edison, H. (1981), 'Short-Run Dynamics and Long-Run Equilibrium Behaviour in Purchasing Power Parity Theory: A Quantitative Reassessment', unpublished PhD dissertation, University of London.

Edminster, L.R. (1926), *The Cattle Industry and the Tariff* (New York: Macmillan).

Eichengreen, B.J. (1983a), 'The Causes of British Business Cycles, 1833–1913', *Journal of European Economic History*, 12(1), 145–61.

(1983b), 'Asset Markets and Investment Fluctuations in Late Victorian Britain', *Research in Economic History*, 8, 145–79.

(1984), 'Central Bank Cooperation Under the Interwar Gold Standard', *Explorations in Economic History*, 21(1), 64–87.

(ed.) (1985a), *The Gold Standard in Theory and History* (New York: Methuen).

(1985b), 'International Policy Coordination in Historical Perspective: A View from the Inter-War Years', in W.H. Buiter and R.C. Marston (eds), *International Economic Policy Coordination* (Cambridge: Cambridge University Press), 139–78.

(1985c), 'Editor's Introduction', in B.J. Eichengreen (ed.), *The Gold Standard in*

Theory and History (London: Methuen), 1–35.

(1986), 'Unemployment in Interwar Britain: New Evidence from London', *Journal of Interdisciplinary History*, 17(3), 335–58.

(1987), 'Conducting the International Orchestra: Bank of England Leadership Under the Classical Gold Standard', *Journal of International Money and Finance*, 6(1), 5–29.

(1989), 'The Gold Standard Since Alec Ford', in S.N. Broadberry and N.F.R. Crafts (eds), *Britain in the World Economy 1870–1939* (Cambridge: Cambridge University Press).

(1990), 'Relaxing the External Constraint: Europe in the 1930s', CEPR Discussion Paper No. 452.

Eichengreen, B.J. and Sachs, J. (1985), 'Exchange Rates and Economic Recovery in the 1930s', *Journal of Economic History*, 45(4), 925–46.

Eichengreen, B.J. and Hatton, T.J. (1988), 'Introduction', in B. Eichengreen and T.J. Hatton (eds), *Interwar Unemployment in Historical Perspective* (Dordrecht: Kluwer), 1–59.

Engle, R.F. and Granger, C.W.J. (1987), 'Cointegration and Error Correction: Representation, Estimation and Testing', *Econometrica*, 55(2), 251–76.

Engle, R.F. and Yoo, B.S. (1987), 'Forecasting and Testing in Cointegrated Systems', *Journal of Econometrics*, 35, 143–59.

Evans, M.K. (1969), *Macroeconomic Activity: Theory, Forecasting and Control* (New York: Harper and Row).

Falkus, M. (1971), 'United States Economic Policy and the "Dollar Gap" of the 1920s', *Economic History Review*, 24(4), 599–623.

Fearon, P. (1987), *War, Prosperity and Depression: The US Economy 1917–45* (Deddington: Philip Allan).

Feinstein, C.H. (1972), *National Income, Expenditure and Output of the United Kingdom, 1855–1965* (Cambridge: Cambridge University Press).

(1988), 'National Statistics, 1760–1920', in C.H. Feinstein and S. Pollard (eds), *Studies in Capital Formation in the United Kingdom, 1750–1920* (Oxford: Clarendon Press).

(1989), 'Wages and the Paradox of the 1880s', *Explorations in Economic History*, 26(2), 237–47.

(1990), 'New Estimates of Average Earnings in the United Kingdom, 1880–1913', *Economic History Review*, 43(4), 595–632.

(1990), 'What Really Happened to Real Wages?': Trends in Wages, Prices and Productivity in the United Kingdom, 1880–1913', *Economic History Review*, 43(3), 329–55.

Feinstein, C.H., Matthews, R.C.O. and Oldling-Smee, J.C. (1982), 'The Timing of the Climacteric and its Sectoral Incidence in the UK', in C.P. Kindleberger and G. di Tella (eds), *Economics in the Long View*, volume 2, part 1 (Oxford: Clarendon Press), 168–85.

Fetter, F.W. (1965), *Development of British Monetary Orthodoxy 1797–1875* (Cambridge, MA: Harvard University Press).

Fisher, I. (1896), *Appreciation and Interest* (New York: Macmillan).

(1907), *The Rate of Interest* (New York: Macmillan).

(1911), *The Purchasing Power of Money* (New York: Macmillan).

(1930), *The Theory of Interest* (New York: Macmillan).

Fishlow, A. (1965), *American Railroads and the Transformation of the Ante-Bellum Economy* (Cambridge, MA: Harvard University Press).

(1966), 'Productivity and Technological Change in the Railroad Section, 1840–1910', in *Output, Employment and Productivity in the United States After 1800* (New York: National Bureau of Economic Research), 583–646.

(1987), 'Market Forces or Group Interests: Inconvertible Currency in Pre-1914 Latin America', unpublished, University of California at Berkeley.

(1989), 'Conditionality and Willingness to Pay: Some Parallels from the 1890s', in B. Eichengreen and P. Lindert (eds), *The International Debt Crisis in Historical Perspective* (Cambridge, MA: MIT Press).

Flanders, A. (1964), 'Collective Bargaining', in A. Flanders and H.A. Clegg (eds), *The System of Industrial Relations in Great Britain* (Oxford: Basil Blackwell), 252–322.

Fleming, J.M. (1962), 'Domestic Financial Policies Under Fixed and Under Flexible Exchange Rates', *IMF Staff Papers*, 9(3), 369–80.

Flora, P. (1987), *State, Economy and Society in Western Europe, 1815–1975* (Frankfurt: Campus Verlag).

Floud, R. and McCloskey, D. (1981), *The Economic History of Britain Since 1700, Vol. 2, 1860 to the 1970s* (Cambridge: Cambridge University Press).

Floyd, J.E. (1985), *World Monetary Equilibrium: International Monetary Theory in an Historical-Institutional Context* (Philadelphia: University of Pennsylvania Press).

Fogel, R. (1964), *Railroads and American Economic Growth* (Baltimore: Johns Hopkins University Press).

(1979), 'Notes on the Social Savings Controversy', *Journal of Economic History*, 32(1), 1–54.

Ford, A.G. (1960), 'Notes on the Working of the Gold Standard Before 1914', *Oxford Economic Papers*, 12(1), 52–76.

(1962), *The Gold Standard 1880–1914: Britain and Argentina* (London: Oxford University Press).

(1963), 'Notes on the Role of Exports in British Economic Fluctuations, 1870–1914', *Economic History Review*, 16(3), 328–337.

(1965), 'Overseas Lending and Internal Fluctuations, 1870–1914', *Yorkshire Bulletin of Economic and Social Research*, 17, 19–31.

(1969), 'British Economic Fluctuations, 1870–1914', *Manchester School*, 37(2), 99–129.

(1971), *Income, Spending and the Price Level* (London: Fontana).

(1972), 'British Economic Fluctuations, 1870–1914', in D.H. Aldcroft and P. Fearon (eds), *British Economic Fluctuations 1790–1939* (London: Macmillan), 131–60.

(1981), 'The Trade Cycle in Britain 1860–1914', in R.C. Floud and D.N. McCloskey (eds), *The Economic History of Britain Since 1700* (Cambridge: Cambridge University Press), 27–49.

(1984), 'Unemployment: Lessons of the Inter-War Years', in K. Cowling (ed.), *Out of Work: Perspectives of Mass Unemployment* (Coventry: University of Warwick).

Foreman-Peck, J. (1983), *A History of the World Economy: International Economic Relations Since 1850* (Brighton: Wheatsheaf).

Fratianni, M. and Spinelli, F. (1984), 'Italy in the Gold Standard Period, 1861–1914', in M. Bordo and A. Schwartz (eds), *A Retrospective on the Classical Gold Standard, 1821–1931* (Chicago: University of Chicago Press), 405–51.

Freeman, R. (1988), 'Labour Market Institutions and Economic Performance', *Economic Policy*, 3(6), 64–80.

Frenkel, J.A. (1971), 'A Theory of Money, Trade and the Balance of Payments in a Model of Accumulation', *Journal of International Economics*, 1(2), 159–87.

(1978), 'Purchasing Power Parity: Doctrinal Perspective and Evidence for the 1920s', *Journal of International Economics*, 8(1), 169–91.

(1981), 'The Collapse of Purchasing Power Parity During the 1970s', *European Economic Review*, 16(2), 145–65.

Frenkel, J.A. and H.G. Johnson (1976), 'Introductory Essay', in J.A. Frenkel and H.G. Johnson (eds), *The Monetary Approach to the Balance of Payments* (Toronto: Toronto University Press), 21–45.

Frickey, E. (1947), *Production in the USA, 1860–1914* (Cambridge, MA: Harvard University Press).

Friedman, M. (1950), 'Wesley C. Mitchell As An Economic Theorist', *Journal of Political Economy*, 58, 237–91.

(1990), 'The Crime of 1873', *Journal of Political Economy*, 98(6), 1159–94.

Friedman, M. and Schwartz, A.J. (1963), 'Money and Business Cycles', *Review of Economics and Statistics*, 45, supplement, 32–64.

(1982), *Monetary Trends in the United States and the United Kingdom* (Chicago: University of Chicago Press).

Fuller, W.A. (1976), *Introduction to Statistical Time Series* (New York: John Wiley).

Gallarotti, G.M. (1989), 'The Anatomy of Spontaneous Order: The Emergence of International Monetary Order Before World War I', unpublished PhD dissertation, Columbia University.

Garber, P. and Grilli, V. (1986), 'The Belmont-Morgan Syndicate as an Optimal Investment Banking Contract', *European Economic Review*, 30(3), 649–77.

Garside, W.R. and Gospel, H.F. (1982), 'Employers and Managers: Their Organizational Structure and Changing Industrial Relations', in C.J. Wrigley (ed.), *A History of British Industrial Relations, 1875–1914* (Amherst, MA: University of Massachusetts Press), 99–115.

Gayer, A.D., Rostow, W.W. and Schwartz, A.J. (1953), *The Growth and Fluctuation of the British Economy, 1790–1850* (Oxford: Clarendon Press).

Geary, D. (1989), 'Introduction', in D. Geary (ed.), *Labour and Socialist Movements in Europe Before 1914* (Oxford: Berg), 1–10.

Germany (1913), *Statistisches Jahrbuch fur das Deutsche Reich* (Berlin: Puttkammer and Muhlbrecht).

Giffen, R. (1892), *The Case Against Bimetallism*, (London: Bell), 2nd edition.

Giovannini, A. (1987), ' "Rules of the Game" During the International Gold Standard: England and Germany', *Journal of International Money and Finance*, 5(4), 467–83.

(1988), 'How Fixed Exchange Rate Regimes Work: Evidence from the Gold Standard, Bretton Woods and the EMS', in M.H. Miller, B.J. Eichengreen and R. Portes (eds), *Blueprints for Exchange Rate Management* (New York: Academic Press), 13–41.

Goodhart, C.A.E. (1972), *The Business of Banking, 1891–1914* (London: Weidenfield and Nicolson).

(1982), 'Monetary Trends in the United States and the United Kingdom: A British Review', *Journal of Economic Literature*, 20(4), 1540–51.

(1984), 'Comment' in M.D. Bordo and A.J. Schwartz (eds), *A Retrospective on the Classical Gold Standard 1821–1931* (Chicago: University of Chicago Press), 222–7.

Goodwin, R.M. (1953), 'The Problem of Trend and Cycle', *Yorkshire Bulletin*, 5(1), 89–97.

Gorton, G. (1988), 'Banking Panics and Business Cycles in the US', (OEP).

Granger, C.W.J. (1969), 'Investigating Causal Relations by Econometric Models and Cross-Spectral Methods', *Econometrica*, 37(3), 424–38.

(1981), 'Some Properties of Time Series Data and Their Use in Econometric Model Specification', *Journal of Econometrics*, 16(1), 121–30.

(1986), 'Developments in the Study of Cointegrated Economic Variables', *Oxford Bulletin of Economics and Statistics*, 48(3), 213–28.

Granger, C.W.J. and Newbold, P. (1974), 'Spurious Regressions in Econometrics', *Journal of Econometrics*, 2(2), 111–20.

Grassman, S. (1980), 'Long-Term Trends in the Openness of National Economies', *Oxford Economic Papers*, 32(1), 123–33.

Greasley, D. (1986), 'British Economic Growth: The Paradox of the 1880s and the Timing of the Climacteric', *Explorations in Economic History*, 23(4), 416–44.

(1989), 'British Wages and Income, 1856–1913: A Revision', *Explorations in Economic History*, 26(2), 248–59.

Green, A. and Urqhard, M. (1976), 'Factor and Commodity Flows in the International Economy', *Journal of Economic History*, 36, 217–52.

Green, E.H.H. (1988), 'Rentiers Versus Producers? The Political Economy of the Bimetallic Controversy', *English Historical Review*, 102, 596.

Gregory, R.G., Ho, V., McDermott, L. and Hagan, J. (1988), 'The Australian and US Labour Markets in the 1930s, in B. Eichengreen and T.J. Hatton (eds), *Interwar Unemployment in Historical Perspective* (Dordrecht: Kluwer), 397–430.

Guilkey, D.K. and Schmidt (1989), 'Extended Tabulations for Dickey-Fuller Tests', *Economics Letters*, 31(4), 355–7.

Haberler, G. (1964), *Prosperity and Depression* (London: Allen and Unwin), 5th edition.

Hall, R.L. and Hitch, C.J. (1939), 'Price Theory and Economic Behaviour', *Oxford Economic Papers*, 2(1), 12–45.

Hanson, S.G. (1938), *Argentine Meat and British Market* (Standard CA: Stanford University Press).

Hardach, K. (1980), *The Political Economy of Germany in the Twentieth Century* (Berkeley: University of California Press).

Harley, C.K. (1976), 'Goschen's Conversion of the National Debt and the Yield on Consols', *Economic History Review*, 2nd Series, 29(1), 101–6.

(1977), 'The Interest Rate and Prices in Britain, 1873–1913: A Study of the Gibson Paradox', *Explorations in Economic History*, 14(1), 69–89.

(1980), 'Transportation, the World Wheat Trade, and Kuznets Cycle, 1850–1913', *Explorations in Economic History*, 17(3), 218–50.

(1986), 'Late Nineteenth Century Transportation, Trade and Settlement', in W. Fischer, R.M. McInnis and J. Schneider (eds), *The Emergence of a World Economy, 1500–1914, Part II: 1850–1914* (Wiesbaden: Franz Steiner Verlag), 593–617.

(1988), 'Ocean Freight Rates and Productivity, 1740–1913: The Primacy of Mechanical Invention Reaffirmed', *Journal of Economic History*, XLVII 4, 851–76.

(1990), 'North Atlantic Shipping in the Late Nineteenth Century: Freight Rates and the Interrelationship of Cargoes', in L.W. Fisher and H.W. Nordvik (eds), *Shipping and Trade 1750–1950: Essays in International Maritime Economic History* (Pontefract: Lofthouse), 147–71.

Harsanyi, J. (1988), 'Bargaining', in J. Eatwell, M. Milgate and P. Newman (eds), *The New Palgrave: A Dictionary of Economics* (New York: Stockton Press), 190–5.

Hart, O.D. and Holmstrom, B. (1986), 'The Theory of Contracts', in T. Bewley (ed.), *Advances in Economic Theory: Papers From the Fifth World Congress of Econometrics* (Cambridge: Cambridge University Press), 71–128.

Harvey, A.C. (1985), 'Trends and Cycles in Macroeconomic Time Series', *Journal of Business and Economic Statistics*, 3(3), 216–27.

(1990), *Forecasting, Structural Time Series Models, and the Kalman Filter* (Cambridge: Cambridge University Press).

Hatton, T.J. (1981), 'Employment Functions for UK Industries Between the Wars', *University of Essex Economic Discussion Paper*, No. 181.

(1983), 'Unemployment Benefits and the Macroeconomics of the Interwar Labour Market', *Oxford Economic Papers*, 35(4), 486–505.

(1985), 'The Analysis of Unemployment in Inter-War Britain: A Survey of Research', *Centre for Economic Policy Research Discussion Paper*, No. 66.

(1987), 'A Quarterly Model of the Labour Market in Inter-War Britain', *Oxford Bulletin for Economics and Statistics*, 50(1), 1–26.

(1988), 'Institutional Change and Wage Rigidity in the UK, 1880–1985', *Oxford Review of Economic Policy*, 4(1), 74–86.

Hausman, W.J. and Watts, J.M. (1980), 'Structural Change in the Eighteenth Century British Economy: A Test Using Cubic Splines', *Explorations in Economic History*, 17(4), 400–10.

Hawtrey, R.G. (1913), *Good and Bad Trade* (London: Constable).

(1934), *Currency and Credit* (Longmans, Green), 3rd edition.

Hendry, D.F. (1983), 'Econometric Modelling: The Consumption Function in Retrospect', *Scottish Journal of Political Economy*, 30(3), 193–220.

(1986), 'Econometric Modelling with Cointegrated Variables: An Overview', *Oxford Bulletin of Economics and Statistics*, 48(3), 201–12.

Heim, C. (1984), 'Structural Unemployment and the Demand for New Labor in Advanced Economies: Interwar Britain', *Journal of Economic History*, 44(2), 585–95.

Hicks, J.R. (1930), 'The Early History of Industrial Conciliation in England', *Economica*, 10(1), 25–39.

(1932), *The Theory of Wages* (London: Macmillan).

(1965), *Capital and Growth* (Oxford: Oxford University Press).

Higgins, B. (1955), 'Interactions of Trends and Cycles', *Economic Journal*, 65(260), 594–614.

Hoffman, W.G. (1955), *British Industry, 1700–1950* (Oxford: Blackwell).

Hooker, R.H. (1909), 'The Meat Supply of the United Kingdom', *Journal of the Royal Statistical Society*, 72, 304–86.

Horner, F. (1802), 'Thornton on the Paper Credit of Great Britain', *Edinburgh Review*, 1, 172–201.

Horton, S.D. (1892), *Silver in Europe* (New York: Macmillan).

Houghton, D.H. (1971), 'Economic Development, 1865–1965', in M. Wilson and L. Thompson (eds), *The Oxford History of South Africa*, II, *South Africa 1870–1966* (Oxford: Clarendon Press), 1–48.

Hughes, J.R.T. (1960), *Fluctuations in Trade, Industry and Finance* (Oxford: Clarendon Press).

Hume, D. (1952), 'On the Balance of Trade', in *Essays, Moral, Political and Literary*, Vol. 1 (reprint of 1898 edn) (London: Longmans, Green).

Hume, L.J. (1970), 'The Gold Standard and Deflation: Issues and Attitudes of the 1920s', in S. Pollard (ed.), *The Gold Standard and Employment Policies Between the Wars* (London: Methuen), 122–45.

Humphrey, D.D. (1955), *American Imports* (New York: Twentieth Century Fund).

Hylleberg, S. and Mizon, G.E. (1989), 'Cointegration and Error Correction Mechanisms', *Economic Journal*, 99 (395), supplement, 113–25.

International Federation of Trade Unions (1913), *Tenth International Report of the Trades Union Movement* (Berlin: IFTU).

International Labour Office (1927), 'The Conciliation and Arbitration of Industrial Disputes: III: Successful Measures Applied in Various Countries', *International Labour Review*, 15(1), 78–97.

(1931), *Principles and Methods of Wage Determination in a Coal-Mining Industry*, Studies and Reports (series D), No. 20 (London: P.S. King).

(1936), *Collective Agreements*, Studies and Reports (series A), No. 39 (London: P.S. King).

(1938), *Labour Courts: An International Survey of Judicial Systems for the Settlement of Disputes*, Studies and Reports (series A), No. 40 (London: P.S. King).

(1939), *The Minimum Wage: An International Survey*, Studies and Reports (series D), No. 22 (London: P.S. King).

Irwin, D.A. (1991), 'Terms of Trade and Economic Growth in Nineteenth Century Britain', *Bulletin of Economic Research*, 43(1), 93–101.

Isles, K. (1934), *Wages Policy and the Price Level* (London: P.S. King).

Jewkes, T. and Gray, E.M. (1935), *Wages and Labour in the Lancashire Cotton Spinning Industry* (Manchester: Manchester University Press).

Johansen, S. (1988), 'Statistical Analysis of Cointegration Vectors', *Journal of Economic Dynamics and Control*, 12(2), 231–54.

(forthcoming), 'A Century of Nordic Cooperation', in R.T. Griffiths (ed.), *1992 in Historical Perspective*.

Johnson, H.G. (1973), 'The Monetary Approach to Balance of Payments Theory', in M.N. Connolly and A.K. Swoboda (eds), *International Trade and Money* (London: Allen and Unwin), 206–24.

(1976), 'The Monetary Approach to the Balance of Payments Theory', in J.A. Frenkel and H.G. Johnson (eds), *The Monetary Approach to the Balance of Payments* (Toronto: Toronto University Press), 147–67.

Johnson, P. (1985), *Saving and Spending: The Working-Class Economy in Britain, 1870–1939* (Oxford: Oxford University Press).

Jonung, L. (1984), 'Swedish Experience under the Classical Gold Standard, 1873–1914', in M. Bordo and A. Schwartz (eds), *A Retrospective on the Classical Gold Standard, 1821–1931* (Chicago: University of Chicago Press), 399.

Kahn, C. (1986), 'The Use of Complicated Models as Explanations: A Re-examination of Williamson's Late 19th Century America', Hoover Institution, Working Papers in Economics, No. E-86-21.

Kalecki, M. (1938), 'The Determinants of Distribution of National Income', *Econometrica*, 6(2), 97–112.

Kemp, T. (1971), 'The French Economy and the Franc Poincaré', *Economic History Review*, 24(1), 82–99.

Kennedy, W.P. (1974), 'Foreign Investment, Trade and Growth in the United Kingdom, 1870–1913', *Explorations in Economic History*, 11(4), 415–44.

(1987), *Industrial Structure, Capital Markets and the Origins of British Economic Decline* (Cambridge: Cambridge University Press).

Keynes, J.M. (1913, 1924 and 1969), *Indian Currency and Finance*, (London: Macmillan for R.E.S.).

(1925), 'The Economic Consequences of Mr Churchill', in S. Pollard (ed.), *The Gold Standard and Employment Policies Between the Wars* (London: Methuen), 27–43.

(1930), *A Treatise on Money* (London: Macmillan).

(1936), *The General Theory of Employment, Interest and Money* (London: Macmillan).

(1939), 'Relative Movements of Real Wages and Output', *Economic Journal*, 49(1), 34–51.

Kindleberger, C.P. (1961), *Foreign Trade and the National Economy* (New Haven, CT: Yale University Press).

(1964), *Economic Growth in France and Britain, 1851–1950* (Cambridge, MA: Harvard University Press).

(1973), *The World in Depression, 1929–1939* (Berkeley: University of California Press).

(1978), *Manias, Panics and Crashes in History* (London: Macmillan).

(1984), *A Financial History of Western Europe*, (London: Allen and Unwin).

(1987), *The World in Depression 1929–1939* (Harmondsworth: Pengiun), 2nd edition.

(1989), *Manias, Panics and Crashes: A History of Financial Crises*, 2nd edn (London: Macmillan).

King, F.H.H. (1987), *The History of the Hong Kong and Shanghai Banking Corporation: The Hong Kong Bank in Late Imperial China, 1864–1902. On an Even Keel* (Cambridge: Cambridge University Press).

King, R.G., Plosser, C.I. and Rebelo, S.T. (1988a), 'Production, Growth and Business Cycles: I. The Basic Neoclassical Model', *Journal of Monetary Economics*, 21(2), 195–232.

(1988b), 'Production, Growth and Business Cycles: II. New Directions', *Journal of Monetary Economics*, 21(3), 309–41.

Kitchen, J. (1930), 'The Supply of Gold Compared with the Price of Commodities', in *Interim Report of the Gold Delegation of the Financial Committee* (Geneva: League of Nations).

Klein, B. (1975), 'Our New Monetary Standard: The Measurement and Effects of Price Uncertainty, 1880–1973', *Economic Inquiry* 13(4), 461–83.

Kondratieff, N.D. (1935), 'The Long Wages in Economic Life', *Review of Economics and Statistics*, 17(1), 105–15.

Kormendi, R.C. and Meguire, P. (1990), 'A Multicountry Characterisation of the Nonstationarity of Aggregate Output', *Journal of Money, Credit and Banking*, 22(1), 77–92.

Kravis, I. and Lipsey, R.E. (1978), 'Price Behaviour in the Light of Balance of Payments Theories', *Journal of International Economics*, 8(2), 193–246.

Kruger, W. (1926), 'Employers' Organizations in Germany', *International Labour Review*, 14(3), 314–44.

Krugman, P. (1979), 'A Model of Balance of Payments Crises', *Journal of Money, Credit and Banking*, 11(3), 311–25.

Kunz, D.B. (1987), *The Battle for Britain's Gold Standard in 1931*, (London: Croom Helm).

Landes, D.S. (1958), *Bankers and Pashas* (London: Heinemann).

Latham, A.G. (1979), *The International Economy and the Underdeveloped World*, (London: Croom Helm).

Layard, P.R.G. (1986), *How to Beat Unemployment* (Oxford: Oxford University Press).

League of Nations, *Statistical Yearbook* (Geneva: League of Nations).

Leamer, E.E. (1985), 'Vector Autoregressions for Causal Inference?', *Carnegie-Rochester Conference Series on Public Policy*, 22, 255–304.

Lee, C.-W. and Petruzzi, C. (1986), 'The Gibson Paradox and the Monetary Standard', *Review of Economics and Statistics*, 68(2), 189–96.

Lewis, W.A. (1949), *Economic Survey, 1919–1939* (London: George Allen and Unwin).

(1978), *Growth and Fluctuations 1870–1913* (London: Allen and Unwin).

Liberal Industrial Inquiry (1928), *Britain's Industrial Future* (London: Ernest Benn).

Liepmann, M. (1938), *Tariff Levels and the Economic Unity of Europe* (London: Allen and Unwin).

Lindbeck, A. and Snower, D.J. (1988), *The Insider–Outsider Theory of Employment and Unemployment* (Cambridge, MA: MIT Press).

Lindert, P.H. (1969), 'Key Currencies and Gold, 1900–1913', *Princeton Studies in International Finance*, 24 (Princeton: Princeton University Press).

Lucas, R.E. (1978), 'Econometric Policy Evaluation: A Critique', in K. Brunner and A. Meltzer (eds), *The Phillips Curve and Labour Markets* (Amsterdam: North Holland), 19–46.

—— (1981), *Studies in Business Cycle Theory* (Oxford: Blackwell).

—— (1987), *Models of Business Cycles* (Oxford: Blackwell).

Lutkepohl, H. (1982), 'Differencing Multiple Time Series: Another Look at Canadian Money and Income Data', *Journal of Time Series Analysis*, 3(4), 235–43.

McCallum, B.T. (1989), 'Real Business Cycle Models', in R.J. Barro (ed.), *Modern Business Cycle Theory* (Oxford: Blackwell), 16–50.

McCloskey, D.N. (1970), 'Did Victorian Britain Fail?', *Economic History Review*, 23(3), 446–59.

McCloskey, D.N. and Zecher, J.R. (1976), 'How the Gold Standard Worked, 1880–1913', in J.A. Frankel and H.G. Johnson (eds), *The Monetary Approach to the Balance of Payments* (London: Allen and Unwin), 357–85.

McCloskey, D. and Zecher, J.R. (1984), 'The Success of Purchasing Power Parity: Historical Evidence and its Implications for Macroeconomics', in M.D. Bordo and A.J. Schwartz (eds), *A Retrospective on the Classical Gold Standard, 1821–1931*, (Chicago: National Bureau of Economic Research), 121–50.

MacDonald, R. and Kearney, C. (1987), 'On the Specification of Granger-Causality Tests using the Cointegration Methodology', *Economics Letters*, 25(2), 149–53.

McGouldrick, P. (1984), 'Operations of the German Central Bank and the Rules of the Game, 1879–1913', in M.D. Bordo and A.J. Schwartz (eds), *A Retrospective on the Classical Gold Standard, 1821–1931* (Chicago: University of Chicago Press), 311–49.

McKibbin, R.I. (1984), 'Why was there no Marxism in Britain?', *English Historical Review*, 99(2), 297–331.

McKinnon, R.I. (1988), 'An International Gold Standard without Gold', unpublished, Stanford University.

Maddison, A. (1964), *Economic Growth in the West* (London: Allen and Unwin).

Mankiw, N.G. (1989), 'Real Business Cycles: A New Keynesian Perspective', *Journal of Economic Perspectives*, 3(3), 79–90.

Martin, D.A. (1977), 'The Impact of Mid-Nineteenth Century Gold Depreciation upon Western Monetary Standards', *Journal of European Economic History*, 6(3), 641–58.

Mathias, P. (1983), *The First Industrial Nation: An Economic History of Britain,*

1700–1914 (London: Methuen).

Matthews, K.G.P. (1986), *The Inter-War Economy: An Equilibrium Analysis* (Aldershot: Gower).

(1986), 'Was Sterling Overvalued in 1925?', *Economic History Review*, 39(4), 572–87.

(1989), 'Was Sterling Overvalued in 1925? A Reply and Further Evidence', *Economic History Review*, 42(1), 90–7.

Matthews, R.C.O. (1959), *The Trade Cycle* (Cambridge: Cambridge University Press).

Matthews, R.C.O., Feinstein, C.H. and Odling-Smee, J.C. (1982), *British Economic Growth, 1856–1973* (Stanford: Stanford University Press).

Maunders, F. (1867), *The Cause and Cure of Monetary Panics* (London).

Meade, J.E. (1951), *The Theory of International Economic Policy* (Oxford: Oxford University Press).

Metcalf, D., Nickell, S.J. and Floros, N. (1982), 'Still Searching for an Explanation of Unemployment in Interwar Britain', *Journal of Political Economy*, 90(2), 386–99.

Meyer, J.R. (1955), 'An Input–Output Approach to Evaluating British Industrial Production in the Late Nineteenth Century', *Explorations in Entrepreneurial History*, 8, 12–34.

Middleton, R. (1985), *Towards the Managed Economy* (London: Methuen).

Mill, J.S. (1848), *Principles of Political Economy* (London: Parker, Son and Bourn).

(1865), *Principles of Politics* (New York: A.M. Kelly), reprint.

Mills, T.C. (1980), 'Money, Income and Causality in the UK: A Look at Recent Evidence', *Bulletin of Economic Research*, 32(2), 18–28.

(1990a), *Time Series Techniques for Economists* (Cambridge: Cambridge University Press).

(1990b), 'A Note on the Gibson Paradox During the Gold Standard', *Explorations in Economic History*, 27, 277–86.

(1991), 'Are Fluctuations in UK Output Permanent or Transitory?', *Manchester School*, 59(1), 1–11.

Mills, T.C. and Wood, G.E. (1978), 'Money, Income and Causality Under the Gold Standard', *Federal Reserve Bank of St. Louis Review*, 60(8), 22–7.

(1982), 'Econometric Evaluation of Alternative Money Stock Series, 1880–1913', *Journal of Money, Credit and Banking*, 14(2), 265–77.

Mills, T.C. and Taylor, M.P. (1989), 'Random Walk Components in Outout and Exchange Rates: Some Robust Tests on UK Data', *Bulletin of Economic Research*, 41(2), 123–35.

Ministry of Labour (1921a–40a), *Gazette* (London: HMSO).

(1934), *Report of Collective Agreements Between Employers and Workpeople*, Vol. I (London: HMSO).

Minsky, H.P. (1986), *Stabilising an Unstable Economy* (New Haven, CT: Yale University Press).

Mitchell, B.R. (1975), *European Historical Statistics, 1750–1970* (New York: Columbia University Press).

(1983), *International Historical Statistics: The Americas and Australiasia* (Detroit, MI: Gale Research Co.).

(1988), *Abstract of British Historical Statistics*, (Cambridge: Cambridge University Press).

Mitchell, B.R. and Deane, P. (1962), *Abstract of British Historical Statistics* (Cambridge: Cambridge University Press).

(1971), *Abstract of British Historical Statistics* (Cambridge: Cambridge University Press).

Mitchell, W.C. and Burns, A.F. (1946), *Measuring Business Cycles* (New York: National Bureau of Economic Research).

Moggridge, D.E. (1969), *The Return to Gold, 1925*, (London: Cambridge University Press).

(1972), *British Monetary Policy 1924–31* (Cambridge: Cambridge University Press).

Moggridge, D.W. (1989), 'The Gold Standard and National Financial Policies, 1919–1939', *Cambridge History of Europe*, Vol. VIII (Cambridge: Cambridge University Press), 250–314.

Morgan, E.V. (1943, rep. 1965), *The Theory and Practice of Central Banking* (Cambridge: Cambridge University Press).

Morgan, M. (1989), *The History of Econometric Ideas* (Cambridge: Cambridge University Press).

Morgenstern, O. (1959), *International Financial Transactions and Business Cycles* (Princeton: Princeton University Press.

Mowat, C.L. (1968), *Britain Between the Wars, 1918–40* (London: Methuen and Co. Ltd.).

Mundell, R. (1963), 'Capital Mobility and Stabilization Policy Under Fixed and Flexible Exchange Rates', *Canadian Journal of Economics and Political Science*, 29(4), 475–85.

(1968), *International Economics* (New York: Macmillan).

(1971), *Monetary Theory* (Pacific Palisades: Goodyear).

(1982), *Purchasing Power Parity and Exchange Rates: Theory, Evidence, and Relevance* (Greenwich, CT: JAI Press).

Nelson, C.R. and Kang, H. (1981), 'Spurious Periodicity in Inappropriately Detrended Time Series', *Econometrica*, 49(3), 741–51.

(1984), 'Pitfalls in the Use of Time as an Explanatory Variable in Regression', *Journal of Business and Economic Statistics*, 2(1), 73–82.

Nelson, C.R. and Plosser, C.I. (1982), 'Trends and Random Walks in Macroeconomic Time Series: Some Evidence and Implications', *Journal of Monetary Economics*, 10(2), 139–62.

Newell, A. and Symons, J.S.V. (1988), 'The Macroeconomics of the Interwar Years: International Comparisons', in B. Eichengreen and T.J. Hatton (eds), *Interwar Unemployment in Historical Perspective* (Dordrecht: Kluwer), 61–96.

Nickell, S. (1985), 'Error Correction, Partial Adjustment and All That: An Expository Note', *Oxford Bulletin Economics and Statistics*, 47(1), 119–29.

(1988), 'Wages and Economic Activity', in W. Eltis and P. Sinclair (eds), *Keynes and Economic Policy: The Relevance of the General Theory After Fifty Years*

(London: Macmillan).

(1990), 'Unemployment: A Survey', *Economic Journal*, 100(2), 391–439.

Nicholson, J.S. (1893), *A Treatise on Money and Essays on Monetary Problems* (London: Adam and Charles Black), 2nd edition.

Nielsen, A. (1917), *Den skandinaviske montunion* (Copenhagen).

Nishimura, S. (1973), 'The Growth of the Stock of Money in the UK, 1870–1913', unpublished paper (Tokyo: Hosei University).

(1988), 'The Mechanism of the Supply of Money in the United Kingdom, 1873–1913', in P. Cottrell and D. Moggridge (eds), *Money and Power* (London: Macmillan), 103–29.

Nugent, J.B. (1973), 'Exchange-Rate Movements and Economic Development in the Late Nineteenth Century', *Journal of Political Economy*, 81, 1110–35.

Nurske, R. (1944), *International Currency Experience* (Geneva: League of Nations).

Officer, L. (1982), *Purchasing Power Parity and Exchange Rates: Theory, Evidence and Relevance* (Greenwich, CT: JAI Press).

(1986), 'The Efficiency of the Dollar-Sterling Gold Standard, 1890–1908', *Journal of Political Economy*, 94(5), 1038–73.

(1989), 'The Remarkable Efficiency of the Dollar-Sterling Gold Standard, 1890–1906', *Journal of Economic History*, 49, 1–42.

Ogden, E.M. (1989), 'The Bank of England as Lender of Last Resort', unpublished PhD dissertation, City University.

Ohlin, B. (1929), 'The Reparation Problem: A Discussion: I. Transfer Difficulties, Real and Imagined', *Economic Journal*, 39, 172–8.

(1967), *Interregional and International Trade* (Cambridge, Mass.: Harvard University Press).

Olson, M. (1974), 'The United Kingdom and the World Market in Wheat and Other Primary Products', *Explorations in Economic History*, 11(4), 325–50.

Palgrave, R.H. (1903), *Bank Rate and the Money Market* (London: J. Murray).

Perren, R. (1978), *The Meat Trade of Britain, 1840–1914* (London: Routledge & Kegan Paul).

Perron, P. (1988), 'Trends and Random Walks in Macroeconomic Time Series: Further Evidence from a New Approach', *Journal of Economic Dynamics and Control*, 12(2/3), 297–332.

(1989), 'The Great Crash, the Oil Price Shock and the Unit Root Hypothesis', *Econometrica*, 57(6), 1361–401.

(1990), 'Testing for a Unit Root in a Time Series with a Changing Mean', *Journal of Business and Economic Statistics*, 8(2), 153–62.

Phelps-Brown, E.H. and Browne, M.H. (1968), *A Century of Pay* (London: Macmillan).

Phelps-Brown, E.H. and Handfield Jones, S.J. (1952), 'The Climacteric of the 1890s: A Study in the Expanding Economy', *Oxford Economic Papers*, 4(3), 266–307.

Phelps-Brown, E.H. and Ozga, S.A. (1955), 'Economic Growth and the Price Level', *Economic Journal*, 65(257), 1–18.

Phillips, A.W. (1958), 'The Relation Between Unemployment and the Rate of Change of Money Wage Rates in the United Kingdom, 1861–1957', *Economica*, 25(4), 283–99.

Phillips, P.C.B. (1986), 'Understanding Spurious Regressions in Econometrics', *Journal of Econometrics*, 33(3), 311–40.

Phillips, P.C.B. and Durlauf, S.N. (1986), 'Multiple Time Series with Integrated Processes', *Review of Economic Studies*, 53(3), 473–95.

Phillips, P.C.B. and Perron, P. (1988), 'Testing for a Unit Root in Time Series Regression', *Biometrika*, 75(2), 335–46.

Pierce, D.A. (1978), 'Seasonal Adjustment When Both Deterministic and Stochastic Seasonality Are Present', in A. Zellner (ed.), *Seasonal Analysis of Economic Time Series* (Washington, D.C.: US Department of Commerce, Bureau of the Census), 365–97.

Pierce, D.A. and Haugh, L.D. (1977), 'Causality in Temporal Systems: Characterizations and a Survey', *Journal of Econometrics*, 5(5), 265–93.

Pigou, A.C. (1927a), *Industrial Fluctuations* (London: Macmillan).

(1927b), 'Wage Policy and Unemployment', *Economic Journal*, 37(3), 355–68.

(1933), *The Theory of Unemployment* (London: Macmillan).

Pippenger, J. (1984), 'Bank of England Operations, 1893–1913', in M.D. Bordo and A.J. Schwartz (eds), *A Retrospective on the Classical Gold Standard 1821–1931* (Chicago: University of Chicago Press), 203–22.

Plosser, C.I. (1989), 'Understanding Real Business Cycles', *Journal of Economic Perspectives*, 3(3), 51–77.

Pollard, S. (1970), *The Gold Standard and Employment Policies Between the Wars* (London: Methuen).

Pool, A.G. (1938), *Wage Policy in Relation to Industrial Fluctuations* (London: Macmillan).

Prebisch, R. (1950), *The Economic Development of Latin America and its Principal Problems* (New York: United Nations).

Pressnell, L.S. (1968), 'Gold Reserves, Banking Reserves and the Baring Crisis of 1890', in C.R. Whittlesey and J.S.G. Wilson (eds), *Essays in Money and Banking in Honour of R.S. Sayers* (Oxford: Clarendon Press), 172–3.

(1978), '1925: The Burden of Sterling', *Economic History Review* 31(1), 67–88.

Prest, A.R. and Adams, A. (1954), *Expenditure in the United Kingdom 1900–1919, Studies in the National Income and Expenditure of the United Kingdom No. 3* (Cambridge: Cambridge University Press).

Ramsbottom, E.C. (1935), 'The Course of Wage Rates in the United Kingdom, 1921–34', *Journal of the Royal Statistical Society*, 98(4), 639.

(1938), 'Wage Rates in the United Kingdom, 1934–38', *Journal of the Royal Statistical Society*, 101, Part I, 202.

(1939), 'Wage Rates in the United Kingdom in 1938', *Journal of the Royal Statistical Society*, 102, Part II, 289.

Rappoport, P. and Reichlin, L. (1989), 'Segmented Trends and Non-Stationary Time Series', *Economic Journal*, 99(395), supplement, 168–77.

Redmond, J. (1984), 'The Sterling Overvaluation in 1925: A Multilateral Approach', *Economic History Review*, 37(4), 520–32.

(1989), 'Was Sterling Overvalued in 1925? A Comment', *Economic History Review*, 42(1), 87–9.

Reich, N. (1938), *Labour Relations in Republican Germany: An Experiment in Industrial Democracy, 1918–1933* (Oxford: Oxford University Press).

Rich, G. (1984), 'Canada Without a Central Bank: Operation of the Price-Specie-Flow Mechanism, 1872–1913', in M. Bordo and A. Schwartz (eds), *A Retrospective on the Classical Gold Standard, 1821–1931* (Chicago: University of Chicago Press), 547–601.

Richardson, J.H. (1933), *Industrial Relations in Great Britain*, International Labour Office, Studies and Reports (series A), No. 36 (London: P.S. King).

(1939), 'Real Wage Movements', *Economic Journal*, 49(3), 425–41.

Rist, M. (1970), 'A French Experiment with Free Trade: The Treaty of 1860', in R. Cameron (ed.), *Essays in French Economic History* (Homeward, Illinois: R.D. Irwin, for A.E.A.), 296.

Robey, R. (ed.), *The Monetary Problem: Gold and Silver* (New York: Columbia University Press).

Rockoff, H. (1984), 'Some Evidence on the Real Price of Gold, Its Costs of Production, and Commodity Prices', in M. Bordo and A. Schwartz (eds), *A Retrospective on the Classical Gold Standard, 1821–1931* (Chicago: University of Chicago Press), 613–44.

Romer, P.M. (1986), 'Increasing Returns and Long Run Growth', *Journal of Political Economy*, 94(3), 1002–37.

(1990), 'Capital, Labor and Productivity', *Brookings Papers: Microeconomics*, 337–67.

Ross, A.M. (1956), *Trade Union Wage Policy* (Berkeley, CA: University of California Press).

Ross, A.M. and Irwin, D. (1951), 'Strike Experience in Five Countries 1927–1947: An Interpretation', *Industrial and Labour Relations Review*, 4(3), 323–42.

Ross, A.M. and Hartman, P.T. (1960), *Changing Patterns of Industrial Conflict* (New York: John Wiley).

Rostow, W.W. (1948), *British Economy of the Nineteenth Century* (Oxford: Oxford University Press).

Runkle, D.E. (1987), 'Vector Autoregressions and Reality', *Journal of Business and Economic Statistics*, 5(4), 437–42.

Sachs, J. (1979), 'Wages, Profits and Macroeconomic Adjustment: A Comparative Study', *Brookings Papers on Economic Activity*, 2, 296–319.

Said, S.E. and Dickey, D.A. (1984), 'Testing for Unit Roots in Autoregressive Moving-Average Models with Unknown Order', *Biometrika*, 71(3), 599–607.

Sargent, T.J. (1973), 'Interest Rates and Prices in the Long Run', *Journal of Money, Credit and Banking*, 5(1), 385–449.

Saville, I.D. and Gardiner, K.L. (1986), 'Stagflation in the UK Since 1970: A Model Based Explanation', *National Institute Economic Review*, 117(11), 52–69.

Sayers, R.S. (1930–3), 'The Question of the Standard in the Eighteen-Fifties', *Economic History*, II, 573, 579, 580, 594–9.

(1936), *Bank of England Operations, 1890–1914* (London: P.S. King and Son).

(1957), *Central Banking After Bagehot* (Oxford: Clarendon Press).

(1960), 'The Return to Gold, 1925', in S. Pollard (ed.) (1970), and also in L.S.

Pressnell (ed.), *Studies in the Industrial Revolution* (1960) (London: University of London: The Athlone Press).

(1976), *The Bank of England 1891–1944* (Cambridge: Cambridge University Press).

Scammell, W.M. (1965), 'The Working of the Gold Standard', reprinted in B.J. Eichengreen (ed.) (1985a), *The Gold Standard in Theory and History* (New York: Methuen), 139–78.

Schumpeter, J.A. (1939), *Business Cycles* (New York: McGraw Hill).

Schwert, G.W. (1987), 'Effects of Model Specification on Tests for Unit Roots in Macroeconomic Data', *Journal of Monetary Economics*, 20(1), 73–103.

(1989), 'Tests for Unit Roots: A Monte Carlo Investigation', *Journal of Business and Economic Statistics*, 7(2), 147–60.

Sells, D.M. (1939), *British Wages Boards: A Study in Industrial Democracy* (Washington, D.C.: Brookings Institution).

Shiller, R.J. (1981), 'Do Stock Prices Move Too Much to be Justified by Subsequent Changes in Dividends?', *American Economic Review*, 71(3), 421–36.

Shiller, R.J. and Perron, P. (1985), 'Testing the Random Walk Hypothesis: Power Versus Frequency of Observation', *Economics Letters*, 18(4), 381–6.

Shorter, E. and Tilly, C. (1974), *Strikes in France, 1830–1968* (Cambridge: Cambridge University Press).

Simon, M. (1968), 'The Pattern of New British Portfolio Investment, 1865–1914', in A.R. Hall (ed.), *The Export of Capital 1870–1914* (London: Methuen), 15–44.

Sims, C.A. (1972), 'Money Income and Causality', *American Economic Review* 62(4), 540–52.

(1982), 'Policy Analysis with Econometric Models', *Brookings Papers on Economic Activity*, 1(1), 107–52.

(1987), 'Comment', *Journal of Business and Economic Statistics*, 5(4), 443–9.

Sims, C.A., Stock, J.H. and Watson, M.W. (1990), 'Inference in Linear Time Series Models with Some Unit Roots', *Econometrica*, 58(1), 113–44.

Sinclair, A. (1962), *Prohibition: The Era of Excess* (London: Faber).

Sisson, K. (1987), *The Management of Collective Bargaining: An International Comparison* (Oxford: Basil Blackwell).

Smith, P.H. (1969), *Politics and Beef in Argentina* (New York: Columbia University Press).

Solomou, S. (1987), *Phases of Economic Growth, 1850–1973* (Cambridge: Cambridge University Press).

Stern, F. (1980), *Gold and Iron. Bismarck, Bleichroder, and the Building of the German Empire* (London: Allen and Unwin).

Stewart, M. (1967), *Keynes and After* (Harmondsworth: Pengiun).

Stock, J.H. (1987), 'Asymptotic Properties of Least Squares Estimators of Cointegrating Vectors', *Econometrica*, 55(5), 1035–56.

Stock, J.H. and Watson, M.W. (1988a), 'Variable Trends in Economic Time Series', *Journal of Economic Perspectives*, 2(3), 147–74.

(1988b), 'Testing for Common Trends', *Journal of American Statistical Association*, 83(404), 1097–107.

Strand, N.V. (1942), 'Prices of Farm Products in Iowa, 1851–1940', *Research Bulletin* 303, Agricultural Experiment Station, Iowa State College of Agricultural and Mechanical Arts.

Sweezy, M.Y. (1941), *The Structure of the Nazi Economy* (Cambridge, Mass.: Harvard University Press).

Tarling, R.J. and Wilkinson, F. (1982), 'The Movement of Real Wages and the Development of Collective Bargaining in the UK, 1855–1920', *Contributions to Political Economy*, 1(1), 1–23.

Tarshis, L. (1939), 'Changes in Real and Money Wages', *Economic Journal*, 49(1), 150–4.

Taussig, F.W. (1917), 'International Trade Under Depreciated Paper', *Quarterly Journal of Economics*, 21, 330–403.

Taussig, F.W. (1927), *International Trade* (New York: Macmillan).

Taylor, M.P. (1986), 'On Unit Roots and Real Exchange Rates: Empirical Evidence and Monte Carlo Analysis', unpublished, Bank of England.

(1988), 'An Empirical Examination of Long-Run Purchasing Power Parity Using Cointegration Techniques', *Applied Economics*, 20(10), 1369–81.

(1989), 'Error Correction, Cointegration and the Forward-Looking Model: The Demand for UK Broad Money During the International Gold Standard', mimeo, City University Business School.

Taylor, M.P. and McMahon, P.C. (1988), 'Long-Run Purchasing Power Parity in the 1920s', *European Economic Review*, 32(1), 179–97.

Thomas, B. (1973), *Migration and Economic Growth* (Cambridge: Cambridge University Press).

Thomas, M. (1988), 'Labour Market Structure and the Nature of Unemployment in Interwar Britain', in B. Eichengreen and T.J. Hatton (eds), *Interwar Unemployment in Historical Perspective* (Dordrecht: Kluwer), 97–148.

(1991), 'How Flexible Were Wages in Interwar Britain?', unpublished paper, University of Virginia.

Thomas, R.L. and Stoney, P.J. (1972), 'Unemployment Dispersion as a Determinant of Wage Inflation in the U.K., 1925–66', in M. Parkin and M.T. Sumner (eds), *Incomes Policy and Inflation* (Manchester: Manchester University Press), 201–36.

Thornton, H. (1978), *An Enquiry into the Nature and Effects of the Paper Credit of Great Britain* (reprint of 1802 edn) (Fairfield, NJ: Augustus M. Kelly).

Tiao, G.C. and Hillmer, S.C. (1978), 'Some Consideration of Decomposition of a Time Series', *Biometrika*, 65(3), 497–502.

Tjostheim, D. and Paulsen, J. (1982), 'Empirical Identification of Multiple Time Series', *Journal of Time Series Analysis*, 3(4), 265–82.

Tobin, J. (1961), 'Money, Capital and Other Stores of Value', *American Economic Review*, Papers and Proceedings, 51, 26–37.

Treu, T. and Martinelli, A. (1984), 'Employers Associations in Italy', in J.P. Windmuller and A. Gladstone (eds), *Employers Associations and Industrial Relations: A Comparative Study* (Oxford: Clarendon Press), 264–93.

Triffin, R. (1985), 'The Myth and Realities of the So-Called Gold Standard', reprinted in B.J. Eichengreen (ed.), *The Gold Standard in Theory and History* (London: Methuen), 121–40.

Tsiang, S.C. (1959), 'Fluctuating Exchange Rates in Countries with Relatively Stable Economies', *IMF Staff Papers*, 7(2), 244–73.

United States (1925), 'Collective Agreements in Czechoslovakia', *Monthly Labour Review*, 21(3), 15.

(1935a), 'Collective Bargaining in France', *Monthly Labour Review*, 41(4), 959–61.

(1935b), 'Types of Employer–Employee Bargaining', *Monthly Labour Review* 41(6), 1445.

(1939), 'Collective Bargaining with Employers' Associations', *Monthly Labour Review*, 49(2), 302–10.

Urquhart, M.C. (1986), 'New Estimates of Gross National Product, Canada 1870–1926', in S. Engerman and R.E. Gallman (eds), *Long-term Factors in American Economic Growth* (Chicago: University of Chicago Press).

van Aarsten, J.P. (1939), 'Italy', in H.A. Marquand (ed.), *Organized Labour in Four Continents* (London: Longmans, Green), 191–228.

van Voorden, W. (1984), 'Employers Associations in the Netherlands', in J.P. Windmuller and A. Gladstone (eds), *Employers Associations and Industrial Relations: A Comparative Study* (Oxford: Clarendon Press), 202–31.

Viner, J. (1924), *Canada's Balance of International Indebtedness* (Cambridge, M.A.: Harvard University Press).

Watson, M.W. (1986), 'Univariate Detrending Methods with Stochastic Trends', *Journal of Monetary Economics*, 18(1), 49–75.

Webb, S. and Webb, B. (1897), *Industrial Democracy* (London: Longmans, Green).

West, K.D. (1988), 'On the Interpretation of Near Random Walk Behaviour in GNP', *American Economic Review*, 78(1), 202–9.

Whale, P.B. (1937), 'The Working of the Pre-War Gold Standard', *Economica*, 11(1), 18–32.

Whitaker, J.K. and Hudgins Jr., M.W. (1977), 'The Floating Pound Sterling of the Nineteen-Thirties: An Econometric Study', *Southern Economic Journal*, 43(4), 1478–85.

White, H.D. (1933), *The French International Accounts, 1880–1913* (Cambridge, Mass.: Harvard University Press).

Wicksell, K. (1907), 'The Influence of the Rate of Interest on Prices', *Economic Journal*, 17(66), 213–20.

(1918), 'International Freights and Prices', *Quarterly Journal of Economics*, 32, 401–10.

Williams, D., Goodhard, C.A.E. and Gowland, D.H. (1976), 'Money Income and Causality: The UK Experience', *American Economic Review*, 66(3), 417–23.

Williamson, J.G. (1964), *American Growth and the Balance of Payments* (Chapel Hill, NC: University of North Carolina Press).

(1974), *Late Nineteenth Century American Development: A General Equilibrium History* (New York: Cambridge University Press).

Williamson, O.E. (1985), *The Economic Institutions of Capitalism: Firms, Markets, Relational Contracting* (New York: The Free Press).

Willis, H.P. (1971), *A History of the Latin Monetary Union* (New York: AMS Press).

Winch, D. (1969), *Economics and Policy: A Historical Study* (London: Hodder and Stoughton).

Worrall, T. (1989), 'Labour Contract Theory', in F. Hahn (ed.), *The Economics of Missing Markets, Information, and Games* (Oxford: Clarendon Press), 336–59.

Wright, J.F. (1984), 'Real Wage Resistance: Eighty Years of the British Cost of Living', *Oxford Economic Papers*, 36(4), 152–67.

Yeager, L.B. (1976), *International Monetary Relations* (London: Harper and Row).

Yeager, M. (1981), *Competition and Regulation: The Development of Oligopoly in the Meat Packing Industry* (Greenwich, Conn.: JAI Press Inc.).

Zevin, P.B. (1989), 'Are World Financial Markets More Open? If So, Why and With What Effects', unpublished.

Index